GRANT MORRISON

Great Comics Artists Series
M. Thomas Inge, General Editor

Marc Singer

GRANT MORRISON
Combining the Worlds of Contemporary Comics

University Press of Mississippi / Jackson

www.upress.state.ms.us

The University Press of Mississippi is a member of the Association of American University Presses.

Copyright © 2012 by University Press of Mississippi
All rights reserved

First printing 2012

∞

Library of Congress Cataloging-in-Publication Data

Singer, Marc.
 Grant Morrison : combining the worlds of contemporary comics / Marc Singer.
     p. cm. — (Great comics artists series)
 Includes bibliographical references and index.
  ISBN 978-1-61703-135-9 (cloth : alk. paper) — ISBN 978-1-61703-136-6 (pbk. : alk. paper) — ISBN 978-1-61703-137-3 (ebook) 1. Morrison, Grant—Criticism and interpretation. 2. Comic books, strips, etc.—United States—History and criticism. I. Title.
 PN6727.M677Z86 2012
 741.5'973—dc22   2011013483

British Library Cataloging-in-Publication Data available

Contents

vii	Acknowledgments
3	Introduction: A Union of Opposites
24	**CHAPTER ONE** Ground Level
52	**CHAPTER TWO** The World's Strangest Heroes
92	**CHAPTER THREE** The Invisible Kingdom
136	**CHAPTER FOUR** Widescreen
181	**CHAPTER FIVE** Free Agents
221	**CHAPTER SIX** A Time of Harvest
251	**CHAPTER SEVEN** Work for Hire
285	Afterword: Morrison, Incorporated
293	Notes
305	Bibliography
317	Index

Acknowledgments

This book would not have been possible without the advice and support of my friends and colleagues. Craig Fischer, Roger Sabin, Will Brooker, and Gene Kannenberg Jr. generously gave their time to read the manuscript and offer feedback. Joseph Witek, Jason Tondro, Steve Holland, Randy Scott, the Michigan State University Library Special Collections, and the George Washington University Gelman Library provided me with sources and images. Charles Hatfield's guidance was invaluable. I also wish to thank Walter Biggins for his good counsel and Seetha Srinivasan and Tom Inge for their encouragement.

An earlier version of my section on *Arkham Asylum* appeared in the Fall 2006 issue of the *International Journal of Comic Art*. I owe editor-in-chief John Lent and exhibition review editor Mike Rhode a debt of gratitude for all they have done to promote the field of comics scholarship.

Finally, I want to thank Christy and Eric for giving me the best support and distraction (respectively) any scholar could hope for.

EDITIONS, PAGINATION, CITATIONS, AND DATES

Grant Morrison's work has been published and republished in multiple formats. In the interest of consistency, I have chosen to refer to the original comic books whenever possible—a decision that also foregrounds their publication as periodicals. For serials published in anthologies such as *2000 AD* or *Crisis*, I have assigned page numbers by chapter, not by their position in the anthologies (many of which were unpaginated and which remain out of print). I have cited Morrison's comics by issue or chapter number and page number, with volume or "Phase" numbers represented in Roman numerals when necessary. For example, (*Zenith* III.1.5) refers to *Zenith* Phase III, chapter 1, page 5, while (*Doom Patrol* 34.22) refers to *Doom Patrol* issue 34, page 22.

Publication dates also pose a challenge when citing periodical comic books. Because American comic books are typically postdated for two or three months after their release, the copyright dates do not always reflect the actual year of publication; comics released at the end of the year are dated for the next year. When these dates diverge, entries in the bibliography will cite the published copyright dates, but any references in the text will use the actual years of publication. I hope these practices will preserve some sense of the original production contexts for these comics.

GRANT MORRISON

INTRODUCTION

A Union of Opposites

At first glance, Grant Morrison might appear to be an unlikely subject for a scholarly study of comics. In a time when graphic novels have finally gained entry to the classroom, the art museum, and the *New York Times Book Review*, he continues to work on periodical comic books; in a medium where memoirs, histories, and other nonfiction works have garnered the most critical approval, he still writes serialized superhero adventures; in a field that exalts creators who write and draw their own comics, he collaborates with artists who bring his scripts to life. Upon closer examination, however, Morrison is one of a handful of writers who have imported the auteurist sensibility of alternative comics and graphic novels to the popular genres and characters that dominate the American and British comics industries. From his beginnings in the "ground level" comics of the 1970s to his most recent work for Vertigo, an imprint of industry giant DC Comics, Morrison has always sought to synthesize the various cultures of contemporary Anglophone comics, alternating between corporate-owned superhero titles and creator-owned work in other genres. His independent streak motivates him to craft stories of considerable range and depth without becoming trapped by genre formulas or conventions; his pop aesthetic leads him to tell these stories in broadly accessible narrative forms, avoiding the equally pernicious trap of the limited audience. He appropriates the most sophisticated techniques of postmodernist literature, drama, television, and film and applies them to popular genres, maintaining his artistic ambitions while working within the comics industry mainstream.

His comics include popular superhero franchises, highly personal stories, and, most remarkably, highly personal stories set within popular superhero franchises. His work regularly violates the conventions of realism, the physical boundaries of the space-time continuum, and the ontological boundaries that separate fiction from reality, but these transgressions enhance rather than inhibit his ability to address the concerns of postmodern culture.

Morrison's comics harness superheroes, fantasy, and other popular genres to formulate self-reflexive critiques of these genres' conventions, histories, and ideological assumptions, as well as more wide-ranging examinations of the ethics of writing. They promote political, economic, and artistic autonomy while recognizing the consequences of unbridled individualism. They create and explore multiple scales of order, intertwining narrative worlds through elaborate synecdoches. Perhaps most significantly, they challenge structuralist and poststructuralist theories that characterize language as an unending chain of arbitrary signifiers, defined by social convention and bearing no connection to the concepts they signify. Morrison grounds this challenge in comics' capacity for visual representation and the fantasy genres' propensity for literalizing meanings that would otherwise be figurative. From the popular medium of comics and the demotic genres of superheroes, science fiction, and secret agents, he questions the major intellectual currents of twentieth-century linguistics, philosophy, and literary theory.

This variety of subjects and styles has been matched by Morrison's assortment of authorial personas. Over the course of his career he has played the part of the young radical, the team player, the company man, the revisionist, the nostalgist, the postmodernist, the magical guru, the drug user, the straight-edger, the public speaker who lectures corporations on branding, and the countercultural icon who appears in music videos, among many others. In his interviews Morrison assumes an engaging and mercurial (if not always wholly reliable) presence, providing thoughtful commentaries on his own work while playing up whatever character he has adopted at that moment. He has worked in multiple media, including music, short stories, screenplays, video games, and two award-winning plays for the Edinburgh Fringe Festival ("Work Outside Comics"), but his emphasis always remains on comics, which he has written (and occasionally drawn) with few interruptions since 1978.

He takes inspiration from all of these forms of expression, mixing popular, canonical, and avant-garde sources. Morrison has cited the influence of Nicolas Roeg's nonlinear films and Lindsay Anderson's satires, Dennis Potter's self-reflexive television dramas and David Rudkin's occult, pagan plays, but he has also cited British television series such as *The Avengers, The Prisoner, Jason King,* and *Doctor Who* (Meaney 347–48; Neighly 248). His literary influences tend towards dissidents and outsiders like the Romantics, the Decadents, and the beatniks (Hasted 71), yet his tastes can also accommodate the fantasy and science fiction novels of Michael Moorcock and Philip K. Dick and the unsparing realism of Philip Larkin's poetry. Musically,

Morrison was "utterly transformed" by the punk movement that emerged when he was a teenager in the mid-1970s (Hasted 55). He adopted many elements of the punk philosophy, including its antiestablishment ideology and back-to-basics aesthetic, though not its nihilism or scorn of technical virtuosity; like many punk acts that signed with major record labels, he has also been willing to work with major publishers in order to maximize his audience. Nor has punk been his only musical influence: during the 1980s he played in Glasgow bands such as the Mixers, who developed a garage sound that combined proto-punk enthusiasm with sixties pop and psychedelia ("The Mixers"), and the Fauves, which traded the punk influence for Morrissey courtesy of Morrison's witty, self-deprecating lyrics ("The Fauves"). Ironically, his influences within comics display the least variety. Although he acknowledges pioneering 1960s writers and artists such as John Broome and Jack Kirby, accomplished 1970s craftsmen like Len Wein and Jim Starlin, and innovative contemporaries such as Bryan Talbot and Alan Moore, all of these figures worked in superheroes or science fiction (Meaney 348–49; O'Donnell). Rather than looking to underground and alternative comics artists, Morrison imports his wide range of literary and cultural influences, diversifying the popular genres with inspirations from outside the medium.

His comics have prompted an equally diverse, if still nascent, body of criticism that runs the gamut from academic scholarship to journalism to the discourses of fandom. Articles on his comics, particularly *Animal Man* and *The Invisibles*, regularly appear in the *International Journal of Comic Art*, the *Journal of Popular Culture*, and other academic journals. Angela Ndalianis's collection *The Contemporary Comic Book Superhero* and Geoff Klock's psychoanalytic genre history *How to Read Superhero Comics and Why* both devote more than one chapter to selected comics by Morrison. His work inspires Steven Shaviro's "theoretical fiction about postmodernism," *Doom Patrols*, and receives effusive praise in Douglas Wolk's more journalistic essays in *Reading Comics*. Most of the discussion still takes place within comics fandom, however, including Patrick Meaney's documentary film *Grant Morrison: Talking with Gods* and the few books dedicated solely to Morrison. Timothy Callahan's *Grant Morrison: The Early Years* discusses five series from the late 1980s and early 1990s, while Patrick Neighly and Kereth Cowe-Spigai's *Anarchy for the Masses* and Patrick Meaney's *Our Sentence Is Up* are companions to *The Invisibles*, annotating that series and interviewing Morrison and his collaborators.

Morrison fandom maintains an active presence on the Internet, where fans debate and decipher his comics in online communities formed through blogs and websites. These communities have produced perceptive readings of Morrison's stories; some of the interpretations in this book were first developed while I participated in these forums, both as a reader and on my own now-defunct blog, and I have not shied away from citing online work when it has shaped my own understanding of Morrison. Whether it takes place online or in print, however, fan discourse is often content to annotate, rationalize, or simply celebrate Morrison's comics; critical appraisal is rare, though hardly nonexistent. This study examines Morrison's work through the interrelated discourses of literary criticism, critical theory, and comics scholarship, seeking to interpret and evaluate his comics while situating them within the evolution of his career, the cultures of contemporary comics, and postmodern culture at large. It also examines Morrison's work as literature: without ignoring the art that gives his comics their form, or the artists who have collaborated so productively with him, I am most interested in Morrison as the prime mover who conceives his stories in their earliest stages and develops them into fully realized scripts that influence his comics' visuals as well as their text. While the artists, letterers, colorists, and other members of the production team all shape the final product, most Morrison comics are unmistakably Morrison's comics, displaying the hallmarks that have made him one of the most distinctive writers in the field.

WORKING METHODS

In a 2005 online poll, a group of fifty comics bloggers voted Morrison their favorite writer by a commanding margin, sixty points ahead of his nearest competitor. The voters were self-selected and the results statistically meaningless, but the poll generated an astute analysis of Morrison's widespread appeal by blogger and comics critic Joe McCulloch ("Thoughts"). McCulloch attributed Morrison's popularity to his prolific output in 2005, his use of varied genres and styles, and his ability to straddle two different aesthetics of making comics, aesthetics that Eddie Campbell terms "comic-book culture" and "the graphic-novel sensibility" (Deppey, "Eddie Campbell" 82, 83). According to Campbell, comic book culture focuses on comics published as periodicals, in popular genres (e.g., superheroes), by multiple creators with specialized jobs in an assembly-line division of labor; the graphic novel sensibility prioritizes finite stories in other genres by solo or auteurist creators. These terms parallel Mark Rogers's distinction between industrial and artisanal methods of production (509–13), which classifies these aesthetics by the modes of production they use rather than the formats and genres they privilege. While Rogers observes a clear dichotomy between these modes of production (513–16), McCulloch notes that Morrison has been able to bridge them, working in collaboration with other creators to produce periodical superhero comics featuring corporate-owned characters while still telling finite stories with "a strong authorial voice and career-spanning thematic concerns" ("Thoughts"). This combination of styles explains his appeal to fans of both the sensibility of the graphic novel and the culture and format of the comic book; Morrison's career suggests the two modes do not have to be antithetical.

Although he drew his earliest comics, Morrison has followed the industry's standard division of labor since the mid-1980s, writing scripts for other artists to illustrate. He typically works in the "full script" style, in which the writer breaks down each page into panel descriptions that dictate the action and setting as well as the dialogue (Salisbury 9). After submitting his scripts he has little contact with most of his artists, even if they request visual references or authorial feedback; Jill Thompson has said this lack of contact extended even to his editors on *The Invisibles* (Neighly 43). E-mail has made him somewhat more accessible to his collaborators, although Cameron Stewart says that his questions for Morrison are usually transmitted through various intermediaries, either the series editor or Morrison's wife, Kristan. The notable exception is Frank Quitely, who maintains regular contact with Morrison since they both live in Glasgow (Callahan 262).[1]

Despite this lack of communication, Morrison often builds rich creative partnerships with his artists, and collaborators such as Phil Jimenez praise him for his ability to think visually in his scripts (Neighly 137). A former artist himself, Morrison builds his stories around images, often sketching thumbnail layouts of the entire comic before adding the dialogue and panel descriptions as he works up the full script (Salisbury 213). He also revises his scripts after he sees the finished art (Meaney 306); Stewart reports that the scripted dialogue is "often a temporary placeholder, and he writes the final dialogue that appears in print after he receives the artwork" (Stewart), a method somewhat closer to the "Marvel style" of plotting in which the writer dialogues pages after they are drawn (Salisbury 9). Although Morrison generally dictates the page and panel breakdowns, he is more than willing to adjust to his artists' ideas—as he must be, since his published scripts and thumbnails show that even his most faithful or literal interpreters make some changes to the framing, layout, or content of their pages.[2]

This division of labor, and Morrison's general lack of contact with his artists, means that his work can vary with the quality of his collaborators.

He is not always able to determine who he works with, especially on high-profile projects for the superhero publishers; his tenures on popular titles such as *JLA*, *New X-Men*, and *Batman* are frequently marked by last-minute fill-in artists who are hired to keep the production on pace, a consequence of the companies' need to maintain their cash flow by releasing comics on regular monthly schedules (Rogers 514). This is not to say that Morrison's more independent, creator-owned comics do not also suffer from their own production difficulties. Several of Morrison's collaborators complain that they receive his scripts a few pages at a time, sometimes weeks late; Phil Jimenez cites these delays as the reason he left *The Invisibles* (Neighly 136). Freed from the commercial imperatives of the more lucrative superhero properties, these comics can at least be held back until they are complete. In recent years, superhero publishers have also begun to allow popular writers and artists to finish comics at their own pace, in the interest of higher sales and more unified collected editions for the expanding bookstore market; Morrison and Quitely took three years to produce twelve issues of *All Star Superman*. On the other hand, the titles that are part of the companies' shared narrative continuities must still maintain monthly schedules, and the companies still require a steady stream of product.

Morrison has worked for the major American and British comics publishers for most of his career, yet he has maintained many of the advantages of independent comics artists. Although Rogers observes that artisanal production methods typically allow the single creator more freedom (515), Morrison is one of the rare writers able to push the formal and generic boundaries of comics storytelling through the industrial system. Some of these projects have seen print through Vertigo, or the titles that led to the creation of Vertigo, which publishes a marginally wider range of genres and sometimes allows creators to retain ownership of their characters; others were released through independent publishers in the British comics industry. These venues have allowed Morrison to write in any genre or style, yet he has also pursued his own interests within the industrial system in no small part because those interests include the popular genres and characters published by the major companies.

The superhero genre fascinates Morrison and serves as the subject of many of his works, which range from revisionist critiques to classicist revivals to avant-garde experiments—or sometimes, as in *Animal Man*, all three at once. These comics are rich in references to the genre's past but, with a few notable exceptions, they generally do not support the nostalgic and teleological narrative implied by fandom's names for the stages of superhero history

(Woo 272)—the declining scale of the Golden Age, Silver Age, Bronze Age, and so forth.[3] Instead, Morrison crafts palimpsests that combine elements from all of these periods (Salisbury 223–24) and pastiches that fuse superheroes with other genres; his superhero comics are informed by their past, but never limited by it. Morrison views superheroes not simply as popular, profitable, or storied characters but as vehicles for generating and embodying a host of potential meanings, a function that elevates them from corporate franchises to metaphors for the human mind.

MAGIC WORDS, MAGIC PICTURES

Morrison works almost exclusively in fantasy genres and generally shuns the realistic style common to many alternative comics and graphic novels. While his comics are filled with authorial surrogates and experiences drawn from his own life, Morrison typically frames them in science fiction or superhero narratives that make the autobiographical material more palatable to him and, he believes, to a larger audience. He is particularly reluctant to write about his hometown of Glasgow, Scotland, regarding the local literary tradition as provincial and predictably dour. As he told Nick Hasted,

> I hate the whole Glasgow writing scene. I hate the fact that anyone who lives in Glasgow is somehow required to write about "my life in the tenements," or "my days in the shipyard canteen." It's so artificial, and so parochial. There's a level of sheer bullshit nostalgia attached to the Glasgow literary scene, and I was more interested in trying to reach an international audience, and talk about things which were more wide-ranging. (Hasted 54)

Rejecting the social realism of the "angry young men" school of British writing, Morrison turns to fantasy to present his life in terms he believes are more widely accessible to audiences beyond Glasgow. He nevertheless insists that these fantastic elements have some basis in reality; in the letter column printed in the second issue of *The Invisibles*, he protests, "Nobody ever believes me when I tell 'em that the so-called 'weirdest' bits of my comics are actually the most autobiographical" (*Invisibles* I.2, "Invisible Ink").

Morrison was born in 1960 to a bohemian household that furnished no shortage of unusual experiences for his future comics writing. His parents, Walter Morrison and Agnes Lygate, were activists who protested against nuclear weapons through organizations such as the Scottish Committee of 100 (Christie). As a child, Morrison would sometimes accompany his father on excursions to photograph missile bases and bomb shelters, an experience he credits with inspiring the spy missions and break-ins of *The Invisibles* (Meaney 337–38). Morrison's parents and his uncle Billy also introduced him to both comics (Hasted 54) and magic (Neighly 237), two fields of creative activity that he has combined throughout his career. His comics dramatize his beliefs in magic and occultism, share his stories of divine revelations and near-death experiences, and articulate a quasi-Gnostic cosmology that maintains the physical universe is a construct suspended in a higher-dimensional space of living information. While readers are never obligated to share these beliefs and always have the option of approaching Morrison's work strictly as fiction, any attempt to study his writing must also seek to understand his cosmology, given the powerful and reciprocal influence each exerts on the other.

Morrison has been practicing magic since he was nineteen (Neighly 237), but the incident that reshaped his world-view and inspired many of his comics transpired in 1994 on a hotel roof garden in Kathmandu, Nepal. As he tells it, he was visited by silvery blobs who took him outside spacetime and into a medium of pure information, where they explained the structure of the universe to him. Morrison first alluded to this experience in the second *Invisibles* letter column, which he was composing at the time of the encounter; the contact happened between the ninth and tenth paragraphs (*Invisibles* I.2, "Invisible Ink"). He would elaborate on the incident years later in interviews with Mark Salisbury (209–10), Patrick Neighly (240–42), and Patrick Meaney (292–95); in "It was the 90s," a short story written for Sarah Champion's anthology *Fortune Hotel*; and in the final issue of *The Invisibles* (III.1, "Invisible Ink"). These accounts become progressively more confident: in the first letter column in 1994, Morrison would demur that the reality of the encounter "remains open to question"; in the Salisbury interview, conducted in 1998 and published in 1999, he not only insists that the encounter happened, he rejects the possibility that it was a hallucination caused by the hashish pellets he had eaten; and in the final letter column of 2000, he mocks his skeptics.[4] Morrison argues that the contact had much more in common with shamanic initiations and alien abduction experiences than with any drug trip, a subject in which he claims some expertise. He also downplays other physiological and environmental factors that might account for his visions. In most of his retellings, Morrison mentions that he had recently climbed the 365 steps that lead to the temple at Swayambhunath, a journey promising enlightenment in this life to the pilgrim who makes the climb without stopping once. Juxtaposing the climb with the contact experience, Morrison implies that he received the promised enlightenment; although he sometimes mentions the heat, the high altitude, and the thin, polluted air in Kathmandu, he never considers how these environmental effects, combined with the hashish, might also have contributed to the evening's revelations.

Morrison eschews any physiological explanations for his encounter, offering psychologistic ones in their place. While he regularly compares the Kathmandu experience to alien abduction, Morrison has clarified for Neighly that he doesn't believe the entities he met were aliens; he speculates that the experience "might just be a human developmental potential [...] it might just be the brain opening up" (242–43). This interpretation is characteristic of Morrison's approach to magic, which seeks to balance credence in the supernatural with scientific or pseudo-scientific explanations typically rooted in psychology. In his "Preface" to Richard Metzger's *Book of Lies* he insists he is "a hard-nosed skeptic" (9) whose belief in magic is based on empirical observation and personal experience, and he maintains that readers can confirm his statements by trying his experiments for themselves. He undercuts this rational posture, however, when he concedes these experiments may not work for everyone and blames any failures on the budding magician's aptitude, not the magic itself ("Pop Magic!" 20). Morrison insists his magic is a set of tools, not a belief system, but by casting doubt on anybody who is unable to wield those tools or replicate his results he effectively makes it impossible to falsify the system—and thus disqualifies it from consideration as a scientific discourse (Popper 40–41), whatever he may claim. Nevertheless, Morrison maintains that his particular system of magic, indebted to the individualistic, egalitarian schools of Austin Osman Spare and chaos magic ("Pop Magic!" 18), is empirical, pragmatic, and democratic, capable of being used by anyone who is willing to try.

He can make these claims with some justice since many of his magical exercises are simply methods of altering his own consciousness. He told Jonathan Ellis that he sees magic "as a kind of 'special attention'—the magician watches and listens to the world very closely and uses his/her knowledge of the obvious to do things which seem baffling or supernatural to people who have not been trained to be quite as closely observant" (Part 8). Under this special attention, even the most innocuous objects or incidents can assume a dreamlike, oracular significance ("Pop Magic!" 17). Magical consciousness is a means of making sense of the world, one that Morrison concedes is not so different from more mundane practices: he told Ellis, "My 'reality tunnel,' as Robert Anton Wilson calls it, is one that allows me to conveniently frame every experience and state of consciousness, good or bad, in the context of my magical initiation and progress. The disciplines of magic bring structure, meaning and pattern into the apparently unstructured, senseless and painful times of anyone's life. As do the grounding disciplines of earning a living and sharing a relationship" (J. Ellis Part 5).

That said, he does not view magic solely as a mode of perception or an interpretive filter. Magical consciousness is only the first step for Morrison, who believes anyone can apply magical practices to alter themselves or their environment. He maintains that he healed Jill Thompson's cat (Neighly 65–66) and cured his own cat's cancer (Neighly 247), and he famously invited readers of *The Invisibles* to participate in a ritual to boost the comic's sales by masturbating to a magical sigil printed in the letter column (I.16, "Invisible Ink"). As part of that ritual, however, Morrison instructed those same readers to promote the series to friends and Internet groups, a less occult means of expanding his audience.

Many of his magical techniques are simply ritualized procedures for motivation and self-actualization, such as his method of summoning gods and archetypes. Morrison freely admits these archetypes are not divine beings but rather "Big Ideas" ("Pop Magic!" 21), names given to powerful emotional states, abstract concepts, and other aspects of the human mind; he suggests "Reductionists may come to an understanding of magic by considering 'Mount Olympus' as a metaphor for the collective Human head" ("Pop Magic!" 22). To remind would-be initiates that these are ideal constructs and not actual deities, he recommends invoking fictional characters, beings known to be unreal, by imitating their qualities. Since the goal of these invocations is to assume those same qualities—"Summon James Bond before a date by playing the themes to *Goldfinger* and *Thunderball* while dressing in a tuxedo" ("Pop Magic!" 23)—these fictional summonings can become exercises in method acting and self-fulfilling rituals of impersonation. Morrison does not attempt to conceal the performative, illusory, or downright deceptive aspects of these practices; one of the first instructions he gives to the aspiring magician in his "Pop Magic!" essay is that adage of self-help programs, "Fake it till you make it" (16).

Morrison has followed these methods himself, summoning guides, benefactors, and role models ranging from comic book characters to real-life celebrities. He invoked John Lennon before beginning his longest and most ambitious series, *The Invisibles* (Hasted 75), and then wrote the ritual into the first issue by taking the character King Mob through the same procedures

Introduction: A Union of Opposites   13

Figure 0-1. *The Invisibles* I.1.18. Art by Steve Yeowell. © Grant Morrison.

(fig. 0-1). Morrison has created many authorial surrogates in his career, but he forged a particularly strong connection with King Mob: rather than basing the character on himself he began to model himself after the character, shaving his head, studying the martial arts, and hanging out in fetish clubs (Salisbury 210; Ness). He soon discovered that events he wrote into King Mob's life were happening in his own; after putting the anarchist assassin through a grueling ordeal of torture and bacterial invasion in volume one and nearly dying of a staph infection himself, he decided to go easier on his surrogate and give him a sexy girlfriend in volume two (Salisbury 210, 212; Neighly 246–47).

This only partially planned correspondence between the author and his character became another kind of magical summoning, one in which Morrison created the Big Idea he invoked. He would later identify this type of magical working as a "hypersigil," a narrative symbol that incorporates and transforms its author's life (Neighly 247; "Pop Magic!" 21). Once again, the ritual could just as easily be described as a self-actualization technique—desiring to reinvent himself as a James Bond-style hero, Morrison wrote the kind of character he wanted to become and then adjusted his behavior to become him—although the near-simultaneous infections of character and author suggest a deeper synchronicity. His acknowledgment of the performative and self-fulfilling qualities of his magical practices does not in any way diminish his belief in the reality of magic.

Morrison's magical beliefs often invite comparison with those of another contemporary comics writer, one to whom Morrison frequently finds himself compared, Alan Moore. Like Morrison, Moore identifies himself as a magician and views his beliefs and practices as an extension of his writing; he too believes that gods exist as stories or ideas within the human mind, and he has publicly dedicated himself to the worship of a fraudulent god (Campbell 4–5). Moore, however, regards both magic and comics writing in predominantly linguistic terms: he told Eddie Campbell, "I eventually learned that magic was what Aleister Crowley referred to as 'a disease of language,' and came to understand that magic is indeed mostly a linguistic phenomenon and was therefore what had been lying at the end of the path beyond mere craft all along" (4). Moore's career has reflected this development as his interests have shifted from comics to novels and shamanic performance pieces that are preoccupied with language as both subject and mode of expression. Annalisa Di Liddo observes that Moore's comics, prose, performances, and magical study are all shaped by his belief in "the supremacy of language as the primary instance of representation," which "results in his view of the word as the first step in all creative and

Figure 0-2. *Vimanarama* 3.5. Art by Philip Bond. © Grant Morrison and Philip Bond.

cognitive acts [...] the starting point of creation" (Di Liddo 30). Morrison, on the other hand, understands magic in primarily visual terms. Most of his public explanations of his magical practices revolve around sigils, symbols that condense written statements of desires or goals into iconic form ("Pop Magic!" 18). He also interprets the conventional representations of gods such as Hermes as "a condensation into pictorial form—a sigil, in fact—of an easily recognizable default state of human consciousness" ("Pop Magic!" 21). Pictures, rather than words, facilitate Morrison's access to these states of consciousness.

This pictorial priority is also reflected in his comics, which routinely stress the inadequacy of language. This claim may seem counterintuitive at first:

Morrison's work is filled with secret vocabularies that control human consciousness, drugs that erase the distinctions between words and the objects they describe, living symbols composed of pure meaning, and realms inhabited by beings made entirely of language. Nevertheless, he supplies these fantastic languages to address a shortcoming in actual human language, the inescapable difference between the verbal or written sign and its referent. This slippage has shaped the modern understanding of language since the "linguistic turn" of the twentieth century, which argued that signifiers do not enjoy any absolute or mimetic relationship to the concepts they signify, only arbitrary, socially and contextually determined ones.[5] Morrison's comics seek to evade, defy, or reverse this view by enhancing or transforming language through the addition of visual representations. *The Invisibles* may state that Key 17 eliminates the difference between word and object, but it can only simulate the drug's effects once artist Phil Jimenez translates verbal signs into the images perceived under its influence. *Vimanarama* may send its young protagonist to an afterlife composed entirely of language and may even unravel him into a cluster of linguistic descriptors, but it can only represent this linguistically determined reality because Philip Bond's art gives the words materiality and graphic presence (fig. 0-2). In both cases, Morrison positions these visual representations as necessary intermediaries between words and objects.

Even when his comics do not explicitly address the limitations of language, Morrison uses visual modes of signification to bypass the symbolic deferrals of verbal signs. One of his most radical techniques emerges from his superhero comics, which he populates with characters who serve as physical incarnations of fears, desires, or abstract concepts: the imprisoned criminals of *Arkham Asylum* embody Batman's repressed anxieties, while the surreal menaces of *Doom Patrol* reify Crazy Jane's traumas at the hands of oppressive authority figures. Morrison also applies this technique to his protagonists, writing superheroes as embodiments of humanity's best qualities and highest aspirations in projects like *JLA* and *All Star Superman*. These characters generate meaning through the concretizations and personifications of hypostasis rather than the abstractions of conventional figurative language: unlike metaphors, which defer their meanings onto absent signifiers (Mellard 519), or allegories, which refer to meanings quite separate from their allegorical vehicles (de Man 189), Morrison's hypostases embody the states they represent through their behaviors and, frequently, through their uncanny anatomies. They express meaning through form and action rather than denoting it through symbolic proxies. While poststructuralist theorists such as Paul de Man celebrate allegory for its confirmation that language can never achieve unity between sign and object, Morrison embraces hypostasis precisely because it challenges this dissociation and reopens the possibility of a mimetic art.[6]

As visual narratives with a proclivity for physicalized representations of emotional traumas and tensions, superhero comics make an ideal staging ground for such a challenge to poststructuralism. Scott Bukatman describes the mechanics that underwrite these hypostases when he locates the superhero body as both focus and vehicle for a host of "body narratives, bodily fantasies, that incorporate (incarnate) aggrandizement and anxiety, mastery, and trauma. [...] The superhero body is everything—a *corporeal*, rather than a *cognitive*, mapping of the subject into a cultural system" (49; his emphasis). This corporeal mapping enables "a symbolic return to a presymbolic space of primal drives and primal fears as well as later anxieties that are at once psychoanalytical, social, and historical" (Bukatman 53). Superhero comics are therefore ideal vehicles for what Slavoj Žižek calls "embodiment in the real" (99), hyper-literalized representations that bypass the symbolic order of language and signification to represent primal drives and fears through figures that are not symbols, figures that externalize their meanings into physical forms. Given this practice's centrality to superhero narratives, it is not surprising that Žižek should state, "As a rule, these embodiments of pure drive *wear a mask*" (172n2; his emphasis), or that he cites as one example none other than the Joker from Tim Burton's *Batman* film. The Joker's hideous, permanent grin, the source and expression of his madness, demonstrates that "The real is thus not an inaccessible kernel hidden beneath layers of symbolizations, it is *on the surface*" (Žižek 172n2; his emphasis), hypostatized in his own form.

Morrison's literalized embodiments, like his magical languages, cannot escape signification: at most they trade symbolic representations for imaginary ones, verbal abstractions for visual simulations. Yet that exchange allows Morrison to sidestep the endless substitutions and deferrals of poststructuralist theories of language. His comics seek a nonlinguistic, presymbolic referentiality through the concretization of symbolic meaning, promising mimetic representations of the abstract and the impossible. This mimetic counterrevolution is abetted by his choice of medium and genre; comics allow him access to visual as well as verbal representation, and superhero stories, like the genres of science fiction (Delany 92; McHale, *Constructing* 246) or the fantastic (Todorov 76–77, 79), routinely literalize meanings that other, more realistic genres represent as metaphor. Individually, either medium or genre would permit Morrison to bypass the abstractions of symbolic language, but together they enable the creation of figures that are at once mimetic and expressionist, figures whose meaning lies in their own form and not in their reference to some other, absent signifier. Morrison's hypostases are reified ideas, emotions, or states of consciousness, not unlike his concept of gods—which may explain why he regularly conjures superheroes alongside other, more traditional divinities as personifications of human intellect and fortitude ("Pop Magic!" 23; Neighly 244–45).[7] Morrison approaches the craft of writing comics with the same pictorial and idealist framework he brings to the craft of magic. For the purposes of this study, his magical beliefs are most important as a guide to interpreting his writing, not a key to the structure of the universe.

WORLDS WITHIN WORLDS

In addition to magical sigils and hypostatic embodiments, Morrison's comics are equally reliant on the techniques of postmodernist literature, drama, and film, most notably metafiction. His work is characterized by a pervasive self-consciousness that can manifest as flagrant experiments with narrative forms, general commentaries on the practice of writing, or more industry-specific examinations of the dynamics of writing corporate-owned characters in a shared narrative continuity. This self-reflexive habit has come to define his career while helping to inaugurate a decades-long trend towards metacritical commentary in other contemporary superhero comics. Morrison's metafictions also form an instructive contrast with his interest in hypostasis and presymbolic representation. Peter Sattler has observed that many scholars celebrate comics for the attention they draw to their own artifice, while many artists prize comics for their directness and their ability to represent interior states with immediacy (220n7). Morrison, however, does both, interrogating his comics' narrative conventions and ideological assumptions while harnessing their ability to bypass the mediations of language. This dual impulse raises a possible contradiction: how can Morrison approach his texts with self-conscious irony while also claiming they offer unmediated representations?

The answer lies in the type of metafiction he practices. Patricia Waugh identifies two poles of metafictional writing, "one that finally accepts a substantial real world whose significance is not entirely composed of relationships within language; and one that suggests there can never be an escape from the prisonhouse of language and either delights or despairs in this" (53). While

Morrison occasionally gestures towards this latter, poststructuralist style of metafiction—*The Invisibles* ends with the comic book turning into a sentence, then an abstracted image, then the blank page—his comics generally accept the existence of a world outside text and language: *Animal Man* even sends its protagonist there (or rather, to its closest possible fictional simulation) to confront his author, Grant Morrison, who confesses frustration at his inability to change the world through his writing. Although Morrison depicts language as the foundation of identity and ideology in *The Invisibles*, *Vimanarama*, *We3*, and elsewhere, he never abandons his interest in the world outside the text. Even his most antirealistic works explore issues of authority and independence, freedom and control, in areas ranging from artistic production to animal rights to political and economic oppression. These interests take his metafictions beyond language into a world governed by material as well as semiotic power. Morrison's commitment to mimetic representation enables him to challenge poststructuralist assumptions about language, signification, and the metaphysics of presence, promising readers hypostases of unmediated experience even as he exposes the processes of his comics' creation.

Rather than simply depict one world, however, Morrison presents multiple worlds that operate on variable narrative and ontological scales. His comics embed stories within stories and worlds within worlds, ascending or descending through different levels of magnification and nesting. He connects these scales through synecdochic or fractal structures in which the part (the embedded narrative or world; also the individual scene, page, or panel) reflects and reproduces the whole (the overall story or cosmos; also the issue or series). He frequently explains these structures through analogies to holograms, which encode the entire image onto each portion of the recording medium, or to the dictum "As above, so below," a principle of Hermetic magic that asserts a fundamental correspondence between microcosm and macrocosm. These explanations present another fusion of scientific and magical discourses—hardly surprising, as Morrison's comics routinely blend the real and the fantastic, sometimes by blurring the distinctions between worlds that run on wildly divergent physical laws or narrative logics. Brian McHale classifies such techniques as "ontological pluralizers" and contends that this plurality of worlds is characteristic of postmodernist fiction (*Constructing* 125–26, 180); Ronald Sukenick suggests these techniques produce an information overload that reflects "the kind of formal organization implicit in contemporary life" (19).[8]

These methods also reinforce Morrison's interest in reconciling concepts Western culture tends to lock into binary oppositions. His metafictions and multiply nested worlds collapse distinctions between fiction and reality, treating the comics page as a mimetic representation while simultaneously calling attention to its graphic artifice. His penchant for embodying abstract concepts balances the literal and the figurative, the material and the ideal, within the human form; his magical languages and iconic sigils fuse word and image in an attempt to transcend the difference between sign and object. This distaste for binaries extends to a mistrust of other philosophical or ideological extremes, including some of the core values of his favorite genres—notably the superhero's role as the defender of a social order that Morrison does not always support. He therefore attempts to synthesize these conflicting ethical codes in his treatment of genre, his ongoing reconciliation of opposites, and his oscillation between two seemingly contradictory modes of comics production.

ALTERNATING CURRENTS

This book follows Morrison through the various stages of his career as he moves between periods of more mainstream or independent work, not to provide an exhaustive survey of his comics (which would be impossible in a single volume) but to chart his attempts to combine the best features of these aesthetics and to trace the development of his most important themes and techniques. Chapter 1, "Ground Level," argues that Morrison's early work in the British comics industry sets the parameters for his career. Starting in the "ground level" comics that sought to bridge the undergrounds and the mainstream, Morrison initially follows the conventions established by his peers and his immediate predecessors, from the New Wave science fiction of Bryan Talbot to the revisionist superheroes of Alan Moore. The revisionist influence is especially prominent in his first major work, *Zenith*, which presents a cynical take on shallow and materialistic superheroes, but while he was writing superheroes for *2000 AD*, Morrison was also working for smaller independent publishers like Trident, style magazines like *Cut*, and more experimental comics like *Crisis* and *Revolver*. Series such as *The New Adventures of Hitler*, *St. Swithin's Day*, and *Dare* express Morrison's anger and frustration at the policies of Margaret Thatcher; along with the later phases of the long-running *Zenith*, they would also establish his own distinctive voice. These comics alternate between mainstream and independent work, between superheroes and other genres, and between convention and innovation, beginning a pattern that Morrison has followed throughout his career.

Chapter 2, "The World's Strangest Heroes," looks at Morrison's first work for American publisher DC Comics, work that continues to define his reputation: *Animal Man*, *Arkham Asylum*, and *Doom Patrol*. Like his early British work, these comics initially participate in the then-dominant style of realistic, revisionist superheroes. To break away from that style, Morrison institutes the mode of writing he is still best known for today, a mode that combines metafiction, surrealism, the absurd, and above all a strategy of physical embodiment. Through his personified terrors in *Arkham Asylum*, his metafictional narratives in *Animal Man*, and his rejection of reductive philosophies and ideological extremes in *Doom Patrol*, Morrison turns long-standing superhero conventions into powerful and variable tools for dramatizing ethical, cultural, and psychological questions that lie well beyond the genre's typical concerns.

Chapter 3, "The Invisible Kingdom," explores Morrison's role in the foundation of Vertigo, an imprint of DC Comics that sought to occupy the space between superheroes and alternative comics by publishing work in other popular genres, typically fantasy and horror. The imprint's positioning resembles Morrison's own career—both are indebted to superhero comics but not bound by their conventions—and in fact, Vertigo was built on the work of Morrison and his peers in marginal DC superhero titles like *Animal Man* and *Doom Patrol*. After briefly considering the comics that inaugurated Morrison's involvement with Vertigo, *Sebastian O* and *The Mystery Play*, this chapter examines his long-running series *The Invisibles*, in which Morrison adapts the structures of superhero comics, spy movies, and other popular genres to articulate a philosophy of government, ethics, identity, and art that seeks to balance the freedom of the individual with their responsibilities to the larger community. The series also provides Morrison's most explicit renunciation of philosophical binaries as his heroes must learn to fight an authoritarian enemy without re-creating its logic and values.

Chapter 4, "Widescreen," accounts for Morrison's unlikely transition from unorthodox Vertigo creator to one of the most popular and influential writers in superhero comics. The chapter begins with a look at *Flex Mentallo*, the metafictional Vertigo miniseries that signaled Morrison's rekindled interest in superheroes, before turning to *JLA*, the DC Comics series that helped to establish not one but two trends in nineties superhero comics: a retro movement that rejected the innovations of the revisionists in favor of nostalgia, and a widescreen style that focused on over-the-top action. Despite his role in launching both of these trends, however, Morrison's approach clashes with the nostalgic imperatives and sometimes reactionary politics of the retro and widescreen movements. His comics instead attempt to move the superhero genre forward by demolishing many of its most basic conventions, including the superhero's role as defender of the status quo. This project is most clear in Morrison's work for Marvel Comics early in the new millennium: while *Marvel Boy* and *Fantastic Four 1234* amount to conventional widescreen and retro comics, *New X-Men* enacts some fundamental changes to Marvel's premier superhero franchise. Morrison recasts the comic as a science fiction series and orients the title towards the future rather than its own convoluted history. Like *JLA*, *New X-Men* presents its protagonists as potentially progressive and transformative figures rather than conservative ones bound by social or generic convention.

Chapter 5, "Free Agents," sees a similar resistance to convention in a quartet of more personal, creator-owned projects Morrison wrote for Vertigo: *The Filth*, which coincided with the end of Morrison's tenure at Marvel, and a trio of miniseries, *Seaguy*, *We3*, and *Vimanarama*, which followed his departure. All of these comics fuse genres into unlikely combinations—Jack Kirby-style superheroes and musical comedies, for example, or *Incredible Journey*-style animal adventure and science fiction techno-thriller—and all feature protagonists who fight forces of authority that seek to impose identities upon them as a means of social control. While these series enact Morrison's own struggles for artistic independence, they also link that struggle to other efforts to find autonomy within the political, economic, and religious hegemonies of the early twenty-first century.

Chapter 6, "A Time of Harvest," looks at Morrison's next attempt at revitalizing the superhero genre in *Seven Soldiers*. An ambitious formal experiment comprising seven interlocking miniseries, *Seven Soldiers* tries to reverse generic ossification and exhaustion by melding superheroes with elements from other genres such as westerns, science fiction, and horror. The resulting hybrids, however, are no more limited to generic metacommentary than were Morrison's Vertigo miniseries. The project uses the conventions of fantasy to depict a twenty-first-century society in social and environmental decline even as it looks for critiques of modernity that are not reactionary in their political implications. *Seven Soldiers* carves out a space between postmodern capitalism and reactionary antimodernism in its search for sustainable methods of social organization—a search that parallels its attempt to develop sustainable, mature genres of popular fiction. It also continues Morrison's ongoing challenge to the linguistic assumptions of poststructuralism while looking for new strategies of signification that are not subject to manipulation by the political and economic forces Morrison holds responsible for modernity's ills.

Finally, Chapter 7, "Work for Hire," examines Morrison's subsequent work writing DC Comics' most popular and lucrative superheroes. Comics from this period such as *All Star Superman*, *Batman*, and *Final Crisis* are almost textbook illustrations of postmodern self-consciousness: Morrison multiplies his protagonists into a dizzying profusion of reflections, parodies, analogues, and counterparts, while he collapses decades of publication history into transhistorical pastiches. This approach has produced some substantive works—*All Star Superman* uses Superman's rich history to stage an argument about the power of ideas to affect the world—yet many of these comics are trapped by their own self-reflexive commentaries and by a set of themes that have become overly familiar from prior Morrison comics. These series are too invested in the concerns of corporate superhero comics and too far removed from the more independent, personal material that has always been a key part of Morrison's work. A brief afterword, "Morrison, Incorporated," looks at some recent comics that suggest Morrison is moving back to creator-owned work once again, and reiterates the importance of understanding his career as a fusion of contrasting styles, genres, and modes of production. Never content to settle on a single aesthetic for long, Morrison continues to merge elements from the many cultures of contemporary comics, demonstrating that, in the right hands, even the most familiar genres have limitless potential.

Chapter 1

GROUND LEVEL

The reconciliation of mainstream and independent sensibilities that has been central to Grant Morrison's career was initially made possible by the unique topography of the British comics industry in the 1970s and 1980s. British comics had never been dominated by superheroes the way American comic books were after the 1960s, and writers had more opportunities to experiment with different genres. Morrison was also fortunate to reach artistic maturity during the adult comics boom of the late 1980s, a period when his fusion of sensibilities was not only tolerated but rewarded. The boom years offered writers a healthy mixture of mainstream and alternative outlets, and a growing number of corporate-owned comics were becoming open to adult subject matter and independent creative autonomy (see Sabin, *Adult Comics* chapters 6 and 7). These venues allowed Morrison to adopt a number of styles, enabling his rapid development; he told Mark Salisbury he was lucky to have "two outlets from the start. One for the avant-garde stuff [...] and one for really mainstream commercial work" (207). His earliest strips, written squarely in the science fiction and superhero genres and dominated by his adolescent influences, quickly yielded to a revisionist sensibility that challenged the conventions of the genres that inspired him. That revisionism itself proved transitory as Morrison moved on to other genres, shifted his focus to more explicit political critiques, and ultimately arrived at a more self-critical outlook that refuses to accept on faith the generic or ideological assumptions of any comics, even his own.

Morrison's first published work appeared in the Scottish anthology *Near Myths* (1978–80), one of the "ground level" comics of the late 1970s that positioned themselves "half-way between 'underground' and 'above-ground'" (Sabin, *Adult Comics* 73). The ground levels operated within mainstream genres—usually science fiction or fantasy—yet approached them with an underground comix sensibility that encouraged experimental layouts and narrative techniques, graphic sex and violence, and complete creative control and ownership by the artists. Or, as Morrison described them to Nick Hasted, "It was this concept that you could do comics that borrowed the best elements of the underground, and married them to the reader-accessibility of mainstream comics. In actual fact, it was a recipe for disaster" (Hasted 56). *Near Myths* failed to reach wide distribution and was canceled after five issues, making it one of the longest-running British ground levels (Sabin, *Adult Comics* 73). The title nevertheless launched Morrison's career and marked his first efforts at synthesizing the tropes of popular fiction with the auteurist production methods of the undergrounds and alternative comics; he wrote and drew his *Near Myths* stories, in keeping with the underground ethos that privileged comics by single creators (Hatfield 16, 18). As we might expect of most eighteen-year-old auteurs, however, these stories are highly derivative, with the *Gideon Stargrave* serial particularly indebted to the New Wave science fiction of Michael Moorcock and the comics of Bryan Talbot, whose own Moorcock-inspired *The Adventures of Luther Arkwright* ran alongside Morrison's work in *Near Myths*. The art is similarly indebted to Talbot and to American comics artists Jim Steranko, Neal Adams, and Jim Starlin, aping their baroque page layouts and use of screentones. The *Near Myths* stories attempt to combine mainstream accessibility with underground experimentation, but in this novice work, Morrison's most overtly experimental gestures inevitably prove to be his most imitative ones.

His next project showed more genuine innovation while remaining indebted to its influences. *Captain Clyde* (1979–82), Morrison's first superhero work, ran in three Glasgow newspapers published by the Govan Press. The strip combined traditional superheroics with the first stirrings of what would later be termed revisionism, grounding its mystically powered protagonist in the real world: Glasgow-based superhero Captain Clyde is unemployed and living on the dole, just as Morrison was at the time (O'Donnell), reflecting the deep recession and soaring unemployment of the early Thatcher years (Hitchcock 320). These gestures towards quotidian realism aside, the art and plotting are still derivative of Starlin, Adams, and the more cosmic, psychedelic side of 1970s American superhero comics (fig. 1-1). Morrison has acknowledged that the strip's ventures into realism were tentative, telling his friend Tony O'Donnell, "Looking back, I wish I'd made it even more realistic but this was before *Marvelman*, and while I'm proud of my few innovations, I was still thinking in a sort of Marvel Comics slam-bang way a great deal of the time." *Marvelman* (1982–84), later reprinted and continued in the United States as *Miracleman* (1985–89), was an Alan Moore superhero serial that

Figure 1-1. *Captain Clyde*. Art by Grant Morrison. © Grant Morrison.

"took a kitsch children's character" from the 1950s and "placed him within the real world of 1982" (Parkin 23); it ran in *Warrior*, a comics magazine aimed at older readers, alongside Moore's dystopian thriller *V for Vendetta* (Parkin 21). *Warrior* and the superhero realism of *Marvelman* were timely discoveries for the twenty-two-year-old Morrison, rekindling his interest in writing comics and demonstrating their capacity for mature work just as *Captain Clyde* was canceled (O'Donnell). Morrison renewed his attempts to break into the industry, though he wrote only one script for *Warrior* before that magazine folded due to poor sales, legal disputes, and creative conflicts. To support himself, he turned to more mainstream outlets aimed at younger readers.

Since 1979, Morrison had been writing and, on one occasion, drawing comics for *Starblazer*, Scottish publisher DC Thomson's youth-oriented science fiction magazine. After the collapse of *Warrior*, he also wrote episodes of the licensed comics *Doctor Who* and *Zoids* for Marvel UK and scripted a number of *Future Shocks*, short science fiction stories with twist endings, for IPC's *2000 AD*. This system of producing a high volume of short scripts was a rite of passage for British comics writers in the early 1980s—a literal rite of passage in the case of *2000 AD*, since writers had to produce a requisite number of *Future Shocks* before they could graduate to an ongoing series (Hasted 57). Lance Parkin describes the short story system as

> a remarkably good apprenticeship. It meant that a writer could see how different artists interpreted scripts, made a number of contacts in the comics' scene, learned what was popular with audiences and what editors were looking for. In terms of storytelling, it imposed an economy and efficiency to the narrative and forced writers to come up with imaginative solutions and striking images and ideas. (19)

Morrison arrived at *2000 AD* at an auspicious moment. The core group of writers and artists who had built the anthology into a smash hit—Pat Mills, Kevin O'Neill, Dave Gibbons, Alan Moore, and others—were being lured away by American publishers who could afford to pay royalties, and *2000 AD* had to bring in a second generation of talent to replace them (Sabin, *Adult Comics* 60). After Morrison completed his *Future Shocks* apprenticeship, he was given the writing duties on *Zenith*, *2000 AD*'s first superhero serial and Morrison's first major work (Bishop 120).

Morrison was writing a feature attraction for one of Britain's best-selling comics, but he would continue to work for other venues that offered more creative latitude. His comics became more daring both artistically and politically, generating no small amount of controversy. In the late 1980s and early 1990s he wrote serials for *Cut*, one of several music and style magazines that commissioned comics during the adult comics boom (Sabin, *Adult Comics* 110), and *Trident*, the flagship anthology of Trident Comics, one of many independent publishers founded at the height of the boom (*Adult Comics* 97). His work also ran in *Crisis*, a politically engaged foray into mature comics published by Fleetway (the new owners of *2000 AD*), and *Revolver*, a "less serious-minded follow-up" designed in response to criticisms that *Crisis* was dull and humorless (*Adult Comics* 106–7). These venues were all short-lived, but they occupied territory similar to Morrison's initial publication in the ground levels and his later work for Vertigo. All of these publishers sought, with varying degrees of success, to carve out interstitial markets within the comics industry—markets that fell between younger and older readers, new and familiar genres, mainstream content and independent creative practices. The adult comics boom of the late 1980s would collapse by the early 1990s (*Adult Comics* 110–11), but Morrison would continue to seek out this middle ground in nearly all his projects.

His British work sets the template for the rest of his career as it moves between mainstream and alternative projects, with each mode informing

Morrison's style and inspiring him to adopt new storytelling techniques or pursue new ambitions. These comics also feature his first explorations of ideas that would preoccupy him for years to come, which he similarly organizes around the opposition and synthesis of conflicting values. Morrison's early British work is driven by tensions between youth and maturity, idealism and cynicism, influence and independence, and traditionalist and revisionist approaches to genre. He becomes increasingly less likely to resolve these conflicts in favor of one side or the other, however, as he settles into a dialectical aesthetic that combines these tensions productively to create works of nuance and substance—even when he writes about characters who are anything but substantive.

ZENITH: REIGN OF THE SUPERBRATS

Zenith (1987–92) was the first superhero feature to run in *2000 AD*, part of a concerted effort to give the comic "more of the look and feel of an American product" even as its most popular creators were leaving to work for American publishers (Sabin, *Comics, Comix* 140). Notwithstanding the growing availability and popularity of American superhero comics in the British market (Sabin, *Adult Comics* 60), the mandate to develop a new superhero for *2000 AD* posed a challenge for Morrison. In his "Introduction" to the collected *Zenith* Phase I, Morrison admits that American-style superheroes had never been especially popular in British comics and acknowledges that "in order to have any degree of success, I'd have to attempt a uniquely British approach to the basic premise of people with superhuman abilities and ludicrous costumes." His solution was elegant in its simplicity: he stole.

> Well, what would *you* have done? Fifty Golden Years of superhero history were stacked like tins on a supermarket shelf, just begging to be slipped into my pockets and sneaked through the checkout.
>   I stole from Superman's 1938 debut and from Britain's own *Captain Hurricane*. I stole from Alan Moore's groundbreaking *Marvelman*, from *Dr. Strange*, *The Flash*, and from *The X-Men*. Delirious with the joy of crime, I even stole from my own previous work and used the contraband to lay the foundations of a fictional world.
>   In the first series of *Zenith*, collected in this volume, all these purloined elements combined to create an instantly recognisable

scratch-mix superhero mythos, designed to encourage certain assumptions based on the reader's previous exposure to the conventions of superhero comics. ("Introduction," *Zenith Book One*)

Contrary to Morrison's claims, this combination of transhistorical bricolage and self-conscious recycling of convention is not so much uniquely British as it is distinctly postmodern. His magpie aesthetic is transatlantic, cosmopolitan, rooted in a global cultural and economic transformation that promotes pastiches and simulacra while disregarding national borders. *Zenith* instead gains local resonance by grafting the conventions and plot structures of American superhero comics onto British characters, settings, and cultural references.

The longest storyline, Phase III's "War in Heaven," is Morrison's version of DC Comics' apocalyptic *Crisis on Infinite Earths* (1985), a limited series about an extradimensional menace that threatened to wipe out a plenitude of parallel universes. Many of these universes were populated by characters DC had acquired from defunct publishers such as Fawcett, Charlton, or Quality Comics; the multiverse served as an intradiagetic space for ordering and containing DC's corporate intellectual properties. Morrison follows this practice in *Zenith* Phase III, creating alternative Earths to house characters from different British comics publishers—all the DC Thomson heroes live on Alternative 666, for example, although Morrison gives them thinly disguised pseudonyms as he didn't have the rights to use them in a Fleetway comic ("Zenith Phase Three Scorecard"). Assembling all the British superheroes of the previous thirty years into a common narrative framework where they can meet, fight, and join forces, Phase III creates an American-style narrative continuity for British comics.

Zenith's attitude towards these pilfered goods is an equally important part of its adaptation to the British readership. Morrison presents the familiar characters and conventions of superhero comics through a skeptical, sardonic style that, despite its transatlantic origins, had become associated with British writers by the late 1980s. That decade saw a vogue for "revisionist superheroes" (Sabin, *Adult Comics* 97), stories that attempted to represent superheroes realistically, cynically, or with a mature artistic sensibility. Roger Sabin calls this movement "arguably the most artistically interesting phase in mainstream comics history" and defines these comics as titles that

> featured more politics, social parody and moral ambiguity, as well as liberal helpings of cinematic sex and violence. [...] Yet the comics were

still essentially superhero-orientated. For the publishers also recognized that it would be commercially unwise to stray too far from established formulas. (*Comics, Comix* 160)

Sabin traces the origins of the revisionist superheroes to Frank Miller's work on *Daredevil* for Marvel Comics and Alan Moore's reinvention of *Swamp Thing* for DC Comics, both in the early 1980s. But the revisionist impulse was if anything even more prevalent in Britain, where it surfaced in other genres, generally science fiction comics, as early as the late 1970s. Moore's *Marvelman* and *V for Vendetta*, Pat Mills and Kevin O'Neill's *Nemesis the Warlock*, Bryan Talbot's *The Adventures of Luther Arkwright*, and *2000 AD*'s lead feature, John Wagner, Alan Grant, and Carlos Ezquerra's *Judge Dredd*, all question, overturn, or mock some of the core assumptions of their genres—notably the idea that the hero must be noble, selfless, and morally upright—while delivering unflinching sex, violence, and political commentary.

Released in the wake of the two most successful and influential revisionist superhero comics, Frank Miller's *Batman: The Dark Knight Returns* (1986) and Alan Moore and Dave Gibbons's *Watchmen* (1986–87), *Zenith* grounds its heroes in contemporary British culture while distancing them from older conventions of the costumed crimefighter. Thus, Robot Archie, long-running star of the children's adventure comic *Lion*, is reconceived as Acid Archie: the bulky 1950s robot has joined the late eighties acid house and rave culture, spouting catch-phrases and painting flowers and smiley faces on his metal body (fig. 1-2). The heroes original to *Zenith* are equally media-obsessed, spending more time releasing singles and appearing on talk shows than they do stopping crime or rescuing people. Zenith, the title character and the first second-generation superhuman, has parlayed his celebrity into a recording career while his highly publicized misbehavior has earned him the tabloid nickname "Superbrat."

This rejection of traditional superhero tropes in favor of the transient tastes of pop culture also extends to the characters' costumes. Morrison explains how Brendan McCarthy, who collaborated with him on *Zenith*'s design, "overturned the conventional notions of superhero *couture* and produced a series of remarkable costume designs which owed more to styles invented by Quant, Westwood and Gaultier than to Superman's blue long-johns" ("Introduction," *Zenith Book One*). Morrison, regular series artist Steve Yeowell, and fill-in artist M. Carmona would gradually add more designs representing different stages in Zenith's career, establishing the protagonist as a shameless mimic who copies any popular trend. In this

Figure 1-2. *Zenith* III.1.5. Art by Steve Yeowell. © Rebellion.

fictitious history, Zenith debuts in 1983 wearing a hussar's jacket and frilled shirt reminiscent of Adam and the Ants (Interlude 3), then spends 1987 to 1990 (Phases I through III) with a prominent quiff (and equally prominent jawline) inspired by Morrissey. When he returns two years later in Phase IV, Zenith has jumped onto the rave bandwagon and traded in his leather jacket for a tracksuit. These looks are overtly derivative, meant to suggest that Zenith is a canny and cynical self-marketer who will adopt any persona to keep up with changing tastes. He scoffs at sixties nostalgia at the beginning of Phase I only to incorporate psychedelic guitars and imagery into his videos by the start of Phase IV, all so he can keep one step ahead of the vapid boy bands who are supplanting him as the kings of manufactured pop in Phase III. Even his public movement in Phase IV towards making more personal, mature music is just one more persona; when Zenith watches a tape of an interview where he claims "the important thing was just the need to express myself" (IV.1.1), he is moved to comment, "I'm a pretty good liar" (IV.1.2).

This brazen image manipulation is just one part of Morrison's generally revisionist take on superheroes. Zenith is shallow, selfish, arrogant, and (save for one rare outburst of heroism in Phase II) not terribly effective as a superhero. According to Morrison, this spoiled young man was drawn from life:

> I wanted to make him as much like me as possible. He was interested in stuff that I was interested in, and I was thinking what I would be like if I was a superhero. Back then that seemed radical, saying, "What would it actually be like?" To just sit down and work through that, and think, well, of course I wouldn't go out and save the world. I'd make lots of records, shag lots of girls and drink a lot. (Hasted 57)

Morrison would not remain interested in this type of realism for long (Bishop 120), but *Zenith*, written at the height of the revisionist trend, presents superheroes as manipulative and self-interested celebrities rather than the selfless champions of comics tradition. Their petty motives and personal failings produce what Morrison terms "designer superheroes in a Nietzschean soap opera, an everyday tale of extraordinary folk" ("Introduction," *Zenith Book One*). In this respect *Zenith* follows in the footsteps of *Marvelman* and *Watchmen*, which also seek to establish a mode of superhero realism by questioning the characters' motives, exposing their pathologies, and otherwise revealing them as flawed, fallible human beings, although Morrison does so with humor rather than pathos.

Zenith nevertheless displays all the hallmarks of an early revisionist superhero comic. The violence is amplified, with superhuman battles that slaughter combatants and level cities; the devastated London of Alternative 666, littered with bodies massacred by sadistic superheroes, is especially reminiscent of Johnny Bates's destruction of London in *Miracleman* 15, which was released the previous year. The references to sex are generally not explicit, although they depart considerably from the chaste norms of the genre: Zenith is propositioned by a preoperative transsexual superhero and is understandably disturbed when he learns that one of the two women he sleeps with in Phase II was cloned from his mother. The comic also emulates its revisionist predecessors in its attempt to dignify the superhero action with quotes from literary masters like the opening line from William Blake's poem "The Tyger," which serves as a key plot point in Phase I (and had recently served as the epigraph to issue 5 of *Watchmen*). Political references are even more abundant, from the ruthless, upwardly mobile Tory MP Peter St. John to the anarchist superhero collective Black Flag. Politics, parody, realism, cynicism, moral ambiguity, naked literary ambition, liberal helpings of sex and violence—*Zenith* fulfills all the requirements of the 1980s revisionist superhero genre. The best example of Morrison's early debt to revisionism, however, and his most explicit political commentary, came in another genre entirely.

DARE: THE CONTRADICTIONS OF PROTEST

Dare, with art by Rian Hughes, began as the flagship feature of *Revolver* in 1990; it was completed in *Crisis* in 1991. Combining science fiction iconography with didactic political critique, the series is both a bitter attack on the Conservative Party's dominance under Prime Minister Margaret Thatcher, who had been in office since 1979, and a cynical revision of the classic British comics hero Dan Dare. Created in 1950 by artist Frank Hampson, Dan Dare was the star of *Eagle*, the weekly comics magazine that made adventure and science fiction comics successful genres in Britain (Sabin, *Adult Comics* 25). *Eagle* was moralistic, Christian, and unabashedly imperialist, and *Dan Dare, Pilot of the Future* set the tone, chronicling Dan's conquest of alien worlds (Sabin, *Comics, Comix* 49). Dan Dare is the antithesis of everything Morrison stands for, making the *Revolver* revival an unusual clash of sensibilities; *Dare* assails the original strip's imperialism, recasting its iconic characters in the worst possible light as a means of expressing its revulsion at the politics of the Thatcher era (Sabin, *Comics, Comix* 140).

This Dan Dare is an injured war veteran, living on a meager pension and hooked on pain medication. The Treens, a Venusian race and Dare's greatest enemies, have become a racial underclass on Earth, forced to work in sweatshops and live in ghettos. In a military incident shortly before the last general election, Dare led a task force that broke a Treen labor uprising and murdered hundreds of innocents, including children. Other members of the regular cast are equally compromised: Albert Digby, Dare's loyal sidekick, has fallen out with Dare and fallen in with a terrorist cell; Sir Hubert Guest, Dare's commanding officer, betrays him to the government; Professor Jocelyn Peabody commits suicide after learning the full measure of her own involvement in a repulsive government conspiracy; Sondar, Dare's Treen ally, is torn apart in race riots. Every character has fallen from the uncomplicated patriotism and moral clarity of the *Eagle* strips, and their fates are all tied into the same scheme; Dare discovers that the nation's ruling Unity Party has been collaborating with the Mekon, the Treen dictator, to murder young workers and produce Manna, a miraculous food substitute that will supposedly solve England's food shortages. This *Soylent Green* scenario grows even worse: Manna, which is made from the sexual secretions of a Treen biocomputer, alters the physiology of its consumers and their unborn children. Still worse: Dare is implicitly raped by the Mekon and infused or impregnated with the Manna. His only remaining course of action is to collaborate with Digby's cell and destroy London with a fusion bomb.

Dan Dare may not be a superhero, but *Dare* is a prime example of the revisionist style as it hardened into cliché by the early 1990s. As Roger Sabin observes in *Adult Comics*, revisionist superhero comics "were by far the biggest bandwagon" following the success of *Watchmen* and *The Dark Knight Returns*, generating many imitators (97–98). When they were not directly copying their predecessors, these later revisionist works increased the violence and brutality in an escalating effort to shock readers. In *Batman: The Killing Joke* (1988), the Joker paralyzes Batgirl and photographs her naked body; in *Batman: The Cult* (1988), Batman is brainwashed into committing murder for a maniacal cult leader who bathes in human blood; in "A Death in the Family" (1988), the Joker beats Robin to death with a crowbar after readers voted on whether the sidekick would live or die by calling a premium-rate telephone number. Robin's death won by seventy-two votes (Sabin, *Comics, Comix* 167). *Dare* is more sophisticated than these efforts: while other late revisionist works simply amplified the sex and violence, *Dare* criticizes the ideology that underwrote its iconic characters. Nevertheless, the vicious and unremitting abuse Morrison heaps on Dan Dare and his friends is of a piece with the revisionist superhero comics of the late 1980s and early 1990s.[1]

This revisionist impulse generates a pronounced tension between Morrison's script and some aspects of Hughes's art, a tension that appears to be rooted in their starkly different attitudes towards their source material. In a dual interview with Nigel Curson, Morrison advertises his disdain for his subject, explaining that *Dare* "doesn't use the minutiae of the Dare mythology, since I really don't know much about it. It does have the Anastasia and Spacefleet Headquarters and that kind of wet dream stuff, for anyone who wants to see it" (Curson 26). While Morrison dismisses Frank Hampson's iconic spaceships and locales, Hughes strikes a very different note:

> **Rian:** I'd like to make known my complete respect for the worth and integrity of the original, and I hope that whatever we come up with has a value. We're not, I hope, out to trash anything for cheap effect.
> **Grant:** I don't know the mythology so much as I know it as a cultural icon.
> **Rian:** He is a symbol that transcends comics ... even people who aren't familiar with the story will use the adjective Dan Dareish to describe things that are of the Boy's Own fifties style. British deco, Meccano annuals, Corgi Collector's Club.
> **Grant:** I've got nothing but disrespect for these kind of things.
> (Curson 27)

Morrison appears to be referring to the fifties iconography and style, not the comic, but those are by his own admission the only things he knows about

Figure 1-3. *Dare* 2.8. Art by Rian Hughes. © Rebellion.

Dan Dare. Hughes at least appreciates *Dan Dare, Pilot of the Future* for its design sensibility, even if his art in *Dare* owes more to European comics artists such as Yves Chaland and Serge Clerc than to Hampson's meticulous realism. As a result, *Dare* is pulled between Morrison's downbeat script and Hughes's elegant retro-modernist design—the series loves the look of Dan Dare's world even if it cannot abide its ideology. Sometimes this contrast becomes self-defeating; Morrison's repeated statements that Dare campaigns for the Unity Party because he needs the money would appear to be contradicted by his sleek deco house, constructed and furnished in a style that, in our world at least, connotes opulence (fig. 1-3).

After dismissing the parts of the Dan Dare tradition that most appeal to his artist, Morrison concedes that the Pilot of the Future isn't all bad: "Initially it might seem that what we're trying to do is take the piss out of that whole fifties ideal of the imperial strong-jawed hero, but in actual fact there is a core of that which is actually quite worthy and quite honourable, and we also want to show that as well, and to show how that can easily be perverted" (Curson 27). Morrison is not willing to shed every trace of the original Dan Dare's heroism and integrity, which reasserts itself when Dan strikes back at his enemies. He tells them, "Once upon a time, I believed in an England that was fair and honourable. I'm almost glad you taught me that England only ever existed in my head. It means it can never really be destroyed" (4.16). Morrison and Hughes contrast this ideal England against the crimes and betrayals of the actual nation Dare has served, a nation transparently modeled on Margaret Thatcher's Britain.

The parallels between *Dare*'s nation and Thatcher's are not inconspicuous and only require explication for an international audience unfamiliar with thirty-year-old British politics. Gloria Monday, the Unity Party prime minister, is a direct analogue for Thatcher; Dare's preelection invasion of the Threshold processing station and suppression of the Treen workers has obvious parallels to both the 1982 Falklands War, which revived Thatcher's flagging popularity before the election of 1983, and to Thatcher's breaking of the miners' strike in 1984–85.[2] But *Dare* goes beyond Thatcher's policies to expose her vision of England as a sham. Gloria Monday convinces Dare to support her by appealing to his idealism, telling him, "we need a strong, unifying symbol for this campaign, a personification of the values that we represent. Patriotism. The strength of the individual. An optimistic, enterprising spirit. I'm talking about you, Colonel Dare" (1.15). Perhaps Dare did embody these qualities once, but the Unity campaign built around them is a lie. This point is driven home in a scene in which Dare appears to be

Figure 1-4. *Dare* 3.3. Art by Rian Hughes. © Rebellion.

standing bravely in front of the *Anastasia*, jaw held high, planting a territorial flag on the soil of some newly discovered, fog-shrouded planet—until the next panel pulls back to reveal Dare standing on a television set, filming a political advertisement (fig. 1-4). It's not just the Unity Party that turns out to be a façade; Dan's own heroic imperialism is just as artificial.

Dare also interrogates the values that Monday and Thatcher claim to represent, including their common appeal to patriotism. Dan is twice told to "Think of England," once by a photographer shooting an ad for the Unity Party (2.7) and again by the Mekon as he prepares to violate Dan (4.12). In this second context the phrase recalls Victorian women's instruction to "lie back and think of England," another indication of the sexual nature of the violation that soon follows. But this second utterance is not so different from the first—both times, the phrase is associated with acts of exploitation. The second time is simply more transparent, recasting Dan's first, voluntary exploitation by the government as an act of prostitution. The Unity Party's nationalistic appeals are little more than pretexts for submission or abuse.

Morrison subjects Thatcher's neoliberal, free-market philosophy to even harsher criticism by repeatedly imagining unregulated capitalism as a form of cannibalistic digestion. Digby uses this metaphor to describe the

Figure 1-5. *Dare* 2.10. Art by Rian Hughes. © Rebellion.

relationship between Britain's wealthy, finance-driven south and its impoverished, postindustrial north: "Sometimes, I think this country's turned into one great digestive system; down south, you've got the consumer system gobbling up everything in its path. And then it all passes through the system and the shite's dumped on us" (2.16).[3] After the truth about Manna persuades Dan to see things Digby's way, he incorporates another version of this metaphor in his final address to the Unity Party leadership: "The machine eats us up and shits us out. It doesn't care what or who it destroys, as long as it keeps turning, eating, excreting" (4.16). Manna itself is the most horrific expression of this metaphor: the unemployed are shipped off-planet with promises of work, slaughtered and broken down into biomass, and fed into the Treen biocomputer. The grossly genital computer then impregnates and replicates itself, producing secretions that are processed into Manna and fed back to the English. The cycle is self-generating and self-devouring, as repetitive and self-enclosed as Gloria Monday's philosophy of political power—"its pursuit becomes an end in itself" (4.11)—and like that power, it is maintained by exploiting and consuming the poor.

For all of Morrison's outrage at Britain's treatment of its underclasses, however, *Dare* maintains a chilly distance from the people on whose behalf it protests. The comic focuses on old *Dan Dare* characters or Unity Party leaders, with the poor literally relegated to the background. One of the most overtly political scenes in the series, in which a nameless member of Digby's cell confronts Dan with all the misery he has ignored, is presented from the remote vantage of a descending rocket. Hughes's art displays the crumbling deco grandeur of the buildings while Morrison's dialogue inveighs against their unsuitability for habitation, but the people who inhabit them are visible only as tiny dots in snaking food lines (fig. 1-5). Later scenes show scavengers rifling through trash cans and addicts buying drugs from a Treen dealer, but *Dare* is short on evidence of the regional division, racial discrimination, and economic devastation cited in its characters' heated lectures. To provide such evidence would take the narrative closer to social realism, and Morrison prefers to work with fantasy. He instead translates his criticisms of Thatcherism into science fiction allegories for the Falklands War, the miners' strike, and the relentless consumption of capitalism. The result is yet another tension in *Dare*, this time between Morrison's political aims and his own preferred mode of writing. The social critique is overshadowed and sometimes nullified by the science fiction, particularly the outlandish Manna plot, which works as a metaphor for runaway capitalism but cannot function the way the Treen massacre does as a coherent analogue and critique of specific Tory policies. A study in contradictions, *Dare* cannot quite reconcile all its conflicting impulses, especially its ambitions to comment meaningfully on real-world politics and its investment, however cynical, in its fantastic design and subject matter.

THE NEW ADVENTURES OF HITLER AND ST. SWITHIN'S DAY: ANGRY YOUNG MEN

By the time he began working on *Dare*, Morrison had already written two other series that addressed or at least flirted with addressing contemporary British politics. Both comics proved controversial, cementing his early reputation as the *enfant terrible* of the British comics industry. *The New Adventures of Hitler* (1989), with art by Steve Yeowell, first ran in *Cut*, a Scottish style magazine. The series follows a twenty-three-year-old Adolf Hitler as he visits Liverpool in 1912, searching for the Holy Grail. Morrison's use of Hitler as a comedic buffoon proved too much for several members of the *Cut* staff, including editor Alan Jackson and columnist Pat Kane, who resigned in protest (Wilson 23). Morrison would later assert that Kane had not even read the story and simply quit after seeing the title as a means of asserting his left-wing credentials (Hasted 81), which may explain why Part One is titled "What Do You Mean, Ideologically Unsound?"[4] The controversy was then picked up in *The Sun*, one of Rupert Murdoch's tabloids, whose reporters accused Morrison of being a Nazi ("Interview with an Umpire" 1).

That same year, *St. Swithin's Day* (1989) ran in *Trident*, the flagship anthology of independent publisher Trident Comics. This short serial, illustrated by Paul Grist, is one of Morrison's most realistic works, based on a set of diaries Morrison kept when he traveled around Britain at age nineteen (Hasted 78). The protagonist is an anonymous, disaffected, angry nineteen-year-old in the Holden Caulfield tradition, though an element of fantasy creeps in as readers discover the boy plans to assassinate Margaret Thatcher. *The Sun* ran a story ("Death to Maggie book sparks Tory uproar") and Conservative MP Teddy Taylor denounced the comic; this time, however, the only effect was to generate publicity and boost sales (Hasted 81).

These comics share many similarities beyond their timing and their contentious public reception. Both series feature alienated young men who undertake insane, self-appointed missions. Both are written as exercises in psychological realism, although neither one fully commits to a realistic style as they probe the fevered imaginations of their delusional protagonists.

Both protagonists narrate their stories, casting themselves as sensitive artistic types while unwittingly revealing their neurosis or dementia. Both men conduct hallucinatory conversations at café tables where their imaginary partners encourage their delusions. And both stories express Morrison's displeasure and frustration at ten years of Thatcherism—although *The New Adventures of Hitler* is far more direct in its criticisms whereas *St. Swithin's Day*, despite its sensationalist assassination plot, isn't really about politics at all.

More than simply playing Hitler for laughs, *The New Adventures of Hitler* attempts to connect its protagonist's monstrous and messianic ambitions to British (or, more precisely, English) history and culture. The opening page juxtaposes one of Hitler's aimless strolls with a choir singing the hymn "Jerusalem," whose first lines, taken from William Blake's preface to *Milton*, are "And did those feet, in ancient time / Walk upon England's mountains green?" The lines refer to the apocryphal story that Jesus visited England with Joseph of Arimathea—the same story that has brought Hitler to England in search of the Holy Grail—but intercutting them with Hitler's walking feet turns the hymn into a double entendre: the choir appears to be asking if the debunked stories of Bridget Dowling, the sister-in-law who claimed that Hitler lived with her and her husband Alois in Liverpool in 1912, could be true. The last page of the series revisits this juxtaposition, intercutting Hitler's departure with the hymn's final verse:

> I will not cease from mental fight,
> Nor shall sword sleep in my hand,
> Till we have built Jerusalem
> In England's green and pleasant land.

Blake's utopian pastoral vision now alludes to Hitler's determination to build a thousand-year Reich and spread it to the rest of the world—including England, where he vows to return in the comic's final panel. Even if we account for the obvious irony in the contrast with Blake, whose poems and prints are cited with far greater sympathy and appreciation elsewhere in Morrison's work, the association implies that all utopias and all nationalisms share something in common with Hitler's dreams of fascist domination and Aryan purity.

The series is especially critical of English nationalism, comparing Hitler's belligerent, genocidal policies to England's history of political, racial, and class oppression and implying that England inspired the Nazi leader.

Figure 1-6. *The New Adventures of Hitler* 4.2. Art by Steve Yeowell. © Grant Morrison and Steve Yeowell.

Hitler fantasizes two meetings with John Bull, the traditional personification of England, envisioned by Morrison and Yeowell as a crass, nationalistic thug who urges Hitler to embrace tyranny. Bull cites with approbation the Peterloo Massacre and England's imperial ventures in Ireland, India, North Africa, and the Boer War, the conflict that gave the world the concentration camp. Morrison suggests this history inspired Hitler's own ambitions, but his criticisms are by no means restricted to equations with Nazism. The mere idea of English nationalism appalls Morrison; when Bull guides Hitler to the Holy Grail, calling it "the spirit of everything that made this island nation great [...] The proudly beating heart of Merrie Englande" (11.2), Morrison and Yeowell represent that heart, that spirit, as an overflowing toilet.

This grotesque image should not be read as simple regional alienation or resentment on the part of its Scottish writer. Morrison has expressed a deep affection for Britain and British culture, including such iconically English artifacts as George Formby songs and *Carry On* films (Hasted 80), but he regards Bull's ideology of English national greatness as the root of Britain's racism and imperialism.

Morrison connects that ideology to Britain's then-current leadership when Bull pronounces, "That's what this country needs: a mad vicious bitch in the driving seat" (4.2). The comment ostensibly refers to Queen Victoria, but the colorists superimpose Thatcher's face on the window and tablecloth lest any reader miss the obvious implication (fig. 1-6). This version of John Bull is the living embodiment of the Thatcher constituency; his claims to be "a plain-speaking man [....] Salt of the earth" (4.1) reflect Thatcher's appeal to the presumed simplicity and moral superiority of her middle-class and petit-bourgeois base, while his disdain for both "arty-farty, too-clever-by-half rubbish" (4.1) and "the defeatist bleating of the barmy Bolshies" (11.2) capture that base's dual class resentments towards any leftists who are either more educated or less wealthy than they. Bull's leering comments about the waitress, on the other hand—"Curvy waitress Kate knows which side *her* bread's buttered on! And when her customers want *service*, she'll bend over backwards to make sure they get it! 'Fancy a *tart*, sir?'" (4.3)—mimic the tittering Page 3 captions of the Murdoch tabloids that supported Thatcher. Bull is the obscene, flatulent, grotesquely scatological embodiment of the ascendancy of Thatcher and her supporters, characterizing them all as racist, sexist, nationalist, proto-fascist boors.[5]

St. Swithin's Day cannot match the intensity of *Hitler*'s disgust at Thatcher and Thatcherism, nor does it really try. The nameless protagonist—we might as well call him the Neurotic Boy Outsider, after the description he scrawls on his own forehead—fantasizes about killing Thatcher, but he scarcely hints at his reasons. His imaginary conversation partner wonders "if her blood'll be blue" (2.5), and a crowd is seen protesting Thatcher's cuts to higher education, but the comic barely touches on politics; Morrison captures the impotent fury of leftists unable to stop Thatcher but never articulates any criticisms of Thatcher's policies or ideology. Even the Neurotic Boy Outsider recognizes that politics are something of a red herring: he is more interested in the media attention he will garner, and he only steals the obligatory would-be assassin's copy of *Catcher in the Rye* to give the experts something to analyze after he is caught (4.1, 4.3). Like its protagonist, the comic repeatedly feints at a political message that cannot be reconstructed from its scant evidence; the Neurotic Boy Outsider's dance on the grave of Karl Marx seems just as significant as his plot to kill Thatcher, and just as impenetrable.

The series instead focuses on the emotional turmoil of a disaffected adolescent. The Neurotic Boy Outsider's self-description, along with his stolen volumes of Salinger and Rimbaud, mark him as a prime example of the type; his most coherent and revealing statement may be his lament, "I hate being 19. I want to be 19 forever" (4.4). Morrison told Nick Hasted, "A lot of people have thought [*St. Swithin's Day*] was a political strip, but I don't think it was political at all. [...] The important stuff was the whole atmosphere of someone being 19, and that real hothouse way of thinking" (Hasted 79). The assassination attempt is concocted to satisfy an adolescent desire for attention rather than any political gripe, as indicated by the boy's final thoughts before he approaches the prime minister: "They won't see me. Nobody's ever seen me. Nobody ever noticed. Nobody ever cared. And it's HER fault it's always raining!" (1.4). This is the Outsider's only complaint against Thatcher, blaming her for his isolation and depression; it highlights the impossibility of extracting any political agenda from his actions, except perhaps a caution about the futility of building Thatcher up into an omnipotent menace responsible for all of Britain's ills, even the weather. In that sense, *St. Swithin's Day* can be read as a gentle warning to frustrated leftists like Morrison himself, rather than the criticism of right-wing nationalists seen in *The New Adventures of Hitler*.

Like *Hitler*, *St. Swithin's Day* depicts a young man in the grip of severe mental problems. The final chapter reveals that the gun the Neurotic Boy Outsider has been cradling throughout the series is just as imaginary as his café-table conversation partner. While this twist suggests that the Outsider is far less menacing than previous chapters have implied—that his only goals are to scare Thatcher and gain some attention in the resulting media spotlight—the gun's graphic presence in earlier chapters and the Outsider's elaborate explanation of how he came across it (delivered to the equally imaginary girl in the café) indicate he is deeply delusional. The serial ends with another delusion as the Outsider imagines himself on a train while Thatcher's security detail beats him into unconsciousness or perhaps even death. The early implications that the Outsider is a Travis Bickle or John Hinckley-style assassin turn out to be a ruse, but the Outsider's commitment to his fantasies makes him a danger to himself.

Aside from these few delusional objects and scenes, which Grist generally renders in the same style as the rest of the story, *St. Swithin's Day*

Figure 1-7. *The New Adventures of Hitler* 9.1. Art by Steve Yeowell. © Grant Morrison and Steve Yeowell.

confines the symptoms of its protagonist's mental illness to his solipsistic narration and strange behavior. *The New Adventures of Hitler*, on the other hand, incorporates the art and coloring into its portrait of madness. Hitler offers Morrison many more opportunities to demonstrate that madness, of course: messianic visions, precognitive flashes, a sinister trolley, a wardrobe that is haunted by John Lennon and Morrissey. But that insanity also manifests in Yeowell's art and particularly in the coloring by Nick Abadzis, Steve Whitaker, and John Buckle. The team eschews naturalistic coloring, washing the backgrounds and occasionally the foregrounds in wallpaper and endpaper patterns, maps, rows of text, and swirls of color. Minor details expand to fill the field of vision when they attract Hitler's attention, and characters occasionally turn transparent in a graphic illustration of the future dictator's sociopathy: he literally sees through the people around him as if they are not real (fig. 1-7). The expressionist coloring places the reader inside Hitler's subjective point of view even when he is depicted on-panel; this deeply unsettling technique extends Hitler's irrationality into the normally objective space of visual representation, forcing readers to see the world as Hitler sees it and leaving no escape from his madness. As a political critique the series may be heavy-handed and facile, but as a portrait of derangement it fully exploits all the possibilities of its format. Even more than its contemporary *St. Swithin's Day*, *The New Adventures of Hitler* graphically delineates the dangers of becoming consumed by fantasy, a powerful critique of imagination and idealism from a generally imaginative and idealist writer.

ZENITH PHASE IV: THE HORUS PARADOX

The later phases of *Zenith* also demonstrate a growing suspicion of idealism while displaying Morrison's increasing command of his medium and his genre, and expanding his repertoire beyond the revisionist tropes and rampant pastiches of the earlier storylines. Morrison hints at this progression as far back as his "Introduction" to Phase I, where he assures readers that his reliance on their familiarity with superhero conventions is only setting them up for later surprises: "In the forthcoming three books [...] those assumptions are cheerfully trashed when the comfortable world of heroes and villains metamorphoses into something rare and strange" (*Zenith Book One*). Phase IV in particular destabilizes the moral absolutes of superhero comics while it questions the certainties of Morrison's own politics. The resulting storyline is more nuanced, generically and ideologically, than any of Morrison's prior British work.

True to Morrison's word, these metamorphoses do not emerge out of nowhere. From its inception, *Zenith* complicates Morrison's anti-Thatcher politics through its selfish yuppie hero and its heroic Tory MP. Peter St. John was once Mandala, hippie superhero and member of Cloud 9, a 1960s superteam who renounced their intended role as soldiers and became countercultural icons. As Mandala, he protested the Vietnam War and meditated with the Beatles; as Peter St. John, he joined the Tories and became a member of parliament, though he is not above using his telepathic abilities to influence or even murder people who threaten his ruthless ascent to prime minister. A conservative who has abandoned his youthful idealism in favor of amoral political calculations, St. John should by all rights be a prime target for Morrison's scorn. Much like Dan Dare, he allows himself to be co-opted by the Thatcher government, yet he never has that redemptive moment of conscience when he rejects what he has become. That's because his moment of conscience came decades before *Zenith* began, when he was one of the few members of Cloud 9 to object to the group's plan to wipe out the human race and become mankind's evolutionary successors.

The other surviving members of Cloud 9 are still closely identified with the counterculture—Zenith repeatedly refers to Lux, Spook, and Ruby Fox as hippies—but after fighting by Zenith's side in Phases I and III, they become his most monstrous antagonists in Phase IV. Cloud 9 joins forces with the anarchist superheroes of Black Flag to form the Horus program, which promises to conquer "pollution, famine, overpopulation" and other social problems and "offers humanity a chance to drag itself up out of the evolutionary mud" (IV.1.3). This scenario recalls the end of Alan Moore's *Miracleman*, in which left-wing superheroes take over the world's governments and reshape everything from the economy to energy consumption to online dating. Unlike *Miracleman*'s autocratic utopia, however, the Horus program turns out to be a sham. Its architects are only interested in their own ascension, regarding humanity as a separate, backward species ready for extermination:

> **Lux:** I can't believe that you, of all people should want to stand in the way of evolution, Peter. We're not monsters, we're the next stage. We can't afford to be dragged back down into the mire by creatures whose time has come and gone.
> **St. John:** I'm all for ascending to paradise, David, but I'm not entirely sure we have the right to kick away the ladder behind us. (IV.2.2)

Ironically, St. John's faith in humanity's capacity for continued evolution displays the last vestiges of his old hippie idealism. He tells Zenith that he resisted his teammates' plans because he "wanted to lift humanity up to our level. I really thought that was possible but you have to remember that this was the '60s and I also thought that *Sergeant Pepper* contained the greatest music ever made" (IV.9.3). Although he feels obliged to distance himself from his sixties tastes, St. John still sides with humanity against the Horus plan to create a new master race. Perhaps Morrison simply acknowledges that genocide is beyond the pale even for Tories (a concession *Dare* does not make), or perhaps he concedes that idealism is not limited to leftist and countercultural ideologies.[6]

He certainly acknowledges that idealism can be a dangerous prerequisite for utopian thinking. Casting the previously sympathetic Cloud 9 and Black Flag characters as genocidal villains is the ultimate expression of a general skepticism towards utopias that runs throughout *Zenith* and across Morrison's career. This suspicion of utopias is characteristic of the British revisionist style in general, also surfacing in the chilling, slightly inhuman paradise of *Miracleman*, Adrian Veidt's plan to save the world by murdering millions in *Watchmen*, or the short-lived, unsustainable urban paradise created by the angry nature god of *Swamp Thing*. Like these works, *Zenith* is as critical of left-wing utopianism as it is of right-wing utopias.[7] When Lux announces that "A new age is dawning," an exasperated Zenith quips, "Oh no! Not another one" (IV.2.1)—and with good reason. All of the villains dream of creating perfect societies of one stripe or another, from the Nazi cultists in Phase I to Michael Peyne, the doctor who created the Cloud 9 superhumans because he wanted to build a better world free of humanity's moral failings. The critique of utopianism turns satirical in Phase II, when computer magnate Scott Wallace—essentially Richard Branson if Branson became a James Bond villain—decides to take over the world because he thinks he can do a better job running it. Wallace follows no particular ideology and hasn't thought about what kind of world he would build or how he would govern it; Zenith talks him out of his plans by reminding him that running the world would be hard work. In an unwitting foreshadowing of Phase IV, Zenith asks Wallace, "why do you think superhumans have never tried to take over the world? I'll bet we could. Thing is, nobody wants the hassle" (II.14.3). Cloud 9 is willing to take on the hassle, but Morrison presents cynics like Zenith and Peter St. John as the better option. Superhumans who work within human institutions and live by human rules, they fight to protect their world even as they jockey for fame or influence within it. The four phases of *Zenith* argue that the self-centered pop star and the cutthroat Tory politician are less dangerous than the utopian dreamer of any ideology.

The Horus program works an equally surprising reversal on the generational politics common to most Morrison comics. One of Morrison's most consistent and enduring character types has been the rebellious teenager who seeks to upset the social order, as seen in figures from the Neurotic Boy Outsider to Dane McGowan of *The Invisibles* to Marvel Boy, Klarion the Witch-Boy, and Seaguy. Morrison often describes these characters as avatars or invocations of Horus, the youthful Egyptian god who, as he told Jay Babcock, embodies "that very powerful energy of adolescent rebellion which seems to have entered the world, overcoming traditional systems, disordering the past in order to create something new" (Babcock 30). Zenith, an insouciant brat who scoffs at his elders, is arguably an early draft of this stock type, but his rebellions are too confined to the evanescent tastes of fashion and pop music to qualify him as a "ferocious fiery adolescent who's throwing down all the bricks in order to build something else up" (Babcock 30). He only rebels within a culture industry that thrives on instantaneous obsolescence, and he copies other successful artists rather than creating anything new. A far better example of an early Horus figure can be found in *Kid Eternity* (1991), written for DC Comics and published the year between *Zenith* Phases III and IV. In that limited series, Morrison reinvents an obscure child superhero from the 1940s as an agent of the Lords of Chaos, beings who seek to overturn a cosmic hierarchy by elevating humanity to enlightenment and godhood. This plan conforms to Morrison's antihierarchical and humanist values—yet it also matches the stated goals of the Horus program, which similarly positions itself as challenging the dominant social and evolutionary order.

Of course, the Horus program is not really interested in elevating humanity any more than the fortysomething Baby Boomers of Cloud 9 are really rebellious youths. Phase IV not only upends Morrison's preferred symbology, character types, and political oppositions, it turns age itself on its head. The Horus faction of Cloud 9, all of them old enough to be Zenith's parents, have halted or reversed their aging to the point where Ruby Fox calls the twenty-four-year-old pop star an "old bore" (IV.2.2). Cloud 9 also reverses the aging process of Michael Peyne, whose narration of Phase IV regresses *Flowers for Algernon*-style from the horrified reminiscences of an old man to the comments of a callow teenager to the scrawls of a child. But *Zenith* was about people who refused to age long before Phase IV wrote this desire onto the characters' bodies. Almost every character is too attached to his or her youth, whether it's Ruby Fox, who "spent two decades looking over [her] shoulder, wishing [she] could be beautiful again" (I.5.5), or Zenith himself, who frets that he's "over the hill" (III.1.3) when his singles start to slip off the charts. The only exception is once again Peter St. John (Callahan 31), who makes no effort to conceal or alter his age, who castigates Ruby for her unhealthy obsession with the past, and who insists that his own past as a member of Cloud 9 is dead and buried. The Tory politician is not only the voice of conscience but also the voice of maturity.

Zenith does not fully depart from Morrison's typical pattern of youth challenging old age. The young protagonist battles plenty of patriarchs and predecessors, including the first superhumans from the 1940s, the Horus faction of Cloud 9, and the Lloigor, an ancient race of elder gods; Phase II, the most formulaic storyline, forces him to fight and kill his own father, whose brain-damaged body has been placed inside a ridiculous robotic suit. If the earlier renditions of this vulgarly Oedipal narrative are fairly unimaginative, Phase IV inverts them by confronting Zenith with enemies younger than he is, including his own son, whose body has been co-opted by one of the Lloigor. The members of Horus have themselves become Lloigor, making the rebellious children—or those who refuse to let go of their childhood—indistinguishable from the corrupt elders. By uncoupling biological age from chronological age, age from idealism, idealism from ideology, and ideology from morality, Morrison collapses the simplistic, morally freighted oppositions that structure many works of popular culture, including some of the earlier phases of *Zenith*. Characters are measured by the actions they take, not by their age or political ideology. Morrison sabotages the rigid, structurally dictated morality that governs more unreflective genre work and replaces it with the dynamic, adaptive moralities of Zenith and Peter St. John. *Zenith* becomes more sophisticated than its origins, revising the assumptions of its genre and its author.

Phase IV ends with a strikingly literal example of the series outgrowing these restrictive generic conventions and reductive ideological oppositions. The Lloigor appear to triumph, slaughtering Zenith, St. John, and Acid Archie and conquering the world before they grow to fill the entire cosmos—at which point they realize they are trapped in a "prison universe" (IV.14.4), a microcosm held in the hand of smug, victorious Peter St. John.[8] The readers are as surprised as the Lloigor to discover that everything since the end of chapter two has transpired inside the Chimera, a formless, shape-shifting superhuman who has replicated the universe in miniature. Rather than confront Horus in the kind of battle superhero comics demand, a battle he cannot win, St. John allows them to deceive and imprison themselves. This refusal to play to the genre's expectations, this portrayal of genre as a trap, is one of the central ideas of Phase IV, paralleled by Zenith's dissatisfaction with the confines of pop music and prefigured by a seemingly innocuous comment earlier in the storyline.

After the Horus group has begun its plans to take over the world, an irate MP demands to know whose side Peter St. John will take. St. John, ever the paragon of maturity, replies that his opponent "attempts, in his time-honoured fashion, to reduce complex issues to the level of schoolyard brawls but I'm afraid I cannot come out to play with him today" (IV.5.3). The stinging rejoinder hints at St. John's indirect, nonconfrontational strategy for dealing with Horus, but it also works as a comment on the difficulty of addressing politics or other complex issues through the conventions of superhero comics—at least as those conventions existed before the revisionist movement challenged and expanded them. In its simplest form, the superhero genre reduces ideological positions to outlandish caricatures and pits them against each other in battles that are no more sophisticated than schoolyard brawls. By the time he wrote Phase IV, Morrison had already scoffed at this practice in the final issue of *Animal Man*, and *Zenith* contributes another, somewhat more muted criticism of the idea that costumed combat can accurately represent complex issues, let alone resolve them.

All of Morrison's early British comics outgrow their generic archetypes, from *Dare*'s revulsion at its patriotic military hero to *St. Swithin's Day*'s demystification of the sensitive social outcast. These comics are especially suspicious of their self-obsessed young protagonists (although the embittered, aging Dan Dare does not fare any better) and of any narrative that would axiomatically assign them moral authority because they are young and alienated—qualities that also describe Morrison's Hitler. Compared to his later works, the comics written closest to Morrison's own adolescence and early adulthood are the least likely to romanticize this period. These series instead emphasize the importance of growth and maturation, if only through its disastrous absence. This progress cannot be attributed to Morrison's British work alone; by the time he began Phase IV, Morrison had already become bored by *Zenith* and was more interested in his growing body of work in American superhero comics (Bishop 157). While he would continue to contribute stories to *2000 AD* through the mid-nineties, including the controversial satire *Big Dave* (Bishop 160–64, 168), he had largely moved on to the American comics industry. Although his American comics initially participated in the same revisionist impulse as his British work, Morrison would soon develop a distinctive style that continues to define his writing to this day.

Chapter 2

THE WORLD'S STRANGEST HEROES

In 1986, DC Comics editor Karen Berger traveled to London to recruit new talent from the British comics industry ("Afterword"). DC had already hired Brian Bolland, Dave Gibbons, Alan Moore, and other creators away from *2000 AD*, with dynamic results on comics like Moore's *Swamp Thing*. By 1986 the company was looking to replicate the phenomenal success of Moore and Gibbons's *Watchmen*, a work that, along with Frank Miller's *The Dark Knight Returns*, generated tremendous sales and media attention and sparked a wave of imitators (Sabin, *Adult Comics* 91–98). DC returned to Britain hoping to find more creators who could bring a fresh perspective to their superheroes—in Morrison's view, "Purely because of the critical success of Alan Moore" (Hasted 58).

Grant Morrison was among the writers invited to pitch projects to Berger. His proposals for *Animal Man* and *Arkham Asylum*, like his early work in *Captain Clyde* and *Zenith* Phase I, participated fully in the revisionist mode, but he would quickly chafe at the confines of the style and at the powerful influence of Alan Moore. As Morrison told Nick Hasted,

> at one point there was a sense that we were all marching into the future together waving the same flag, then I realized that we weren't, which is probably why I criticized Alan quite a lot, which is why he doesn't speak to me anymore. But I really felt the need to get out from under his shadow, because it had become so oppressive, and we were all being expected to do as he did. (Hasted 59)

He alludes to criticisms like the one he made in his "Drivel" column for the British comics fanzine *Speakeasy*, where he accused Moore of plagiarizing Robert Mayer's novel *Superfolks* in *Marvelman*, *Watchmen*, and "Whatever Happened to the Man of Tomorrow?" ("Drivel" 55).[1] He also played out this anxiety of influence in his comics, where he would build up to a dramatic break with the revisionist style, particularly over the revisionists' claims to bring realism to superhero comics. In his introduction to the collected edition of *The Dark Knight Returns*, Moore praises Miller's portrayal of Superman for the way it "manages to treat an incredible situation realistically and to seamlessly wed the stuff of legend to the stuff of twentieth century reality" ("The Mark of Batman"). But this putative realism was too often used as a synonym or euphemism for the lurid sex, graphic violence, and heavy-handed parody Sabin attributes to the revisionist movement (*Comics, Comix* 160); the "twentieth century reality" Moore lauds in *The Dark Knight Returns* includes cannibalistic gang members, topless Nazis, foul-mouthed flying robots, and a yuppie caricature named "Byron Brassballs."

In 1993, after the revisionist movement had peaked, Morrison told Paul McEnery, "The idea that you could bring something as ridiculous as superheroes into the real world seemed to me completely insane" (qtd. in Bukatman 75). By that point he had already broken from the revisionists in his own comics, developing a style that attempted to address serious moral, cultural, and psychological issues without resorting to sensationalistic "realism" or renouncing the more fantastic and outlandish conventions of the superhero genre. Building on his early British work, Morrison came to rely on metafictional devices, synecdochic narrative structures, absurdist humor, and, perhaps most importantly, a figurative strategy that literally embodied meaning in the traumatized forms of his characters. This mode of expression did not come all at once, however, but emerged fitfully in his first American comics.

ANIMAL MAN: BEYOND METAFICTION

One of the two concepts Morrison pitched to Berger in their London meeting was *Animal Man* (1988–90), a reworking of a 1960s hero so obscure that his greatest exposure in the previous two decades had been as a member of a team of similarly marginal characters, the aptly named Forgotten Heroes. Even his secret identity, "Buddy Baker," suggested a character both generic and incomplete. Buddy presented a slate so blank that the project would eventually force Morrison to develop a personal style distinct from those of other revisionist writers. Although he initially conceived *Animal Man* as a finite four-issue miniseries, DC asked Morrison to extend the story into an ongoing monthly comic book (Callahan 251). Morrison had scripted the first four issues in the style of Alan Moore, with poetic narration and

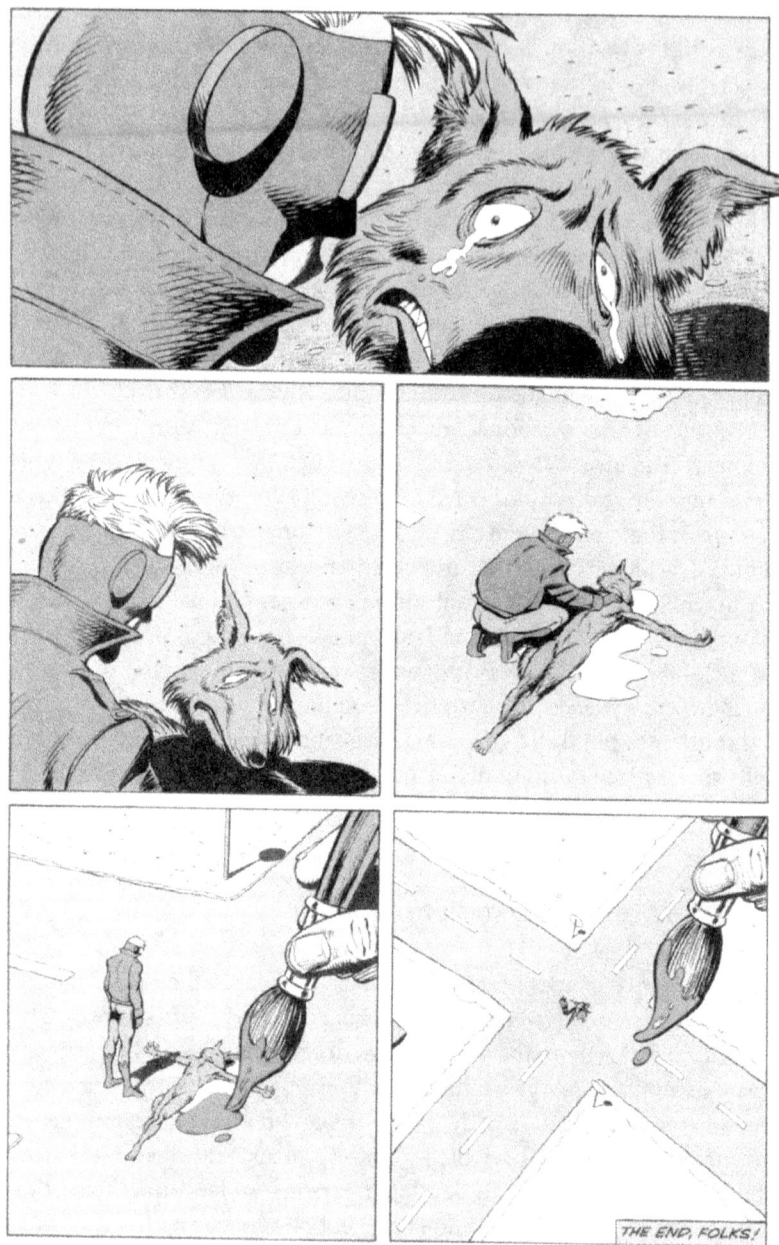

Figure 2-1. *Animal Man* 5.24. Art by Chas Truog. © DC Comics.

ironic scene transitions that would have been at home in *Watchmen* or *Swamp Thing* (Hasted 59), but the unforeseen expansion left him looking for a more original voice. As he writes in the "Intro" to the first *Animal Man* trade paperback, "I suddenly found myself lost for ideas. Having no desire to produce yet another grittily realistic exploration of what it is to be superhuman and/or an urban vigilante with emotional problems, I cast desperately around for a new direction."

He wasted no time in finding one. Issue number 5 of *Animal Man*, "The Coyote Gospel," the first story planned as part of an ongoing series, introduces Buddy to an anthropomorphic coyote named Crafty, a transparent stand-in for the Warner Bros. cartoon character Wile E. Coyote. Crafty, frustrated with the endless torments of his violent cartoon existence, confronts his paintbrush-wielding God and is banished for his insolence to "the dark hell of the second reality"—Buddy Baker's reality, the baseline diegesis of the *Animal Man* comic book—where he endures even more realistically painful punishments in order to redeem the suffering of his fellow cartoon characters (5.20). On the final page, as this cartoon Christ lies bleeding on a crossroads, God's hand and brush intrude into the space of the panels to paint the blood red (fig. 2-1). As Timothy Callahan (73) and Steven Zani (237, 239) note, the device is reminiscent of Chuck Jones's 1953 Warner Bros. cartoon "Duck Amuck," although this demonstration of the creator's power is far more sinister.

This story would become "the template for the further development of the entire series" (Morrison, "Intro"). From "The Coyote Gospel" forward, *Animal Man* is increasingly dominated by metafictional occurrences. A computer screen, first seen in issue 8, displays the musings and narrative commands of some sinister creator; this proves to be the screen of Grant Morrison, who enters the narrative as a character beginning with issue 14. The aliens who gave Buddy his powers reveal that he is a revision of an older character from the 1960s; these aliens also destroy an antagonist by reversing artist Chas Truog's drawing process, breaking the villain down into his component lines and bursting his speech balloon like a soap bubble (fig. 2-2). Soon after, Buddy meets a physicist named James Hightower who has been following a trail of clues planted by Morrison, clues that lead to the realization that he and Buddy are fictional characters. They undertake a peyote-fueled vision quest in the Arizona desert, leading to one of the most transgressively charged moments in the series, if not in Morrison's entire career, when Buddy looks back over his shoulder, stares directly out of the page, and screams "I can see you!" at the reader (19.11). Even this moment

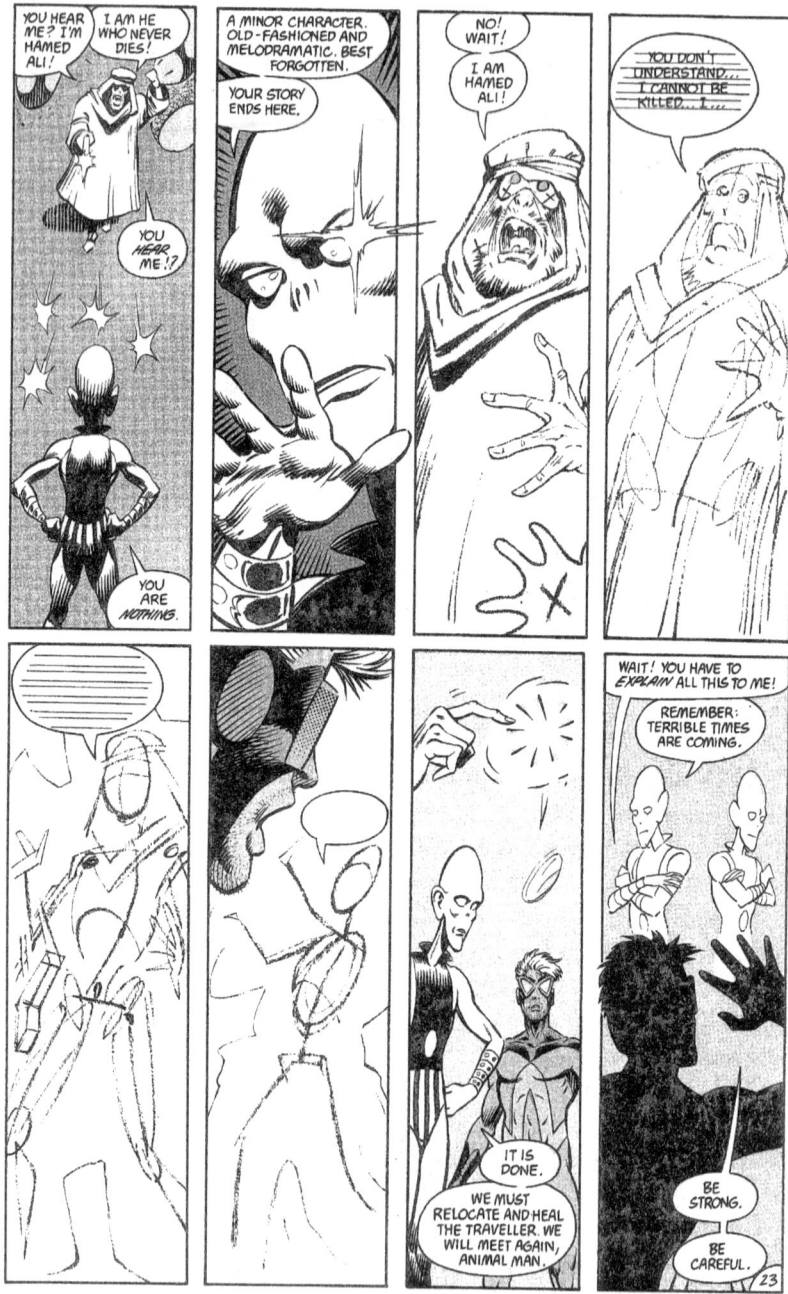

Figure 2-2. *Animal Man* 12.23. Art by Chas Truog. © DC Comics.

of self-awareness is not the end of the comic's metafictional odyssey: in the final issue, after a grueling ordeal in which Buddy loses his family, travels through time, prevents the return of all the characters who were deleted from DC Comics' narrative continuity in *Crisis on Infinite Earths*, and journeys through a Limbo of forgotten comic book characters, he literally meets his maker—Grant Morrison himself.

Metafiction would become a staple of superhero comics over the next two decades, with a number of titles presenting self-reflexive commentaries on the history of the genre or incorporating their own histories of extranarrative revisions and revamps into the narrative proper.[2] But in 1988, when most superhero comics with literary aspirations were proclaiming their realism, Morrison's metafiction was unusual and daring, setting *Animal Man* apart from its contemporaries (Zani 234).[3] Too many scholarly treatments, however, have evaluated the series only as metafiction, leading them to overlook other, equally important features of Morrison's newly emerging style and, in some cases, to discount the work's formal and thematic complexity. In *Comic Book Culture*, for example, Matthew Pustz focuses exclusively on the metafictional elements, concluding the title was innovative only for "comic book fans unfamiliar with contemporary metafiction [...] readers with a broader understanding of contemporary literature might have seen *Animal Man* as a relatively simple exercise in postmodernism" (127, 129). While Pustz correctly observes that Morrison's metafictions are far less revolutionary outside the world of superhero comics, his summary is too reductive, depicting the comic as little more than a series of self-referential games. Contrary to the claims of its critics and some of its most effusive proponents, *Animal Man* is not solely concerned with metafiction, and Morrison applies its metafictional elements towards representing a host of thorny moral, ethical, and theological dilemmas.

Even the narrative structure is not governed exclusively by metafiction. At least as important, and closely intertwined (but not interchangeable) with his metafictional concerns, is Morrison's interest in fractal geometry and holographic scale. Issue 6, the first after "The Coyote Gospel," introduces this new element and points to one of the series' chief organizing patterns. Rokara Soh, an "art martyr" from the fascist planet Thanagar, has created a doomsday weapon that operates on fractal principles. As he explains to Buddy, "A fractal shape is one which reveals more detail, more information, upon closer examination. It can be magnified indefinitely and still reveal new complexities" (6.17). The next page shows an image of the Mandelbrot set, a fractal that possesses partial self-similarity: at certain points, the fractal generates identical shapes at increasingly smaller scales. *Animal Man* follows a similar structure, in which even the most apparently self-contained stories often feature a plot or detail that reflects the themes or structure of the series as a whole. Because issues 5 and 6 introduce the metafictional and fractal models Morrison will follow, either one might be said to represent the entire series in miniature—but then, so might several other issues.

Animal Man further explores ideas of scale and self-similarity through repeated references to the implicate order theory of quantum physicist David Bohm, which Morrison's author-surrogate (that is, Morrison himself, in the comic) summarizes as "A vision of a vast, interconnected universe where every part contains the whole. Where the universe is a mirror reflecting itself" (14.6). This theory provides a cosmological underpinning for many of Morrison's formal games—his use of the classic Silver Age villain the Mirror Master takes on new resonance in light of the comic's self-reflexivity and self-similarity—and for the synecdochic variations of scale that have always featured prominently in Morrison's work. On two different occasions, for example, characters in *Animal Man* face a wall of darkness only to discover it is the pupil of a colossal eye, which quickly recedes back to normal size (17.21, 19.4–5).[4] Other variations of scale prove far more serious, while also moving well beyond the parameters of Bohm's theory. The universe of *Animal Man* is in fact not one but several universes. Crafty forsakes his cartoon world for the "hell above" (5.20) of Buddy's world, the shared world of most DC Comics characters. But Buddy learns to see one level higher, into our world: "I saw into another world and it was worse than this one. It was like I glimpsed heaven and ... and it wasn't paradise. It was more like hell" (19.13). Each world grows progressively more realistic, from children's cartoons to superhero comics to our own reality; unfortunately, each world also becomes more dominated by pain and tragedy, to the point where Buddy wonders, "What if God's reality [...] what if it's so bad that he had to imagine us to help make life bearable?" (19.13).

The nested realities of *Animal Man* do not end with these three worlds. The series also presents a number of intermediary realities, including the white void that exists between panels—which characters periodically breach and which "represents the middle ground between [Buddy's] reality and the higher world" (24.2)—and the comic book simulacrum of Glasgow where Buddy meets a comic book simulacrum of Grant Morrison. Nor do the cascading realities end with our world. An insane criminal called the Veil, who has also discovered that he is a comic book character, recites the series' now-standard discovery that he is not real. But he continues, "And there's something worse. The creators . . . *they're* not real either" (24.14). His comments hint at the disturbing end (or rather, the disturbing lack of ending) of all metafiction: as Jorge Luis Borges writes in "Partial Magic in the *Quixote*," its ceaseless regressions "suggest that if the characters of a fictional work can be readers or spectators, we, its readers or spectators, can be fictitious" (196).

As Borges's comments on *Don Quixote*, *Hamlet*, the *Ramayana*, and the *Thousand and One Nights* suggest, such nested worlds are a common metafictional device with a long history in literature. However, Morrison's interconnected universes and implicate orders also imply an ethical framework that could alleviate some of the pervasive suffering he describes. In issue 17, Buddy—who became a vegetarian back in "The Coyote Gospel"—catches his son, Cliff, eating a burger. His arguments for vegetarianism, based on the environmental damage done by large-scale industrial cattle farming, are presented in unconsciously Bohm-like terms: "nothing exists in a vacuum, Cliff. Everything is connected" (17.10). Buddy learns his own lesson when three firemen are injured as a result of an animal rescue in which he took part. In an interconnected world, any act, even the most innocent or well intentioned, can have disastrous consequences for other beings. Two issues later, Hightower explains how interconnection and implicate order theory can provide a basis for ethics: "everything in the universe is connected, you see. From atoms to galaxies. We're all responsible. Every decision we make affects the future of the whole universe" (19.15).

Unfortunately, while Buddy pursues his vision quest with Hightower, learning an implicate ethics and discovering the nature of reality, his family is murdered by a consortium of businessmen seeking to silence his outspoken views on animal rights. Buddy's heroics fail at least as often as they succeed, so much so that in the series' penultimate issue he inventories everybody he has failed to save, from manic-depressive super-villains to a dolphin mother and child whose brutal slaughter can be viewed as a fractal foreshadowing of his own family's murder; "All of us," he laments, "victims of this pointless cruelty" (25.20). That cruelty has been a theme of the series from its first issues, which revolved around the abuses of hunting and animal experimentation but also paused to highlight a cat killing a mouse to feed her kittens (2.1); violence is universal in *Animal Man*, visited upon and by animals and humans alike. Many of the problems that frustrate Buddy, like the depletion of the ozone layer or "the dog fights and the stray cats and all the little cruelties that go on every day" (17.17), would seem to be either too large or too small to fall in any superhero's jurisdiction. Those crimes that are more suitably superheroic in scale, like murder, prove equally beyond Buddy's control. The only option that remains is for Buddy to follow in Crafty's footsteps and petition his own creator—Grant Morrison—to end this endless, senseless brutality.

Morrison's commentary is not limited to fictional characters. As he makes clear in the final issue, Buddy and Crafty's position is analogous to our own: we, too, are at the mercy of an inscrutable, capricious higher power, buffeted by tragedies we cannot control, and unlike them, we don't even have anybody we can complain to (26.7). Animal Man's torment at the hands of his writer becomes a surprisingly apt metaphor for humanity's existential helplessness. Yet the Grant Morrison who appears in *Animal Man* is not God, nor even the Satanic, demiurgic figure he describes himself as, the figure who steps in to persecute and corrupt somebody else's innocent characters (26.3), although he certainly appears that way to Buddy. In reality, our reality, he is even more helpless than his characters; in many respects, fictional characters like Animal Man have some major advantages over mere mortals like Grant Morrison. In response to Buddy's demand to know if he's real or not—a question that will echo throughout Morrison's career—the author replies, "You existed long before I wrote about you and, if you're lucky, you'll still be young when I'm old or dead. You're more real than I am" (26.9–10). He paraphrases a point made by Hightower two issues earlier: as works of art these characters are not only real, but potentially immortal (24.17).

Morrison also knows these characters can exert agency and influence in the real world. He makes this claim most forcefully in *Animal Man* 13, an issue Callahan characterizes as a message-oriented interlude with no connection to the series' larger philosophical and metafictional concerns (85–86). In fact, the issue argues that fictional characters are potentially just as real and as powerful as the people who create and invest them with meaning. Mike Maxwell, a washed-up American superhero operating in Africa under the embarrassingly imperialist name of B'wana Beast, tells his black South African successor that "the Beast belongs to mythology" and that "It's beyond politics" (13.16). Maxwell's insistence that politics and superhero mythology are mutually exclusive is indicative of his origin in Silver Age DC comics, which generally avoided or ignored political topics, although Morrison implies it stems from Maxwell's own guilt that he hasn't used his powers to confront the problems facing Africa (13.7). The new Beast, anti-apartheid activist Dominic Mndawe, counters that in South Africa "nothing is 'beyond politics'" (13.16) and dispels Maxwell's rigid partitioning with the toast "Today's politics is tomorrow's mythology" (13.17). In his first act as the Beast—now given the marginally less embarrassing moniker of Freedom

Beast—he creates a simulacrum of a unicorn as a living refutation of an Afrikaner police officer's claim that the dream of ending apartheid "is like the unicorn; it exists only in a sick fantasy" (13.14). The officer learns, fatally, that fantasies, mythologies, and symbols can exert real political power through their capacity to inspire action. *Animal Man* 13, while still the politically earnest message issue Callahan describes, also participates in the exploration and valorization of the ideal that runs throughout the series. The ideal surfaces again in Hightower's connection of the morphogenetic field that bestows Animal Man's powers to Plato's theory of forms (18.17), in his association of the "heaven" Buddy sees—our world—with Bohm's higher, implicate order (19.15), in the army of fictional characters that threatens to invade our reality, and in Morrison's own defense of the durability and potency of fiction in the final issue.

This ideal philosophy is accompanied by an attack on realism—or, at least, the violence and cynicism that had come to be equated with realism in the revisionist superhero comics of the late 1980s. *Animal Man* briefly descends into this mode after Buddy's family is killed, but only to reject it. Issue 21 opens with Buddy donning a black-and-white leather costume from his punk days in the early eighties, comparing himself to Travis Bickle from *Taxi Driver*, and narrating his transformation in the clipped, faux hard-boiled style of the time: "I can't afford to think, only react. Like an animal. I must let myself go. Become an animal" (21.1). If Morrison's early issues were written in a naïve imitation of Alan Moore, with their overwrought scene transitions and ironic juxtapositions of word and image, issue 21 is a deliberate and acerbic parody of Frank Miller. Neither Buddy nor his series can sustain this brutal cynicism for long, however, and each subsequent issue grows more outlandish than its predecessor. Buddy first travels through time (issues 22 and 23), then confronts the ontological confusion caused by the return of all the parallel universes and superfluous characters DC Comics erased in *Crisis on Infinite Earths* in an attempt to streamline their narrative continuity (issues 23 and 24). This return of the repressed at least has some in-story pretext in the person of the Psycho-Pirate, the walking plot device who recalls all the deleted realities; no such excuse pertains to issue 25, when Buddy journeys through a Limbo filled with forgotten comic book characters who are aware of their own fictionality. The journey culminates in the metafictional meeting with Morrison, which occupies issue 26; the violent pseudo-realism of five issues earlier now looks cheap and artificial against Buddy's walk through a quiet, down-to-earth representation of Glasgow.

Along the way, Morrison delivers several critiques of 1980s realism. As the borders between realities are breaking down, the Psycho-Pirate involuntarily summons Overman, a degraded version of Superman from a parallel world. Overman and his world are Morrison's inventions but they compile all the clichés of revisionist superheroes in the period immediately after *Watchmen*, from extreme violence and sordid sexual encounters to shallow, pompous political critiques. Yet this debauched "realism" does not prevent Animal Man from delivering Overman a decidedly irrealist defeat, first yanking him bodily out of the comics panel, then confronting him with his own fictionality, and finally watching as he is trapped and crushed by a shrinking panel border—another gag borrowed from "Duck Amuck" (24.13–15). As the panels close in around him, Overman pleads, "I'm not like you! I'm real! I'm realistic!" (23.15). His amendation indicates the profound difference between the *real* and the *realistic*: the revisionist superheroes, for all their creators' claims to realism, turn out to be no more real than the many oddball Silver Age characters Morrison features throughout *Animal Man*.

The final issue is, if anything, even more explicit in its demolition of superhero realism. Morrison initially refuses Buddy's plea to resurrect his family, saying "It wouldn't be realistic. Pointless violence and death is 'realistic.' Comic books are 'realistic' now" (26.13). The unusual context, however, extends this critique from comic book writers outwards to comic book readers and the rest of the human race. Morrison confesses that he killed Buddy's family to wring a "cheap emotional shock" out of his audience (26.7), but he later questions this desire to watch other beings suffer:

> All the suffering and the death and the pain in your world is entertainment for us. Why does blood and torture and anguish still excite us? We thought that by making your world more violent, we would be making it more "realistic," more "adult." God help us if that's what it means. Maybe, for once, we could try to be kind. (26.19)

Other ethical censures of superhero comics similarly outgrow their initial boundaries. Confronting Animal Man with his "ideological opposite," a carnivore named Slaughterhouse who kills and tortures animals for sport, Morrison explains, "The idea is you fight this guy and you settle the moral argument by beating him into the ground." It's a fair encapsulation of how superhero comics typically manage ideological conflicts—but Morrison adds, "Don't laugh. That's the way we do things in the real world, too" (26.15). Just two pages earlier, he has summed up the moral case for animal exploitation in three words: *"Might makes right"* (26.13). It's uncomfortably close to the logic of most superhero comics, in which moral rectitude is proven or at least confirmed by physical domination. By intertwining these ethical and philosophical dilemmas with superhero conventions through metafiction, rather than the cynical bloodshed and superficial political engagement of revisionist "realism," Morrison has found a greater purpose for his criticisms of the genre: in calling for more ethically responsible comics, he also challenges us to treat each other and the rest of the planet more responsibly. By issue's end, he has put this ethics of compassion into practice by granting Buddy's request. Returning to his home, Buddy discovers that his family is still alive, their death erased with that most trite of authorial cop-outs—it was all just a dream. Even if we cannot expect such mercy from our own hypothetical creators, Morrison suggests, we can at least show it to and model it for each other.

With its resurrection of forgotten 1960s characters and its explicit reaction against the excesses of 1980s revisionism, *Animal Man* might be regarded as one of the earliest entries in a retro-Silver Age nostalgia movement that would come to prominence in the 1990s in such titles as Alan Moore, Rick Veitch, and Steve Bissette's *1963*, Kurt Busiek and Alex Ross's *Marvels*, and Morrison's own *JLA*. Even the comic's metafictional elements have antecedents in the Silver Age, when the Flash would periodically travel to a parallel universe and meet his editor, Julius Schwartz (Hasted 61). But the series cannot be reduced to a commentary on other comics or a set of metafictional games. From "The Coyote Gospel" to Buddy Baker's meeting with Grant Morrison, the comic's treatment of animal rights and the human condition feeds seamlessly into its metafictional speculations, and vice versa: the metafiction brings Morrison's impassioned outcries a narrative sophistication and formalistic detachment that mitigates their potential for didacticism, while the themes of cruelty and compassion lend the metafiction an ethical purpose that elevates it from a strictly literary dilemma to a moral and theological one. *Animal Man* turns out to be larger than any single theme or technique; everything is connected to form a narrative rich with meaning and purpose.

ARKHAM ASYLUM: WHY SO SERIOUS?

When Morrison pitched *Animal Man* to DC Comics, he also proposed *Arkham Asylum* (Hasted 58; Callahan 251), a graphic novel exploring the madhouse that holds Batman's most deranged foes. Although the book wasn't completed and published until three years later, the timing could not have been more perfect: released in December 1989, in the wake of the record-breaking Tim Burton *Batman* film, *Arkham Asylum* was a smash hit. Readers primed for solemn, atmospheric Batman stories by Frank Miller's *The Dark Knight Returns*, Alan Moore and Brian Bolland's *The Killing Joke*, and Burton's film bought the graphic novel in droves; according to editor Karen Berger, it had sold "close to a half million copies" by 2004, making it "the best-selling original graphic novel" in American superhero comics ("Afterword"). Beyond its timing, another significant factor in the book's success is no doubt Dave McKean's art, which blends painting, drawing, photography, and mixed-media collage to confront readers with striking page designs, expressionistic figures, and densely packed, often inscrutable symbols. Berger suggests one reason for McKean's appeal when she remarks that "his influences weren't comics oriented, but a mix of contemporary illustration and design, which was something entirely different from what any of us was used to seeing in traditional comics" ("Afterword"). It was also entirely suited to the audience's newly whetted appetite for sophisticated superhero comics that advertised their aspirations to artistic maturity. McKean's art and Morrison's script fit the bill, presenting Batman's night in Arkham Asylum as an initiation rite in which he faces his deepest fears and darkest impulses, personified in the forms of his worst enemies.

Unfortunately, they also rely on a pungent mixture of symbols and allusions that overburdens the story and oversells the comic's efforts at being taken seriously. (The graphic novel's full name, borrowing a line from Philip Larkin's "Church Going," is *Batman: Arkham Asylum: A Serious House on Serious Earth*.) Morrison represents Batman not simply as a man confronting his own considerable psychological demons but also as a Christ figure, suffering and symbolically dying for the inmates he battles; this most stale of literary metaphors is laid down before the story even begins, in a sequence of extranarrative frontispieces featuring a crumbling manuscript titled "The Passion Play as It Is Played To-Day," a handful of nails, the plan of a building (presumably the eponymous asylum) that shares the cruciform layout of cathedrals, a giant letter *chi*, and a fossilized bat. With such unearned and redundant symbolism filling its pages, it is little wonder that, as Morrison would later complain to Nick Hasted, he "ended up being accused of doing the most pretentious Batman book ever" (67). Morrison would later maintain his story was intended as a critical reinterpretation of serious, grandiose, revisionist superhero works like *The Dark Knight Returns* or *The*

Killing Joke, but these claims are only partially supported by the comic and its script. *Arkham Asylum* both critiques and participates in some of the worst excesses of eighties superhero comics.

Although *Arkham Asylum* was published just months before the *Animal Man* issues that parodied Frank Miller and scoffed at "realistic" superheroes, the script was drafted back when Morrison was conceiving those first four issues of *Animal Man* in imitation of Alan Moore. *Arkham Asylum* is similarly indebted to revisionist superhero comics, drawing on Miller's interpretations of a Batman riven by psychological turmoil and a Joker designed to provoke sexual panic. Andy Medhurst and Will Brooker both cite Morrison's Joker as one of the most extreme examples of a troubling trend in the late 1980s that displaced any anxieties or ambiguities in Batman's sexuality, especially intimations of homosexuality, onto his archenemy (Medhurst 161; Brooker, *Batman* 246). In point of fact, Brooker and Medhurst are too modest—*Arkham Asylum* extends this displacement even further until almost everyone in the asylum exhibits some form of deviant sexual behavior. Clayface fetishizes department-store mannequins, a bit of Batman lore that predates Morrison.[5] The Mad Hatter is portrayed as a child molester in a sinister allusion to persistent rumors about Lewis Carroll's sexual proclivities.[6] Maxie Zeus claims he is "Zeus Arrhenothelus. Part man. Part woman" as he shocks a security guard into electroconvulsive ecstasy. Zeus later tells Batman that "The AC/DC altar awaits"; Morrison's script notes that the pun on the bisexual connotations of AC/DC "is quite deliberate" (47).[7] Amadeus Arkham, the asylum's insane founder, dons his mother's wedding dress, and even the clown fish in his aquarium are capable of changing their sex.

The most infamous instance of cross-dressing, however, was expunged from the script: in Morrison's first draft, the Joker wore make-up and black lingerie in a parody of Madonna (12). The editors at DC Comics and their corporate owners at Warner Bros. vetoed the Madonna look because, as Morrison tells it, they believed readers would "immediately assume Jack Nicholson [who played the Joker in the Burton film] is a transvestite" (Hasted 67). However insipid its logic or its motives may have been, at least the corporate interference nixed yet another association of the Joker's psychosis with this blameless form of gender performance. Unfortunately, the association of the Joker with homosexuality remains. Medhurst tabulates all of the stereotypical signifiers that brand the Joker as gay, culminating when the villain gropes Batman and makes a lewd reference to his sidekick, Robin. While Batman is understandably upset at this manhandling, his overcompensating response—"Take your filthy hands off me! [. . .] Filthy degenerate!"—displays all of the "homophobic ferocity" Medhurst describes (161).

In 2004, as part of the *Arkham Asylum* 15th Anniversary Edition, DC published Morrison's original script and thumbnail layouts, as well as a set of contemporary annotations in which Morrison attempts to reposition his work as a criticism of the very same revisionist trends it exemplifies. He takes particular care to clarify—or revise—the comic's sexual subtexts, maintaining that "The repressed, armoured, uncertain and sexually frozen man in *Arkham Asylum* was intended as a critique of the '80s interpretation of Batman as violent, driven, and borderline psychopathic" (5). Morrison's clarifications seem not only belated but all too convenient, an attempt to control his image retroactively from a later critical moment with a much lower tolerance for homophobic stereotypes. In fact, several passages in the original script endorse the sexually frozen portrayal of Batman, whom Morrison describes as "quite incapable of sustaining any kind of relationship with a woman" because "Batman doesn't like women" (61). Morrison's subsequent annotations attempt to spin these comments back into a critique of the 1980s Batman: "Again, this appraisal of Batman's sexuality applies only to the 'damaged' version of the character presented within these pages. I prefer to think of him now as Neal Adams drew him—the hairy-chested globetrotting love god of the '70s stories" (61).

Nevertheless, the script also supports Morrison's claims that the story was written to confront and purge Batman's anxieties, and not simply to displace all forms of sexual deviance onto his enemies. Lucy Rollin argues that the Joker's chaotic behavior, including his ambiguous sexuality, allows him to assume the role of a psychoanalyst, guiding Batman through a therapeutic exploration of his own unconscious (8). At the narrative's climax, Batman frees the asylum inmates and returns Two-Face's trademark silver dollar, restoring him to a more functional mode of insanity and undoing the damage his psychiatrists have wrought in their efforts to cure him. The crimefighter reconciles himself to his foes and tacitly accepts his own place in the asylum among them. A surprisingly lucid Joker—wearing a trenchcoat and drawn in a scratchy sepia-toned style that make him almost indistinguishable from McKean's rendition of Batman's friend and confidant, Commissioner Gordon—waves goodbye, telling Batman, "There's always a place for you here." Morrison's annotations to this scene make the redemptive effects of the ordeal even more explicit, arguing that Batman has "integrated his psychological demons and emerged stronger and more sane" (66). Rather than demonizing the inmates for their deviance, *Arkham Asylum* reconciles

Batman with the manifold modes of deviance he battles every night on the streets of Gotham City.

If Morrison's annotations attempt to redeem his portrayal of the villains' sexual abnormalities, then his original script makes the same point while offering a revealing glimpse into his methods. The script describes Clayface as

> an avatar of filth and corruption, the personification of pestilence and infection, whose impure touch carries instant contagion. Alert readers will perceive him as AIDS on two legs and realise that he represents the fear of what lies beyond the curtain in the Tunnel of Love. If we take all the encounters with villains as corresponding to various psychological states, then this one is Batman's fear of sexuality as something intrinsically unclean. (36)

The description of Clayface as "AIDS on two legs" might easily be taken as more evidence of homophobia and sexual panic if Morrison did not stress that Clayface embodies *Batman's* fear of sexuality. The inmates are not sexual others to be rejected, but externalizations of Batman's own fears and desires. Richard Reynolds and Geoff Klock have both observed that Batman's major antagonists all reflect some aspect of his own character (Reynolds 68; Klock 35–36); Morrison capitalizes on this longstanding tradition by linking the Arkham inmates to Batman's sexual anxieties, not simply to displace and combat them but to reflect them back at him.[8] Rollin, working without access to Morrison's script and annotations, observes that the inmates "become projections of [Batman's] own psyche" (10), an interpretation she supports with this comment from the Mad Hatter: the criminal tells Batman, "Sometimes I think the asylum is a head. We're inside a huge head that dreams us all into being. Perhaps it's your head, Batman. Arkham is a looking glass. And we are you." Morrison's 2004 annotation of this scene notes simply, and a little defensively, "The Mad Hatter obligingly explains the book for anyone who hasn't figured it out yet" (42); the graphic novel projects Batman's anxieties corporeally onto his enemies and architecturally onto the asylum that contains them.[9]

Filled with characters and locations that are at once concrete entities and manifestations of the protagonist's psyche, *Arkham Asylum* presents Morrison's first substantial use of hypostasis. This initial foray is strictly psychoanalytic, harnessing the unnatural bodies and extraordinary spaces of superhero comics to embody presymbolic trauma and terror. Morrison's 2004 introduction names "psychoanalytical theory" as one of his inspirations

(15th Anniversary Edition), although he tends to cite Jungian archetypes rather than the Lacanian concepts that inform Slavoj Žižek's "embodiment in the real." Nevertheless, when one Arkham inmate suggests taking off Batman's mask to expose his real face, the Joker snaps, "That *is* his real face," providing further confirmation for Žižek's insight that masks function as surface manifestations of meaning (172n2). In that same sequence, Morrison's script describes the frightening, totemic bat that Batman sees in a Rorschach inkblot as "primal, atavistic, the embodiment in one picture of the rage and terror that fuels Batman's existence" (21). Everything in the narrative is symbolic in a manner that obviates the deferred meanings of conventional symbolism: Morrison describes Arkham Asylum as "an avatar of itself, the archetypal Asylum" (44), and says the titanic insignia on the Bat-signal is "stronger and more real than the man it represents" (8). Finally, the 2004 annotations describe Doctor Cavendish, the secret antagonist who nearly kills Batman in the story's climax, as "the very embodied heart of [Batman's] own insanity" (60). All of the figures Batman encounters in *Arkham Asylum*, from his worst enemies to his own mask, hypostatize the traumas that created him and the anxieties that result from them.

While Morrison's figurative strategy renders further symbolic representation unnecessary, McKean's art does not follow suit. Morrison, seeking to account for the graphic novel's troubled reception, told Nick Hasted,

> I imagined it being done by someone like Brian Bolland, and my vision was of it being ultra-real to the point of being painful. [...] But then when Dave McKean did it it became something quite different, because he wanted to make it more abstract. And I think that in a lot of ways, the ways we both approached it clashed in the middle. [...] I think it would have been easier for people to deal with if it had been a lot more concrete. (64–65)

If this willingness to shift the blame onto his collaborator—which only intensifies in the 2004 annotations—appears disingenuous, the script seems to bear it out, as Morrison's notes call for a physical presence and a depth of field that McKean does not provide.[10] Morrison's description of the Mad Hatter's room provides an excellent case in point:

> Imagine now that you can hear Jefferson Airplane's "White Rabbit" begin to play here and continue throughout this scene. We're in a big room that's littered with all sorts of curious stuff. (A tip of the hat here

to the Batman tradition of giant props.) The floor is marked out with black and white chess squares and we can see huge chess figures—ivory white and dark red—standing or lying fallen around the room. [...] There is also a giant teapot and a huge mirror with a baroque frame. Throw in anything else you feel might add to the atmosphere. A liquid slide projector fills the room with psychedelic swirls and whorls of marbled colour. Sweet, cloying drifts of smoke fill the room. It looks most of all like a 1967 nightclub—a hallucinogenic paradise. (40)

Establishing a detailed physical environment, Morrison's script displays familiarity and comfort with abandoned visual conventions such as the giant Dick Sprang props that once populated the Batman comics of the 1940s and 1950s. Morrison's interpretation of the Mad Hatter reflects the juvenilia and camp of Batman's past portrayals, yet these props appear nowhere in McKean's art, dissipating much of the scene's atmosphere (fig. 2-3). Other details present in the script but absent from the art include important plot points that set up the sudden reappearance of doctors Cavendish and Adams at the story's end, elaborate explanations of the various symbols, and harrowing descriptions of an asylum taken over by its inmates: "There is a cryptic splash of blood across the reception desk, a discarded gun" (13). The script is grounded in concrete detail, yet McKean's art abandons the verisimilitude necessary for this approach, leaving a story that is almost purely, unbearably symbolic.

Morrison also provides his own, less easily embodied symbolism, particularly in the graphic novel's most overwrought scene. It occurs when Batman, distraught by a few simple psychological tests and the memory of his parents' murder, shatters a mirror, jabs a shard of glass through his hand, and mutters "Mommy?" as he staggers down the hall. Morrison's script describes the "ritual symbolism" (31) of the bloodletting for almost a full page, with reference to Pisces, the moon, Christ, Osiris, the vesica piscis, Stonehenge, Avebury, the transsexual clown fish, the Mad Men of Gotham, and "the holographic process in which intersecting circular wave patterns produce three dimensional images" (32), another reference to David Bohm's model of an interconnected universe. These interlocking symbologies are remarkably consistent and complementary in Morrison's handling, yet he provides no indication of how McKean might work them into the story other than saying "Batman is here inflicting upon himself one of Christ's wounds and it's all got something to do with fish, okay?" (32). McKean, for his part, more than doubles the scene's length and introduces a new set of

Figure 2-3. *Arkham Asylum*. Art by Dave McKean. © DC Comics.

symbols when Batman looks into a mirror and either sees the young Amadeus Arkham or becomes the young Bruce Wayne; whichever is the case, these images condescend to the reader, explaining a theme of childhood trauma that is already painfully apparent. Both creators contribute to the scene's overweening self-importance and pandering symbolism, but each one provides their own independent set of symbols, leading, as Morrison remarked in the Hasted interview, to "two symbol systems merrily fighting each other, with the reader trying to make sense of it all" (65–66).

In *Batman Unmasked*, Will Brooker imagines what would have happened if Dave McKean and Brian Bolland had switched art duties on *Arkham Asylum* and *The Killing Joke*. He argues that McKean's art complements Morrison's allusive and intertextual script with its stunning collages (Brooker, *Batman* 271–72), while Bolland's more conventional and hyper-detailed representational style, by contrast, "would have illuminated every corner of *Arkham Asylum*, turning ambiguity to stolid detail and making the lunatic house a 'real' place of objects and rooms rather than the state of mind implied by McKean's painting" (*Batman* 272–73). Brooker concludes that both artists are well matched to their respective works, privileging the more direct stylistic correspondences between script and art. Yet even if we set aside Morrison's stated preference for Bolland's style, the disjunctions between the art and script of *Arkham Asylum* suggest that Morrison's symbolically overburdened story would have benefited had it been grounded in Bolland's solidity and verisimilitude. Lucy Rollin argues that McKean's art constitutes a graphic expression of the unconscious (4–7), but Morrison's comments in the script and annotations imply that concrete images may be just as suggestive as overtly symbolic ones. For Morrison, the most terrifying expressions of the real are found not in McKean's encoded symbolisms and expressionist flourishes but in hyperrealistic renderings of impossible figures that embody otherwise inexpressible fears and desires. The ultra-realistic art Morrison would have preferred, with its concretely rendered characters and lavishly realized settings, would have been well suited to this mode of representation. McKean's more abstracted images, on the other hand, forgo the grounding in the physical world that might have redeemed the pedestrian, even hackneyed nature of the comic's metaphors. His abandonment of verisimilitude and depth of field all but annihilate Morrison's externalized embodiments, converting presymbolic manifestations into more conventionally figurative, less potent symbols. While Morrison bears the responsibility for many of the pretensions of *Arkham Asylum*, his assessment of its clashing art and writing styles and their competing symbolic systems perceptively diagnoses one of the comic's greatest weaknesses, its failure to exploit the mimetic power of its most resonant representational technique.

According to Morrison, the negative reaction to *Arkham Asylum* led to a temporary retreat from experimentation. He followed the contentious graphic novel with *Batman: Gothic* (*Legends of the Dark Knight* 6–10, 1990), a five-part Batman story that featured more conventionally revisionist elements; the artist was Klaus Janson, who had previously collaborated with Frank Miller on *Daredevil* and *The Dark Knight Returns*. Morrison told Nick Hasted, "I had been so shocked by the bad reception [of *Arkham Asylum*] that I wanted to show people that I could just write a straight thing as well" (70). However, the story is not quite the "completely normal Batman comic" Hasted describes (70). Inspired by Morrison's fascination with Romantic poets and Gothic novels (Callahan 250), the story is rife with the same kinds of literary allusions, dream images, and religious symbols that permeate *Arkham Asylum*. There are fewer differences between these two Batman projects, and more continuity between those projects and Miller's revisionist interpretation, than Morrison would later acknowledge. He would break newer ground on a contemporaneous project that featured less popular and less profitable characters, leaving him free to challenge the audience's expectations of what a superhero comic could be—and to develop his hypostatic strategies with new collaborators.

DOOM PATROL: MISSING FACES AND REPLACEMENT HEADS

In the spring of 1988, Morrison was invited to take over DC's *Doom Patrol* series ("A Word"). Unlike the virtually unknown Animal Man, the Doom Patrol came with a long tradition. Created in 1963 by writer Arnold Drake (with an assist from Bob Haney) and artist Bruno Premiani, the Doom Patrol were "the World's Strangest Heroes," the first DC Comics characters to show the influence of the angry, alienated monster-heroes of the newly ascendant Marvel Comics (Jones and Jacobs 100–01). After enjoying a brief vogue for eccentric and camp heroes in the mid-1960s, the Doom Patrol's original series was canceled due to falling sales; a team of far more conventional replacements introduced in the 1970s never found the same success. By the late 1980s, the Doom Patrol had become yet another generic team of mutant outcasts in the mold of Chris Claremont, Dave Cockrum, and John Byrne's tremendously popular *Uncanny X-Men*. As Morrison opined in a *Doom Patrol* letter column, "In these days of angst-ridden mutants and grittily realistic (yawn) urban vigilantes, the Doom Patrol no longer seem quite as extreme as they did back in 1963" ("A Word"). To differentiate them from both Chris Claremont-style mainstream superheroics and Frank Miller-style revisionism, Morrison writes, "I decided straight away that I would attempt to restore the sense of the bizarre that made the original Doom Patrol so memorable" ("A Word").

Morrison's *Doom Patrol* (1988–92) is indeed bizarre, featuring a number of experimental techniques: nested narratives, automatic writing, characters who speak only in anagrams or acronyms. Artist Richard Case, not to be outdone, draws two issues as pastiches of twentieth-century art styles in a story set inside an infinitely recursive painting that has devoured Paris. If *Animal Man* contrasted its fractal structures and metafictional encounters against Buddy Baker's ordinary middle-class home life, *Doom Patrol* is self-consciously avant-garde from start to finish, bombarding readers with one strange new twist after another. Over the course of his four years on the title, Morrison would refine many of his signature themes and techniques, most notably his distrust of binary oppositions and his reliance on hypostatic figures that write meaning directly onto the human form. He and Case restore the Doom Patrol's eccentricity primarily by recalling and amplifying the body traumas that made Drake and Premiani's team not only memorable, but frequently unsettling.

Cliff Steele, the only member of the original Doom Patrol to survive relatively unchanged onto Morrison and Case's team, demonstrates their back-to-basics approach. A human brain transplanted into a robot body after a devastating racing accident, Cliff proved eminently expendable for Drake and Premiani, who melted his face (*My Greatest Adventure* 82), dipped him in molten lead (*MGA* 84), exchanged his brain with an archenemy's (*Doom Patrol* I.93), ran him through a machine press, (*DP* I.94) and had him tear off his own limbs to escape a series of deathtraps (*DP* I.87). Morrison and Case maintain the tradition while raising the stakes: during their tenure Cliff changes bodies several times, including an alien repair-job with arachnoid legs and a somewhat too advanced model that decides it wants to live independently of his brain. Morrison's real innovation, though, is to have Cliff feel the shock of wounds that other superheroes routinely shrug off with preternatural calm. Previously, the only acknowledgement of his accident was a surly, grudge-carrying personality typical of the Thing and other monstrous Marvel heroes. Morrison is the first writer to treat Cliff as an amputee, feeling phantom pains and longings from a body that no longer exists. In the first and last issues of Morrison's run, he has signed himself into a psychiatric hospital to cope with this trauma and with the loss of his teammates.

Possibly because it holds no lucrative trademarks that need to be preserved for movie adaptations and lunch boxes, the Doom Patrol has always had a higher body count than most super-teams; as Cliff remarks in Morrison's first issue, "The Doom Patrol kills people. It chews them up and vomits out the bits" (19.12). One of its living casualties is Larry Trainor, who served in the original Doom Patrol as Negative Man, a superhero whose only power was hosting a radioactive spirit that crippled him whenever it left his body. Morrison once again ups the ante, fusing Larry and the spirit with Dr. Eleanor Poole to form Rebis, a biracial hermaphrodite. Rebis is covered from head to toe in bandages just as Negative Man was, but this time they conceal a gradual degeneration of hir body, hinted at by foul odors and troubling self-examinations. By the end of Morrison's run, the first body has decayed completely and Rebis has created a new one by impregnating and giving birth to hir new self.

The third member of the original Doom Patrol, Rita Farr a.k.a. Elasti-Girl, could grow, shrink, or stretch her malleable body, but the glamorous Hollywood star never shared the uncanny appearance of her teammates. This perhaps explains why she was the only member to stay dead after Arnold Drake killed off the Doom Patrol at the end of their first series (*DP* I.121). Morrison replaces her with Kay Challis, Crazy Jane, a woman with an unusual case of multiple personality disorder: each of her sixty-four personalities has its own superhuman ability. The physical plasticity of Elasti-Girl, already somewhat redundant with Cliff's endlessly destructible and reconfigurable body, becomes the psychological plasticity of Crazy Jane—although many of Jane's personalities also subject her to physical transformations, changing her into a clawed, blue-skinned crone or a giant with a flaming sun for a head. By making the third member of the Doom Patrol as outlandish as the other two, Morrison completes Drake's project. The damaged bodies and shattered psyches of the Doom Patrol subvert the power fantasy that underwrites most superhero comics, presenting characters that are not more desirable than the readers, but far less so. As Morrison comments, "the fundamental, radical concept" of the Doom Patrol was that "here was a team composed of *handicapped* people. These were no clean-limbed, wish-fulfillment super-adolescents who could model Calvins in their spare time" ("A Word"; his emphasis).

The physical and psychological traumas of the Doom Patrol signal how superheroes can convey other meanings beyond the power fantasies projected upon their more idealized colleagues. Nearly all of the characters in Morrison's *Doom Patrol* embody various traumas, emotions, or concepts through their distorted and mutable figures. Morrison uses Cliff's human brain and artificial physique to stage a satirically literalized conflict between mind and body in issue 34; much later in the series, Jane observes that his hard metallic exterior also works as a trope for his emotional isolation, telling him "It's not just bullets and missiles that can't get through that goddamn armor, is it?" (60.13). Both male and female, black and white, Rebis describes hirself as "the avatar of contradiction" (28.3). Hir successful creation of a new body at the end of Morrison's run is the result of a long effort to transcend these dualities, only one example of the comic's deep suspicion of binary oppositions. And Jane's sixty-four personalities are formed as a response to sexual abuse by her father, each one representing a different reaction, coping strategy, or aspect of the original self. The mind that houses and connects them is literalized as an underground transit system with each personality inhabiting her own station; the most traumatized selves are located in the deepest stations, of course, with the lowest level reserved for a well leading to a "buried and forgotten section" (30.9). That well contains a monstrous representation of Jane's father, and the entire architecture of the underground concretizes Jane's psychological repression of the abuse that created her. While *Doom Patrol* uses a variety of strategies for generating meaning, hypostasis and physical embodiment are the keys to representing and understanding the traumas that structure the series.

The most serious distortions of the human figure, however, are reserved for a gallery of antagonists and supporting characters who make Rebis, Jane, and Cliff look downright normal. Morrison and Case are especially fond of designing characters whose heads have been replaced by any number of inappropriate objects—celestial bodies, geometric shapes, fingerprints, clocks, candles, mirrors, telephones, church towers, and lava lamps, to name a few (fig. 2-4). Other figures hew somewhat closer to conventional human anatomy but still don't present faces to the world, either because their features are obscured by the masks and helmets that anonymize the religious inquisitions and secret police organizations to which they belong, or because they have had their faces multiplied, scrambled to other locations on the body, or wiped clean entirely by some obscure and ominous power (fig. 2-5). These figures almost always represent threats to rationality and psychological harmony: if the missing faces wipe out the ego and annihilate the individual, the replacement heads topple the seat of reason, supplanting it with the imagery of the unconscious. Both constitute graphic demonstrations of

Figure 2-4. The Candlemaker. *Doom Patrol* 60.24. Art by Richard Case. © DC Comics.

Figure 2-5. The Keysmiths. *Doom Patrol* 63.13. Art by Richard Case. © DC Comics.

the absurd, surreal threats the Doom Patrol fight to contain—forces of totalitarian control, eruptions from the unconscious, or intrusions from other realities that do not follow the same laws and logic as our own.

Although Morrison does not explicitly sort his villains into missing faces and replacement heads, he does provide his own rough taxonomy of these bizarre menaces. In his final issue of *Doom Patrol*, a psychiatrist, believing the various monsters battled over the course of the series to be nothing more than symbolic defense mechanisms Jane has erected to conceal the trauma of incest and rape, conducts a fairly astute reading of Morrison's work:

> Keysmiths, Scissormen, Men from N.O.W.H.E.R.E.—they all seem to represent faceless forces of authority, but it's an authority that's incomprehensible ... and inhuman. The other characters [Jane]'s spoken about—Red Jack, Shadowy Mr. Evans, the Candlemaker—are all nightmarish male oppressor figures. The omnipotent bad father. (63.11)

The doctor offers a valid symbolic interpretation of *Doom Patrol*, yet she also indicates, unwittingly, that these figures are something more than symbolic—they are *incomprehensible* to symbolization, horrifically real expressions of authority and terror. She also separates the antagonists into two categories that roughly conform to Morrison and Case's figurative divide. The sinister organizations are literally "faceless," and the bad fathers she cites all sport some form of replacement head: Red Jack's is a floating, empty mask, the Candlemaker's a flaming candelabra, and the Shadowy Mr. Evans, although possessed of a relatively normal face, does come with a cranial-mounted periscope. Morrison does not maintain a rigid and absolute separation of these categories—many of the more abstract replacement heads are effectively faceless operatives working for conspiracies like the Cult of the Unwritten Book or religious orthodoxies like the Insect Mesh—but he does use them to draw a clear distinction between solitary foes and collective ones, and the different dangers they pose.

Some readers of *Doom Patrol* focus only on the collective enemies, casting the Doom Patrol as heroic nonconformists. Steven Shaviro suggests that "Stability, normality, conformity, and everyday boredom are always the real enemies" (6) in the series, but this tells only half the story at best. Agents of conformity are frequent antagonists in *Doom Patrol*, particularly in the middle third of Morrison's run, when the team finds itself dragged into an alien religious war and targeted by a government conspiracy that seeks "to exterminate all eccentricity and irrationality in this crazy ol' world" (44.6). Josh Lukin classifies these foes as "advocates of a sterile, Enlightenment-based rationalism which seeks to crush wonder and imagination" (86), but Shaviro—and, to some extent, Morrison—makes no distinction between rationalisms that seek to eradicate difference and those that merely contribute to everyday boredom. Conflating the latter with the former, Shaviro reduces cultural oppression and resistance to matters of style, enlisting the Doom Patrol in a purely aesthetic struggle that celebrates all of the transformations of postmodern capitalism, from the liberating to the trivial to the dehumanizing, with equal vigor as forms of revolutionary transgression.[11]

Certainly, *Doom Patrol* provides plenty of easy targets for the type of cultural subversion exalted by Shaviro. The most obvious of these authority figures is Mr. Jones, a former government agent who lives in a postwar suburban rambler with a white picket fence—a domestic idyll so familiar that its critique has become as much of a cliché as the idyll itself. Mr. Jones, who plays a sitcom laugh track while he torments his wife and dog, assembles a team of "normalcy agents" to ensure "a quirk-free world. A normal world where decent people know what's around the corner" (35.15). This insistence on normality, predictability, and decency is joined, predictably enough, to a murderous intolerance when Jones sends his agents to destroy Danny the Street, a sentient transvestite thoroughfare—a street with "macho" businesses like hardware and military surplus stores "dressed up in fairy lights and lace curtains" (35.18). The subversion Shaviro celebrates rarely cuts any deeper than setting up and tearing down these paper-thin representatives of a conformity that postwar America never welcomed as unproblematically as Morrison presents it here. Jones is nothing more than the necessary straight man for the freewheeling absurdity and hipster irony Shaviro attributes to *Doom Patrol*, and so long as the Doom Patrol find themselves battling him and his kind, they make excellent touchstones for Shaviro's book.

But Jones is only one kind of antagonist. Lukin observes that another recurrent menace is the sadistic artist or creator who tries to remake reality, or believes he has made this one (86). Two of Lukin's examples, Red Jack and the Candlemaker, are omnipotent bad fathers, types of the primal bad father who raped Jane and who haunts the series. These nightmarish fathers are the figures of an authority marshaled not for normality and social control but for the violation of all normality, all social law. Even when they are not literal rapists like Jane's father, patriarchs and patriarchal creators are still suspect in *Doom Patrol*—none more so than the icily paternalistic Niles Caulder, a.k.a. the Chief, founder of the original Doom Patrol. Morrison exposes the wise leader, scientist, and mentor of the Drake and Premiani series as a façade for a much more sinister individual who experiments on animals and murders his teammates when he thinks they threaten his plans.[12] Perhaps even worse, from Cliff's point of view, the Chief also engineered the catastrophes that created the original Doom Patrol, including Cliff's racing accident, to provide him with human subjects.[13] No longer satisfied with these small-scale experiments, he has initiated a global apocalypse that will reshape the world according to his own designs. Announcing his intention to populate the world with a new form of life, the Chief elevates himself to godhood—a godhood framed in the scientific language of catastrophe theory and nanotechnology, but no less absolute than the divinity claimed by Red Jack or the Candlemaker. Whether their power is rational or supernatural in origin, lone authorities are as dangerous as collective ones in Morrison's series.

Unlike the inquisitions, cults, and government agencies who hound the Doom Patrol, however, the solitary tyrants often present themselves as rebels in defiance of some higher authority. Red Jack alleges that he was imprisoned by other, unnamed deities for the crime of creating the universe (24.9), and the Chief says he was inspired by Victor Frankenstein's "Promethean dream" to create life (57.18). No one affects the posture of the Romantic rebel artist better than the Shadowy Mr. Evans, who calls himself Satan and claims he has "selflessly endeavored to lift the chains of sordid repression from the shoulders of mankind"; he fumes because humanity has "rejected [him] in favor of mad Ialdabaoth, the stern and frowning dad of this world" (48.14). While his self-pitying rhetoric may cast him as a foe of the oppressive father, his actions reveal he is no better than his enemy. His sexual liberation of Happy Harbor, Rhode Island, reduces the town to a paraphiliac orgy culminating in gang-rape sprees and the surgical violation of coma victims (48.4–5), and his home contains a torture chamber for anyone who criticizes his performances. Evans might pose as a rebel who seeks to shatter the repression and neurosis of Mr. Jones's normalcy—he even shows Cliff a "sad tableau of 'ordinary life'" in which a bored housewife reads a magazine called *Suburban Lifestyle* (48.16)—but the unchained desire of Happy Harbor is no less dystopian than the enforced conformity of the world Jones made, and Evans's aggressive, pandemic sexualization is violent enough for Jane's psychiatrist to classify him with the other omnipotent bad fathers. Exactly one year after the Mr. Jones issues, Morrison complicates their simplistic conflict between the freaks and the authorities by confronting the Doom Patrol with a parody of Romantic liberation as extreme and grotesque as Jones's parody of social conformity.

Nobody complicates the ideology of *Doom Patrol* more than Mr. Nobody, leader of the Brotherhood of Dada. While all the other antagonists can be categorized as faceless agents of authority or lone omnipotent oppressor-creators, the two incarnations of the Brotherhood of Dada are the sole examples of a third category—the rival team of outcasts and misfits. Following time-tested superhero convention, Morrison designs each member of the first Brotherhood as a counterpart of the Doom Patrol: Rebis's bandaged appearance and variety of abilities are reflected in the Quiz, a mysophobe who seals herself inside an insulated suit; Crazy Jane's fragmentation into multiple personalities is perfectly inverted in the Fog, who absorbs the personalities of the victims he ingests; and if Cliff Steele is a brain without a body, then Sleepwalk, who exhibits tremendous strength while somnambulating, might be termed a body without a conscious mind.[14] In another comic book this clash of opposites might seem trite, yet Morrison designs the Brotherhood of Dada as reflections of the Doom Patrol not to make them better sparring partners but to unsettle the Doom Patrol's belief in their own role as defenders of the status quo.

Mr. Nobody is a minor, all-but-forgotten member of the Brotherhood of Evil, a criminal organization from the Drake/Premiani *Doom Patrol*, but he does not appropriate their name, which would lock his team into a simple moral binary typical of most Silver Age comics. He instead rejects this dualism and gives his team another purpose:

> "Good"! "Evil"! Outmoded concepts for an antique age. Can't you see? There is no good, there is no evil in our new world! Look at us! Are we not final proof that there is no good, no evil, no truth, no reason? Are we not proof that the universe is a drooling idiot with no fashion sense? From this day on we will celebrate the total absurdity of life, the gigantic hocus-pocus of existence. From this day on, let unreason reign! The Brotherhood of Evil is dead! Long live the Brotherhood of Dada! (26.23–24)

Nobody rejects all dualisms, telling a group of onlookers that Dada is "the point at which yes and no and all opposites meet" and promising to lead them into "the empire of the senseless" (27.19). Whenever he encounters the Doom Patrol, he presents himself as an emancipatory figure who only wants "to break the crushing monotony of life! To set the world free! […] Every man his own master with the freedom to say 'no'" (29.4). If this last claim contradicts his earlier attempt to demolish all binary oppositions, it also casts the Brotherhood as harmless scamps or heroic rebels who bring the freedom of absurdity to a regimented world—making them perfect counterparts to the

Doom Patrol. Most superheroes battle "to preserve society, not to re-invent it" (Reynolds 77), and the Doom Patrol, for all their oddities, are no exceptions. They defend reality against all manner of strange threats, working "to establish order in a chaotic world" (Callahan 157). Without rejecting this longstanding convention of the genre or changing the Doom Patrol's mission, Morrison presents their opposite numbers in the Brotherhood of Dada with considerable sympathy.

Yet Nobody also murders several people, tries to kill the Doom Patrol, twice attempts to drag the world into an infinitely recursive painting, and subjects the city of Venice to an acid trip that causes at least one woman to have a nervous breakdown—although Nobody is quick to disclaim responsibility for this last assault, blaming a repressive society for the woman's paranoia (50.18). While Nobody's justifications may seem facile or self-serving, Morrison appears to endorse them when half the Doom Patrol decides they agree with him. After Nobody enlists the second Brotherhood of Dada in a series of Merry Prankster-style antics and a quixotic campaign to become president of the United States of America, Crazy Jane refuses to fight him and Danny the Street claims he didn't mind when they hijacked him. As outcasts and targets of persecution themselves, Jane and Danny can muster neither the interest nor the legal rationale for stopping a crime wave so bizarre it doesn't break any laws. (As one character notes, the Controlled Substances Act makes no provisions for school buses powered by the hallucinogenic bicycle of Albert Hoffman, discoverer of LSD.) The Brotherhood of Dada nearly supplant the Doom Patrol as heroes of their own comic book until Cliff insists that he has to stop the Brotherhood even if he can't quite articulate why: "Because if we don't... then... then the Brotherhood is right and there's no point... no point to anything. I can't live that way" (51.20).

Cliff's need to preserve meaning and resist Nobody's empire of the senseless is soon echoed by John Dandy, one of the U.S. government's literally faceless operatives, who tells Nobody "This country made sense once" (52.20) and implicitly blames him for its slide into meaninglessness. When Cliff finally intercedes, however, it's to rescue Nobody (unsuccessfully) from assassination by Dandy and the government. Cliff may side with the freaks against the authorities, but he never quite accepts Nobody's rhetoric about the liberatory power of strangeness and unreason. He justifies his presence at Nobody's fatal rally and delineates his rules of engagement with reference to the universal standards of the Enlightenment rationalism Nobody rejects, insisting that "the Brotherhood of Dada has as much right to free speech as anyone else"; when government forces make the more serious infringement on the Brotherhood's rights, Cliff attempts to save them, but he is just as prepared to destroy their school bus if they try to dose Washington, D.C. as they did Venice (52.4). Later, when the other members of the Doom Patrol once again waver over whether they should stop the Chief's apocalypse since it may result in the creation of a better world, Cliff swiftly settles the debate by asserting that "people ought to be allowed to choose what happens to them" (62.3). These stands on principles of life, free expression, and self-determination make Cliff Steele and the rest of the Doom Patrol defenders of liberal democratic social order even when that society ostracizes them, and even when they must protect it from its own legally empowered guardians.[15] Despite their outlandish appearances, their traumatic pasts, and their sympathy for the Brotherhood, the Doom Patrol are not agents of unreason like Nobody's groups. Their defense of universal self-determination positions them between and in opposition to the oppressive hierarchies, tyrannical creator-fathers, and destructive subversives who rampage through their series; the Doom Patrol are not challengers of social conformity but mediators between authority and desire.

EMBODIED AUTHORITIES, IMAGINARY TERRORS

The heroes' roles as ideological mediators and the comic's interest in embodied representation both come to the foreground when the Doom Patrol are dragged into an alien war midway through Morrison's run. The centuries-long conflict between the Orthodoxy of the Insect Mesh and the Ultraquist Geomancers presents an unusual collision of sources, combining the violent religious schisms of early modern Europe with the outlandish science fiction of Jack Kirby's "Fourth World" comics.[16] Prior to the Doom Patrol's arrival, the war has been fought primarily through weaponized neuroses, plagues that destroy words and therefore compromise the objectivity of the physical world, psychosomatic projections, and "words that kill" (38.20). Rhea Jones, the former Doom Patrol member kidnapped by one side as part of a stratagem to end the war, is a "lodestone" who bonds with the electromagnetic field of her planet, "becoming that world's expression in the flesh" (40.15). These weapons and tactics mirror Morrison's own figurative techniques in *Doom Patrol*: abstract concepts and psychological states take physical forms in a war that is not only fought through hypostasis, but also over hypostasis.

The Orthodoxy and the Ultraquists battle over the Judge Rock, a giant floating head that is "part city, part shrine, part promise, part avatar of the potential for earthly paradise" (38.20). The Rock is later revealed to be a lapsed angel once tasked with transforming Eden "from a physical reality into an abstract idea" after the fall (41.19)—in other words, reversing a hypostasis back into conventional symbolic abstraction. Instead of discharging its duties, the Rock stole a cutting from the tree of knowledge and fled the Earth to create its own prelapsarian paradise, a world that never experienced the linguistic fall into purely symbolic meaning. This revelation explains why the war between the Orthodoxy and the Ultraquists has been fought with so many hypostatic combatants: their world neither mandates nor recognizes the difference between ideas and objects. This is also why their war has dragged on without end; the Judge Rock, Rhea explains, "had no imagination. The only working dynamic it could think of was conflict. Haven't you ever wondered why your societies are so simplistic, your struggles so meaningless?" (41.20). The aliens discover they are only tropes and their conflict has been nothing more than an embodiment of duality (41.23)—always a dangerous notion in *Doom Patrol*. The Doom Patrol end this allegory by crashing the Judge Rock and planting the cutting in the debris, releasing the creative energy of the tree of knowledge and giving the aliens new ideas that do not revolve around dualistic conflict.[17]

The Judge Rock is not the only authority figure to be knocked down a peg in the final pages of the space war; after Cliff objects when Rhea leaves the Doom Patrol to explore the universe, Jane gently chides him, "You're not her dad, Cliff" (41.23). This becomes a pattern in *Doom Patrol*, with young women like Rhea, Jane, and Dorothy Spinner all learning to become self-reliant and either outgrowing or actively facing down the authorities in their lives. These authorities are invariably male, whether they are terrifying oppressors like Jane's father or benevolent (if somewhat overprotective) guardians like Cliff. Unlike every other father figure in the series, however, Cliff accepts his loss of authority with grace. There is no question as to what sets him apart: the disfiguring accident that robbed him of his body has not only made him a better person, as the Chief boasts (57.27), it has also stripped him of the ultimate symbol of male power. When Cliff enters Jane's mind to pull her out of a comatose state—comas come thick and fast in this series where the mind and body are routinely separated—he encounters personifications of each of her sixty-four personalities. He can only persuade them to allow him access to the deepest, most private levels of her subconscious by stripping down, exposing his smooth, sexless metal groin, and proclaiming, "I'm not a man" (30.18). Cliff's gender identity is never in flux the way Rebis's is—he even begins a gradual and halting romantic relationship with Jane—but his accident has made him the only man in the series to surrender his authority voluntarily. He is also the only man to undergo his own story of trial and maturation as he learns to see past his idealization of Niles Caulder and gives up everything—his brain, his consciousness, even a chance at a new, human body (62.7)—to end the Chief's catastrophe program.

He is not, however, the only character to lose his body. The pages of *Doom Patrol* contain several full-body amputees, unfortunates who feel bodily desires more acutely than those who still have bodies. Cliff sets the tone for these explorations of the interdependence of mind and body in Morrison's first issue:

> You know, they say that amputees feel phantom pains where their limbs used to be. Well, I'm a total amputee. I'm haunted by the ghost of my entire body! I get headaches, you know, and I want to crap until I realize I don't have any bowels. And ... when I look at a woman, sometimes I ... (19.12)

The amputated antagonists condense these yearnings into parody. One of the Sex Men, government agents detailed with containing outbursts of sexual desire, expresses interest in sleeping with Jane only after he has been decapitated (48.20). The Brain, an enemy of the original Doom Patrol, has grown frustrated by his long existence as a brain in a tank; he tells his confederate, "I'm tormented by thoughts of strip chess. Pure mind just isn't enough, Mallah. I long for a body" (34.10). Conversely, in that same issue one of Cliff's robot bodies longs for a life independent of Cliff's mind and attempts to murder his brain. If the minds crave the completion of bodies, the bodies seem to have little use for the mind.

When the Brain's henchman, a hulking gorilla with surgically enhanced intelligence, proclaims himself and his master "A vivid and explicit expression of Cartesian dualism" (34.12), he provides yet another reminder of Morrison's penchant for hypostatic demonstrations of abstract concepts, but he is unaware that the more serious, or at least higher-stakes, dramatization of that dualistic tension is happening between the two components of Cliff Steele. The Brain and Mallah serve only to satirize that conflict, and Morrison's signature style, in a hypostatic theatre of the absurd. That satire displays Morrison's usual mistrust of dualisms, Cartesian or otherwise—the robot body's attempt to separate itself from the mind leads to destruction, but so does the Brain's attempt to place his mind in a body—yet it also exhibits some signs that Morrison has rigged the conflict. The two disembodied brains representing pure mind are both completely helpless, and both desperate for bodies, while the robot and gorilla bodies both possess intellects that permit them autonomy; so, to a lesser degree, do the book's many sleepwalkers, dreamers, or psychically active coma patients like Sleepwalk of the Brotherhood of Dada, Rhea Jones, Cesarina the Somnambulist, the denizens of Orqwith, or Ilse Krauss. If Morrison ends his twinned mind/body conflict on a note of uncertainty and irresolution with a quote from the Smiths song "Still Ill"—"Does the body rule the mind or does the mind rule the body? I don't know" (34.24)—then his sympathies, here and elsewhere in *Doom Patrol*, seem to lie with the bodies that are so frequently animate vehicles for his ideas.

This emphasis on the physical and embodied is a major departure from the Gnostic ideas that otherwise shape much of *Doom Patrol*. The Gnostics, early Christian sectarians who sought mystical, esoteric knowledge, believed the body and the material world are innately corrupt, creations of a flawed, subordinate god known as the demiurge and sometimes identified as Ialdabaoth (Harris 109–09). Morrison appropriates this cosmology into *Doom Patrol*, patterning a number of its menaces after the demiurge or the archons that serve him. Red Jack claims to be a Gnostic creator-god punished by a higher power; similarly, the leaders of the Cult of the Unwritten Book are described as both Archons and demiurges (33.13–14). The Archons turn out to be a pair of Punch and Judy puppets worn by a dead king and queen, their necks broken, who are themselves moved by marionettes' strings pulled by an unseen puppeteer—a graphic demonstration of the limitations of the demiurge, who is always at the mercy of some even more remote power. Other, less explicitly Gnostic storylines follow the cosmology almost as transparently. After she destroys and remakes the Judge Rock, Rhea tells the aliens, "Now you don't have to pray to a hollow head-in-the-clouds. The creator's come down among you, not as a judge, but as a sort of imaginative energy" (41.20). She has replaced the callous and inflexible authority of Ialdabaoth with the creative potential of the Supreme God whose emanations formed the universe and the other divinities (Harris 89–91).

The Gnostic cosmology enables Morrison to pit the Doom Patrol against a series of stand-ins for the Judeo-Christian God, all of whom claim absolute power and authority over the material world, while preserving some space for a higher power that is not malevolent and cannot be bested by a team of comic book superheroes. Rather than turn the comic into a Gnostic gospel, however, Morrison selectively abandons, complicates, or inverts the cosmology when it would contradict other aspects of his series; his antagonists are themselves Gnostics as frequently as they are the archons and demiurges the Gnostics reviled, and it can be difficult to distinguish the two. The Cult of the Unwritten Book summons the Decreator, an "anti-god" who will unmake the universe, because the cultists "believe matter and physical manifestation to be corrupt" (32.6). The Shadowy Mr. Evans claims to be a Gnostic liberator who rebels against Ialdabaoth, but he is just as sadistic and dangerous as the demiurge; Red Jack, on the other hand, claims to be both the demiurge imprisoned in the world of matter and the higher beings who imprisoned him there (24.9). Rhea's transformation of the Judge Rock breaks down this opposition in a similar fashion by suggesting the stern judge can become the creative force. Judge and creator, archon and liberator, demiurge and Supreme God all meld together, making the Gnostic renunciation of the material world as simplistic and questionable as any other binary opposition.

Doom Patrol is, if anything, more likely to find danger and corruption originating in the realm of the ideal. Many of the antagonists are purely abstract, conceptual, or imaginary: a fictional city that intrudes into and begins to engulf the real world (in a story based on Jorge Luis Borges's "Tlön, Uqbar, Orbis Tertius"); a young girl's imaginary friends and terrors, given substance by her psychic powers; warring aliens who exist only as hypostases of dualistic conflict; and other nightmarish personifications of fears both individual and collective. The series' signature question is Cliff Steele's exasperated "Is this real or isn't it?" (21.17), which will be repeated by several characters with only minor variations until Morrison's departure. In this respect, *Doom Patrol* forms a surprising contrast with *Animal Man*; where the prior series exalts the ideal and finds in fiction the possibility for a compassion that seems to be absent in the real world, *Doom Patrol* recognizes that ideas can pose their own hazards and perform their own kind of violence. Whereas Buddy Baker discovers his own fictionality and attempts to enter the real world that created him, the Doom Patrol—who inhabit the same fictional universe as Buddy and even meet him briefly (28.1–2)—prevent a number of imaginary invaders from entering and remaking the world their series always presents as real.[18] *Doom Patrol* reverses *Animal Man*'s privileging of the ideal, valuing the concrete and physical over the purely cerebral not only in its preference for hypostasis over metafiction, but also in the moral weight it assigns to each category as the grotesquely embodied Doom Patrol push back one imaginary threat after another.

This exposure of the potential tyranny and terror of the ideal does not constitute a defense of materialism. The sentient robot body that proclaims itself "a materialist at heart" (34.8) is played for laughs just as much as the talking gorilla who thinks he and his brain-in-a-tank pal are a living proof of Cartesian dualism, and the mindless or unconscious bodies that battle the Doom Patrol are just as dangerous as the bodiless spirits or conceptual menaces. The psychological and ideological threats may outnumber the strictly material ones, but Morrison's suspicion of binaries bars him from embracing either extreme. His Doom Patrol act as mediators in the book's philosophical and theological conflicts much as they do in its political and social ones. Patrolling the no man's land between authoritarian creators and libidinous rebels, between government conspiracies and anarchist absurdities, Cliff, Jane, and Rebis protect mundane society and consensus reality from any and all forms of ideological extremism.

Morrison's interest in mediating between the ideal and the real explains the two endings of *Doom Patrol*. In the penultimate issue, after the rest of the Doom Patrol has decamped to Danny the Street—now expanded into Danny the World, a storybook planet of infinite possibilities—Dorothy Spinner decides to remain behind. The last line of the issue is her request, delivered to one of her imaginary friends, to "Take me to the real world" (62.24). In a series that regularly ends its storylines with young women asserting their independence, Dorothy's decision to leave her protectors and live in the real world provides one final moment of maturation. Morrison's last issue is a wrenching reversal, however, as Jane finds herself trapped in a dreary world where psychiatrists keep telling her the Doom Patrol and its adventures are merely figments of her imagination.[19] After Jane disappears, rescued by Cliff and Danny, a narrator—most likely a sympathetic psychiatrist desperate to believe Jane has not committed suicide—insists, "There is another world. There is a better world. Well . . . there must be" (63.24). These words, Morrison's last in *Doom Patrol*, accompany scenes of Jane returning to Danny, rejecting the real world that turns her heroic adventures and companions into so many symbolic filters for a dismal and sordid past.

These twinned and diametrically opposed finales encapsulate much of the ambivalence of *Doom Patrol*. Reality is the site of adult responsibility and oppressive rationalism, the imagination a source of juvenile terrors and surreal solace. This ambivalence, and the ever-present tension between the real and the imaginary, might suggest why Morrison is drawn to hypostasis: the trope produces bodies that are both literal and figurative, physical and conceptual. Hypostasis allows Morrison to transcend the dualities that are the series' one constant enemy, uniting the best aspects of the material and the ideal. Underneath its self-conscious weirdness *Doom Patrol* may be a deeply conventional superhero comic in many ways, chronicling the adventures of a team of outcasts who preserve the status quo against ideological and ontological disruptions, but instead of offering a cast of idealized figures suitable for reader identification or desire, Morrison and Case summon a host of freakish, impossible anatomies capable of addressing a limitless range of ideas. The series is at its most eccentric, experimental, and significant when it speaks about and through the mutable bodies of the world's strangest heroes.

THE HILARITY OF INFLUENCE

No discussion of *Doom Patrol* would be complete without some acknowledgment of Morrison's humor. Nearly all his comics display a keen sense of the absurd and a knack for droll dialogue—the Joker even slips a couple of good lines into the otherwise somber *Arkham Asylum*—but the later issues of *Doom Patrol* are particularly rich with parodies of other comics, from an affectionate homage to Stan Lee and Jack Kirby's *Fantastic Four* (*DP* 53) to a more devastating jab at the early-nineties mutant comics of Chris Claremont, Jim Lee, and Rob Liefeld (*Doom Force Special* 1). When Morrison was denied permission to use occult investigator John Constantine (created by Alan Moore, Steve Bissette, and John Totleben in *Swamp Thing*), he devised stand-in Willoughby Kipling, a smug coward who carries Constantine's penchant for alcohol abuse to parodic excess. In its fiftieth issue, *Doom Patrol* even parodies itself as Morrison and a gallery of guest artists invent a series of ludicrous scenes from the Doom Patrol's history; on the final page, Case draws an assortment of Doom Patrol merchandise including a toy brain in a jar and a Crazy Jane doll with interchangeable heads (50.40). Most of the parodies, however, take aim at Morrison's contemporaries. *Doom Patrol* 45 features the Beard Hunter, a comic book fanboy turned hitman who patterns himself after the Punisher, paraphrases Wolverine, and speaks in the terse narration common to many of Morrison's parodies of violent superhero comics: "I'm the best there is at what I do. What do I do? I hunt beards" (45.3–4). In that same issue the Bearded Gentlemen's Club of Metropolis boasts a portrait of Alan Moore, draped in shadow and looking much like the photograph that graced the back cover of early editions of the *Watchmen* trade paperback; the portrait is cheekily labeled "Our Founder" (figs. 2-6, 2-7). Morrison told Timothy Callahan the picture was the work of artist Vince Giarrano, just as he said it was cover artist Simon Bisley's decision to

The World's Strangest Heroes   89

Figure 2-6. Detail from the *Watchmen* 1988 trade paperback, back cover. © DC Comics.

Figure 2-7. *Doom Patrol* 45.9. Art by Vince Giarrano. © DC Comics.

draw an unshaven Flex Mentallo to resemble Moore on the cover of *Doom Patrol* 36 (Callahan 262–63). Even if he disclaims the overt jokes at Moore's expense, these parodies separate Morrison's *Doom Patrol* from Moore's work no less than they disparage the angst-ridden mutants and grittily realistic urban vigilantes that so bored Morrison in that early letter column.

Morrison would have a more difficult time separating himself from the literary and artistic influences that pervade his first American comics. Early issues of *Doom Patrol* reference Borges, De Quincey, Wordsworth, Byron, Shelley, Wilde, Plath, and Peter Barnes's play *The Ruling Class*; Crazy Jane names herself after a painting by mentally ill Victorian artist Richard Dadd (and indirectly alludes to a cycle of poems by William Butler Yeats); and the Painting that Ate Paris is filled with quotations of nearly a dozen modernist art movements. *Batman: Gothic* evokes Gothic and Romantic writers from Horace Walpole and M. G. Lewis to Byron and Edgar Allan Poe; *Arkham Asylum* contains enough literary, religious, mystical, and psychoanalytic allusions to warrant its own annotated script; and even *Animal Man*, a series more likely to reference obscure 1960s comics characters, features the authorial presence that Morrison would later describe as "this Satanic, Byronic figure" (Hasted 62). These works advertise Morrison's influences, with *Doom Patrol* in particular seeking to place itself in continuity with literature and the visual arts more so than with other comics. The allusions grow thick enough that Morrison's authorial surrogate in *Animal Man* muses, "What'll it be next? Choice extracts from the *Oxford Dictionary of Quotations*? Trotting out the Nietzsche and the Shelley and the Shakespeare to dignify some old costumed claptrap?" (14.7). These lines are none too subtle shots at Alan Moore—the first chapter in the American publication of *Miracleman* ended with a Nietzsche quote and the final lines of Shelley's "Ozymandias" closed the penultimate issue of *Watchmen*—but they also take aim at Morrison's own increasing reliance on literary allusions to provide his comics with a high-cultural pedigree. *Animal Man*'s critique of the artificiality of revisionist superhero comics applies to its author's literary aspirations as well.

This marks the point at which Morrison's allusions begin to question the necessity of seeking legitimacy through imitations of other art forms. *Animal Man* 14 was published in June 1989; the next month, *Doom Patrol* 26 began the story of the first Brotherhood of Dada and the Painting that Ate Paris. These issues reference mass culture almost as frequently as they do high art: Mr. Nobody's lair contains Raoul Hausmann's *Mechanical Head* and a small collection of Dadaist readymades, but it is also filled with children's toys, seventies comic books, posters for the Osmonds and the Bay City Rollers, all the cultural detritus of the decade of Morrison's adolescence (26.8). Associating the Dadaist supervillain with the children's culture of the 1970s is an art-historical non sequitur but it makes perfect sense. The Dadaists ignored or assaulted distinctions between high and low culture, incorporated commonplace materials into their art, collaged images together, and blended image and text (Hugnet 15–34, 43), just like Morrison's own chosen medium. The storyline ends with Dadaist art sapping the energy of the other artistic movements contained within the Painting that Ate Paris and stripping away the significance of language itself, reducing all other modes of painting (and, implicitly, of writing) to nonsense (29.19, 29.23). After such a climax, any further references to literature or painting are pointless; absurdity stands triumphant thanks to the very qualities Dada shares with comics.

Morrison continued to cite works of art and literature, but after his first year on *Doom Patrol* he would tend to mine his influences for ideas, not parade them as aspirational peers. He continued to reference other comics as well, primarily for purposes of parody or to set his own works apart: after *Arkham Asylum* and the first four issues of *Animal Man*, Morrison would no longer limit himself to the conventions of superhero revisionism. The metafictional ethics of "The Coyote Gospel" and the embodied traumas of *Doom Patrol* would steer Morrison towards new themes and new means of exploring them, distinct from the revisionists' bids for literary respectability or their confusion of violence and sexuality with artistic maturity. *Arkham Asylum*, a standalone graphic novel locked into the moment of its creation, is the work of a writer fully invested in these assumptions, but *Animal Man* and *Doom Patrol*, serials unfolding over the course of nearly five years, show Morrison tabulating and then synthesizing and transcending his influences. All these comics are indebted to the first wave of revisionists, but *Animal Man* and *Doom Patrol*, like Morrison's subsequent works, are no longer bound by them.

Chapter 3

THE INVISIBLE KINGDOM

By the early 1990s, DC Comics had cultivated six series—*Swamp Thing, Hellblazer, Sandman,* and *Shade, the Changing Man,* along with *Animal Man* and *Doom Patrol*—based on obscure superhero or horror properties and aimed at mature readers. All of these series except *Doom Patrol* had been edited or developed by Karen Berger and all had been written by British writers, most of whom Berger had recruited. DC Comics president Jenette Kahn and editorial director Dick Giordano asked Berger to develop a new publishing imprint that would unify and expand these titles into a line of mature comics (Contino, "A Touch of Vertigo"). Berger named the imprint Vertigo and began seeking out new titles, a mission that was aided by another company's misfortunes. Disney Comics had been planning their own mature readers imprint, Touchmark Comics, under the direction of Art Young, a former DC editor and onetime assistant to Berger. Young enlisted several veteran writers, including Morrison, but poor sales and an overextended line led Disney to scrap their plans for Touchmark amid a general wave of cancellations in 1991. Berger hired Young as her senior editor and British liaison, acquired the Touchmark comics, and was able to double the size of Vertigo's publishing plan before the imprint debuted in January 1993.[1]

Since the imprint's inception, Berger has sought to distinguish Vertigo titles from the superhero comics that dominate the American comics industry. In her view, the line offers greater realism, sophistication, and the irreverent "outsider's perspective" of the British writers she recruited, factors that attract a more adult audience (Contino, "A Touch of Vertigo"). Yet the imprint would continue to draw nourishment from the superhero comics that had inspired its core titles; in its first six months, Vertigo launched new series about vintage superheroes like the original Sandman from the 1940s and published comics about risible or forgotten DC characters like Brother Power the Geek and the Tattooed Man. When the line did branch out, it tended to go only as far as other popular genres like fantasy or horror—rare in the comics industry of the 1990s, but hardly unheard of. The result was an imprint caught between publication models and, sometimes, between audiences; Dana Jennings writes, in a *New York Times* profile of Berger, that "Fans of the small, independent presses say Vertigo is too mainstream, tainted by being part of DC. Superhero fans meanwhile accuse Vertigo of being too avant-garde" (C8). Vertigo occupies an undefined middle ground between corporate comics and alternative ones, popular genres and more personal work—exactly the space Morrison has gravitated towards throughout his career. Given his formative role writing two of the six core series and contributing one of the Touchmark projects, it is not surprising that the imprint's positioning should resemble Morrison's. Both are indebted to superheroes and other popular genres but are not bound by them. This has made Vertigo an ideal home for Morrison's more independent works, which break out of superhero conventions without wholly rejecting popular tastes.

Ironically, Vertigo did not publish any comics written by Morrison in its first two months. *Animal Man* had long since been handed off to other writers, and his run on *Doom Patrol* ended the month before Vertigo launched. Morrison's presence was soon felt in the third month, however, with the debut of *Sebastian O*, a three-issue miniseries by Morrison and Steve Yeowell originally commissioned for Touchmark. The next two years saw the publication of Morrison's original graphic novel *The Mystery Play*, the one-shot special *Kill Your Boyfriend*, and the ongoing series *The Invisibles*, Vertigo's first creator-owned ongoing series (Neighly 16). These comics show Morrison gradually awakening to the new possibilities opened by Vertigo, which promised to combine the creative freedom of independent comics with the production values and, at least potentially, the audience of mainstream comics. In practice, the imprint often fell short of that promise: audiences failed to materialize, editors censored issues of *The Invisibles* (Neighly 37–40, 249), and the line developed a confining house style of its own. Vertigo nevertheless allowed Morrison to tell new stories outside the dominant genres of American comics. *Sebastian O* and *The Mystery Play* largely rework old material, but *The Invisibles* and its parodic reflection, *Kill Your Boyfriend*, shed generic constraints to tell stories about countercultural rebellion and the inevitability of co-optation—a fate they try to avoid through their unsparing self-criticism. Vertigo may be poised uneasily between mainstream and alternative models, but Morrison uses that liminal space to create comics that trade on familiar genres while challenging the prevailing ideologies that shape contemporary Western culture.

SEBASTIAN O AND *THE MYSTERY PLAY*: DANDIES, MESSIAHS, ASSASSINS

Morrison's first Vertigo projects stick to familiar territory, compiling and repeating elements from his previous works. *Sebastian O* (1993) might appear more original at first glance: it tells the story of a fugitive dandy in an alternate Victorian England that possesses advanced technology but retains a nineteenth-century design sensibility, a world of motorized hansom cabs and virtual reality simulators that resemble diving helmets. Beneath the steampunk science fiction, however, the miniseries follows the plot structures of the super-spy genre; Nick Hasted detects the influence of 1960s television shows and Morrison adds that Sebastian O is inspired by Michael Moorcock's Jerry Cornelius (Hasted 71). Morrison had already drawn on these sources in comics such as *Gideon Stargrave* and *Steed and Mrs. Peel* (1990–92), an adaptation of *The Avengers*. *Sebastian O* transplants the spy formulas to a steampunk setting but otherwise follows them to the very end, when a seemingly dead henchman returns to ambush Sebastian well after the master villain has been vanquished. The miniseries anticipates the genre's influence on *The Invisibles* and particularly on the character of King Mob, who, like Sebastian O, combines the dandy and the assassin into a single figure.[2]

Even the plot twist that moves the miniseries beyond the typical concerns of the spy genre echoes an earlier comic. Sebastian's archenemy, Lord Lavender, has created a virtual reality that he describes with appropriately Victorian terminology as a "magic lantern simulation" (3.16). In the final issue, Lavender tells Sebastian that they are inside this simulation, that the whole world is a computer program under his control. The sudden revelation of a new, outer level of reality, the wrenching adjustment of scale, the discovery that the world is only a simulacrum—Morrison had done this before, in collaboration with Yeowell, and with the same vocabulary. The narrator of *Zenith* Phase IV dismisses the Lloigor's destruction of London as a "magic lantern apocalypse" (IV.14.2) since it transpires within Chimera's perfect simulation of the universe. Unlike that earlier series, though, *Sebastian O* never steps outside the simulation and its protagonist scarcely displays any shock at this ontological bait and switch.

Perhaps this is because Lavender's magic lantern simulation is only the last in a series of artificial worlds. Sebastian, Lavender, and the other major characters are all former members of the licentious "Club de Paradis Artificiel"; Sebastian's home is fully mechanized, filled with secret passages and moving rooms; his friend the Abbé has constructed a Mechanical Garden filled with clockwork plants; and the lesbian George Harkness has created a less technologized simulation of heterosexual domesticity by dressing as a man, adopting a masculine name, and indulging in masculine pastimes such as hunting while in the company of her lover. As dandies and decadents, Sebastian and his peers already live in simulacra of their own creation. Sebastian proudly declares, "It is our duty to be as artificial as possible" (1.14), and so Lord Lavender assumes he will be untroubled by the thought that the rest of world is equally artificial (3.15). He may be right, although Sebastian's final line, asking his butler to pass the laudanum, might suggest some barely-acknowledged desire to drown this truth in a narcotic haze (3.24). Lavender's magic lantern simulation is a fantastic literalization of the all-encompassing artifice of the *fin de siècle* Decadence movement, turning the standard science fiction trope of virtual reality into a tribute to Morrison's artistic forerunners. Ironically, this acknowledgment of the Decadents' influence is one of the most original and inspired elements in an otherwise derivative miniseries.

The Mystery Play (1994) makes greater claims to autonomy, positioning itself as a serious work free of Morrison's usual generic influences, but it too recalls prior comics. An original graphic novel with moody painted art by John J. Muth, the project follows the pattern of an unlikely but obvious predecessor, *Arkham Asylum*. Joe McCulloch traces the substantial parallels between the two plots, noting that both comics introduce outsiders into closed communities, subject the outsider to a series of arcane philosophical exchanges with the various inhabitants, bombard the outsider with heavy-handed symbols and allusions, blend subjective perception and hallucination with external reality, and culminate in cathartic finales in which the Christ-like outsider accepts and purges the sins of the community before he departs ("Please God"). *The Mystery Play* manages to be even less subtle than *Arkham Asylum* about its religious overtones: not only is the plot built around the murder of the actor playing God in a revival of a medieval mystery play cycle, but its Christ-figure outsider—an escaped mental patient posing as a detective investigating the murder—assumes the identity of "Carpenter." *The Mystery Play* reads like an attempt to re-create the success of *Arkham Asylum* by replicating its plot and atmosphere, although without Batman to attract readers such an attempt seems quixotic at best. The graphic novel achieved *Arkham*'s reputation for ponderous symbolism and "purposefully chaotic" storytelling (Tong 50), but not its sales.

One theme does set *The Mystery Play* apart from its predecessor. As McCulloch observes, the investigation unfolds as a sequence of dialogues between Carpenter and the town's various residents. Rather than duplicate

Arkham's psychoanalytical hypostasis, however, in which the inmates reflect and embody Batman's fears and desires, *The Mystery Play* crafts an epistemological allegory that bounces Carpenter against characters (some real, some hallucinatory) who advocate other systems of producing knowledge. A coroner stresses the importance of breaking problems down to their component parts while he conducts an autopsy; the actor who plays Satan transforms into the real thing and insists the only meaning is that which we impose on a senseless world; the mayor propounds a cloying, transparently false religious symbolism to burnish the town's image and his own reputation; and the minister scoffs at any symbolic or metaphysical interpretations. Carpenter takes Morrison's standard holistic position that all events are interconnected, and he attempts to perceive the implicate order that gives those events meaning. The detective defends Morrison's epistemology while his suspects either deny the possibility of meaning or attempt to limit its scope by separating facts rather than connecting them; it is probably no coincidence that the actor playing Satan is named Severs. The graphic novel is as much an updated morality play of allegorical conflict and instruction as it is a mystery play restaging the Passion.

More interested in interrogating these systems of knowledge than it is in solving the murder, *The Mystery Play* is perhaps best understood as a "metaphysical detective story," part of a subgenre that "parodies or subverts traditional detective-story conventions [. . .] with the intention, or at least the effect, of asking questions about mysteries of being and knowing which transcend the mere machinations of the mystery plot. [. . .] Rather than definitively solving a crime, then, the sleuth finds himself confronting the insoluble mysteries of his own interpretation and his own identity" (Merivale and Sweeney 2). Metaphysical detective stories generally emphasize the impossibility of attaining positivistic knowledge in an uncertain world, an argument *The Mystery Play* shares with an earlier Morrison crime story, *Bible John: A Forensic Meditation* (1991). Published in *Crisis* and illustrated by Daniel Vallely, Morrison's former bandmate in the Mixers and the Fauves, *Bible John* is the story of the fruitless search for a real-life serial killer who murdered three women in Glasgow in the late 1960s. The story makes no efforts at true-crime realism, however, as Morrison and Vallely attempt to identify the murderer through cut-up techniques and other divinatory methods, including a Ouija board ("Q&A: Grant Morrison"). Because Bible John was never captured, the artists are free to advance patently fictitious theories about his motivations, attributing the murders to Thuggee rituals, the nearby American nuclear submarine base, the violent zeitgeist of the sixties, even the moon landing, which they interpret as "the ultimate symbolic submission of the feminine principle" (4.8). Unable, despite these supernatural inquiries, to propose any definitive solutions to the murders, Morrison and Vallely instead examine the ways they and other investigators fill the many absences and lacunae that surround the killings. Their visual and verbal collages become textual equivalents of the composite portrait that remains the only, imperfect clue to Bible John's identity; like that composite, the torrents of information collected in the comic approximate the truth yet provide no reliable answers. The final chapter identifies *Bible John* as a story about "the ordering and reordering of data" and "the human need to impose significance upon a chaos of information" and speculates that we use the violent irrationality of murder—or stories about murders—to restore a mythic dimension to modern life (6.5; see also Hasted 72–73).

Bible John anticipates many of the themes of *The Mystery Play*; indeed, Morrison compares the police reconstructions and retellings of the Bible John murders to "Mystery plays, Passion plays" (4.1), deploying the metaphor that would structure his later work. Like its predecessor, *The Mystery Play* surveys different methods of organizing information into knowledge and reconnects secular modernity to the numinous and sacred; God's murder and its subsequent investigation both lend spiritual significance to a generic English town that is otherwise devoid of meaning. However, *Bible John* concludes that all interpretations are arbitrary and "all meaning is self-imposed" (6.5), a position akin to Severs/Satan's argument in *The Mystery Play*, whereas that later graphic novel's sympathies align more closely with Carpenter's belief that the chaotic excess of information resolves into an implicate order when viewed from the proper perspective. If *Bible John* offers a deconstructionist argument that maps, pictures, and other modes of representation can never fully capture their subjects, only the assumptions and biases of their makers, *The Mystery Play* holds out the possibility that every material phenomenon is itself a sign rich with meaning, awaiting the right interpreter.

Unfortunately, Morrison is content simply to reiterate these ideas rather than engage more substantively with them. The townspeople's various systems of knowledge serve only to pose weak challenges to Carpenter's methodology, not to be examined as viable epistemologies in their own right, and the detective's holism is already well known to readers of Morrison's other comics. The religious allegory that structures and, ultimately, limits the story is similarly unembellished. Having established the parallels between his plot and the Passion, Morrison does little with them except to let events play out to their predetermined end—and while the Christian allegory concludes with leaden predictability at Carpenter's crucifixion, the murder plot that serves as its vehicle and dramatic engine goes unresolved. The graphic novel falls victim to its own didacticism, so satisfied with the delivery of its statements about knowledge and faith that it makes little effort either to push them into new inquiries or to flesh out the bare-bones mystery that conveys them.

Despite their forays into gray areas of ontological and epistemological doubt, Morrison's first Vertigo comics do not take full advantage of the imprint's intermediate positioning between genre stories and auteurist comics. *Sebastian O* is too dedicated to re-creating its influences to spend much time pursuing the implications of its worlds of artifice, while *The Mystery Play* overspills with ideas that overwhelm the minimal plot. Morrison would not fully exploit the possibilities Vertigo offered him until his next major project, which balances features from both of these comics in a more sophisticated and durable combination. Like *The Mystery Play*, *The Invisibles* is a comic about the "primacy of ideas," dedicated to dramatizing and testing Morrison's beliefs (Neighly 230); like *Sebastian O*, it offers solid genre storytelling, particularly in the spy genre, that grounds those ideas and prevents the series from lapsing into naked didacticism. While neither work realizes its full potential, both *Sebastian O* and *The Mystery Play* shape the series that would define Morrison's tenure at Vertigo.

THE INVISIBLES: PERMANENT REVOLUTION

The Invisibles (1994–2000) is by design a series in constant flux. Running for three volumes over nearly six years, the comic evolves from a wide-ranging survey of Morrison's philosophy to a grueling year-long trial of initiation and rebirth, then to a violent action movie in volume two, then to a self-reflexive, self-critical text disgusted with violent action movies, and finally back to a survey of Morrison's substantially changed philosophy in volume three.[3] This refusal to settle on a single genre or direction makes *The Invisibles* an ideal vehicle for all of Morrison's interests, from the popular to the esoteric. The series incorporates virtually every one of his influences, evoking sources as diverse as Bryan Talbot, Michael Moorcock, Philip K. Dick, Robert Anton Wilson, Vodou, chaos magic, Situationism, Romantic poetry, linguistic theory, 1960s spy series, and more; Patrick Neighly and Kereth Cowe-Spigai trace these intertexts in their companion volume, *Anarchy for the Masses* (2003). Despite its investment in science fiction and fantasy, however, the series is also drawn from Morrison's life: *The Invisibles* fictionalizes his experiences traveling around the world, experimenting with magic and drugs and cross-dressing, surviving a near-fatal staph infection, and being shown the structure of the universe on a hotel roof garden in Kathmandu. *The Invisibles* is, in short, a narrative expression of Morrison's life, thought, and creative ambitions in the last decade of the twentieth century and its many changes track his own.

These shifting identities owe as much to Morrison's rotating artistic partners as they do to his own evolving interests. *The Invisibles* pairs Morrison with familiar collaborators like Steve Yeowell and introduces him to new ones like Phil Jimenez and Chris Weston; with the exception of volume two, which is drawn exclusively by Jimenez and Weston, each storyline and sometimes each issue has a new artist. The penultimate storyline, "The Invisible Kingdom" (III.4–2), sports sixteen different artists, reuniting most of the people who had previously illustrated the series and giving Morrison an opportunity to draw a page himself. The artistic transitions reinforce and sometimes influence the series' changes in genre and tone: when the first volume attempts to conform to the prevailing Vertigo mode, Jill Thompson draws several issues in the style she brought to other Vertigo titles such as *Sandman* and *Black Orchid*. Superhero artist Phil Jimenez illustrates "Entropy in the UK" (I.17–19), a storyline that delves behind a secret agent's romanticized self-image, and returns for the action-oriented volume two. Philip Bond's more cartoonish art is perfectly suited to the biting media commentary of the "Satanstorm" arc that kicks off volume three (III.12–9), and when Thompson returns to illustrate part of "The Invisible Kingdom," she does so in the looser, more anarchic style of her *Scary Godmother* series. The changing cast of artists is generally well-matched to Morrison's protean style, possibly to a fault—several of his collaborators, including Jimenez (Neighly 100) and Weston (Neighly 203), believe the inconsistent look of volume one hurt the comic's sales.

External factors also account for many of the book's commercial troubles and a few of its reinventions. *The Invisibles* had the misfortune to debut just before the dramatic collapse of the direct market in comic book distribution and retail. The late 1980s and early 1990s had seen a sudden increase in speculative comics collecting, which fueled an industrywide expansion of retailers and publishers.[4] These sales proved unsustainable, however, and the equally sudden implosion of the speculator bubble led to the failures of thousands of comic book stores, the consolidation of several distributors into one monopoly, the disappearance of many smaller publishers, and the bankruptcy of industry giant Marvel Comics (Gabilliet 148–52). *The Invisibles* very nearly followed them into cancellation: sales dropped from 64,000 at the beginning of the series to only 20,000 within a few months (II.7, "Invisible Ink"). Morrison attributes the decline to the dense literary, historical, and philosophical content of "Arcadia," the second storyline, which he believes gave *The Invisibles* "some strange, unkillable reputation as a difficult book" (II.7, "Invisible Ink"). On the other hand, Stuart Moore, the series' first editor, has offered another explanation more attuned to the impracticalities of the direct market: "*The Invisibles* was always a pretty challenging book. [. . .] I always thought it was a specialized taste, and you can't really judge its actual readership by the first four issues, which were ordered before retailers had much feedback on its sell-through" (Neighly 56). Because comic books are nonreturnable, sales figures measure sales to retailers, not readers; and because retailers must order comics months in advance of publication, they often purchase the first three or four issues of a new series without any sales data (Gabilliet 143–44). Moore suggests the initial orders for *The Invisibles* were unrealistic, reflecting optimistic retailers and not actual sales to readers. Those retailers would not have had an opportunity to adjust their orders downwards until around the time "Arcadia" began, postponing the loss of sales.

Whatever the cause—"Arcadia," artistic instability, general inaccessibility, or the beginnings of a massive downturn in the comics market—the falling sales forced Morrison to adjust the comic's tone more than once. The second year features fewer philosophical discussions and more character-oriented stories, as well as more action; according to Morrison, "by the time I got to 'Sheman' I thought the age of experimentation was over" (Neighly 59). This is true only in a relative sense, as "Sheman," the first storyline of the second year, still weaves plotlines from three different time periods together to articulate a theory of synchronic time; it also initiates an ambitious year-long storyline that often revisits the same events from multiple perspectives. But Morrison was concerned enough about the series' future that in the letter column to issue 16, he asked readers to masturbate to a magical sigil on Thanksgiving Day, 1995, as part of an exercise to increase sales. Morrison maintains that the ritual saved the series, whereas Jimenez credits his arrival for "Entropy in the UK" and his glossier, more commercially accessible art (Neighly 68–69). Possibly the reversal in fortunes had something to do with Morrison's instruction that fans should attempt to recruit new readers for issue 17 after they finished charging their sigils—although he would characterize this plea as part of the magical process, "to give coincidence a pathway along which to move" (I.16, "Invisible Ink"). He provided more pathways for coincidence when he restarted the series in a second volume that moved the characters to America, increased the sex and violence, and signed Phil Jimenez as the regular artist in a successful bid to attract new readers. *The Invisibles* would not return to its original English setting and its rotating artists until volume three, by which point it was consolidating past plotlines and gearing up for the finale.

Both creative and commercial factors make *The Invisibles* a multifaceted, multivalent series that reinvents itself at least once each volume. The series adopts diverse implied authors, narrators, cosmologies, and genres while questioning the ideological assumptions of each of its constituent elements. This constant self-examination ultimately leads Morrison to revise his own premise of a war between the forces of freedom and oppression, and to develop alternative narratives that complicate the simple dualism of most genre fiction. *The Invisibles* pursues intellectual solutions rather than martial ones, arguing that liberation is best achieved not through violence but by changing our models of language and selfhood. Morrison abandons the binaristic metaphysics of symbolic language and Romantic individualism, proposing instead a synthetic metaphysics that elides the differences between sign and object, self and other. Ambitious though these ideas are, they are not especially hard to ferret out, nor are they buried behind obscure allusions and oblique metaphors—or rather, not exclusively so, since Morrison crafts a holographic structure that advertises his meaning at multiple scales of the narrative. The challenge of reading *The Invisibles*, then, lies in sorting out and prioritizing the most important concepts from the flood of signals sent by an evolving series whose only constants are contradiction and change.

HOLOGRAPHIC TIMESPACE

The Invisibles tells the story of a secret war between a conspiracy dedicated to bringing every aspect of human existence under its control and a network of anarchists dedicated to stopping them. The agents of liberation are members of the Invisible College, also known as the Invisibles; the forces of authority are led by the Archons of the Outer Church, whose name indicates that the series adheres—at least initially—to a Gnostic cosmology familiar from earlier Morrison comics. At the end of the first volume, an agent of the Archons describes the universe as a trap designed to contain a rebellious demiurge (I.25.1, 22), not unlike Chimera's false cosmos in *Zenith*, and characters routinely leave the physical world to enter higher realities governed by the Archons or the Invisible College. These intimations that humanity inhabits an illusory prison world were appropriated by the Andy and Larry Wachowski film *The Matrix*, which Morrison maintains lifted its plot, imagery, and atmosphere, including its "entire gnostic theme," from *The Invisibles* (Neighly 236).[5] Unlike his imitators, however, Morrison rejects the suspicion of the material world that underwrites the Gnostics' dualistic cosmology. In the final issue, a young Invisible named Reynard asserts that the physical universe holds as much possibility for transcendence and growth as the ideal, because it is part of the ideal: "The Gnostic error is to hate the material world. [...] The material world is the part of heaven we can touch" (III.1.12). This sentiment is not confined to the end of the series; midway through volume one the Barbelith entity tells Dane McGowan, "The soul is not in the body. The body is inside the soul" (I.16.13), one of many statements that suggest continuity, not opposition, between the physical and the spiritual.

Morrison also complicates the series' investment in Gnosticism by introducing several competing cosmologies. In the first issue of volume three, Mr. Six and Elfayed, instructors at the Invisibles' training academy, acknowledge that their students have "been told a number of ... contradictory stories about the nature and origin of our universe" (III.12.8), an admission that could just as easily be directed at the readers. Many of these stories replace theological explanations with metafictional ones, implying the world of *The Invisibles* is a work of fiction written by one of its characters or a virtual reality video game designed by another protagonist. The most consistent and reliable cosmology in the series holds that the universe is actually a hologram formed by the overlap of two higher-dimensional meta-universes (II.6.21). Morrison associates this theory with the Gnostics through the vesica piscis, a religious symbol made from the intersection of two circles, which he believes to be a diagram of the intersecting universes (fig. 3-1).[6] Unlike Gnostic cosmology, however, the holographic model does not regard the material world with antipathy; while Morrison sets up a dualistic opposition between the "healthy" and "sick" meta-universes, the fact that they combine to generate our universe suggests an interest in synthesis rather than Manichaean conflict.

Holograms also provide a handy metaphor and an intradiegetic explanation for the fractal self-similarity that structures the series. Just as each part of a hologram encodes the whole image, so does each storyline, each issue, each page, and each panel have the potential to reflect and condense

Figure 3-1. *The Invisibles* II.6.21. Art by Phil Jimenez. © Grant Morrison.

the ideas that direct *The Invisibles* as a whole. Accordingly, a certain amount of redundancy is hardwired into the series as Morrison elaborates on the same themes in multiple locations and across multiple discourses. The series confirms its holographic model of the universe through the mystical teachings of the Invisible Academy, but it first articulates that model through the physics of Takashi Satoh, who explains,

> Think of timespace as a multidimensional self-perfecting system in which everything that has ever, or will ever occur, occurs simultaneously. I believe timespace is a kind of object, a geometrical supersolid. I believe it may even be a type of hologram in which energy and matter themselves are byproducts of the overlapping of two higher systems. (II.5.16)

Takashi's theories also reinforce the unified, synchronic model of time offered in the previous volume by an Aztec god who states that "All times are the same time" (I.14.1), an idea *The Invisibles* will return to throughout its duration. In the syncretic discourse of *The Invisibles*, science, religion, and magic are all equally capable of explaining the origin and structure of the universe.

That structure bears a remarkable resemblance to the formal structure of Morrison's chosen medium, the comic book. Takashi, more perceptive than he knows, asks,

> Where is the past? Where is the future? Undeniably, they exist, but why can't you point to them? The only way to do that is to jump 'up' from the surface of timespace and see all of history and all of our tomorrows as the single object I believe it is. (II.5.16)

In other words, the only way to perceive time in its full multidimensionality is to assume the vantage point of the comic book reader, poised above the surface of the page. If Takashi knew he was in a comic, he could point to the past or the future simply by indicating previous or subsequent panels. Because they coexist on the space of the comics page, even panels that depict different moments in time are contemporaneous parts of the graphic composition. As Scott McCloud observes in *Understanding Comics*, in the world of comics "Both past and future are real and visible and all around us" (104). *The Invisibles*, or any other comic, assumes the very structure Takashi describes: a universe in which events occur simultaneously and form one single object.

Morrison and his collaborators can therefore exploit the formal possibilities of comics to illustrate his theories of time and space. Phil Jimenez is especially adept at manipulating the pacing and layout of panels to dramatize different subjective experiences of time: discontinuous transitions capture the scattered attention of drug use, alien contact, and other altered states of consciousness, while cascades of tightly focused panels show the adrenalized intensity of movement and physical exertion. Some formal games, like a scene in which two Invisibles bend back and reach through panel borders (II.6.22), are transparent metafictions in the style of *Animal Man*, but others supply more serious illustrations of the nature of time in Morrison's universe. Jimenez is fond of showing multiple images of a character moving through a continuous space (II.1.20, II.7.14), a technique that conflates different moments in time into a single panel (fig. 3-2). By the end of the series this technique has become an important part of Morrison's cosmology, representing "life casts" (Neighly 210n14.3) that show every moment of a person's existence at once. These life casts are records of an organism's passage through space and time and graphic demonstrations of what timespace might look like from Takashi's external vantage point (fig. 3-3).[7] Time in *The Invisibles* may be simultaneous, yet it is anything but

The Invisible Kingdom   105

Figure 3-2. *The Invisibles* II.1.20. Art by Phil Jimenez. © Grant Morrison.

Figure 3-3. *The Invisibles* vol. 7: *The Invisible Kingdom* 254. Art by Cameron Stewart.
© Grant Morrison.

homogeneous as these formal experiments demonstrate a variety of modes of experiencing and representing time within a synchronic universe.

THE DECENTERED TEXT

The contradictory cosmologies and varied representational strategies are merely two expressions of the series' preference for dialogic or heteroglossic discourses over monologic ones. *The Invisibles* is deeply suspicious of any kind of authority, including narrative authority, which it seeks to undermine or disperse at every opportunity. Readers are introduced to this decentered aesthetic when a foul-mouthed teenaged hoodlum named Dane McGowan is inducted into an Invisibles cell populated by a motley group of countercultural types including Lord Fanny, a transgender woman and shaman; Boy, an African American woman and former police officer; Ragged Robin, the world's first time traveler; and King Mob, a super-assassin who likes to wear fetish gear. The Invisibles are so committed to their battle against tyranny that they refuse to establish any hierarchies within their own cell, rotating roles, selecting leaders, and assigning duties by drawing slips of paper. This antihierarchical attitude carries over into Morrison's composition of the series: *The Invisibles* nominates multiple authors and narrators (Wolk 261–63), including nearly every member of Dane's cell. The superabundance of storytellers has the effect of distributing authorial control from Morrison to his characters and ultimately to his readers.

King Mob's cover identities mark him as the most obvious authorial stand-in. He writes horror novels under the name Kirk Morrison, and he pretends to be a reincarnation of Gideon Stargrave, linking him to Morrison's first published comics in *Near Myths*. Unlike other Morrison avatars, however, he does not exert control over the text; he represents Morrison's romanticized self-image, but he rarely directs the story. Dane, on the other hand, tells the entire story of *The Invisibles* to a childhood friend in a framing narrative that makes him one of the series' authors; Fanny uses her magic to "alter the fragile structure of time and space" and write herself a more favorable fate (I.15.16–17); and Ragged Robin writes a fan-fiction version of *The Invisibles* before she travels back in time to take part in the story she helped create. Robin tells King Mob—her lover and Morrison's analogue— "I fell in love with the picture of the author. Then it turned out there was no author. Or maybe the author was me" (II.21.18). Robin represents a reader who has both taken over and lost control of authorship; in either case,

Morrison places responsibility for the series out of his hands.[8] The final issue shifts even more responsibility onto the readers with the revelation that *The Invisibles* has become a virtual reality game that allows players to experience the story from the perspective of any one of its three hundred characters (III.1.7)—which is to say, the series ends with a transparent figure for its own reading experience, acknowledging its potential for immersion and encouraging readers to become active participants like Robin. Morrison implies that readers can select any character to be the protagonist, an egalitarian and rather hyperbolic claim, though it does support his statement that the book's "central character" is Audrey Murray, a woman who appears in only two issues (Neighly 218). Murray is a representative of one of the book's recurring themes rather than the focus of its plot, but *The Invisibles* does distribute the starring roles among the five members of Dane's cell, with frequent digressions putting supporting characters in the spotlight.

The cast is as diverse as it is expansive. Unlike *Dare*, which both addresses and displaces racial issues by representing nonwhite races as alien Treen, *The Invisibles* incorporates a variety of experiences by writing characters across a broad range of racial and gender identities. Morrison resolves the previously irreconcilable tensions of *Dare*, finding a way to write about minority experiences without violating the tone of the series or pushing the social concerns to the margins. The stories that focus on the African American Invisibles agents Boy and Jim Crow are organized around black mythologies, drawing upon religions like Vodou and the Dogon people's worship of the Nommo as well as more contemporary urban legends about government programs to round up black dissidents or release crack cocaine onto American streets. While these issues look beyond black sources—Boy's stories cite the Black Iron Prison from Philip K. Dick's *VALIS* and the ubiquitous WASTE signs from Thomas Pynchon's *The Crying of Lot 49*—they appropriate elements from science fiction and conspiracy literature and repurpose them to address black themes and concerns in a manner consistent with the style that Mark Dery terms Afrofuturism (180). With its bricoleur's aesthetic and its mixture of social realism and visionary imagination, Afrofuturism meshes well with the fantastic elements of *The Invisibles* while allowing for racial critiques from black perspectives.[9] The series adapts Afrofuturist strategies to other nonwhite experiences by fusing science fiction and fantasy elements with Hindu, Buddhist, Aztec, and Aboriginal Australian beliefs, expanding the cast even further.

Morrison's handling of these perspectives is not always smooth. Boy is underdeveloped compared to the other Invisibles, and Fanny, the only

Latina character and the most prominent queer one, bears the weight of too many clichés.[10] Because so many of these characters are magicians or shamans, the series threatens to reinforce the exoticizing stereotypes of the noble savage or the magical negro, which assert that nonwhite people are more spiritual, intuitive, or possessed of special powers or awareness. Yet the series usually complicates or confounds these stereotypes through the sheer breadth of its cast. Jim Crow and Papa Skat are both affiliated with Vodou loa, but Boy is a down-to-earth agent with no magical abilities. Several Asian characters display an advanced understanding of time (Neighly 126n1.1), but Billy Chang achieves his insight through the study of the occult, Takashi Satoh through physics, and Takashi's great-grandfather through Eastern philosophy and art. Not every nonwhite character is magical, nor is every magician nonwhite—two of the most prominent mystical mentors, Mr. Six and Tom O'Bedlam, are white Englishmen, and Mr. Six shares his duties with the Egyptian Elfayed. *The Invisibles* is simply too sprawling, its cast too large and too diverse, ever to be that reductive.

The heterogeneous cast explains why the series has so many identities. Each member of the Invisibles inhabits a different genre, from Robin's science fiction to King Mob's spy movies, novels, and television shows. Boy puts an Afrofuturist spin on conspiracy literature and Dane's journey takes him from kitchen-sink realism to fantasy and back again. No one has more generic models than Lord Fanny, whose identity is so fluid that "Sheman," the story of her upbringing and shamanic initiation (I.13–15), can only take the form of a manic pastiche. Morrison and Jill Thompson present several scenes in the style of other comics, including Alan Moore and Dave Gibbons's *Watchmen*, Frank Miller's *Sin City*, Rob Liefeld's grotesquely hypertrophied work for Marvel and Image, and Jaime and Gilbert Hernandez's *Love and Rockets*. Morrison has said he borrowed the bricolage technique from Oliver Stone's film *Natural Born Killers* (I.17, "Invisible Ink"; Neighly 59), but in his and Thompson's hands it becomes an elegant visual equivalent of Fanny's cross-dressing, a creative transvestism that distills the heteroglossia of the series as a whole. *The Invisibles* dresses in many styles over its six-year run, but it interrogates or resists each one in a way that demands a flexible and multifaceted view of genre.

SECRET IDENTITIES

Although it is Morrison's most sustained work for Vertigo, *The Invisibles* is in many respects a superhero book, following the conventions of the superhero genre even as it presents them in a manner more consistent with Vertigo's positioning outside the mainstream American comics industry. The series had its genesis in several different ideas for revamping obscure DC Comics heroes like the Boy Commandos and the Whip (Neighly 14–15). Morrison quickly discarded these properties in favor of new characters for whom he holds the copyrights, but their superheroic origins survive in the thinly disguised conventions that shape the series.[11] Each Invisible adopts a codename, though these names are not flashy advertisements of power or virtue but rather oblique references to the ideologies they battle against.[12] Several wear costumes, ranging from King Mob's distinctive mask to Ragged Robin's doll-like make-up to Jolly Roger's skull-and-crossbones emblem. Even Lord Fanny's cross-dressing constitutes a form of costuming, the adoption of a "spirit mask" (I.13.4) and "she-male chain-mail" (I.13.5) that confer shamanic powers. All of the Invisibles possess special abilities, ranging from combat training to magical or psychic powers, and they routinely break the law in the service of a higher morality; they differ from superheroes only in that they show no loyalty to the state whose laws they disregard. Nevertheless, the Invisibles fulfill most of the seven traits in Richard Reynolds's definition of the superhero genre (16) and all three of the qualities in Peter Coogan's more streamlined definition of the superhero, which boil down to a mission to fight evil and injustice, extraordinary powers, and a split identity, including an emblematic costume (30–39). The Invisibles fit so comfortably within the superhero genre that in the second volume they are joined by Mason Lang, an American billionaire who is modeled on Batman's secret identity, Bruce Wayne (Neighly 257).

While it is rife with superhero conventions, *The Invisibles* still violates one of the most fundamental assumptions of the genre, an assumption Richard Reynolds lays bare:

> A key ideological myth of the superhero comic is that the normal and everyday enshrines positive values that must be defended through heroic action—and defended over and over again almost without respite against an endless battery of menaces. [...] The normal is valuable and is constantly under attack, which means that almost by definition the superhero is battling on behalf of the status quo. [...] The superhero has a mission to preserve society, not to re-invent it. (77)

Reynolds does allow that superheroes frequently break the letter of the law in order to uphold higher principles (16), and arguably the Invisibles' conduct can be made to fit this pattern. Much like Morrison's Doom Patrol, the

Invisibles defend liberal democratic values of freedom and self-determination even as they battle nominally democratic governments that have failed to secure those rights (and in many cases have worked covertly to undermine them). Nevertheless, the Doom Patrol and other superheroes contain threats to the social order, restoring the world to the status quo ante; the Invisibles are the threat to the established order, seeking to reinvent society in ways the superhero genre does not normally permit. *The Invisibles* occupies the unusual position of a comic book that fulfills many of the genre's conventions while violating its central ideological axiom.

This work is best understood through a model of genre that recognizes the distinction between semantics and syntax. In *The American Film Musical*, Rick Altman observes that genres are typically defined through both semantic methods that itemize common elements and syntactic methods that classify relationships between elements: "The semantic approach thus stresses the genre's building blocks, while the syntactic view privileges the structures into which they are arranged" (95). Most definitions of the superhero genre, including Reynolds's and Coogan's, tally its semantic elements (costumes, powers, secret identities, and the like), although both authors venture into the syntactic when they consider the relationship of superheroes to their societies—that is, the ideological positioning of most superhero narratives. These definitions tend to shift unconsciously between semantic and syntactical modes. If we pay explicit attention to both, we can view *The Invisibles* as a hybrid book that incorporates many of the semantic elements of superhero comics—often recasting them slightly to align with the semantics of the spy, science fiction, or conspiracy genres—while turning their ideological syntax on its head. Coogan, perhaps to compensate for the broad applicability of the semantic approach (Altman, *Film Musical* 96), attempts to banish such hybrid or borderline cases from the superhero genre by ruling that they belong to other genres (Coogan 47–58). Altman's model eliminates the need for such rigid partitions, both because he observes that genres are often shaped by "inter-generic relationships" (*Film Musical* 114) and because his semantic/syntactic approach provides critics with a useful vocabulary for classifying works that combine the semantic conventions of one genre with the ideological syntax of another (*Film Musical* 117).[13]

The Invisibles is never fully satisfied with any of the genres it draws upon: much as it inverts the ideological structures of the superhero comic, so does it chafe against the narrative style of the Vertigo comic. Although several writers, including Morrison, contributed to the founding of Vertigo, the imprint quickly developed a house style that sought to emulate the success of a single author. Just as Morrison felt that he and his fellow British imports were encouraged to follow in Alan Moore's footsteps in the late 1980s, he lamented the dominant influence that Neil Gaiman's *Sandman* exerted on Vertigo in the 1990s: "Even now, because *Sandman* is so successful, what they want is a lot of *Sandman*. And despite protestations to the contrary, there's still a definite pressure there. The more like *Sandman* it is, the better. The more people we have talking for 24 pages or longer the better. Don't put in any action scenes, because that's no longer what's acceptable" (Hasted 59). He could easily be describing the first storyline in *The Invisibles*, "Down and Out in Heaven and Hell" (I.2–4), which he had just finished writing at the time of this statement. The story depicts Dane McGowan's induction into the Invisibles, which consists mostly of a walking tour of London interspersed with quotes from *King Lear*, images of William Blake's Urizen, potted theses about the true natures of gods and cities, and archetypal scenes of heroic initiation taken directly from the Joseph Campbell monomyth. These self-consciously literary airs were a poor fit for Morrison; barely halfway through the story, Dane himself is moved to complain, "I can't be arsed with any more of this walking around, talking shite" (I.3.16).

Yet for all of Morrison's evident unease at aping Gaiman's comics, the first volume of *The Invisibles* is also deeply indebted to *Sandman* and the Vertigo house style in terms of its pacing and episodic structure. One of Gaiman's most influential and enduring practices in *Sandman* was his alternation between longer, clearly delineated story arcs and collections of self-contained, single-issue stories, many of which focused on minor supporting characters or viewed the protagonist from a new perspective. The self-contained stories fleshed out the world of *Sandman* and provided breathers between arcs, while the arcs turned out to be the ideal length for collection in trade paperbacks. *Sandman* settled into a steady rhythm of serials and short stories that was well suited for developing a new audience of comics readers and a new market in bookstores. The first volume of *The Invisibles* follows the same pattern, particularly in issues 10 through 12, which leave the main cast to introduce new Invisibles agents and explore the lives of supporting characters. These issues, and the second year of comics that follows them, adapt Gaiman's alternating story structure and rotating protagonists but shed his bookish subject matter and scripting style in favor of more science fiction, spy, and action movie elements—which the series will test and reject in turn.

KILL OVERLOAD

The transition from long-winded literary survey to super-spy adventure begins with issue 9, "23: Things Fall Apart," which continues the cliffhanger ending and the art team (Jill Thompson and Dennis Cramer) from "Arcadia" but moves the book into a radically different mode. The Invisibles escape an ambush and Dane flees the team in a combat filled with commandos, car chases, bombs, bullets, and at least a dozen violent deaths. But this issue also begins the series' criticism of the action movie conventions it adopts with such high zest, signaling that the Invisibles' violence is neither psychologically healthy nor morally justifiable. The jaded, desensitized King Mob cracks jokes throughout the issue, at one point quipping "Life just gets cheaper and cheaper" as he guns down two soldiers (I.9.21); by the issue's end even his teammate Boy objects to his gallows humor (I.9.23). By contrast, Dane shoots one enemy soldier and is appalled by his actions. The murder haunts him for the rest of the series and he never kills again.

The self-criticism continues in issue 12, "Best Man Fall," a story that forces readers to reevaluate the characters' moral standing through a shift in point of view. "Best Man Fall" tells the story of security guard Bobby Murray through a sequence of discontinuous vignettes that suggest the proverbial life flashing before his eyes as he is about to die. An early scene showing Bobby falling in battle during the Falklands War encourages this interpretation, but this turns out to be a feint—he survives his injuries and several vignettes are set after his recovery. The cause of Bobby's reminiscences and the reason for his presence in an issue of *The Invisibles* gradually become apparent as he takes a job with a private security firm, dons a familiar helmet and bulletproof vest, and responds to an alarm at his workplace: Bobby Murray is one of the guards King Mob kills when he rescues Dane from an enemy brainwashing facility in the first issue. Morrison replays the same combat in two radically different contexts. The first time, Bobby dies as one of several casualties of the premier issue's violent entertainments (I.1.34–35); the second time, his death becomes a tragedy as readers have full awareness of the life being extinguished (I.12.17, 20, 23). Similarly, King Mob looks like a standard (if strangely garbed) action hero when Dane witnesses his daring rescue, but from Bobby's point of view in issue 12, he appears callous, even sociopathic—signs that he is not the romantic hero Dane initially believes him to be and that his murders are not heroic deeds to be celebrated or consumed uncritically. It should be noted, however, that Bobby Murray is no innocent victim either. He turns a blind eye to his employers' abuses to collect a steady paycheck and takes out his frustrations by beating his wife. He is no more romanticized than King Mob, but by showing us his entire life—without excuse or condemnation—Morrison forces us to acknowledge the human cost of the violence that entertains us.

As the violence intensifies, so does Morrison's critique of the genres that rely on it. In an effort to give the series a stable artistic identity and reverse its falling sales, Phil Jimenez signed on as the regular artist for volume two and Brian Bolland provided covers. Both artists brought a glossy, glamorous look that suited the second volume's new setting in America and its new emphasis on lurid, Hollywood-style sex and violence. The first storyline, "Black Science" (II.1–4), is so indebted to Hollywood—both in its torrent of self-reflexive movie references and in its imitation of the narrative structure of the big-budget action movie, from the opening fight scene to the climactic explosion—that it spawns its own sequel a year and a half later in "Black Science 2" (II.17–20). But while the mayhem escalates dramatically in volume two, Morrison's self-critique keeps pace. The third chapter of "Black Science" repeats the life-of-a-henchman trick from "Best Man Fall," but Morrison and Jimenez compress it from an issue to a single page. As King Mob shoots Lieutenant Martin Lincoln, panels depicting scenes from Lincoln's past spray out as if expelled from the wound (fig. 3-4). His life is graphically spilled onto the page, and readers are reminded—or, if they are new readers attracted by the second volume's change in direction, given a crash course—that no lives are truly expendable in *The Invisibles*. Morrison repeats the trick once more in the very next issue, when a dying soldier looks up at King Mob and mistakes him for a childhood memory of meeting the angel of death in a junkyard (II.4.13)—a near-perfect reiteration of Bobby Murray's childhood fear of an old gas mask in a coal cellar, which foreshadowed his death at King Mob's hands, although this time the reverie lasts just one panel. These accelerating repetitions demonstrate Morrison's recurring claim that time is compressing as the world advances closer to the apocalypse (see I.13.2 and III.1.15), but they also force readers to accept the humanity of the Invisibles' victims as their kills increase with a frequency and brutality that disgust even King Mob.

By the fourth and final issue of "Black Science," the killing has become so constant that King Mob confesses he's on "kill overload," sickened by the pace and volume of his murders: "If we don't get out of here soon I'm going to start questioning the already fucking dubious morality of my actions" (II.4.13). He does just that in the next storyline, when a brief respite allows him to admit what he's become and how he became it. He tells Robin, "It was

Figure 3-4. *The Invisibles* II.3.9. Art by Phil Jimenez. © Grant Morrison.

all those Moorcock books; I wanted to be Jerry Cornelius, the English assassin. I wanted the guns and the cars and the girls and the chaos . . . Shit. I've ended up a murderer. My karma's a bloody minefield" (II.6.23). His determination to remake himself in the image of his pop culture icons—here he mentions Michael Moorcock's Jerry Cornelius stories, but other passages advertise the influence of James Bond, *Barbarella*, *The Prisoner*, and other spy or science fiction stories—has made it too easy for him to dehumanize and murder his enemies. Despite this self-awareness, the next issue sees him backslide even further. He only kills two people in "Time Machine Go," vicious killers who are about to torture and murder his friends, but their execution is so bloody and presented in such grisly detail that King Mob vomits after he is done (II.7.8). This scene may be another example of Morrison's penchant for holographic compression, since it plays out in miniature the progress of King Mob and *The Invisibles* as a whole over the course of volume two. The series overindulges in exploitative sex and violence so it can purge itself by volume's end, an approach that allows Morrison to wallow in the most brutalizing and objectifying practices of popular culture while he denounces them—and to pick up some new readers along the way.

King Mob may throw his gun into a pond and declare "Bond is dead" (II.22.16) at the end of volume two, but his renunciation of violence is not yet complete. He initially trades his Bond-inspired self-image for a less lethal but no less combative one modeled on Bruce Lee, using martial arts to disarm or disable his enemies. He continues on this trajectory until he nearly dies at the end of volume three, when he is saved by the intervention of a passing stranger who turns out to be Audrey Murray, the widow of the guard he killed in the first issue. Although she does not know she has rescued her husband's murderer, she cites Bobby's death as the reason she couldn't leave a stranger to die (III.2.20). The perseverance and compassion that led Morrison to name Audrey the series' central character also make her a far healthier role model than King Mob, and one of many characters who promotes empathy and mercy over destructive conflict.

King Mob's ex-girlfriend Jacqui, who once participated in and fueled his retro-sixties fantasies, warns him that he has built his identity around the enemies he battles and claims that the battle is the only thing sustaining his enemies (II.5.12); for support she quotes no less an authority than *VALIS*, the source of much of Morrison's cosmology in *The Invisibles*. King Mob rejects her claims with some vehemence, and some justice, as the Archons' conspiracy would seem to operate just fine without his interference, yet *The Invisibles* repeatedly hints that Jacqui is right on the larger metaphysical point. The series questions one of the fundamental conventions of the formula adventure story, which in its most unreflective form "requires a basic antagonism between hero and villain" (Cawelti, *Adventure* 33). Morrison cannot let this dualism go unchallenged, and he spends much of the series unsettling the Invisibles' beliefs not only in the morality of their methods but also in the rightness of their struggle with the other side—or the existence of another side to struggle against. Defying the bedrock principles of its contributing genres, *The Invisibles* refuses to assume that freedom and control, rebellion and authority, or good and evil are easily identifiable and mutually exclusive concepts (James 435–36).

The first chapter of "Arcadia" (I.5) is particularly rich with microstatements that foreshadow and condense Morrison's dismantling of this dualistic premise. The most charged of these statements occurs when King Mob attends a performance of the *Mahabharata*, the Indian martial epic, told by a *dalang* versed in the art of *wayang kulit*, Indonesian shadow puppet theater. His guide explains, "The dalang is more than a puppeteer. His skill makes us believe that we see a war between two great armies, but there is no war. There is only the dalang" (I.5.1). The scene implies the war between the Invisibles and the Outer Church is equally illusory, equally orchestrated. If this insinuation, which seems obvious in retrospect, should prove too unthinkable for the fifth issue of a series that appears to be organized around a great war between the forces of freedom and control, Morrison reinforces it with a surplus of equivalent statements throughout "Arcadia." An insane pianist imagines black keys warring with white ones but notes that the same hand plays both. A blind chess player, who may be one of the secret powers of the universe, sits perpendicular to the assembled pieces on his board and manipulates both sides. And when Dane McGowan, always willing to question the Invisibles' dogma along with everybody else's, asks how he can be certain he's really joined the Invisibles and not the Outer Church, Boy is unable to answer him (I.5.11).

Within less than a year, the very idea that there are separate sides to join will be shattered. Dane recalls a part of his initiation that was suppressed during "Down and Out in Heaven and Hell," an encounter with Barbelith, a mysterious satellite and a sort of cosmic placenta designed to help deliver humanity into the next stage of consciousness. Barbelith promises to show Dane the truth and then asks him "Which side are you on?" The corresponding image shows a Möbius strip—a strip with only one side (fig. 3-5). This statement of unity would seem to be contradicted by the Invisibles' violent battles with the Archons and their servants, who plan

Figure 3-5. *The Invisibles* I.16.13. Art by Paul Johnson. © Grant Morrison.

to enslave humanity; even if the Invisibles run the risk of defining themselves through their enemies, becoming like their enemies, or sustaining their enemies through conflict, their war still has real consequences for the human race. By the final issue, however, the King Mob of 2012, who has renounced violence for more than a decade, has formed a different view of the Archons. He describes them as "inoculating agents" that mark our transition out of "larval consciousness": "The inoculation is conceptualized by the developing larva as an invasion of threatening 'not-self' material ... the confronting and integration of 'not-self' being a necessary stage in the development of the maturing larva's self-awareness" (III.1.13). The Archons are nothing more than our own fears of the other, the not-me, given monstrous shape. Their home in the Outer Church manifests all our worst fears about the fate of the human race (Neighly 29), which we might interpret as the dystopian or apocalyptic consequences of our fears of the other. Morrison argues it is still necessary to overcome these fears, but this struggle must be internal and psychological before it can be extended to social relations.

This turn from physical confrontation and dualistic conflict to psychological self-examination and mutual interdependence defies the logic of the spy story, the action movie, the anarchist tract, and the conspiracy narrative just as much as the Invisibles' revolutionary goals flout the normative values of the superhero genre. *The Invisibles* challenges the assumptions, formulas, and ideological structures of all the genres it draws upon, telling a story of superheroes who seek to overturn their society, killers who renounce violence, and revolutionaries who realize there is no external enemy. The series possesses a wide-ranging semantics and a thoroughly subversive syntax that make it *sui generis*, a work only Morrison could have produced.

THE LANGUAGE OF THE ANGELS

The reformed King Mob who confronts the last Archon in 2012 eschews bullets and explosives in favor of language and ideas, and he dispels the Archon without firing a shot. His gun discharges a flag blazoned with an onomatopoeic "POP"; the Archon interprets it as a command and bursts on the spot. This fatal literalism is only possible because King Mob has exposed the Archon to a drug that erases the distinction between language and reality, making the scene one of the most dramatic illustrations of a recurring argument about the power of language to shape our perceptions. Like many readers, Douglas Wolk believes the series essentially restates the Sapir-Whorf hypothesis, which holds that language "gives form to our experience of the world" (Eco, *Serendipities* 77–78) by dictating our cognitive categories.[14] Wolk says Morrison's strong interpretation of the Sapir-Whorf hypothesis is "prima facie ridiculous if taken literally" (272), but *The Invisibles* is not as invested in linguistic relativism as Wolk claims. The series considers both relativist and universalist ideas about language as it wades into an even more fundamental (and long-settled) dispute between mimetic theories that posit a correspondence between sign and object and a structuralist linguistics that attributes a sign's meaning to social conventions. Morrison concocts several different languages or linguistic devices to dramatize these theories in the service of a larger project to transcend language and symbolic communication entirely.

The most striking of these devices are the drugs that appear to render linguistic signs as real as the objects they describe. In "Entropy in the UK," Sir Miles Delacourt, chief human agent of the Archons, interrogates King Mob by injecting him with Key 17, which "scrambles perceptual information reaching the secondary visual cortex. It makes him unable to tell the difference between the word describing an object and the object itself" (I.18.6). The drug recalls Don DeLillo's *White Noise*, in which the psychoactive drug Dylar creates addicts who cannot distinguish between word and object, and Philip K. Dick's *Time Out of Joint*, in which the military simulates an entire town by conditioning its inhabitants to interpret words written on paper as if they were the things they represent. The most overt influence on the interrogation sequence is George Orwell's *Nineteen Eighty-Four*, as Morrison

Figure 3-6. *The Invisibles* I.19.7. Art by Phil Jimenez. © Grant Morrison.

restages the scene in which O'Brien tortures Winston Smith into seeing four fingers as five. Rather than rely on electric shocks, however, Sir Miles simply writes "FIVE FINGERS" on a piece of paper, which King Mob mistakes for reality—and, because artist Phil Jimenez is complicit in the illusion, we see the extra finger as well (fig. 3-6). Morrison and Jimenez collapse the distinction between word and image, re-creating the effects of taking Key 17. The result is an artificial hypostasis that turns linguistic symbols into concrete (if hallucinatory) embodiments of the objects they denote.

This direct and total correspondence between sign and referent furnishes Morrison with an opportunity to examine language's power to shape perception. Sir Miles explains that the alphabet is "designed to set limits upon humanity's ability to express abstract thought. What you see depends entirely upon the words you have to describe what you see. Nothing exists unless we say that it does. The drug we gave you is called Key 17, and with its help, we can conjure reality out of a few words scrawled on paper" (I.19.7). Key 17 is itself a nightmarish hypostasis of both the Sapir-Whorf hypothesis and of interpellation, the process by which ideological superstructures such as language dictate subjectivities to their own users. The drug literalizes the cognitive shaping of Sapir-Whorf linguistic relativism and the discursive hailing of Althusserian ideology, presenting both as implements of social control.

Key 17 also provides a fantastically literal illustration of the poststructuralist sentiment that "language goes, as they say, all the way down" (J. Berger

343), that our experience is always mediated through and shaped by language. The protagonist of *Time Out of Joint* formulates a strong version of this argument, starting from the structuralist position that all words derive their meanings from arbitrary social conventions:

> Central problem in philosophy. Relation of word to object ... what is a word? Arbitrary sign. But we live in words. Our reality, among words not things. No such thing as a thing anyhow; a gestalt in the mind. Thingness ... sense of substance. An illusion. Word is more real than the object it represents.
> Word doesn't represent reality. Word *is* reality. For us, anyhow. Maybe God gets to objects. Not us, though. (Dick, *Time* 60)

Poststructuralist linguistics follows from the same starting point, yet there is a fundamental difference between its contention that linguistic signs can only refer to other signs and the concretized languages of *Time Out of Joint* and *The Invisibles*. In these worlds, reality is literally made of language—but that language is mimetic, referring to objects and concepts that exist outside language and conjuring them in ways that negate the symbolic substitution that poststructuralism presumes is inescapable. In addition to the neurochemical tricks of Key 17, *The Invisibles* is awash in languages that can summon or reshape reality, including "the secret common language of shamans—that language whose words do not describe things but are things" (I.15.15) and the "liquid logic processors" of the twenty-first century, which drop Ragged Robin into "a warm ocean of living words" (II.20.2–3) that she uses to write her version of *The Invisibles*. Whether magical or technological, these mimetic languages are at once confirmations that language structures experience and defiant assertions of its referentiality. Language may go all the way down in *The Invisibles*, but these signs correspond to their referents in a manner that poststructuralist theory deems impossible.

Other apparent endorsements of the poststructuralist view of language prove equally contradictory and ambivalent. A member of Cell 23, a meta-Invisibles cell that specializes in deprogramming other Invisibles operatives, tells the protagonists that "Reality is all about language" (II.13.5), but he does not argue that the languages that shape our experience derive their meanings only from social convention. In the very next panel, and for the next five pages, Cell 23 assaults the Invisibles with words from a secret, sixty-four-letter alphabet, words that can hijack the language processing areas of the brain, simulate alien contact, or simply turn off human consciousness.

If reality is "all about language" in the world of *The Invisibles*, it is not so in the strictly conventionalist sense of the poststructuralists, let alone the linguistic relativism and determinism of the Sapir-Whorf hypothesis. The Invisibles have never heard Cell 23's keywords before and don't even know most of their alphabet, yet the words still have their intended effect; social convention cannot determine their meaning or explain their cognitive impact. Cell 23 may tell the Invisibles "There are ... things all around. Things you never see because you don't have the words, you don't have the names" (II.13.8), reiterating the Sapir-Whorf hypothesis, but their keywords testify to a Chomskian universalist grammar locked deep in the human mind. The series alternates between universalist and relativist approaches to language and highlights whichever one has the most narrative potential for any given scene.

These universal and mimetic languages hold out the possibility of recovering another tongue long sought by scholars. In *The Search for the Perfect Language*, Umberto Eco describes the long tradition of attempts to recover the perfect, primal, Adamic language of direct correspondence that preceded the Tower of Babel, if not humanity's expulsion from Eden (7–10); to re-create this language is to reverse the Fall. Key 17 alludes to this potential in its very name, which Morrison derives from the Tower, a trump in the major arcana of the Tarot, widely read as a depiction of the fall of the Tower of Babel (Ouspensky 17; Raine 70). The major arcana are often identified as "keys" in the English esoteric tradition that Morrison follows (see, for example, Kathleen Raine), and the Tower, although given the number sixteen, is the seventeenth key since the first trump, the Fool, is assigned the number zero. "Key 17" therefore refers to the Tower, to Babel, and to the Biblical loss of the perfect language, a loss that the drug attempts to undo through neurochemistry. But if some of the languages of *The Invisibles* seek to reverse this linguistic fall through the mimetic method of total correspondence between word and object, others operate under the poststructuralist principle of wholly arbitrary relations between sound and meaning.

At the end of "Arcadia" Ragged Robin discovers the head of John the Baptist, which speaks in random sounds that different listeners interpret as prophecies or commands. She describes this infinitely mutable language as glossolalia, the speech of religious ecstasy; the blind chess player concurs and identifies glossolalia as "The true tongue, lost after Babel. The language of the angels" (I.8.18). Yet because everybody hears the head's speech differently, projecting their own meanings upon it (I.8.11), the glossolalia would appear to have more in common with the post-Babel welter of languages and interpretations, not the universal tongue that preceded the tower's fall. The chess player resolves this contradiction by further describing glossolalia as "the language of ecstasy and dreams. The primal tongue of fire. It is the original voice of the unconscious mind" (I.8.19). His account combines the Biblical with the psychoanalytic, casting the fall of the Tower of Babel, itself a reenactment of the Fall from Eden (J. Berger 341), as a fall from the unconscious into symbolic reasoning and language. The significative substitutions and deferrals of the symbolic order are equivalent to the confusion of languages after Babel, the loss of the original, Adamic language of mimesis, and ultimately the loss of innocence and bliss—whether that blissful state is imagined to take place in Eden or the womb.

With its endless, arbitrary permutations defined only by the assumptions of the listener, glossolalia would appear to be the conventionalist counterpoint to Key 17 or the secret language of the shamans, in which words are the things they denote and can therefore have no other meanings. Yet Morrison's glossolalia is no less primal or prelapsarian a tongue, and even the languages of correspondence leave some room for interpretation. After the Invisibles gain access to Key 17, they tinker with the drug's hypostatic effects by exposing its subjects to more abstract triggers. The experimentation begins when King Mob and Lord Fanny neutralize an enemy agent by dosing her with Key 17 and showing her a mug that reads "World's Greatest Dad," which she translates into an idealized image of her own father—still a fairly concrete referent, although the superlative calls for some element of imaginative projection. As the Invisibles become more adept in the drug's use, upgrading it to Key 23 and Key 64, they gradually introduce more ambiguous phrases.[15] When they raid Westminster Abbey to disrupt Sir Miles's coronation of the Archons as kings of the Earth, they bewilder their opponents by dosing them with Key 23 and bombarding them with scraps of paper covered in abstractions—*life, tomorrow, death, chaos, love, control, release, melt, gestate*, and so forth (III.2.6–7). Without any concrete referents, each viewer's interpretation would have to be dictated by their own assumptions and experiences. If even the concretized, fully interpellated words of Key 17 and its descendents can be polyvalent, then there is no perfect language of absolute meaning.

Absolute meaning is instead the province of the Invisibles' enemies. One of several glimpses into the Outer Church reveals a gigantic floating cube engraved on every face with the words THIS SCULPTURE MEANS TOTAL CONTROL ONLY (II.3.14–15); this is the Archons' version of art, a sculpture that attempts to dictate and limit its own interpretation. The Archons have made the Outer Church into a place where "Things are stripped of all meaning, all significance, all association but that which is determined by Control" (II.3.10). The result, a univalent world in which all art, language, and meaning are reduced to propaganda, is hardly preferable to a world in which signs bear no relation to their referents and all meanings are arbitrary. The Invisibles seek to bypass both the tyranny of absolute correspondence and the chaos of floating signifiers by using a language of subjective experience.

Mason Lang, one of America's wealthiest men, makes an unlikely Invisible. He joins the organization as a result of a childhood alien abduction in which he is taught a "meta-language" of "emotional aggregates. [. . .] One word, one sound, represents a whole complex of ideas and associations and feelings" (II.1.11–12). This meta-language circumvents even the hypostases of Key 17 and the language of the shamans; if they reinforce the power of the signifier by granting it a mimetic presence, Mason's emotional aggregates constitute a language of the real that sidesteps symbolic communication entirely. Mason might understand the aggregates as words or sounds, but Dane and Fanny are able to express them through the nonverbal, nonsymbolic, expressive medium of dance (II.7.18).[16] As a shaman, Fanny is also capable of summoning the shimmering liquid substance known as "magic mirror" or "logoplasm"—literally, "word liquid" or "living word substance," a name that suggests a considerable overlap with the meta-language. Dane describes the mirror as looking "like pictures and feelings" (II.22.9); Fanny, preparing to release the mirror, insists she speaks through feelings, not words (II.20.13); and Mason first encounters the meta-language after drinking a "liquid software" from what he believes is the Holy Grail (II.1.11). Whether it is expressed through speech, dance, or logoplasm, the meta-language of emotional aggregates does not introduce any symbolic mediation; pictures and feelings are communicated to the witness or listener without any need for words. At the same time, each expression conveys a complex of ideas and feelings, preserving the potential for multivalence and avoiding the dangers of the Outer Church.

King Mob is not especially fluent in this meta-language, but when he attempts to articulate one particularly charged emotional aggregate he inadvertently describes the magic mirror's origins and its effects: "It was like a whole universe of love. A place where there's nothing left of us but pure, uncut heart. A place outside time where there are no lies and no misunderstandings because everyone is part of everyone else" (II.5.15). Jimenez illustrates the passage with an image of the logoplasm in which two silvery blobs—likely representative of King Mob and Jacqui—interpenetrate and meld with one another. Since Morrison's holographic text is multiply redundant, other characters confirm this account with their own recollections of intersubjective unity beyond the boundaries of time and space. One mortally wounded soldier explicitly connects this unity to Morrison's models of prelapsarian language and consciousness in his dying words:

> Momma if I could talk I'd tell you I see the the holy light momma I'm in the holy light. [...] It's the first light momma and there's an angel here but it can't speak ain't none of us can speak here in this land there are no tongues momma how come we forgot all this and this land? (II.4.10)

The address to his mother and the mention of "the first light" imply that this soldier, in his final moments, has returned to a prenatal space, a land that everybody forgets upon their birth into the world. Instead of the primal language of correspondence, however, this land has no language at all. Language is unnecessary because, as King Mob remembers, everyone is part of everyone else: symbolic communication is as unnecessary as lies and misunderstandings are impossible. The ultimate achievement of the metalanguage, then, is to render symbolic language entirely useless.

The series culminates in an analogous linguistic regression and return on its final page, when Dane addresses the readers directly with an anecdote from his training:

> My mate Elfayed told me something when I was little and wanking about twenty times a day: "We made gods and jailers because we felt small and ashamed and alone," he said. "We let them try us and judge us, and, like sheep to the slaughter, we allowed ourselves to be ... sentenced.
> "See! Now! Our sentence is up. (III.1.22)

This passage cannot be excerpted or separated from the page, however, as the graphic design is central to its meaning (fig. 3-7). While Dane speaks these words, artist Frank Quitely and letterer Todd Klein magnify them until they fill the panels, becoming the images before they disappear completely in a blank, unbordered, open-ended space.[17] Wolk summarizes this sequence by noting that "words dispense with and replace drawings [...] the word becomes the visible representation of its invisible power" (277). He also detects another layer of meaning behind the colossal "UP" that expands beyond Quitely's panel borders, proposing that it is "in a way, a call for its medium to grow up" (Wolk 277). Like most metafictional readings of

Figure 3-7. *The Invisibles* III.1.22. Art by Frank Quitely. © Grant Morrison.

Morrison's work, this seems plausible but also far too modest in its expectations. Comics had been growing up for decades when this issue was published in April of 2000; Morrison aims for something higher.

Read not as the last word in Dane's sentence but, in the penultimate panel, as a sentence unto itself, the terminal "UP" becomes a far less bounded linguistic suggestion, what Morrison elsewhere in *The Invisibles* terms an Ericksonian command or an instance of neuro-linguistic programming (III.6.15). The final issue, page, sentence, and word successively condense the message of the entire series, distilling it down to a monosyllabic instruction that urges readers to improve their psychological and social well-being (Neighly 214). Mass action on the "UP" would end our willing surrender to the authorities, institutions, and ideologies we have created. As the final panels make clear, the end of our self-imposed sentence would also mean the end of the language that has sustained these systems. Morrison, Quitely, and Klein convert verbal symbols into visual representations before annihilating them completely, transforming Dane's words from conventionally symbolic representations to specular, imaginary ones and finally into the undefined, unrepresentable space of the real. This Lacanian regression figuratively restores *The Invisibles* to our original natal state at the precise moment that the placental Barbelith manifests on Earth to guide everyone into a new state of plenitude and completeness that Morrison calls the supercontext: the linguistic regression primes us for psychological and social rebirth.

ROMANTIC UTOPIAS

This drive to recover a primal state of bliss implies a Romantic world-view common to many of Morrison's prior comics. His early work is rich with Romantic ideas: rebel creators, sensitive artists, and tyrannical authorities abound, as do allusions to Blake, Byron, Shelley, De Quincey, and other Romantic writers. Christopher Murray describes Morrison's work as "a contemporary, post-modern re-imagining of the notion of the 'Romantic sublime'" (35) and identifies *The Invisibles* as the culmination of a Romantic influence that extends back to *Zenith*. The "Arcadia" storyline writes this influence into the series by making George Gordon, Lord Byron, and Percy Bysshe Shelley agents of the Invisible College and forerunners of Morrison's protagonists. This, however, is the high-water mark for Morrison's Romanticism. After "Arcadia," overt references to the Romantics recede from his work, both because Morrison has become far less interested in establishing a literary pedigree and because his philosophy changes considerably over the course of *The Invisibles*. The series begins by adopting many of the Romantics' beliefs, including their conflicted views of revolution and utopia, but Morrison gradually develops new theories of identity and selfhood that lead him to a radically different concept of liberation.

"Arcadia" opens with a debate between Byron and Shelley as they ride along the shores of the Adriatic, unwittingly inspiring Shelley's poem "Julian and Maddalo: A Conversation".[18] Like the eponymous characters of that poem, Shelley and Byron debate the responsibilities of artists and the possibility of utopia:

> **Byron:** I do know this; men are like sheep and will obey anyone who kicks their arses hard enough!
> **Shelley:** I disagree. There is a drive in men towards liberty. As poets, it is our duty to turn our faces up from the mire, to look up and tell our fellow men that we have seen a better world than this.
> **Byron:** I love the world. I love the whole turning, farting, pissing, shitting mess. I'm not so sure I could come up with a better one or even if I'd wish to see it made perfect. What would we write about? (I.5.3)

One of the keys to understanding *The Invisibles*, and Morrison's writing in general, is to recognize that both of these poets speak for Morrison. As he told one reader in a subsequent letter column, "The Shelley/Byron debate surprised me because I started out on Shelley's side but ended up siding with Byron. Some combination of both would seem to be the sanest response to living and dying in the modern world, whether that's the modern world of 1818 or 1995" (I.9, "Invisible Ink"). Morrison is the idealist and the realist, the utopian and the cynic; *The Invisibles* attempts to reconcile these conflicting outlooks, although most of the evidence in "Arcadia" would seem to come down on Byron's side.

The story is haunted by the French Revolution and particularly by the Reign of Terror, which serves as Byron's final answer to Shelley's utopian dreams, proof that "there was not one damned utopia that did not set its foundations in human suffering and pain. It begins with fancy words but always ends in blood" (I.5.4). Other scenes set during the Terror echo this critique, identifying the guillotine as "the prototype Murder Machine. Mass execution turned over to the bureaucrats. The living and the dead totted up as credits and debts in an accountant's ledger. The shadow of the scaffold cast across the Twentieth Century" (I.6.20). The guillotine initiates and embodies the worst aspects of modernity, converting people into commodities or statistics and mechanizing mass murder with brutal, rationalistic efficiency. Morrison cements his criticisms by introducing both Enlightenment rationalism and modern technology to a more perverse example of eighteenth-century utopianism when he restages and revises the Marquis de Sade's novel *The 120 Days of Sodom*. As de Sade's fantasy of unrestrained sexual license descends into rape, mutilation, and murder, his imaginary libertines brand their captives with bar codes (I.7.11) and ultimately annihilate themselves in a nuclear explosion. One of the libertines recognizes the blast as "The light of reason" (I.7.18), marking planetary extinction as the terminus of the Enlightenment and recalling Byron's earlier warning, "the brighter the light, the darker the shadow" (I.5.5). "Arcadia" plumbs the dark side of Enlightenment rationalism and utopianism, finding they lead only to better technologies of extermination and control.

The storyline references several planned utopias, including Robert Southey and Samuel Taylor Coleridge's unrealized attempt at pantisocracy and the cultural revolutions of the 1960s. All of these projects founder on the same basic problem of human nature: people want to be led. Byron laments this trait and de Sade builds his erotics around it, but the dilemma is expressed most poignantly by a former acid casualty in a San Francisco bondage club:

> In the '60s you had your Timothy Learys and what's his name? "Cuckoo's Nest." Kesey. All those guys. They were at the wheel, they could see the road ahead, right? They told us all we had to do was get fucked up on LSD and we'd all turn into super-people and build the promised land out of rainbows and flowers. [...]
>
> When I finally came down it was 1985. Shit. From free love to safe sex, huh? Whatever happened to the revolution? (I.8.1)

King Mob connects this seemingly unmotivated interlude to de Sade, the French Revolution, and the Romantics, and outlines one of the basic principles of the series:

> He was talking about revolutions. Or the revolution. I suppose there only is ever one.
>
> I think he felt let down by his driving instructors. He thought he just had to sit back in his seat and be taken everywhere. He didn't realize they were just showing him what to do. (I.8.3)

Even in his past attempts at revolution, the ex-hippie was only following others instead of working to liberate himself; no doubt that explains why, with sublime irony, he has ended up as a slave at a bondage club. His example prompts de Sade to repeat Byron's belief that we all want somebody else to tell us what to do, but King Mob and the Invisibles resist the idea of leading others into a perfect world. They instead claim they want to give everybody, even their enemies, a chance at living in their own personal utopias (I.8.6).

This aligns the Invisibles with Shelley's dogged idealism, which Morrison tests but does not slight. For all that history confirms Byron's pessimism, Shelley never abandons his belief in utopia. Wracked with guilt over his daughter's death, Shelley insists, "I know where utopia lies. It is here. Where is the love, beauty, and truth we seek but in our mind? [. . .] Here. Waiting for us to grow up and recognize it and come home" (I.8.13). Tapping his forehead, the poet redefines utopia from a social project to a personal ideal capable of promoting individual development. He also reveals why so many heads have rolled through "Arcadia," from guillotined aristocrats to the lost head of John the Baptist, each serving as a visual reminder of the only space where it is safe to build a perfect society. Despite its revolutionary trappings, *The Invisibles* exchanges social answers for existential ones and advocates for an idealist view of the world rather than any particular political ideology.

Morrison does not view *The Invisibles* as an apolitical work, but he recognizes that it departs from the explicitly political content of *Dare* or *The New Adventures of Hitler*. Fearing those comics would become defined too narrowly and dated too quickly by their attacks on Thatcher, he shifted to political content that "attacks the foundations of evil politics, rather than attacking figureheads" (Hasted 79). *The Invisibles* locates those foundations in the human psyche and their escape in the imagination. When Dane, assaulted by images of humanity's violence and cruelty during his initiation, screams that he wants to fix the world, Barbelith tells him, "'Then fix yourself. The world will follow. Everything will follow. 'As above, so below'" (I.21.23). Barbelith quotes the Hermetic principle which asserts that the universe reflects the self and vice versa, their similarities persisting across orders of magnitude in a manner consistent with Morrison's interest in fractals, holograms, and implicate order theory. Yet in this context it is also a straightforward admission, consistent with "Arcadia," that utopian projects are doomed to fail unless people first address their own desires for domination, submission, destruction, and all the other impulses that undermine social progress. Morrison does not believe such personal growth can be dictated, only modeled and motivated, and so his Invisibles resist being cast as leaders or messiahs; they might illuminate the path for others, but ultimate responsibility rests on each individual.

This fundamentally Romantic view of self-directed liberation governs volume one but becomes complicated in later volumes by Morrison's changing beliefs. At the start of the series, the antagonists are all authoritarian caricatures dedicated to the destruction of the individual (James 441). In the first issue, the evil headmaster Mr. Gelt blames the celebration of "individualism and self-reliance" for a "rising tide of anarchy and violence" (I.1.24), which he attempts to correct through surgery and psychological conditioning. As late as the end of the second volume, Mr. Quimper, another agent of the Outer Church, describes individuality as a "sickness" that prevents people from fulfilling their proper functions as cogs in a vast social machine (II.19.3). By the end of the series, however, the Invisibles themselves have become suspicious of individuality, critiquing it not out of a desire for machinelike conformity but rather from the belief that the individual self is one of the factors blocking human development. This dramatic change owes much to the work of author and pop psychologist Ken Wilber, which Morrison has cited in interviews about *The Invisibles* (Neighly 232, 247) and in *The Invisibles* itself (III.8.5). Wilber, by his own admission, initially held a Romantic view of a humanity alienated from the lost presence of a primal, unified state, but problems with that model led him "to abandon a pure Romanticism for a more evolutionary or developmental view" in which humans are growing towards spiritual awareness, not struggling to regain it (1). Morrison's own beliefs have followed a similar track, partially due to Wilber's influence, in a progression that unfolds over the course of *The Invisibles*.

Although its heroes initially work to liberate humanity into a multitude of individual utopias, the series increasingly views the individual self as incomplete or problematic. At first, the Invisibles simply augment or protect themselves by generating additional personalities. In "Entropy in the UK," King Mob creates fictional personas based on Gideon Stargrave to deflect a telepathic interrogation; in "House of Fun" (I.22–24), Invisibles veteran Mr. Six heals an abscess in reality by sacrificing his civilian identity as Brian Malcolm. He then rejoins Division X, a deep-cover Invisibles cell whose members have based their personalities around characters from 1970s British cop shows. As the series transitions into the highly self-reflexive volume two, the Invisibles become increasingly aware and skeptical of the artificial, performative aspects of their identities. In the "auto-critique" section of issue 13, exposure to one of the primal 64-letter words causes the protagonists to place themselves under *détournement*, replacing their normal dialogue with Situationist criticisms of the false and exploitative images of revolution they promote (II.13.6–7). These identities, especially King Mob's super-spy posture, are revealed as fictional shells, behavioral constructs only slightly more mundane than the "fiction suits" that enable ascended characters to move through the narrative as other people. One such character, the former Invisible John-a-Dreams, reenters the narrative as at least two separate entities on opposite sides of the war between the Invisible College and the Outer Church.

If the ability to assume additional personalities allows freedom of action and the expansion of perspective, the converse is that being limited to just one personality limits psychological development. The blind chess player tells Dane, on the verge of enlightenment, that "'Ego' scaffolding necessary to your development must now be husked before it constricts your growth" (III.2.13). In Morrison's holographic view of history, this means the ego also constricts social development and traps humanity in intersubjective conflict. Reynard, a young Invisible in the year 2012 who believes she has replaced the unitary self with the cycling identities of the "MeMePlex" (III.1.2), tells an older Dane that stable personalities and radical separations of self and other were responsible for war because "You tried to hammer your enemies into shape: you wouldn't understand how you allow them to define the boundaries of your self-sense" (III.1.5). The Invisibles of the twenty-first century appear to have come around to Jacqui's point of view that an identity based on conflict with or difference from the other depends on that other for its own definition.

To end this conflict, the Invisibles work to abolish the individual self and elevate humanity to a state of being they call the supercontext, which Reynard describes as follows: "You identify with everything in the universe that is not-self and dissolve the existential alienation dilemma in unity. All is one and several is none" (III.1.7). In the supercontext, as in the logoplasm, subjectivities are no longer separate. The supercontext's union of the me and the not-me is Emersonian in its promise to transcend the alienation of the individual, and yet the Invisibles are post-Romantic in their blithe assertion that humanity has never really been alienated. In the same issue, King Mob motivates himself for his impending entry into the supercontext by telling himself, "I am part of 'nature.' Every airplane, every power station is a result of 'Nature's' process. We never fell. We were never apart from the world. We lied to ourselves" (III.1.13). Morrison renounces the Romantic myths of separation from nature and a fall from innocence, replacing them with a developmental model in which humanity has always had the capacity to grow into, rather than recover, a unified and transcendent subjectivity.

RESISTANCE IS USELESS

Brimming with Morrison's new confidence in humanity's developmental potential, the final issues of *The Invisibles* accept and even celebrate some social phenomena that earlier issues would have viewed with skepticism. This late passivity is on display in a television announcement overheard in the final issue (possibly a newscast, possibly a promotion for the new *Invisibles* virtual reality game). The speaker draws a troubling analogy as he or she asks whether the multiple personalities of the MeMePlex are "The end of notions of territory and boundary? The very concept of the individual, like that of the bounded nation-state[,] was not designed to survive the last millennium and must be transcended: hence this emergence of the so-called 'MeMePlex'... or multiple personality disorder as a lifestyle option" (III.1.6). This passage applies postmodern economics to the psyche, promising the MeMePlex will erase intersubjective boundaries just as postmodern capital, moving from country to country with little to no impediment, effectively ignores national borders. Nothing in the issue contradicts or challenges this call for a globalization of the self; certainly nothing duplicates Michael Hardt and Antonio Negri's contemporaneous observation that "the current global tendencies toward increased mobility, indeterminacy, and hybridity are experienced by some as a kind of liberation but by others as an exacerbation of their suffering," let alone their contention that these economic transformations are most apparent among "The losers in the processes of globalization" (Hardt and Negri 150). The indeterminate, hybrid, psychologically mobile identities of Morrison's future Invisibles might be just as harmful to some people, but the final issue only welcomes this transformation—a reaction typified by the joyous rave Dane joins as the supercontext arrives and the comics page breaks down, annihilating panel borders no less than psychological or national ones (III.1.21–22). The comic devotes little consideration to the possible drawbacks of using globalization and multiple personality disorder as models for human development.[19]

Morrison and his characters are quite comfortable modeling the new, decentered human self on the practices of global capitalism because they believe they have successfully co-opted those practices. King Mob promotes the Invisibles philosophy by turning it into a lucrative virtual reality game that capitalism will market to the point of its own destruction. He justifies his corporate sell-out to Dane by quoting his teenage idols, the Sex Pistols—"I use the en-eh-mee" (III.1.8). Morrison espouses the same strategy in his interviews, telling Patrick Neighly his plan for *The Invisibles* "was to dress revolution in the clothes of MTV and of fashion shoots so that people would absorb it. They'd absorb ideas so toxic and so destructive it would undermine their normal consensus reality" (Neighly 253). Neighly remarks on the "irony in the fact that *The Invisibles* is a revolutionary tract unwittingly published by AOL Time Warner, the largest media conglomerate in the world" (253), but it is not clear who is exploiting whom. The revolution proposed in *The Invisibles* is so focused on individual development rather than collective action—and, in the end, so complementary with transformations in global capitalism—that it poses no threat to Time Warner, only a revenue stream. Morrison, like King Mob and like the Sex Pistols, may claim to use the enemy, but they have also used him.

To his credit, he is well aware that co-optation can cut both ways. The auto-critique sequence in volume two admits that the Invisibles are all commercialized fantasies of rebellion, especially when King Mob declares, "The most pernicious image of all is the anarchist-hero figure. A creation of commodity culture, he allows us to buy into an inauthentic simulation of revolutionary praxis. [. . .] The hero encourages passive spectating and revolt becomes another product to be consumed" (II.13.6). Every word of it is true, and yet even this bracing self-criticism is not entirely trustworthy. The reliance on theoretical jargon, so alien to King Mob, is more characteristic of the Cell 23 agents who trigger the auto-critique; one of them boasts, with audible scorn, "we have the keys to a wider world which you have not been educated to comprehend. [. . .] We have words and concepts for things you aren't even able to imagine in the rudimentary vocabulary of your slave language" (II.13.7). Cell 23 deploys the deep-structure command language of the 64-letter hyperalphabet as the most arcane of all academic vocabularies, a magnified version of the Situationist jargon they place in King Mob's mouth. Their palpable condescension, their tactic of wielding words as weapons ("Hit them with some vocabulary"), and their command of not one but two impenetrable argots brands Cell 23 as an unflattering caricature of self-righteous New Left radicals and cliquish academics whose rhetoric limits the effectiveness of their own critiques. If selling out to the culture industry compromises the revolutionary agenda, so does retreating behind an isolating and self-aggrandizing doctrine of intellectual superiority.

Morrison had already fashioned a similar argument about the impotence of critical theory in *Kill Your Boyfriend* (1995), a dark comedy drawn by Philip Bond. The story of a pair of anonymous, disaffected teenagers who go on a killing spree to express their contempt for societal norms, the comic is far more cavalier than *The Invisibles* about treating murder as a form of social protest. The protagonists' adolescent rebellion is directionless, concerned mostly with their discovery of things the readers already know and opinions they have likely outgrown (e.g., "schools are just factories for turning out robots"). *Kill Your Boyfriend* nevertheless offers an effective and timely commentary on *The Invisibles*. Written in the spring of 1994 ("Afterword") as Morrison was beginning *The Invisibles*, the comic presents early versions of many of the same ideas that would preoccupy the long-running series while calling attention to some of its weaknesses and blind spots. The criticism begins in earnest when the murderous protagonists are briefly taken in by a traveling band of students who call themselves "style terrorists" and claim to practice violence as a form of art (30). These students are immediately recognizable as a parodic version of the Invisibles, since they are drawn from the same stock types (the black militant; the Romantic poet; the bald, tattooed, butch lesbian who resembles King Mob) and since they adopt pithy code names like "Drum," "Styx," and "Jailbait." They toss around Situationist terminology and talk about "floating identities" (30), which the Girl (the nameless female protagonist) understands as a set of multiple, mutable, entirely elective personalities she can adopt and discard at will—the MeMePlex five years before *The Invisibles* put a name to it. The students are the Invisibles, played for comedy rather than action.

Action, in fact, is precisely what they are missing. For all their talk of destroying the spectacle, the students never quite get around to staging their violent arts projects. They fear that if they break the law, they will "never get an Arts Council grant or a retrospective at the ICA" (34), revealing their desire for funding and approval from the art institutions they claim to despise.[20] When accused of dragging their heels, they fall back on obfuscating jargon: "Praxis can only come after intensive discourse, you know what I mean? We have to define the parameters of revolutionary activity . . . " (34). If the students look like King Mob's team, they sound like Cell 23, and their timidity indicts both groups—the countercultural clichés and the arrogant intellectuals—for their dependence on the culture they define themselves against. A campfire scene in which the students toast all the signifiers of suburban English life from council estates to garden gnomes suggests feigned irony masking a sincere affection (32)—an affection they share with Morrison, who confesses, "I love all those things about [Britain] that are most ridiculous, like the Blackpool Tower and candy floss and *Carry On* films" (Hasted 80). Blackpool Tower is the climactic destination in *Kill Your Boyfriend*, where the Girl confesses that she likes the shabby holiday town and the culture of spectacle that is most visible there (45). That culture is more robust than its critics, who only pursue easy targets and who reinforce the culture's aesthetic hierarchies in any case: "All you ever do is try to shock old people and the middle classes," the Girl tells the students. "Christ! Anybody can do that" (46).

The Invisibles, of course, go considerably further than tweaking bourgeois sensibilities; they attack centers of political, military, and cultural power using violent methodologies the art students can only theorize. This might seem to make them more comparable to the protagonists of *Kill Your Boyfriend* but for the two comics' radically different attitudes towards conflict. The characters in *Kill Your Boyfriend* are broadly drawn caricatures whose deaths are little more than punch lines, whereas *The Invisibles* takes every life so seriously that three of the protagonists either renounce violence or quit the Invisibles entirely. The adolescent solipsism and us-vs.-them mentality that fuel the Boy and Girl can find no purchase in *The Invisibles*. Every life matters and every opposition, whether it originates in politics, philosophy, religion, genre, or human psychology, collapses by the end of the series. With even the most fundamental binaries shading into continuities, the Invisibles can no longer define themselves as warriors or revolutionaries; they have become guides and rescuers, exponents of Morrison's post-Romantic certainty that the human race always has the potential to improve. It is this capacity for change, not its long run or high page count, that makes *The Invisibles* Morrison's most complex Vertigo comic and one of the cornerstones of his career. The series places its ideas in perpetual dialogue, motivating itself, as it exhorts us, to be better.

Chapter 4

WIDESCREEN

After spending the middle years of the 1990s writing for Vertigo and *2000 AD*, Morrison returned to a superhero genre transformed by the freefall in the American comics market. The collapse of the speculator bubble shuttered stores, devoured distributors, and drove publishers into bankruptcy, but it also empowered veteran creators to reject the style of comics the speculators had supported and then just as rapidly abandoned—namely, the Image style. Image Comics was founded by seven artists who left Marvel when the company would not grant them ownership of the characters they created (Dean Part 1). While Image gave them the creative control they sought, these artists generally chose to work in the same genres and styles they had honed at Marvel: violent superhero comics with hypersexualized characters (Bukatman 57–66). Several other creators—particularly writers, whose work had never been important to the artist-driven Image style—responded by reacting not only against Image but also against the revisionist comics of the 1980s that had preceded them and made their graphic violence and exaggerated sexuality acceptable to the comics market. These writers were themselves lifelong comics fans who had grown up on Silver Age superhero comics and who looked back to that period as they sought to ignore or reverse the trends of the previous decade. In many ways, the superhero genre was just catching up to Grant Morrison, who had revived forgotten Silver Age characters and denounced the excesses of revisionism in the pages of *Animal Man* and *Doom Patrol*. Some of these comics went far beyond Morrison's nostalgia, however, espousing conservative politics and aesthetics that were foreign to Morrison's work. The nineties retro comics were fitting representatives of their times, exemplary products of a decade that was obsessed with the past and a comics market that saw no future.[1]

In *1963* (1993), Alan Moore, Rick Veitch, and Steve Bissette created a deadly accurate parody of early 1960s Marvel comics; the never-completed final chapter would have contrasted its Marvel-style champions against the violent antiheroes of Image Comics, which gamely published the miniseries. *Marvels* (1994), by Kurt Busiek and Alex Ross, revisited more than thirty years of Marvel continuity from the perspective of an awestruck journalist. Ross and Mark Waid brought the same everyman's perspective to DC Comics in *Kingdom Come* (1996), a story in which elderly superheroes come out of retirement to discipline their violent successors, while Busiek and Brent Anderson pursued a less spiteful and contentious brand of nostalgia by inventing their own history for *Astro City* (1995–present). Modeled after the archetypal heroes, locales, and stories of DC and Marvel, the fabricated past of *Astro City* continues to pay tribute to the rich, convoluted narrative continuities that predated the revisionist movement. Alan Moore built a similar continuity in *Supreme* (1996–2000), albeit with a metafictional twist: Moore wrote his reconceptualization of Supreme and the reconstruction of his past into the story, aided by Rick Veitch's spot-on mimicry of Golden and Silver Age Superman comics that had long since been banished from modern DC continuity. Moore's America's Best Comics imprint (1999–2006) displayed an even wider range of references, homaging everything from Winsor McCay's *Little Nemo* to Will Eisner's *The Spirit* to Harvey Kurtzman's *MAD*, incorporating a whole century of American comics into its wistful pastiche. These comics generally shared two qualities, a self-reflexive awareness of superhero traditions and a self-consciously classicist tone, often accompanied by an explicit rejection of revisionism and its legacy.

By the late nineties, the movement had consolidated to the point that Morrison could refer to it in the pages of his superhero comics. *Prometheus* (1998), a one-shot special introducing a new JLA villain, also features a would-be superhero named Retro whose slogan is "Today's hero, yesterday's attitude!" (1.8). He believes his earnest, back-to-basics approach to superheroics led to his selection in a "Join the JLA for a Day" contest, beating out "all those other guys with claws and chains and stuff" (1.8), a disparaging reference to Image-style superheroes. An issue of *The Flash* written by Morrison and Mark Millar and published that same month includes a highly self-conscious conversation that replicates Retro's logic and values.[2] Jay Garrick, the Golden Age Flash, remarks that "A few years ago, for example, everyone wanted someone with claws and a telescopic sight on their team. Now these guys are complaining no one returns their calls anymore. [...] People want heroes again. [...] We've been through the darkness. Now let's see a little light" (134.9). Wally West, the current Flash, goes even more metatextual: he uses fandom's system of dating comics by successive "Ages" and cites Gerard Jones and Will Jacobs as saying that "the Dark Age only just ended in '95 [...] it's still too early to say what this new age is even going to be called yet" (134.10). This lack of a label notwithstanding, all of the heroes agree that they live in a new era—one that, to judge by their conversation, is marked by equal measures of self-reflexivity and traditionalism. While the retro comics might more accurately be classified as a movement rather than an entire age, Morrison was indisputably at its center.

Morrison's nineties superhero comics also anticipated another fad that would not achieve full definition until the end of the decade. Prior to Morrison's arrival, the Justice League of America, like most superhero teams since the 1980s, was written in the style of Chris Claremont's *Uncanny X-Men*, emphasizing character development and interpersonal conflict over plot and action. *JLA* generally pushed these concerns to the margins, focusing on the heroes' efforts to thwart apocalyptic menaces that threatened the planet if not the entire universe. After this approach proved a commercial success—*JLA* was among DC's best-selling comics, often the only DC comic to break into the top ten titles in monthly sales—more superhero books began to feature high-concept ideas and action on a grand scale.[3] This style was soon dubbed "widescreen," a reference to the panoramic tiers of horizontal panels that imitated the aspect ratios of widescreen movies and illuminated the action in lurid detail.[4] Morrison credits himself with originating the widescreen style in the second issue of *JLA* (Lien-Cooper), although the specific pages he cites resemble a standard two-page spread rather than the cinematic action of later widescreen comics (fig. 4-1). The style did not coalesce until Warren Ellis and Bryan Hitch married that action to the clean linework and detailed environments of European comics albums and a slower, decompressed pacing borrowed from manga in their series *The Authority* (1999–2000).

The widescreen comics combined the self-conscious historicism of the retro movement—Ellis populated *The Authority*, its predecessor *Stormwatch* (1996–98), and its contemporary *Planetary* (1999–2009) with thinly veiled analogues of older comics characters—and the sheer spectacle of the Image artists, uniting the decade's dominant trends in superhero scripting and art. *The Authority* was a hit, prompting many subsequent comics to mimic its widescreen visual style; others emulated its callous heroes, who reveled in their own strength and imposed their will on the world. These imitators typically bore titles that advertised the heroes' unparalleled power and authoritarian leanings: *The Monarchy* (2001–02), *The Establishment* (2001–02), *The Order* (2002), *Justice League Elite* (2004–05), and *The Ultimates* (2002–08), perhaps the most successful copy of *The Authority*. These comics were

Figure 4-1. *JLA* 2.16-17. Art by Howard Porter. © DC Comics.

self-conscious, and often derivative, but hardly classicist—*The Authority* and *The Ultimates* were as successful for their shock value, their willingness to breach conventional superhero ethics, as they were for their art.

Morrison was an eager participant in both the retro and widescreen movements in miniseries such as *Marvel Boy* (2000–01) and *Fantastic Four 1234* (2001), the graphic novel *JLA: Earth 2* (2000), and collaborations such as *Aztek: the Ultimate Man* (1996–97) and *The Flash* (1997–98), both written with Mark Millar. These shorter works adopt either the visual style and scope of widescreen or the self-reflexive traditionalism of the retro comics. In his longer, ongoing series such as *JLA* (1996–2000) and *New X-Men* (2001–04), however, Morrison reveals that he does not trust the larger ideological implications of either movement. His most sophisticated and successful superhero comics from the millennial period balance tradition and innovation as they attempt to revitalize the superhero genre without succumbing to the conservative aesthetics or the authoritarian politics of other

1990s reactions against revisionism. To that end, Morrison's series feature inclusive and egalitarian superheroes who share their responsibilities with humanity, inspiring humans to work with them, emulate them, or become superheroes themselves. These series also use metafiction, hypostasis, and other postmodernist narrative techniques while they combine superheroes with other genres ranging from science fiction to autobiography. Even these modest and well-meaning experiments, however, would eventually run up against the genre's entrenched conventions and the comics industry's ownership practices, limiting Morrison's ability to transform the superhero genre single-handedly.

FLEX MENTALLO: WHEN WORLDS COLLIDE

Morrison's first attempt at revitalizing the superhero began at the unlikely home of Vertigo, although its origins predated that imprint. Flex Mentallo debuted as a supporting character in Morrison's *Doom Patrol*, where he initially appeared to be a long-forgotten (if obviously parodic) superhero from the 1950s. "Musclebound: The Secret Origin of Flex Mentallo" (*Doom Patrol* 42) reveals that Flex was once the hapless protagonist of the famous Charles Atlas advertisement "The Insult that Made a Man out of 'Mac,'" which promised to turn 97-pound weaklings into musclemen with Atlas's mail-order workout program (Landon 200–02). Tired of getting sand kicked in his face, Mac orders a training program from a mysterious stranger and becomes an adept of "muscle mystery," which, in Morrison's surreal revision of the Atlas ad, not only improves his physique but also harnesses his muscle power to read minds and perform other psychic feats. After humiliating his beachside bully, Flex becomes a superhero and embarks on a series of strange adventures. Or so he thinks: Flex, it turns out, is actually a fictional comic book character—that is, a comic book character within the world of *Doom Patrol*, making him a fiction within a fiction. Flex is the creation of Wally Sage, a seven-year-old boy whose psychic powers brought his hero to life. At the end of the storyline, Wally has died but Flex remains alive and as chipper as ever, determined to continue fighting crime in a radically different world. In an epilogue, he tells *Doom Patrol* readers, "You know, since I became real, I've begun to notice things about the world I live in. Number one is that the superheroes are so miserable and depressed. It beats me why there should be so many long faces but in my own small way I plan to change all that. It's time to put a smile on the face of the war against crime. So make way for America's merriest crimefighter!" (*DP* 46.3). Flex's faux-Silver Age origins, his dismay at the grim superheroes of the 1990s, and his determination to reverse the trends of revisionism mark him as one of the first characters in the nineties retro movement.[5] He would not resume his mission for nearly five years, however, and when he did he would carry it far beyond simple nostalgia.

America's merriest crimefighter finally returned in the pages of *Flex Mentallo* (1996), a four-issue miniseries published by Vertigo. Morrison's first collaboration with artist Frank Quitely, the miniseries introduces even more ontological confusion to Flex's already questionable existence. No longer part of the Doom Patrol's world in the stranger corners of the shared DC universe, this Flex inhabits a world much closer to our own, a world that once had superheroes but now finds itself in desperate need of their help. Searching for an old (and equally fictional) comrade, Flex becomes caught up in a quest to save his planet, his creator, and his genre from their own self-destructive impulses. *Flex Mentallo* deploys postmodernist narrative strategies and a web of intertextual references to deliver a metafictional commentary, a genre history, a fantasy autobiography, and a manifesto calling for a new phase of superhero comics.

Morrison pursues all of these projects by eliding the distinction between fiction and reality. The Flex Mentallo of the miniseries is still a fictional hero come to life, but his creator is a new Wally Sage who is a musician rather than a powerful psychic and whose life bears more than a passing resemblance to Morrison's own. It isn't clear whether Flex and Wally inhabit the same narrative diegesis or not: Wally's childhood comics appear to predict or create Flex's part of the plot (1.10–11), yet a later scene's word balloon placement implies that Wally lies in an alleyway just around the corner from Flex (1.15). Similarly, Wally's phone can contact a variety of characters from Flex's narrative despite (or perhaps because of) its lack of batteries. It is difficult even to determine how many different diegeses are operating in the miniseries since they all turn out to be nested within each other, frustrating any attempts at cataloging or ranking them. In one scene Wally's apartment opens onto a tiny ceramic village (4.9), which over the course of the miniseries manifests inside a fishbowl, on the moon, and inside one of Wally's childhood dreams. In another scene a superhero from another dimension takes young Wally inside a human brain—possibly his own—and explains that Wally's entire universe is composed of two subatomic superheroes who have occupied (in fact, *become*) every possible point in spacetime by means of a quantum superposition (4.15). Narratives of varying levels of realism and fantasy collapse together until any distinctions between them vanish;

Quitely illustrates this confusion of realities with the recurring image, taken from Silver Age comics, of parallel worlds colliding (2.24, 3.21–22), while Morrison provides a textual counterpart by merging Flex's narration with Wally's (3.17–20). Wally, the extradimensional superheroes, and Morrison all seek to create a world that leaves "No more barriers between the real and the imaginary" (4.15), and so the series ends with two devastating blows to those barriers: Wally transforms into a superhero while a small army of other heroes, liberated from the prison of fictionality, arrives on his world. Both events illustrate the power of ideas and imaginary constructs to direct human behavior, an indication that reality and fiction are already interdependent; Morrison implies that fictional superheroes model the confidence and the selflessness that humanity must adopt in order to save itself.

The confusions of *Flex Mentallo* are not limited to its narrative ontology. In his unpublished essay "Hero of the Beach: Flex Mentallo at the End of the Worlds," Will Brooker argues that Flex's sexuality is just as impossible to pin down: "While his hyperbolically-muscled body and bulging trunks position him as the ultimate in quaintly outdated straight heroic masculinity, precisely the same signifiers cast him as an equally dated gay pin-up, the beefcake idol thinly disguised as a health and fitness illustration" (5–6). Adopting the discourse of queer theorists who emphasize the multivalence and undefinability of queerness, Brooker suggests that because Flex can potentially be read as straight or gay, but never definitively read as one or the other, his comic is "more fundamentally 'queer' than it would have been had Morrison explicitly stated that the hero and Wally enjoyed a gay relationship" ("Hero" 7). Brooker connects this queerness to Flex's multiple, contradictory origin stories and the nonlinear, digressive structure of the miniseries, arguing that these narrative qualities are themselves queer—although this argument depends on a reductive association of linearity with heterosexuality. We need not equate linear narratives with heterosexual ones to observe that *Flex Mentallo* departs from both models, or to note that its treatment of sexuality is just as mercurial as its shifting ontologies. In fact, Flex's polysemic queerness may owe more to his genre than to Morrison's narrative techniques. Aaron Taylor contends that the superhero body, defined by spectacle, freed from the demands of anatomy or verisimilitude or even basic physics, itself "constitutes a polymorphous sexuality, or at least a sexuality that dualistic logic cannot constrain" (346). *Flex Mentallo* certainly capitalizes on this opportunity to unsettle binary logic; when Flex comments that his powers of muscle mystery have given him a "bodymind"

(1.5), that seamless compound word effaces one of the most fundamental dualisms of Western culture.

Like Taylor, Morrison asserts that the superhero genre has always housed fluid, queer sexualities and invited erotic readings alongside more chaste ones (Landon 211). The third issue exposes this secret history by sending Flex to a superhero orgy in which previously repressed subtexts—heterosexual, homosexual, and everything in between, including some configurations that are possible only in the fantastic world of superhero comics—explode to the surface. As Wally inventories the revealing costumes and fetishistic powers he declares, in breathless arousal, "Frederic Wertham was fucking right!" (3.18). Morrison refers (with a slight misspelling) to the controversial work of Fredric Wertham, who argued in *Seduction of the Innocent* (1955) that Batman, Robin, and Wonder Woman all carried none-too-subtle homosexual connotations. For these pronouncements Wertham has been vilified by comics fans and fan-historians, a trend Morrison blithely reverses with Wally's shameless admission. While later comics would embrace these queer readings (*The Authority* features a gay relationship between thinly disguised analogues of Superman and Batman), Morrison is one of the first superhero writers to accept Wertham's interpretations while stripping them of their connotations of guilt and deviance—connotations that owe as much to Wertham's critics as they do to Wertham himself.[6]

This acceptance of the genre's polymorphous sexuality is just one facet of *Flex Mentallo*, which recapitulates the history of superhero comics by organizing each issue around a different era. The first issue is filled with references to Golden Age characters and character types like Superman, Captain Marvel, and kid sidekicks, initiating its metafictional historiography with the genre's earliest and most basic elements. The second issue addresses the Silver Age tendency to multiply, mutate, and expand individual characters or items into entire families, systems, and cosmologies, alluding to that period's plenitudes of parallel worlds and endless spectra of Kryptonite; it also includes a treatise on the Silver Age's transformation of superheroes from "idealized masculine figures" like Flex to softer, more "fluid and feminine" bodies (2.16).[7] The third issue parodies the somber atmosphere, gritty realism, and crude sexuality of the revisionist superheroes—a standard Morrison move, though one other superhero comics were just awakening to—while the final issue attempts to move beyond revisionism into a new stage, christening itself "the first ultra-post-futurist comic" (4.22). If *Flex Mentallo* is a fair representation, this stage is marked by metafictional self-consciousness as "characters are allowed full synchrointeraction with readers" (4.22) and comics produce stories about other comics.

Morrison parallels the development of the superhero genre with the growth of his surrogate reader and author, Wally Sage. The miniseries follows both through their formative years (the Golden Age and early childhood), the unbridled expansion of their imagination (the Silver Age/late childhood), and an angry period of violence, cynicism, and sexual desire (revisionism/adolescence) before achieving a maturity that can accept and integrate all these past stages (self-reflexivity, nostalgia, and adulthood). Notably, revisionist comics are presented not as the culmination of this development but as a stage of transition, more adolescent than adult. The apparent villain of the series, a masked figure who threatens to kill Flex and destroy the world in the name of "bring[ing] some realism" into the story (4.13), is unmasked as the teenage Wally Sage, who spouts common criticisms of superhero comics—"Pathetic fucking power fantasies for lonely wankers" (4.17)—and subjects Flex to a sneering semiotic analysis—"Look at you! A half-naked muscleman in trunks. What's that supposed to signify?" (4.18). Attributing these criticisms to a moody, lonely teenager both defuses them and demolishes revisionism's claims to artistic maturity; as one character remarks, "Only a bitter little adolescent boy could confuse realism with pessimism" (4.17). Morrison sets out to save comic book readers and writers from their embarrassment at the superhero genre's juvenile origins, arguing that a truly mature genre can embrace rather than reject its most naïve, garish, or bizarre elements.

Mapping Wally Sage's life onto the genre's history, Morrison also fits it to his own. Scenes of Wally's youth match Morrison's recollections of his childhood comics reading: he and Wally both have bohemian parents and uncles who read comics, both start collecting comics at age twelve, and both associate early memories of comics with childhood illnesses and operations (*Flex* 1.17–18; Hasted 53–54). Both have politically active fathers who instill fears of nuclear annihilation in their sons, and Wally pursues the career in music that Morrison abandoned in his twenties. *Flex Mentallo* is an autobiographical account as much as it is a superheroic fantasy or a metafictional manifesto. Morrison fuses fantasy and realism to present memories and other autobiographical material that he is unwilling to translate directly onto the page.

This mode of fantastic realism achieves its most perfect visual expression in the third issue when the teenage Wally stares across a bleak postindustrial landscape, looking over a city much like Glasgow but for the titanic stealth bomber that soars overhead, trailing bombs in its wake (fig. 4-2). The surreal

Widescreen 145

Figure 4-2. *Flex Mentallo* 3.10. Art by Frank Quitely. © DC Comics.

contrast is rich with potential meanings. Wally may be completely oblivious to the bomber until the blast destroys him, an interpretation consistent with that issue's presentation of superhero comics as a distraction from real life. As Wally says,

> That's what I remember: hot summer nights, sweltering in my bedroom, reading comics and dreaming and drawing, while life went on outside my window. Imagine a jail cell, yeah? A fallout shelter, where the walls are covered with so many drawings you can't tell it's a prison anymore. It's so bright and colorful; sexy girls, handsome musclemen, adventure. You start to forget it's not real. You don't realize the world's ended for you. (3.10–11)

On the other hand, since Wally is recalling his adolescent neuroses in this passage, the bitter revisionist may be speaking through him; more likely—if such evaluations have any meaning in a series where mutually exclusive narratives happily coexist—the teenager is imagining the bomber, "dream[ing] about the end of the world" (3.10) and demonstrating the self-destructive impulses that will make him the miniseries' chief antagonist in its final issue. In either case, the panel displays Morrison's knack for using fantastic imagery to dramatize material that normally falls under the province of social or psychological realism, even as he offers a critique of escapism.

Wally's apocalyptic fantasies and destructive urges suggest that *Flex Mentallo* is also a deeply personal story of Morrison's battles with depression. Morrison regularly uses his comics as proxies for his own psychological and emotional struggles; in the course of explaining the many autobiographical elements of *The Invisibles*, he told Alex Ness, "I'm desperately writing biography to celebrate life in this world and to negotiate with depression and meaninglessness." He made similar comments to Daniel Robert Epstein, telling him, "I tend to turn events in my life into the symbolic material that fills the stories. All the autobiographical stuff ends up in the work—if I'm feeling depressed, I'll call the depression something like Primordial Annihilator and send the Justice League in to kick its arse." These comments refer to Morrison's final storyline in *JLA* but they could just as easily describe one *Flex Mentallo* plotline in which a wave of nothingness called "the Absolute" devours a multitude of parallel universes. A Justice League-style team of superheroes called the Legion of Legions escapes the Absolute by creating Wally's world and then entering it as fictional characters who survive in the imaginations of children. The all-consuming annihilation of the Absolute hypostatizes the suicidal impulses of the teen Wally Sage; this depressed sixteen-year-old self survives into the adult Wally, who attempts suicide but also saves himself through the memory of Flex Mentallo, the character he created to embody his own confidence and courage.[8] Wally marshals fictional characters to overcome his depression just as Morrison does, and by rekindling Wally's creativity and hope for the future Morrison reinforces his own.

If *Flex Mentallo* is highly effective as a psychological allegory and a fantasy autobiography, it is less effective at imagining the next stage of the superhero genre—or, perhaps, it is all too effective at imagining a stage that relies on recirculating old concepts rather than creating new ones. In one sense the "first ultra-post-futurist comic" ends exactly where it began, in self-reflexive games. The miniseries opens with nostalgia as Flex reminisces about past adventures (each one summarized with a single panel modeled on DC Comics' surreal Silver Age covers) and asks himself, "What happened to the good old days? The heroes and villains, the team-ups and dream-ups? [...] Maybe it is the end of the world and there's nothing left to do but play with our old toys" (1.12). The final issue is more forward-looking, yet its optimism is founded on a reconciliation with those same old toys, an acceptance of superhero comics' past in all its weird glory; the miniseries does not resolve Flex's initial dilemma so much as recast it in a more positive light. At the end of the world or the end of an exhausted genre cycle, only nostalgia and self-conscious play remain.

The covers of *Flex Mentallo* also suggest that the ultra-post-futurist comics of the self-reflexive era cannot break out of this cycle of nostalgia and recapitulation. Illustrated by Quitely and featuring logos designed by Rian Hughes, the covers, like the issues they envelop, summarize the history of American comics, from a gaudy image bursting with captions to a glossy silhouette that parodies *Dark Knight Returns* (fig. 4-3). Their many paratextual devices poke fun at the commodity culture of superhero comics (Brooker, "Hero" 4): even though Flex is a virtual unknown who has appeared in only a handful of comics, his covers are cluttered with fake awards, autographs, parodies of the Comics Code seal ("Approved by the World Body-Building Association"), simulated stamps from a "Used Adult Magazine Centre," and minuscule type claiming that Grant Morrison and Frank Quitely are themselves registered with the English and Scottish patent offices. Like *Supreme*, *Astro City*, and other nineties retro comics, *Flex Mentallo* invents a false publication history for its protagonist, but unlike those series, it builds that history around Flex's commodity value as much as his changing artistic representations. The first three covers trace American comics' ascent from disposable, disreputable entertainment to commodity fetish, from the detritus discarded in an adult bookstore to the collector's item signed by its creators.

Even the final issue, which looks to the future of superhero comics, is not free of this commodification: the cover multiplies the Flex Mentallo property into an entire franchise (fig. 4-4). Quitely places a collage of Flexes in freefall beneath a palimpsest of logos, presumably taken from different stages in the fictitious history of his nonexistent series; the images of Flex include a cartoonish manga version, a genial, smiling Silver Age hero colored with the Ben-Day dots once used in comic book printing, and a screaming Flex drawn in the angular, crosshatched Image style. Other elements of the collage focus on the registered trademark symbol and a fragment of a UPC barcode; the actual barcode for the issue, and the vertical stripe that brands it as part of the Vertigo imprint, are thrown slightly askew and thus are incorporated into the collage as well. The cover reminds readers that Flex is, has been, and always will be a property owned by DC Comics, no matter what guises he takes. It also suggests that an

Figure 4-3. Cover to *Flex Mentallo* 3. Art by Frank Quitely. © DC Comics.

Figure 4-4. Cover to *Flex Mentallo* 4. Art by Frank Quitely. © DC Comics.

ultra-post-futurist Flex will only be a combination of past interpretations, not a new direction. Nostalgic and self-reflexive superhero comics do not transform the genre, or even contribute new elements to it; they simply reshuffle the old ones. In the end, *Flex Mentallo* may be a better manifesto for rejuvenating the genre than it is an example of such rejuvenation. The comic's innovations lie more in its avant-garde narrative techniques, its fusion of realism and fantasy, and its ambiguous, tolerant sexuality, not in its pronouncements about the future of the genre. Morrison would have to lead by example in his next superhero project.

JLA: FANFARE FOR THE COMMON MAN

JLA (1996–2000) transformed Morrison from a Vertigo writer with a cult following into one of the most successful creators in superhero comics. At the time the series was Morrison's highest-profile work in American comics, giving him access to DC Comics' most popular characters and, through them, to a new audience of superhero readers. *JLA* reunited Superman, Batman, Wonder Woman, Green Lantern, the Flash, Aquaman, and the Martian Manhunter, the original lineup of the Justice League of America, but its focus was not purely retrospective; with Morrison's inventive storylines and Howard Porter's kinetic, hyperactive art, well-suited to readers raised on Marvel and Image comics, the series was poised to appeal to new and old readers alike. Despite its cast of tightly controlled corporate properties and its position at the center of the shared DC Comics continuity, *JLA* attempts to revitalize the superhero genre by aligning it with egalitarian rather than authoritarian politics and pursuing novelty over nostalgia. The end result was a comic that thrived in a direct market dominated by superhero titles even as it challenged the superhero genre to outgrow its past practices.

Although they occupied very different positions in the comics market, *JLA* bears many similarities to *The Invisibles*. The two series were written contemporaneously, ending within a month of each other in March and April of 2000. Each series represents, albeit from slightly different angles, Morrison's efforts at remaking popular genres. Much as *The Invisibles* preserves the core semantics of the superhero genre beneath its spy, science fiction, and conspiracy elements, *JLA* adapts superhero conventions to dramatize concepts far outside the genre's usual concerns. The series filters *The Invisibles'* ideas about linguistic determinism through the archetypes of fantasy and science fiction, including a pair of primitive demons who reshape reality by manipulating symbolic icons (*JLA* 7), angels who view the world as a holy text they can rewrite at will (*JLA* 6), and an android who struggles to achieve free will even though her programmers have omitted the word "freedom" from her vocabulary (*JLA* 5). Both series draw on a common mythology: the JLA battles two different evil stars or "anti-suns," paralleling the eclipsed sun that presides over the finale of "The Invisible Kingdom" and tying into a larger Morrison cosmology that extends back to the sinister Black Sun in *Zenith*. The Flash describes his "speed field" as a world of "Silver, morphing hyper-dimensional gels" (3.6), recalling the magic mirror, and Green Lantern compares an odyssey across space and time to an alien abduction (12.2), echoing Morrison's Kathmandu experience. Jason Tondro has shown how *JLA*'s "Rock of Ages" storyline and volume three of *The Invisibles* both restage Arthurian legends of the quest for the Holy Grail. These stories also build up to apocalyptic events that transpire on December 22, 2012, although *The Invisibles* imagines that eschaton as a mass elevation of consciousness whereas *JLA* depicts a more literal Ragnarok provoked by the tyrant god Darkseid.[9] The JLA and Darkseid battle for possession of the Worlogog, a mystical artifact that reflects all of space and time in a holographic scale model, and it is *JLA*, not *The Invisibles*, that features Morrison's most concise description of holographic structure when Superman explains that "Each fragment of a hologram contains all the information of the whole but on a smaller scale" (10.11). The more accessible and commercially successful *JLA* not only raises many of the same ideas as *The Invisibles*, it provides a useful gloss on its difficult contemporary and on Morrison's work in general.

The series would establish a more contentious relationship with other superhero comics, including its peers and successors in the retro and widescreen movements. *JLA* advertises its break from its contemporaries in the first storyline, which takes aim at the increasingly common plot of superheroes abandoning their reactive posture and taking proactive steps to change the world, even to the point of becoming dictators and using their unmatched power to rule humanity. Coogan observes that this is a characteristic plot of the revisionist era (216) and cites several examples: Moore's *Miracleman* and *Watchmen*, Miller's *Dark Knight Returns*, and Mark Gruenwald and Bob Hall's *Squadron Supreme* (1985–86). This plot also surfaces in the nostalgic *Kingdom Come* before it becomes one of the signal features of *The Authority*. As superhero comics have become more aware of the ideological implications of their "might makes right" philosophy, they have shown increasing attention to these fascistic tendencies, whether to criticize them or arguably, in the case of the later widescreen comics, to indulge in them. Aaron Taylor sees these tendencies in Morrison's *JLA* as well; noting that the trade paperback collecting the first storyline is titled *JLA: New World Order,* he states "the title of the comic takes on an ominous tone" and asks "Will [the JLA's] 'New World Order' emulate the supremacist and interventionist policies of certain government administrations?" (347). The title may offer ample opportunity for such readings but it provides scant evidence to support them, as it was devised specifically for the trade paperback and does not appear anywhere in the storyline's original, periodical publication. *New World Order* is not wholly inappropriate to the stories it collects, however, as Morrison's introductory arc does center on a group of super-beings who propose to reshape the planet with their interventionist policies and who eventually attempt an outright takeover of the world—but these are the antagonists, not the heroes.

The Hyperclan are an advance guard for a Martian invasion force who mask their true mission by posing as superheroes and promising to save the world, whether by greening the Sahara desert or executing supervillains on live television. They serve as philosophical foils for the JLA, demonstrating the dangers of authoritarian superheroics, and the storyline ends with Morrison's unambiguous declaration that the supremacist and interventionist policies of the Hyperclan are neither morally defensible nor terribly effective. Most of the aliens' actions are aimed at dominating the human race, either by manipulation or conquest; their one act of charity turns out to be superficial and transient as the fertilized Sahara reverts to desert by the final issue. The heroes of the JLA seize this failure as an opportunity to disavow the Hyperclan's agenda of proactive intervention in human affairs and to define their own mission by contrast:

> **Superman:** The Hyperclan's garden of Eden, crumbling to dust. They said they would fix the world. It doesn't work that way.
> **Wonder Woman:** Then where does that leave us? Are we doing too much or too little? When does intervention become domination?
> **Superman:** I can only tell you what I believe, Diana: humankind has to be allowed to climb to its own destiny. We can't carry them there. (4.19)

Superman takes the Peter St. John position that humanity must be allowed to develop on its own, free from superhuman interference—superheroes are only there "To catch them if they fall" (4.19). The Hyperclan, on the other hand, are as deceptive and domineering as the Horus program. Like *Zenith* before it, *JLA* redefines the superhero genre's maintenance of the societal status quo as a protection of self-determination and a refusal to interfere with and subjugate weaker peoples; Morrison turns the genre's potential conservatism into a progressive repudiation of the use of force to impose political agendas. His comics place the responsibility for social change on the average citizen, not the superhero.

The finale of the first storyline puts this philosophy into action when the JLA, unable to stop the Martian invasion, can only encourage humanity to save itself. The JLA alerts the world that the Martians are vulnerable to fire and the people of Earth act on this information to subdue the invading force on their own. While Morrison and Porter convey this collective action through the risible shorthand of a crowd igniting matches and cigarette lighters—a scene more suggestive of the encore at a rock concert than a desperate insurgency (4.16)—they nevertheless show humanity taking charge of its own fate, with the superheroes simply acting as guides and guardians. Morrison repeats this plot device again at the end of his tenure on the series, when the JLA turns the entire population of Earth into superhumans to resist destruction by Mageddon, the aforementioned "primordial annihilator" (36.5). The newly empowered human race takes to the skies to rescue Superman and repel Mageddon, briefly reversing the usual formula and showing once again that humanity can assume responsibility for itself (*JLA* 41). Morrison's *JLA* considers the very questions Taylor and other critics of the superhero genre raise, rewriting genre conventions to reconcile them with Morrison's progressive politics. Interventionist superheroes such as the Hyperclan and the Ultramarines (*JLA* 24–26 and *JLA Classified* 1–3) are invariably antagonists, and opportunities to criticize the proactive, tyrannical heroes who would dominate later widescreen comics such as *The Authority*.[10] The one time the JLA attempts to enact a large-scale social change—in the graphic novel *JLA: Earth 2* (2000), where they try to liberate an alternate Earth run by criminals—they discover they can no longer distinguish between their humanitarian intervention and the imposition of a new, unwelcome political system (57), and their mission ends in failure. While Geoff Klock claims that this refusal to exercise their power makes the JLA "conservative" in contrast to the "radical" Authority (137), his comments confuse the maintenance of genre conventions with political conservatism—and overlook the many ways Morrison's *JLA* also insists the superhero genre has to move beyond its past and its traditions.

JLA proves highly critical of nostalgia even though it superficially bears all the trappings of the retro-Silver Age style. Morrison restores the Justice

League's original membership and briefly uses the compartmentalized plot structures established by their first writer, Gardner Fox: in the second issue the team splits into smaller groups to investigate mysterious developments in three remote locales, a Fox staple (Jones and Jacobs 42). The JLA confronts many of the original Justice League's villains—Starro the Conqueror, the White Martians, Professor Ivo and T. O. Morrow, the Demons Three, the Key, the Injustice Gang, Vandal Savage, the Shaggy Man, the Queen Bee, the Crime Syndicate—and Morrison even resurrects devices as minor as the scientific "Flash Facts" that once peppered John Broome's *Flash* comics. The series advertises Morrison's familiarity with and affection for DC's Silver Age, but it never mistakes that affection for nostalgia; in *JLA*, only the antagonists pine for an idealized past. The leader of the Hyperclan reminisces about the days when Martians ruled the Earth, saying "Life was good then. Life will be better" (1.18) as he excavates a buried Martian city. When Morrison reveals that the Hyperclan experimented with terrestrial life, sabotaged humanity's evolutionary future, and view mankind as their property (4.12), he exposes their nostalgia as an adjunct to their ideology of despotism and racial supremacy, nothing more than a desire to regain the power they once abused.

The next story is even more explicit in its problematization of nostalgia. T. O. Morrow and Professor Ivo, two vintage mad scientists, create a sentient android programmed to infiltrate and destroy the JLA. After their plan fails, as they await their inevitable recapture, Ivo pours the last of the Dom Perignon and proposes "the one toast that never goes out of style ... to the good old days!" (5.21). The toast is hardly the first sign of their yearning for the past: Ivo and Morrow have deliberately restaged a classic superhero storyline of betrayal and rebellion, one that Morrow himself first enacted with the android Red Tornado in *Justice League of America* 64–65 (1968).[11] Morrow takes considerable pride in reenacting that story, creating another android who can develop a conscience, defy her instructions, and thwart his plans simply so he can boast of his superior programming skills (5.18, 5.20). He does not care that he has created a sentient being only to watch her destroy herself; the nostalgia of *JLA*'s antagonists is callous and self-centered when it is not downright reactionary. It is also self-defeating, as Morrow's fidelity to his past achievements trumps his desire to destroy the JLA.

While excessive nostalgia is either reactionary or fatalistic, the wholesale rejection of the past is no better; one hero's struggle to shed the burdens of tradition causes him to lose his ethical moorings and drives him to treachery. *DC One Million* (1998), a multi-series crossover conceived and authored by Morrison and centered on the JLA, introduces a new cast of superheroes from the 853rd century who have modeled themselves on the protectors of the late twentieth century. Because publishing imperatives required that these new characters be recognizable to contemporary readers—many of the future heroes took over the starring roles in their predecessors' books for one month—the heroes of the future assume a depressing familiarity. The DC universe of 85,271 looks uncomfortably like the DC universe of 1998, as even the most transient properties like *Chase* and *Young Heroes in Love* have apparently survived eighty-three thousand years into the future despite their cancellation immediately after the end of the crossover. With the future offering nothing more than the replication of the distant past, it is no surprise that one hero should rebel against this monotony. The Starman of the 853rd century betrays his teammates, his ancestors, and his entire society as a means of escaping his hereditary role in a stifling family tradition of heroism that stretches back to the 1940s; in a tie-in issue of *Starman* written by James Robinson, he briefly contemplates killing his ancestor Ted Knight, the first Starman, as punishment for founding his lineage.

The future Starman also rebels against his role as chief computer technician for a society that "organizes itself around the processing of information" (*DCOM* 1.8), trading in ideas rather than goods. Contrary to its initial, utopian presentation, the 853rd century circulates and recirculates concepts with such frictionless ease that ideas themselves have become devalued. Starman confesses, "In the System, nothing meant anything because everything was possible. I sold my soul to Solaris because I couldn't think of anything better to do" (*DCOM* 3.18). Klock attributes this disloyalty to the century's freedom from artistic influence and tradition (133–34), but Starman's other statements and actions indicate he is motivated by the excessive burdens of eighty-three thousand years of influence and the impossibility of living wholly free of tradition. He repents his defection and is moved to perform an authentically heroic act of self-sacrifice after he meets Ted Knight: "In the end, what made me turn was remembering that light in Old Man Knight's eyes. The costume. The heritage. Like it was all still new and meaningful" (*DCOM* 3.18). The burdens of inheritance and the devaluation of recycled ideas drive the future Starman to treason, yet his reconciliation with his family tradition—just one generation past its inception, when it was still novel—redeems him. Morrison furnishes no better example to support Klock's argument that the JLA regularly confronts "Text, overdetermination, and the limits of handling information overload" (132); like so many other characters in *JLA*, the future Starman struggles to find meaning in a narrative tradition menaced by the sheer weight of its own accumulated history.

Other characters try to manage the contradictory benefits and burdens of tradition by striking a balance between novelty and nostalgia, viewing the past with ironic self-consciousness. The Key, a longtime foe who has realized the Justice League will always defeat him, constructs a plot that depends on their ability to escape one of his traps (*JLA* 8–9); aware of his own history, an astute reader of his past failures, he tries to avoid repeating the past instead of re-creating it in loving detail as Morrow does. Klock observes that this plot, which locks the JLA in a series of false narrative continuities vaguely modeled on past phases of their publishing history, also banks on the JLA's ability to recognize they are trapped in fictions—that is, to become at least partially aware of their own fictional status (131–32). In that same story, the new Green Arrow, stripped of his own weapons, is forced to use his father's fanciful trick arrows, ridiculous Golden and Silver Age contrivances like the boomerang arrow and the boxing glove arrow, weapons that did not suit the revisionist era's preference for realistic violence. Initially unable to fire these atavistic oddities with any accuracy, Green Arrow learns to master them and stops the Key by accepting the more ludicrous parts of his father's legacy. He does not fully revert to that tradition, however, nor does he completely shed his embarrassment at his father's designs, and the next story finds him using regular arrows once again. The Key storyline suggests that traditions are important, but best handled with a distancing self-consciousness that can acknowledge the past without reconstructing it uncritically.

Perhaps the most direct expression of Morrison's ambivalent relationship with nostalgia and tradition comes in his first issue when, in order to make way for his restoration of the original membership, he must first wipe the slate clean by hospitalizing the previous Justice League and destroying their satellite headquarters. The most prominent detail mentioned in Morrison's narration, a synecdoche for the loss of the satellite and a metonymy for the abolition of the Justice League it housed, is the explosion of the trophy room and the expulsion of its mementos into the void: "Fantastic debris spills into the darkness; spirit jars, a giant hourglass, deadly playing cards, all the trophies of countless, forgotten adventures, emptied into a well of endless ink" (1.17). Significantly, these trophies commemorate the adventures of the original Justice League of America, such as the giant hourglasses that confined several members on the cover of *Justice League of America* 26 (1964)—adventures that the narration specifies were already "forgotten" even before the explosion scattered them into space. Their fate serves as a wry commentary on the DC Comics of the mid-nineties, which (prior to Morrison's *JLA*) sought to ignore, rewrite, or erase the company's Silver Age traditions in the interests of modernizing their characters and competing with Marvel and Image.[12] Viewed in this context, Morrison's metaphor for the depths of space is equally telling: the trophies vanish into a "well of endless ink," their memories figuratively diluted or blotted out by the same medium (typically India ink) that delineates every shape on the comics page. The comics of the eighties and nineties have already annihilated the Justice League's history; Morrison simply makes the destruction official so he can begin again. His narration expresses a palpable regret at the loss of these stories, yet his plotting positions such losses as a necessary prelude to his own resuscitation of the Justice League and his reintroduction—with an ironic, self-conscious twist—of venerable Silver Age characters and conventions.

Despite its emphasis on action and spectacle, *JLA* is more complex than it first seems, a widescreen comic that rejects the exuberantly authoritarian ideology of later widescreen comics and a retro comic that opens with the destruction of its own past. Highly skeptical of the ideological implications of both of these movements, *JLA* attempts to rejuvenate the superhero genre through self-conscious attention to its traditions, updating some and ignoring or altering others to suit Morrison's politics as well as his aesthetics. Contrary to his revisionist predecessors, his retro peers, and his widescreen successors, Morrison attempts to write a politically progressive superhero comic by prescribing a limited role for superheroes and holding humanity responsible for its own fate. Though its narrative scope and its focus on iconic characters were much imitated, Morrison's *JLA* is not much like its successors—not even Morrison's next projects.

MARVEL BOY AND *FANTASTIC FOUR 1234*: MARVEL NIGHTS

After completing *JLA* and *The Invisibles*, Morrison moved to leading superhero publisher Marvel Comics for a four-year stay. This was not his first time working for Marvel; he had written licensed comics for Marvel UK in the early eighties before breaking into the American company with *Skrull Kill Krew* (1995–96), a miniseries with Mark Millar and Steve Yeowell that tried and generally failed to bring *2000 AD*-style audacity to Marvel. These comics occupied the fringes of the Marvel line, places where Morrison could write with a free hand, and his first projects upon his return were no exception. They were published through Marvel Knights, an imprint owned by Marvel and featuring Marvel characters but contracted through Event Comics, a company founded by artists Joe Quesada and Jimmy Palmiotti.

Figure 4-5. *Marvel Boy* 4.5. Art by J. G. Jones. © Marvel Comics.

Quesada and Palmiotti allowed creators to work in their own idioms rather than follow the Marvel house style, and their imprint "emphasized more sophisticated storytelling than that found in [Marvel's] main line" (Deppey, "X-Men" 46–47). While Marvel Knights did not afford the opportunities for genre diversification that Vertigo did—or permit creators to retain the copyrights to their work—it did allow more leeway than Marvel proper, making the imprint a suitable first stop for Morrison. His Marvel Knights comics are bold by Marvel standards, given to cynical reinterpretations of classic Marvel characters and featuring superheroes who fight to destroy rather than protect the existing social order. Neither feature, however, was all that novel in the wider superhero market of the time, and Morrison's early Marvel projects are fairly conventional representatives of the styles *JLA* so scrupulously critiqued.

Marvel Boy (2000–01), for example, is Morrison's first truly widescreen comic. J. G. Jones illustrates the miniseries with all the elements of the aesthetic: tiers of panels drawn in widescreen aspect ratios, grand spectacle, and slowed, decompressed, lovingly detailed violence (fig. 4-5). Morrison would argue that the miniseries broke from the cinematic style, telling Warren Ellis, widescreen's chief proponent and public face, that he

> began to utilise J. G. Jones' preposterous genius to its best effects and decided to rethink the prevailing vogue for cinematic/money shot panel structures and page layouts. Marvel Boy's visual style becomes more like MTV and adverts; from #3 on it's filled with all kinds of new techniques; rapid cuts, strobed lenticular panels, distressed layouts, 64 panel grids, whatever. We've only started to experiment but already *Marvel Boy* looks like nothing else around. [...] Comics don't need to be like films. (W. Ellis, "Come in Alone")

For all his enthusiasm and his determination to distinguish *Marvel Boy* from the crowd, the comic does not live up to Morrison's hyperbole. While Jones designs many pages around unusual layouts and panel shapes, the experiments are not as extreme as Morrison describes—the miniseries features one two-page, twenty-four-panel grid, for example (4.9–10), but nothing with sixty-four panels—and for the most part the comic conforms to widescreen's cinematic stylings.

It also conforms to the widescreen ideology of social transformation through righteous violence. Ellis himself tended merely to pay lip service to the idea of writing superheroes as agents of change: for all that the protagonists of *The Authority* talk about making the world a better place, they only fight conventionally exotic comic book villains like aliens, extradimensional invaders, and an Asian mastermind who displays all the racist markers of the Yellow Peril caricature. After Ellis was succeeded by Mark Millar, however, the Authority began using their considerable power to depose dictators and intimidate governments. Although Millar justifies their actions with liberal interventionist appeals to the human rights of the refugees they defend, the Authority's brutal interventions are licensed by nothing more than their ability to impose their will on weaker beings. Their pretensions of radical political transformation inevitably boil down to a belief that power is its own justification, no different from the rationales of the dictators they depose. *Marvel Boy*, which began just three months after Millar took over *The Authority*, opens fire on the heart of Western capitalism and democracy rather than the foreign proxies of Millar's series but otherwise takes a similar approach, featuring a protagonist with a self-appointed mission to destroy a society he regards as corrupt and illegitimate. Enraged because a human shot down his ship and murdered his crewmates, the young alien warrior Noh-Varr declares war on planet Earth by destroying the United Nations headquarters and writing an obscene message across the island of Manhattan with the rubble of razed buildings—a joke that presumably seemed more amusing when such large-scale urban destruction was, for Western readers and writers, safely confined to science fiction. While one observer issues the preposterous statement that this rampage leaves "zero fatalities" (2.19), the scale of destruction undercuts Noh-Varr's claims to victimization and virtuous revenge.

He finds more solid ethical footing when he faces his enemies directly, battling hypostatized figures of multinational capitalism and global policing instead of crowds of terrified civilians. Morrison pits the alien warrior against the United Nations Bannermen, cloned super-soldiers who provide "first strike global security" (2.6), and Hexus, the Living Corporation, an interstellar parasite that conquers planets through aggressive marketing campaigns before it exhausts their resources and spreads to find new hosts. If Hexus stands for the groundless postmodern corporation then postmodern capitalism itself enters the conflict in the form of Dr. Midas, a multi-trillionaire who boasts of his ability to co-opt any potential challenge and turn it to his advantage. Morrison has said *Marvel Boy* invokes "the incoming current of Horus, the newly arriving Lord of the Aeon" (W. Ellis, "Come in Alone"), aligning its protagonist with the other young rebels who populate his work. Like these other avatars of Horus, Noh-Varr tears down existing systems to replace them with new ones (Babcock 30), challenging the economic and political dominance of global capitalism at the turn of the millennium.

His foes are not simply ideological embodiments in some geopolitical allegory, however; they are equally significant as modernizations and perversions of the classic heroes of Marvel Comics. The Bannermen are modeled on the World War II-era super-soldier Captain America, with comparable shields and uniforms. They also possess "adamantium lacing" (2.6) similar to that of the mutant Wolverine and they have a "gamma-enhanced function" (2.6) that transforms them into monstrous, brutish beings much like the Hulk, just as their name suggests the Hulk's alter ego, Dr. Bruce Banner. Midas literally cloaks himself in the iconography of Marvel's Silver Age, donning a suit of golden armor similar to one worn by Iron Man early in his career; he also hunts Noh-Varr with a Mindless One, one of a race of extradimensional servitors frequently encountered by Dr. Strange. Midas seeks to re-create the cosmic ray bombardment that created the Fantastic Four, Marvel's first superheroes of the Silver Age; when he succeeds, he receives all of their powers and assumes a rocky appearance much like the Thing. Noh-Varr himself serves as a kind of hyperviolent Spider-Man, an alienated teenager whose powers come from insect DNA (1.18). Settling into a dark, inverted retro style, *Marvel Boy* is highly critical of its publisher's most prominent heroes: Iron Man's capitalist acquisition and the Fantastic Four's scientific innovation are both tools of domination for Midas, while Captain America's patriotic militarism has led to the Bannermen, mindless soldiers whose first-strike capabilities are hired out to government agencies. In battling these characters, Noh-Varr defeats stand-ins for a number of Marvel's Silver Age heroes and Morrison stages his own symbolic critique and conquest of Marvel.

Morrison provides another twist on familiar Marvel icons in *Fantastic Four 1234* (2001), a four-issue miniseries with art by Jae Lee. Languid and moody where *Marvel Boy* is frenzied and violent, *1234* is less agonistic than its predecessor but no less skeptical of its publisher's flagship characters. Instead of engaging in symbolic combat against contemporary analogues for classic Marvel heroes, Morrison flirts with cynical, revisionist interpretations of each member of the Fantastic Four. Johnny Storm, the Human Torch, is callous and combative while Ben Grimm, the Thing, is so depressed over his monstrous condition that he betrays the team to their worst enemy. Team leader Reed Richards, Mr. Fantastic, isolates himself in his laboratory, alienating his wife, Susan Richards, until the self-effacing Invisible Woman is tempted by thoughts of adultery. In the miniseries' ultimate revision, Reed is held responsible for the creation of his archenemy, Victor von Doom, who is nothing more than an externalization and solidification of Reed's dark thoughts and murderous impulses (4.1–3). But Morrison immediately undercuts these readings with the revelations that Doom has built a machine that can manipulate the Fantastic Four like game pieces, altering their emotions and rewriting their histories, and Reed has only been in isolation because he has been busy building a machine of his own to counter Doom's moves (4.4–5). The true revisionist in *1234* is not Grant Morrison; it is Doctor Doom, rewriting continuity with his tawdry narratives of betrayal. Morrison concludes the miniseries by reasserting the decency of the Fantastic Four and reassuring the other team members of the wisdom and love of their patriarch. Despite its sultry atmosphere, *1234* ends as a fairly conventional superhero comic that teases revisionist readings only to reject them.

Marvel Boy similarly turns out to be a conventional widescreen comic despite its anarchistic pretensions. Noh-Varr might battle the forces that seek to globalize the industrialized nations' economic and military hegemony, but he himself intends to remake the Earth in the image of his homeworld and to promote the ways of his people, a creed that Morrison, borrowing a phrase from the Dead Kennedys' "California Über Alles," translates as "Zen fascism" (6.21). Noh-Varr is every bit as arrogant, aggressive, and imperialist as the enemies he battles. Like Millar's *Authority*, *Marvel Boy* affects a vaguely leftist critique of Western society even as it indulges in power fantasies about remaking that society through the righteous violence of an autocratic strongman. *Marvel Boy* and *Fantastic Four 1234* are more typical examples of millennial comics than they first appear, notable primarily for allowing Morrison to experiment with and tarnish Marvel properties. These fringe projects conform to the prevailing standards of their market; ironically, Morrison's Marvel work would not become truly revolutionary until he took over the company's premier franchise with *New X-Men*.

NEW X-MEN: SURVIVAL OF THE FITTEST

Before the fifth issue of *Marvel Boy* saw print, Marvel Comics underwent two major leadership changes that would have a profound impact on Morrison's work for the company. In January 2000, Marvel's new owner, Ike Perlmutter, appointed Bill Jemas as president of publishing and new media (Raviv 265–67). In September of that year, Jemas fired Marvel Comics editor-in-chief Bob Harras and hired Joe Quesada to replace him. With Quesada now overseeing the entire Marvel Comics line, and with Jemas determined to attract new readers (Raviv 266), the company became more receptive to the kind of experimentation that previously had been confined to Marvel Knights. As one of their highest-profile experiments, Jemas and Quesada hired Morrison to revamp the X-Men. *New X-Men* (2001–04) continues Morrison's ongoing project to challenge and rewrite superhero conventions, but in a more humane context than the violent destruction of *Marvel Boy* or the faux revisionism of *1234*. *New X-Men* seeks to resuscitate the franchise by distilling the X-Men down to their essential elements and treating those elements more seriously than most previous writers had; Morrison's revolutionary idea is to take Marvel's mutant heroes at face value.

In his initial proposal for *New X-Men*, published in collected editions as the "Morrison Manifesto," Morrison laments the stagnation of nineties superhero comics in general and the X-Men franchise in particular: "In the last decade or so, the tendency at Marvel has been intensely conservative; comics like the *X-Men* have gone from freewheeling, overdriven pop to cautious, dodgy retro. What was dynamic becomes static—dead characters always return, nothing that happens really matters ultimately. The stage is never cleared for new creations to develop and grow. The comic has turned inwards and gone septic like a toenail" (item 2). His solution is to take the X-Men into the future by looking back to their past. The "Manifesto" praises Chris Claremont and John Byrne, whose collaboration on *Uncanny X-Men* (1977–81) built the comic into Marvel's leading franchise but also set the parameters that would define and limit X-Men comics for more than two decades. Morrison exalts their work because "they had the freedom to create new material, reconceptualise the old stuff which still worked and ignore the outmoded elements which had sapped the original *X-Men* series of its vitality" ("Manifesto" item 1). Tasked with simultaneously recapturing their old magic and breaking the grip of nostalgia, Morrison proposes to treat Claremont, Byrne, and their successors as they treated the original Stan Lee and Jack Kirby X-Men: keep what works, ignore the rest, and add new pieces until the comic is vital once again.

New X-Men is therefore poised between its fidelity to classic X-Men comics and its need to attract new readers. Morrison preserves the core syntax of the post-Claremont X-Men comics, their treatment of mutants as both a persecuted minority and as *Homo sapiens superior*, the evolutionary future of the human race. However, he recasts the semantics to downplay the superhero elements, aligning them instead with the science fiction approach of the Bryan Singer *X-Men* film adaptation. Frank Quitely, the first of many artistic collaborators on *New X-Men*, replaces the team's traditional spandex superhero costumes with leather uniforms similar to those worn in the film, while Morrison pares down the unwieldy cast to a mere half-dozen mutants. The series largely ignores the perplexing intricacies of "the most convoluted continuity in comics" ("Manifesto" item 4) and advertises a dramatic break from the past: *New X-Men* sports a new title (the comic was previously known as *X-Men*) and a sleek, symmetrical logo, and Quitely's covers resemble fashion magazines rather than other superhero comics (Klock 174). Even the title of the first storyline, "E is for Extinction" (*New X-Men* 114–116), offers a subtle but scathing correction to the previous decade's X-Men crossovers, which did hideous violence to the English language in the interest of maintaining the "X" brand; "E is for Extinction" promises there will be no more titles like "X-Tinction Agenda" (1990) or "X-Cutioner's Song" (1992–93).

In a break from forty years of Marvel tradition, Morrison insists that the X-Men are not and have never truly been superheroes. A conversation from his first issue, prompted by the new team uniforms, makes the case:

> **Hank McCoy:** I was never sure why you had us dress up like super heroes anyway, Professor.
> **Scott Summers:** The Professor thought people would trust the X-Men if we looked like something they understood. (114.14)

Scott describes the X-Men's superhero guises as a form of social camouflage, one their mentor, Professor Xavier, believes they can now discard in the interest of advancing the acceptance of mutants. In reality the situation is exactly the opposite, with Morrison providing generic camouflage for a successful but stale superhero franchise to lend it an air of novelty. This infusion of elements from other genres builds on the "Morrison Manifesto," where he argues for redefining the X-Men as science fiction:

> The movie wisely went sci-fi instead of trying to appease the superhero crowd and I think we must do the same. The *X-Men* is not a story about super heroes but a story about the ongoing evolutionary struggle between good/new and bad/old. The X-Men are every rebel teenager wanting to change the world and make it better. Humanity is every adult, clinging to the past, trying to destroy the future even as he places all his hopes there. The super-hero aspect should be seen as only a small element in the vast potential of this franchise. (item 4)

Figure 4-6. *New X-Men* 114.1. Art by Frank Quitely. © Marvel Comics.

Figure 4-7. *New X-Men* 114.22. Art by Frank Quitely. © Marvel Comics.

While "good/new" and "bad/old" fall far short of Morrison's usual distrust of binaries—the comic itself would be considerably more nuanced—the manifesto shrewdly casts *New X-Men* as a story of both genetic and generic evolution. The X-Men struggle for survival but they also struggle to grow out of their own creative stagnation, with most of the franchise and genre conventions standing firmly on the side of stasis and extinction. The opening page of Morrison's run shows Scott Summers and Wolverine thoroughly demolishing an aging Sentinel robot, as they have done countless times before, with Scott telling his teammate "You can probably stop doing that now" (fig. 4-6). The page becomes a typically synecdochic or holographic double-entendre conveying Morrison's sense that the X-Men need to break out of their patterns of convention and habit if they are to grow into something new.

As the ailing Sentinel's misfortunes should indicate, the X-Men's foes are also in dire need of evolution and change. In that same issue Cassandra Nova, the antagonist in Morrison's first storyline, mentions that the mutant-hunting Sentinels have always been "spectacularly ineffective against highly adaptive *Homo superior* targets" (114.12)—as they must be, since the X-Men must always defeat them to keep their franchise alive. Nova restores the robots' menace by introducing a new generation of "wild Sentinels" who use spare machine parts "to evolve themselves into more effective forms" (114.20). This new capability balances the X-Men's natural evolutionary advantage, making the wild Sentinels more varied, adaptive, and animalistic.

Significantly, the first wild Sentinels seen in *New X-Men* are small, fast pack hunters who resemble mechanical velociraptors, recalling another recent transformation in the image of a popular movie monster (fig. 4-7). In *The Last Dinosaur Book*, W. J. T. Mitchell interprets the climax of Steven Spielberg's *Jurassic Park*, with its confrontation between a single *Tyrannosaurus rex* and a pack of velociraptors, as a combat between dinosaurs who symbolize two different eras of capital accumulation, the "corporate giantism" of industrial capitalism and the downsized "flexible accumulation" of postmodern capitalism (103n15.1). Modernist and postmodernist forms of capitalism may clash in *Jurassic Park*, but the old order simply yields to the new in *New X-Men* as the wild Sentinels displace their failed predecessors. They share the raptors' "flexibility, rapid strike forces, teamwork, adaptability, steep learning curves," and perhaps even their "gender confusion" (Mitchell 182) since they are led by Cassandra Nova, a being of uncertain genetic provenance who appears to be female yet looks exactly like Charles Xavier. The shift from titanic, static Sentinel robots to swift, adaptive wild Sentinels re-creates Spielberg's transition from *T. rex* to *Velociraptor*, updating the decrepit Sentinels for the postmodern age even as the saurian allusion reminds readers of the threat of extinction and evolutionary failure. In the plummeting comic book market of the early years of the twenty-first century, Morrison sees generic mutation, adaptation, and fusion as the only ways the X-Men, their enemies, and the superhero genre as a whole can survive.

MUTATION AND DIFFERENCE

Because the X-Men are persecuted for their mutant abilities, they have long been read as a free-floating metaphor for any minority group. Chris Claremont, who brought themes of persecution to the forefront during his tenure as writer, has stated that the story of the X-Men "is about racism, bigotry, and prejudice.... It's a book about outsiders, which is something that any teenager can identify with. It is a story about downtrodden, repressed people fighting to change their situation, which I think anybody can empathize with" (qtd. in Jones and Jacobs 251). Richard Reynolds comments, with less certainty, that "the whole theme of the X-Men [...] can be read as a parable of the alienation of any minority" and notes that "gay readings of the mutant subtext have been fairly common" (79); Cheryl Alexander Malcolm reads mutants as "a metaphor for Jews" (144); and Neil Shyminsky collects many similar interpretations from creators, fans, and critics (387). Just because these readings enjoy wide circulation does not, however, mean they are wholly accurate or unproblematic. Reynolds implies they interpret the comics too narrowly (79), while Shyminsky castigates readers and creators who use the mutant metaphor to equate the tribulations of straight, white, male comics fans with the experiences of groups that face systematic oppression (387–89)—as, for example, Claremont's quote conflates the institutionalized outsider status of "downtrodden, repressed" minority groups with the more provisional outsider status of teenagers, many of whom do not belong to any oppressed minority. Shyminsky contends that the mutant metaphor allows the X-Men's predominantly straight, white, male readership to identify with racial or sexual others—not such a bad thing, except insofar as it displaces these others in favor of predominantly straight, white, male mutants and obscures the benefits of the racial and gender privileges they and their readers enjoy. Readings that position the X-Men as an oppressed minority, and especially those that equate systematic discrimination with temporary social ostracism, may efface or even naturalize authentic experiences of oppression.

Morrison inherited this dilemma when he signed on to write the X-Men. His solution is to embrace the minority interpretation, but also to take it more literally and carry it further than any predecessor had done. Rather than confine the association to metaphor, Morrison writes mutants as a diverse and thriving minority group whose experiences of persecution and resistance are not limited to being hunted by giant robots. They have established their own mutant culture, with mutant bands, mutant fashions, mutant icons, even, like so many real minority groups before them, mutant neighborhoods: the Alphabet City section of New York's East Village has become "Mutant Town" (*New X-Men* 127), the site of tenements and riots but also home to the city's most stylish clubs and boutiques. Mutants have attracted enough countercultural chic to generate their own fans, imitators, and appropriators from the dominant culture, creating new challenges to the maintenance of mutant identity. Unlike past treatments that offered a crude, poorly conceived metaphor for civil rights-era racial politics, Morrison uses mutancy as a vehicle for talking about the contradictions and transformations of minority identity in the new millennium. *New X-Men* both literalizes the minority metaphor and updates it for the post-civil rights era.

These mutants live in an age when they are as celebrated as they are reviled for their difference, although the old dangers still persist, sometimes arising from the people who are most attracted to their culture. In one of Morrison's most acerbic statements on contemporary Western society's hypocritical fear of minorities and embrace of minority cultures, a group of young men who are guilty of at least one antimutant hate crime discuss how much they enjoy listening to mutant bands (135.11). Earlier in the series, a teenager shoots a mutant classmate even though he idolizes mutants and wears a T-shirt of Magneto, the radical mutant separatist (118.1–3). Shyminsky interprets this scene as a critique of the X-Men comics' longstanding equivalence between mutants, minority groups, and socially awkward comics fans (400–1), as the shooter is a self-proclaimed geek who wants to steal his classmate's organs and become a mutant himself. He takes his inspiration from John Sublime, a self-help guru who has founded a "third species" of people "who have decided to transcend their species orientation" (*Annual 2001* p.8). This third species, the "U-Men," are humans who seek to release their inner mutant through organ transplants and body modification; Shyminsky interprets them as another criticism of the dominant culture's appropriation of and identification with minority identity. If so, they offer an appallingly literal, biological trope for the dangers of co-optation as they harvest mutant organs from unwilling donors, taking not only their identity and subcultural allure but also their very bodies.

Although Morrison's mutants face new threats of appropriation, the old antimutant prejudice is still alive and well in *New X-Men*, ranging from fantastically horrific acts of genocide to depressingly mundane displays of ignorance. When humans openly express their fear and hatred of mutants, Morrison links their sentiments to contemporary expressions of bigotry. The antimutant protesters who gather outside the Xavier Institute brandish a cross that declares "God hates mutants" (117.5), an allusion to Westboro Baptist Church pastor Fred Phelps's slogan "God hates fags," while a confrontational television reporter asks loaded questions that betray both antimutant bias and other forms of xenophobia, such as his demand to know how many illegal immigrants the school is hiding (118.11). Other bigots, however, are not so easy to spot, and the more sophisticated antagonists target mutants for exploitation or extermination while paying lip service to diversity. In a meeting with two of the X-Men, John Sublime demonstrates most of the tactics that contemporary racists have developed for deflecting charges of racism: he accuses the X-Men of being elitists, claims they are persecuting him, and even accuses them of bigotry, all while declaring his philosophy is about "empowering the different, celebrating the strange" (118.19). Morrison reveals how racist and xenophobic ideologies have adapted to survive despite contemporary Western society's outward observance of the virtues of multiculturalism and tolerance.

Sublime can be read both as a racist projecting his bigotry and his sense of entitlement onto his mutant targets and as an appropriator seeking to steal the qualities that make mutants different—readings that are hardly inconsistent with each other. There is, however, a third, far more disturbing interpretation: that he and his U-Men are also a clear and troubling allegory for transgendered people. Sublime describes the typical U-Man as "a mutant soul born in a frail, powerless human body" (*Annual 2001* p.8), recalling popular descriptions of transgender-identified people as "a man trapped in a woman's body" or vice versa. Similarly, his "third species" appellation evokes attempts to define a third gender outside conventional masculinity and femininity, and his reference to "species orientation" implies that modern medical techniques have transformed the concept of species from a biological classification into a psychological, social, and behavioral one akin to gender identity. What makes these analogies so troubling, of course, is that Morrison also writes the U-Men as murderous poseurs who seek to steal another group's authentic and biologically ordained difference. Not only are they killers, they are not who and what they claim to be.

As much as Morrison's language invites this interpretation, the series also indicates that we shouldn't read the characters too narrowly as metaphoric stand-ins for any real-world groups. To be sure, one X-Man seeks to draw exactly this sort of analogy between mutants and gays, making the case for the X-Men's longstanding gay subtext within the text of the comic. After Hank McCoy inadvertently and inaccurately outs himself as gay, he tells Scott, "I've been taunted all my life for my individualistic looks and style of dress . . . I've been hounded and called names in the street and I've risen above it [. . .] I'm as gay as the next mutant!" (134.11). Contrary to his public statements, however, he's not actually gay; he claims he's maintaining the lie "to challenge preconceived notions about language, gender and species" (131.8). Morrison would offer a similar defense of Hank's storyline, telling Arune Singh, "I was trying to talk about the fact that being gay is just a label. Like 'being' black. [O]r 'being' British. Or 'being' a fan of Madonna." While Morrison generally regards identity as being mutable and self-determined, he forgets that, for most people, racial and sexual identity are neither as elective nor as trivial as tastes in pop music. Fortunately, *New X-Men* offers a more complex portrait of minority identity. Hank admits his gender performance began as a cruel joke calculated to hurt an ex-girlfriend (134.11), undercutting his claims to serve as a role model for gays and suggesting readers shouldn't take his analogy too far. Pursue any of these metaphors long enough and they will all lead to implications just as troubling as the

U-Men's apparent slander of transgendered people; one hopes that no writer working for Marvel Comics would suggest that gays are genetic aberrations or that racial minorities belong to a separate subspecies, yet the X-Men are both. Setting aside Hank's fatuous rationale for his deception, Morrison generally does not write his characters as metaphors, allegories, or any other figurative representations of existing groups. He prefers to treat mutants as a distinct minority, completely real within the fantastic boundaries of their own comic. The U-Men occupy a role within that comic as appropriators of the X-Men's difference, not as a sinister allegory for gender difference in our own world.

Morrison also avoids the common practice of casting the X-Men in a dubious allegory for the civil rights movement in which Professor Xavier stands for Martin Luther King Jr. and Magneto for Malcolm X. While such allegories have been a popular means for some fans and creators to lend the X-Men franchise a borrowed gravitas (see, for example, Skir 21–23), they ignore the substantial differences between these characters and the more complex, far less antithetical civil rights leaders. Malcolm X, after all, did not attack military bases or take over small countries and King did not hide his minority identity (Shyminsky 390), nor did he lead a team of commandos whose primary mission was foiling Malcolm X's dreams of conquest. Morrison wisely forgoes such absurd comparisons as he delineates the internal conflicts within the mutant community over different approaches to liberation politics and equal rights. Rather than invest any one of these approaches with absolute moral authority, Morrison critiques integrationist strategies along with the separatist and supremacist philosophies that have traditionally been the province of the X-Men's enemies.

New X-Men initially holds out the possibility that Professor Xavier has already achieved his dream of mutant integration, that mutants are about to enter their own post-civil rights era. At the beginning of Morrison's second year on the series, mutants and mutant culture are more visible than ever, but it is too early to celebrate a postracial utopia of tolerance and diversity. Subsequent developments will show this progress sabotaged by human and mutant alike; worse, they will suggest that Xavier has always been too slow, too cautious, and perhaps too naïve about humanity's interest in coexisting with mutants. His archrival Magneto and his star pupil Quentin Quire both tell him repeatedly that he has failed to achieve his dream. Even his most loyal student, Scott Summers, is forced to concede that humans will always be at war with mutants after he uncovers a human genocide program (145.14). Ironically, the Professor's greatest achievements during Morrison's run—outing himself as a mutant, raising mutants' public profile, and opening a chain of mutant refuges around the world—are accomplished while Cassandra Nova assumes his identity; Xavier himself admits that Nova took the steps he was afraid to take (128.7–8). If Nova was, as Xavier now believes, simply "an agent of nature, testing its own boundaries, forcing change into stalemated systems" (128.8), then his hypercautious, closeted approach to mutant rights was part of that stalemate.

Perhaps the greatest blow to Xavier's confidence is the apostasy of his student Quentin Quire in the "Riot at Xavier's" storyline (*New X-Men* 134–138). By all rights, Quentin should be the ideal hero-in-training: his gangly, bespectacled appearance, his alliterative name, even his hopelessly unfashionable sleeveless sweater all recall Peter Parker, Spider-Man's bookish alter ego and the classic example of the Marvel superhero as adolescent outsider. Instead, Quentin rejects Xavier's philosophy and changes from the traditional Marvel outsider hero to the more unstable Morrison rebel youth. He even inscribes a deranged slogan ("CRAZY NOW") across his forehead (134.18–19), signaling that he has become Morrison's latest neurotic boy outsider. His first act as the new Quentin Quire is to humiliate Slick, a charismatic mutant classmate, by exposing his true, grotesque appearance; although the humiliation is largely motivated by Quentin's envy and self-loathing, it also takes on political overtones. Slick pretends to be socially conscious, expressing his outrage over the apparent murder of mutant fashion designer Jumbo Carnation by composing a maudlin protest song: "*When will the suffering reach its end? / Can man and mutant meet as friends?*" (134.15). The mawkish lyrics advertise Slick's fawning dedication to Xavier's integrationist dream, but as Quentin points out, the song is an empty gesture that cannot benefit Jumbo Carnation or bring his killers to justice (134.15).

The humiliation of Slick marks Quentin's first break from Xavier's politics. Although he initially justifies his actions by claiming he was defending "the ethos of the Institute" (134.18), Quentin quickly shifts to attacking Xavier himself: "I think all that seems to matter to you now is being on television and telling everyone how wonderful your brave new world is. Well, I live in the brave new world and it's not as shiny and perfect as you'd like to think. You're always selling this future that never arrives, you preach Utopia but you never deliver on this 'dream' we keep hearing about" (134.19). Quentin's lecture betrays his precocious arrogance, his impatience, and his apparently willful ignorance of the steps Xavier is taking to enact that dream. (As the "Riot at Xavier's" story begins, the school is planning to admit its first nonmutant students.) That said, he also has a point—even after the drastic changes initiated by Morrison, Xavier is scarcely closer to achieving his goals than he was when the first issue of *The X-Men* was published in 1963. Morrison has taken the narrative constraints faced by any never-ending, corporate-owned serial—the impossibility of establishing any permanent change to the status quo or bringing the series to a definitive ending—and turned them into indictments of the protagonists' failures to change their society. He does so not to score cheap points against the characters but to generate dramatic tension as the X-Men struggle against this seemingly immutable law of ongoing superhero comics.

Quentin, frustrated by this lack of progress, will resort to the extreme steps of mutant supremacism, antihuman vigilantism, and open rebellion against Xavier, carrying the "good/new" and "bad/old" binarism of the "Morrison Manifesto" to its ultimate, destructive conclusion. However, he is hardly the only mutant to challenge Xavier's dream of peaceful integration. Mutant culture as a whole is turning confrontational—with some justice after the extermination of the mutant nation of Genosha, but also with disastrous consequences. Magneto has become an icon to young mutants, and Jumbo Carnation designs fashions "based on what humans thought we might wear when they were most scared of us" (135.9). Other mutant artists seem equally determined to live down to human culture's worst fears about them. One popular band names itself "Juggernaut" after an infamous mutant criminal; another calls itself "The Coming Race," a reference to the eponymous 1871 Edward Bulwer-Lytton novel about a subterranean Aryan master race. A creepy racialist undercurrent has begun to settle into mutant society: Carnation calls his attackers "big, primitive humans" (134.1) prior to their confrontation, and Quentin and his followers refer to humans as apes and monkeys (135.12)—terms with long histories as racialized insults, indicating that these mutants are just as bigoted as their xenophobic human counterparts.

The cultural nationalism of Quentin Quire and Magneto follows the logic of other protest movements that, by displacing all moral culpability onto their enemies, replicate the prejudice and bigotry they ostensibly challenge. Julia Kristeva exposes the origins and contradictions of this logic in her essay "Women's Time"; while she writes specifically about the more radical elements of second-wave feminism, her comments apply just as well to other separatist movements, including Quentin's:

> As with any society, the counter-society is based on the expulsion of an excluded element, a scapegoat charged with the evil of which the

> community duly constituted can then purge itself; a purge which will finally exonerate that community of any future criticism. Modern protest movements have often reiterated this logic, locating the guilty one—in order to fend off criticism—in the foreign, in capital alone, in the other religion, in the other sex. Does not feminism become a kind of inverted sexism when this logic is followed to its conclusion? (202)

When Quentin Quire assumes all humans are murderers (135.8) as a means of licensing his own genetic condescension, his protest politics become a kind of inverted racism (or, simply, racism). However, his attempt to overthrow Xavier, seize the school, and declare "Year Zero for mutantkind" (136.22) is futile, doomed, suicidal—in short, every bit as theatrical and ineffective as the protest song he mocked a few issues earlier, although his riot does result in the deaths of three students.[13] Magneto, on the other hand, has the power to carry these beliefs to their ultimate conclusion after he nearly destroys the X-Men and conquers the island of Manhattan. With no apparent sense of irony or shame, the Nazi concentration camp survivor sends captive humans to die in crematoria. Magneto's attempts to protect mutants from eliminationist humans have led to an inverted eliminationism, an inverted Nazism.

Xavier's integrationism and Magneto's separatism and cultural nationalism both fail in *New X-Men*. The series calls for a third strategy of mutant liberation politics but never suggests what shape it might take, although Morrison does lay some of the groundwork for it—and gesture towards the foundation of other "third waves" for real-world equality movements—when he identifies the faulty assumptions that have undermined earlier strategies. Quentin, his telepathy boosted to unsustainable levels through abuse of the drug Kick, briefly touches the minds of everyone on the planet and reaches an epiphany:

> **Quentin:** I hear thoughts in Chinese ... and French ... and Arabic ... but ... it's everyone thinking the same stupid thought ... just one thought divided into ignorant boxes ... jabbering so hard it can't hear itself thinking [...] everyone scared of their replacements ... scared of their children ... scared of themselves ...
> **Xavier:** Like a hand scared of its fingers. (138.10–11)

Quentin and Xavier describe what *The Invisibles* called the existential alienation dilemma, a profound sense of isolation that results from our self-image as autonomous individuals and our inability to perceive the commonalities that unite us. *New X-Men* regards this alienation as the ultimate source of social division and prejudice. With his dying words, Quentin suggests he and Xavier were both wrong to blame humans for their problems, asking, "What if the real enemy ... was inside ... all along?" (13), not in human bigots or mutant terrorists but in each person's fear of the young, the foreign, the new, the other, the self.[14] In his last moments, he realizes he has been his own worst enemy. Quentin, like Kristeva, recognizes that evil and guilt can never be transferred wholly onto the enemy scapegoat, that they persist even (or especially) in those who seek to purify their communities. No one enjoys absolute, uncontested moral superiority in *New X-Men*, and Morrison suggests that any successful contemporary equality movement must begin with this realization.

THE TERROR OF THE IDEAL

The real enemies in *New X-Men* are inevitably internal, psychological, or ideal. When the Stepford Cuckoos, a quintet of female students loyal to Xavier, tell Quentin that his rebellion is not a Romantic struggle between anarchy and authority or youth and experience, but simply a battle of "in" versus "out" (137.20), they not only diagnose his need for peer-group acceptance, they also identify the series' recurring interest in exploring the differences between characters' external, social identities and their private selves. Misfit mutants like Beak and Angel Salvador display surprising courage and heroism; Emma Frost cultivates an aura of superficiality to mask a history of tragedy; Hank McCoy invents a gay identity to ease the sting of a failed relationship; Wolverine attempts to recover a forgotten past and supply a missing interiority; Scott Summers and Jean Grey both repress their passions until their marriage collapses; Scott and Emma conduct a telepathic affair that is no less a betrayal for being purely mental; and Xorn, the X-Men's newest member, is actually Magneto, their greatest rival. These are, for the most part, the heroes of *New X-Men*, and when they err, they err in forgetting that ideas, fantasies, or façades can be just as consequential as physical actions. The villains are those who acknowledge no difference between interior and exterior because they project their psyches onto the outside world, reimagining it to conform to their most selfish or hateful impulses.

Weapon XV, the latest generation of mutant-killing super-soldier, could almost be a Morrison protagonist. Born and raised inside an "experimental micro-reality" called The World (143.9), he spends his whole life struggling to see beyond the boundaries of his artificial home. When he bursts through the shell of The World and into the night sky he could be a Gnostic hero shattering his material prison, a Platonist Superman abandoning his cave for a new world of freedom, power, and limitless potential. But Morrison remains suspicious of these idealist doctrines, and so Weapon XV carries his illusions out with him. Having discovered that his World is artificial, he assumes that everything and everyone else is equally unreal (144.12), reserving consciousness and agency only for himself—other beings are simply puzzles to be solved, obstacles to his own growth (144.14–15). Weapon XV quickly reverts to his conditioning, accepting his role as a mutant hunter and his place in the Weapon Plus program's satellite headquarters, another self-contained environment he accurately describes as "a second World" (145.5). His inability to shed his solipsism as easily as he shatters the walls of his material prison leads to his willing confinement in a second, larger prison.

The most terrifying example of this lethal solipsism is Cassandra Nova, the architect of the genocide in Genosha. Nova is first presented as the evolutionary successor to the mutant race, and then as Xavier's unborn twin sister, but the truth is much stranger: she is a *mummudrai*, an alien name for Xavier's antithesis or, in Jungian terms, some combination of his shadow-self and his anima. Jean Grey explains, "Think of it like 'out' is the *mummudrai* of 'in.' 'Yin' is the *mummudrai* of 'yang.' And Cassandra Nova is the *mummudrai* of Charles Xavier. Legend says each of us faces our own personal *mummudrai* in the womb, shortly before birth—it is our first experience of the alien, the 'other,' the different" (126.13). A *mummudrai* is supposed to be bodiless, but because Xavier was, even *in utero*, the world's greatest psychic, this psychological complex has taken physical form, using Xavier's genome to build a mutant body of incomparable power. Her identity and world-view are wholly dependent on Xavier, however, since she is "living emotional energy. [. . .] In Cassandra's mind, our universe and the womb she became aware in are one and the same thing . . . only she and Charles are real" (122.14). She regards the X-Men as antibodies Xavier has created to protect himself from her, and the mutant race as a pestilence to be exterminated in her cosmic game of sibling rivalry. As with Weapon XV, solipsism licenses her attempts at genocide since she does not believe any of her victims are truly alive. An idea given concrete form herself, Nova mistakes her own egocentric ideas for reality.

A seemingly unrelated conversation in the issue immediately following Nova's defeat points out the dangers of this hypostatic confusion of the imaginary and the real, connecting Morrison's preferred figurative technique to the series' themes of the fear of the other. Xavier, attempting to describe the origins of humanity's antimutant prejudice to Xorn, offers this charitable explanation: "A shared ideal is one of the best ways to hold a tribe together in the face of chaos. But now the tribes are all sharing the same tent, and we can all be guilty sometimes of mistaking our ideals for things. Sometimes the idea of the monster is more real than the monster itself" (127.5). Xavier unwittingly sums up Cassandra Nova, clarifying her role in the previous storyline as an idea that has taken physical form, but more importantly, he indicates why such embodiments matter outside the plot machinations of any given X-Men comic book. Nova is not simply a monster created through the reification of an abstract concept; the reification of the abstract is itself monstrous in *New X-Men*, generating hatred and xenophobia as humans and mutants alike project their beliefs and fears onto the other. A few issues later, Morrison drives the point home by providing another, all-too-real example of the potentially disastrous consequences of the reification of the ideal. After Xavier foils an attempted terrorist attack by telepathically forcing a group of hijackers to abandon their ideology, he promises that none of them "will ever again use violence in the service of abstract ideas" (133.10). With its overt evocation of the al-Qaeda attacks of September 11, 2001, the scene offers a grim reminder that monstrous reifications and deadly ideas are not just the province of science fiction.[15]

Whatever their methodology, whatever their cause, however real or fictitious they may be, all of the X-Men's antagonists commit violence in the service of abstract ideas. Morrison provides no greater example of the dangers of reification than Magneto. After his apparent death in Cassandra Nova's Sentinel attack (*New X-Men* 115), Magneto's image begins appearing on T-shirts and posters, many of which bear the slogan "MAGNETO WAS RIGHT" (*New X-Men* 118, 135). A group of followers build a monument to him, and his estranged son says that his "greatest trick is to be more dangerous dead than he ever was alive" (132.9). This new status as a posthumous icon, a posthuman Che Guevara, leads young mutants like Quentin Quire astray, but it also proves dangerous to Magneto himself, who returns only to discover that he has become dwarfed by his own reputation. Crowds of adoring mutants fail to recognize him (147.9, 150.21, 150.25) and he quickly loses control of followers who are more more attracted to the icon than the man. Xavier forces him to acknowledge that his image has taken on a life of its own: "Magneto had become a legend in death, an inspiration for change. Now look at you—just another foolish and self-important old man, with outdated thoughts in his head. You have nothing this new generation of mutants wants ... except for your face on a t-shirt" (150.26). After his plans fail, Magneto chooses the martyrdom he had previously feigned, provoking Wolverine into killing him and leaving the X-Men with the words, "Give me death. Make me immortal" (150.27). Unable to shoulder the responsibilities of leading the mutants attracted by his image as the perfect mutant rebel, Magneto takes the easy way out and becomes that image once again. Only an icon, or a martyr, can no longer disappoint his disciples.

SHADOWPLAY

The reification of his carefully fabricated image is only one of the forces that condemn Magneto to death; he is just as doomed by the expectations, conventions, and stock plots of forty years of X-Men comics. He spends much of Morrison's run executing an ingenious plan to infiltrate the Xavier Institute as Xorn, convert the most vulnerable students to his ideology, and ambush the X-Men. At his moment of victory, however, when he has defeated the X-Men, destroyed the Institute, and taken over the island of Manhattan, he becomes trapped by the contradictory expectations of his followers, who want him to build a workable society yet refuse to listen to him unless he performs the supervillain role they know from the media. When one acolyte tells Magneto that his followers "want you the way you used to be" (147.12), she could just as easily be speaking about readers who demand fidelity to past interpretations of the character. Both audiences demand that he play a character incapable of running the mutant society he has dedicated his life's work to establishing. Rather than create something new, Magneto surrenders to his followers' expectations and reverts to standard supervillain form, wasting his efforts on attempts to exterminate humans and a senseless plan to reverse the Earth's magnetic poles. His decision to embrace the supervillain cliché leads to an equally clichéd death; as Morrison told Jonathan Ellis, "The 'Planet X' story was partially intended as a comment on the exhausted, circular nature of the X-Men's ever-popular battle with Magneto and by extension, the equally cyclical nature of superhero franchise re-inventions. I ended the book exactly where I came on board, with Logan killing Magneto AGAIN, as he had done at the end of [Morrison's immediate predecessor] Scott Lobdell's run" (Part 4). Morrison presents the inevitable recourse to X-Men convention as repetitive, confining, and ultimately fatal.

Magneto is not the only character imprisoned by the circular narratives of the never-ending superhero franchise. Although Morrison expands the

X-Men universe with a wealth of new characters and plot developments (Cassandra Nova, the wild Sentinels, Sublime, the U-Men, Fantomex, Weapon Plus, a host of new students at the Xavier Institute, redesigns of Hank McCoy and Emma Frost, the end of Scott and Jean's marriage, and the beginning of Scott's relationship with Emma), he still pits the X-Men against traditional enemies like the Sentinels, the Imperial Guard, and Magneto. He also re-creates classic storylines such as Jean Grey's death and rebirth as the Phoenix (first told in *Uncanny X-Men* 100–101) or the flashforward to the dystopian future of "Days of Future Past" (*Uncanny X-Men* 141–142). Morrison places his own distinctive spin on both stories, but he nevertheless repeats familiar plot devices that X-Men writers had revisited countless times; his final gift to the X-Men is an attempt to free them from this cycle of repetition. When Jean forgoes another reincarnation, allowing Scott to be happy with Emma instead of grieving for her, she aborts a nightmarish future of perpetual war and releases Scott from a rocky relationship that had dragged on for forty years (*New X-Men* 154). The story follows the "Days of Future Past" formula of proposing and then erasing a potential future, yet it also breaks from that formula in its refusal to restore the series to its status quo.

    Throughout the series, Morrison attempts to strike a balance between satisfying the conventions of the X-Men franchise and taking that franchise in new directions. By the end of *New X-Men*, however, the series feels the weight of tradition too heavily and expresses that burden in openly metafictional terms. In Morrison's final issue, Sublime—who has all but conquered one potential future—admits he has distracted the X-Men with "mindless conflict" and "perpetual struggle" to prevent mutants from achieving evolutionary dominance: "The supermen fight and die and return in a meaningless shadowplay because we make them do it" (154.2). If the reference to shadowplay recalls the illusory, orchestrated conflict of the *dalang* in *The Invisibles*, the plural *we* points not only to Sublime and his henchman but to Morrison, his fellow creators, and their audience. The comment implies their repetition of the same empty battles and exhausted formulas has prevented the X-Men, and the superhero genre as a whole, from developing in new directions. In a series obsessed with evolution and change, Morrison suggests the genre has hit a self-imposed dead end.

    His most damning attack on the superhero genre, however, bypasses the X-Men to take aim at another franchise entirely. At the end of "Assault on Weapon Plus" (*New X-Men* 142–145), the X-Men and their ally Fantomex break into the satellite headquarters of the Weapon Plus program, a project that creates super-soldiers and trains them to exterminate mutants. One room on the satellite contains a round table ringed by chairs bearing the media-friendly codenames of the super-soldiers, a common meeting space for superhero teams such as Morrison's own JLA. Fantomex explains this guise is a marketing strategy "to introduce new strains of highly controversial, genetically-engineered supermen to the public" through a "genetic cleansing operation disguised as a comic book fighting team" (145.14). Weapon Plus has not only bred its soldiers to thwart the evolution of the human species, it will wrap them in the iconography of the superhero to convince the public to accept genocide. The discovery works a bitter reversal on Morrison's earlier attempts to write progressive, egalitarian superheroes. *Flex Mentallo* suggested that superheroes could inspire the noblest aspects of the human character, and *JLA* allowed humanity to determine its own future. In Morrison's Marvel work, however, superheroes are mindless pawns of state power like the Bannermen, Zen fascists like Noh-Varr, or genocidal killers like the Weapon Plus super-soldiers. Whether they support the existing social order or seek to destroy it, his Marvel superheroes practice authoritarian, eliminationist politics and they just might convince the human race to follow them. It is hardly surprising that Morrison chooses not to identify the X-Men as superheroes; his Marvel comics suggest that nothing can change the genre's conventions or its ideology.

New X-Men remains a superhero comic but it reaches beyond the superhero genre, incorporating new elements to rejuvenate the franchise and update its portrayal of minority identity for the post-civil rights era. Unfortunately, most of these innovations did not long outlast Morrison's departure. After months of increasingly contentious relationships with comics retailers and creators, Marvel president Bill Jemas was replaced by new publisher Dan Buckley in October 2003 (Weiland), shortly before Morrison finished *New X-Men* and left Marvel. Almost overnight, Marvel abandoned Jemas's experiments and returned to more traditional, nostalgic approaches (Deppey, "X-Men" 50), particularly in the X-Men franchise. Chris Claremont reassumed his previous centrality to the X-Men titles, reversing Magneto's death and absolving him of his crimes by attributing them to an impostor. In just over a year and a half many of Morrison's contributions, including the explosion of new mutants and the subculture they had created, were undone, erased from the comics. While these changes cannot alter Morrison's completed story, they illustrate the practical limits of working within a shared universe whose properties are shaped by other writers and owned by the publisher. Morrison's next projects would respond to this lack of creative independence by breaking away from superheroes: they would be owned by Morrison, they would fall partially or entirely outside the superhero genre, and, fittingly, they would be published at Vertigo.

Chapter 5

FREE AGENTS

Closed-circuit television cameras record a balding, middle-aged man in unsparing detail as he buys transsexual porn and picks his nose. More cameras track a military scientist as he strolls through a research facility on his way to euthanize his animal test subjects, unaware that they have broken free and are killing his subordinates. Visitors at a theme park are surrounded by omnipresent cartoon eyeballs who ferry kidnapped children down subterranean canals. God reveals the predestined fates of two young lovers while fire-belching demons destroy London, murdering the queen, the prime minister, and the cabinet. These nightmares of surveillance, domination, and violent rebellion appear in a quartet of projects Morrison wrote for Vertigo during and immediately after his time at Marvel: *The Filth* was published concurrently with his run on *New X-Men* while *Seaguy*, *We3*, and *Vimanarama* followed his departure. Each one tells a finite story—*The Filth* is a thirteen-issue limited series, the others three-issue miniseries—and each features original characters owned by Morrison and his artists, freeing them from the constraints imposed by never-ending, corporate-owned franchises.

Like *The Invisibles* before them, these series experiment with other genres without completely abandoning superheroes. From a *JLA* parody in *The Filth* to the Jack Kirby-inspired character designs in *Vimanarama*, the superhero genre informs all of these comics, if only as an object of commentary or satire. Following Morrison's work on some of the highest-profile franchises in superhero comics, the Vertigo projects express his frustration at the corporate creative control, the conservative ideology, and the ossified conventions that make the genre so resistant to change. Morrison responds by breaking down generic boundaries and merging superheroes with other genres, which are themselves subject to examination and critique. *The Filth* parodies the spy genre; *Seaguy* combines the narrative stasis of superhero comics with the aimless, episodic plotting of picaresque narratives and the encoded symbolism of medieval allegory; *We3* fuses the military techno-thriller and the animal adventure story; and *Vimanarama* unites Kirby-style superheroes with science fiction, Hindu and Muslim legend, the film musical, and the romantic comedy in a dizzying pastiche. These projects also look to other media and other comics traditions, drawing inspiration from film, animation, video games, and manga in an attempt to infuse American comics with new idioms and to attract an audience that, like Morrison, is no longer interested in "the storytelling clichés and endlessly recycled images of traditional, mainstream superhero books" (Brady, "Inside Morrison's Head").

Reflecting Morrison's search for creative autonomy within the American comic book industry, these series depict characters who seek independence from the array of social and cosmic forces that seek to control them. They feature secret policemen pressed into duty against their will, animal weapons fighting for survival after the military uses and discards them, a reincarnated princess who resists the relationships dictated by her past life, and an aspiring superhero who seemingly has no responsibilities at all until he discovers the hidden acts of brutality and exploitation that sustain his idyllic society. These protagonists struggle against parents, police, the culture industry, the military, God, destiny, and even language—sometimes successfully, sometimes not, as they attempt to live freely and act ethically in societies that will not allow them any agency. By paralleling and in some cases directly linking these efforts with his own resistance to genre and industry constraints, Morrison extrapolates his creative struggles onto the larger problems facing the world in the first decade of the new millennium.

THE FILTH: STATUS: Q

The Filth (2002–03), a limited series with art by Morrison's *Invisibles* collaborator Chris Weston, wallows in the most oppressive and repugnant aspects of postmodern culture at the beginning of the twenty-first century: the omnipresent surveillance, the murderous ideological extremism, the debased sexuality, the unlimited expansion of the state's power over its citizens, and the conversion of all these indignities into narcissistic entertainment by a compliant culture industry. Morrison would later describe *The Filth* as "a filter or cleansing plant—a colourful pseudo-kidney, if you like" (J. Ellis Part 5), designed to process and purify the negative feelings instilled by this culture. He has also characterized the experience of writing *The Filth* as a magical initiation, an "Oath of the Abyss" that forced him to confront and pass through "all the negative states of consciousness available to us as human beings" (Brady, "A Healing Inoculation"). To begin this initiation, and to research the project, he immersed himself in "books about anti-life, death and decay, shame, dirt, chaos, nervous breakdown, mind control[,] porn, humiliation, cruelty, schizophrenic art and disease pathology" (J. Ellis Part 5), a process so wrenching that Morrison has stated he "almost committed suicide on several occasions and spent most of the year in a state of intense psychological and physical distress" (Brady, "A Healing Inoculation").[1] Stripped of its occult terminology—and setting aside the harrowing effects Morrison describes—this account offers a fairly traditional post-Romantic portrait of the artist who pursues extreme experiences and plunges into dangerous psychological states to create his art, which his audience may then consume with safely vicarious pleasure. *The Filth* casts this Orphic narrative in magical, biological, and sociological terms, bringing its author, its protagonist, and potentially its readers through the darkest states of human experience in order to transcend them.

The series also functions as an inversion or "photo-negative" of Morrison's last work for Vertigo, *The Invisibles* ("Filthy Thoughts"). Like most of his comics, including *Doom Patrol*, *The New Adventures of Hitler*, *St. Swithin's Day*, *Marvel Boy*, *New X-Men*, and nearly all of his Vertigo work, *The Invisibles* focused on subversives, misfits, and outsiders, yet *The Filth* stars the authorities responsible for policing these antisocial elements. (In addition to describing the series' pervasive physical and ideological detritus, "the filth" is also British slang for the police.) The project was based on an unsold proposal for Nick Fury, Agent of SHIELD, Marvel Comics' premier superspy and most sympathetic government agent ("Filthy Thoughts").[2] Marvel's rejection of the proposal allowed Morrison to take his ideas in directions that no superhero publisher would permit for its properties, but the series remains steeped in the semantics of the spy genre, inspired by heroic law-enforcement agencies like SHIELD and the organizations in Gerry Anderson television series ("Filthy Thoughts"). Unlike those series, however, *The Filth* questions the morality of its heroes until it is impossible to distinguish them from the threats they are supposed to contain.

The Filth stars Greg Feely, a middle-aged bachelor with a bad comb-over, an addiction to pornography, and a cat dying of a misdiagnosed malady. Before the first issue is done, Feely is told that nothing in his life is real, that "Greg Feely" is just a parapersonality, an artificial identity created to house Ned Slade, a highly trained agent of the social cleansing organization known as the Hand. Structured around five hand gestures, five planetary correspondences, and five functions—the division known as the Fist handles the martial arts of war and assassination, the Finger manages the "venereal arts" of sex and vice, the Frequency oversees the "mercurial arts" of communication and surveillance, and so forth (2.2–3)—the Hand are brightly garbed secret police who eliminate threats to society, and Slade is a veteran officer who has been recovering from the pressures of his duties by vacationing as the thoroughly mundane Greg Feely. By the end of the series, however, every one of these premises will be challenged if not thoroughly debunked. From the Hand's mission as guardians of society to Greg's true identity, Morrison provides readers with multiple interpretive possibilities.

That multiplicity extends to the series' settings, which include a number of societies located on a variety of physical scales and narrative frames. The most frequent plot features the Hand's battles against invasive forces that degrade what David Allison calls "pocket utopias" ("Déjà Vu"), microworlds that aspire to utopian conditions. These societies are constructed according to several different ideologies ranging from the communitarian "bonsai planet" of the I-Life, microscopic robots who create "simple social structures based on play and co-operation" (2.10), to the luxury-liner city-state of the *Libertania*, which bears many similarities to an unbuilt libertarian tax haven called the *Freedom Ship* (Miéville 251–52). Other utopias are still in the speculative stages even within the pages of *The Filth*, present only as bizarre, unrealized dreams like porn star Anders Klimakks's vision of a world that runs on sex and pornography—"Instead of money, there will be blow jobs. [...] The job of everybody will be to fuck everybody else for the camera to watch" (6.22)—or would-be superhero Max Thunderstone's conviction that everyone could achieve enlightenment if only they would induce temporal lobe epilepsy. These imagined utopias are just as likely to be targeted and destroyed as the achieved ones, which may be just as well since none of these societies are especially desirable: the *Libertania*, riven by class divisions between the upper and lower decks, quickly slides into anarchy and piracy, while the childlike I-Life, who look and act like the Teletubbies, threaten to infect humanity and create "an unstoppable plague of idiots" (2.11).

As foolish or unworkable as these utopias may be, none of them are given the chance to fail on their own (with the arguable exception of the *Libertania*, which has already reached a dangerous tipping point before an intruder nudges it into chaos). Whatever their ideology, they are all invaded by corrupting capitalists who establish new societies structured around the barbarism of unrestrained self-interest or the objectification, degradation, and voyeurism of hardcore pornography; one corruptor, the director

Tex Porneau, combines both of these principles in his mantra "Fuck or be fucked" (5.9). Nevertheless, Porneau and his peers do not simply convert quixotic utopias into neoliberal dystopias of unregulated competition; these perverse tempters go beyond greed, beyond even lust, to revel in pure death drive. Simon (as in "Simon says"), "the world's richest and most perverted man" (1.21), squanders billions for the chance to replace the I-Life's cooperative programming with "the drive towards cannibalistic self-destruction, incest and suicide" (2.16). Porneau co-opts Anders Klimakks's genetically engineered semen to film a rape/snuff movie in which giant sperm attack and kill the women of Beverly Hills. And Max Thunderstone finds his own body co-opted by the Hand and injected with the rogue parapersonality Spartacus Hughes, who has previously sold the I-Life to Simon and destroyed the *Libertania* as part of his project of debasing and remaking the pocket utopias.

This last fate indicates the Hand's role in *The Filth*. Although they neutralize dangerously antisocial individuals like Porneau, the Hand are themselves tasked with preventing these utopias from achieving realization; they are initially sent to Los Angeles not to stop Porneau but to kill Klimakks (6.13). Like the heroes of most formula adventure fiction, the Hand work to preserve the status quo—or, as the Hand officers call it, "Status: Q." Morrison connects this mission to his ongoing critique of the superhero genre via the Status Quorum, a team of comic book superheroes who look suspiciously like Morrison's JLA and whose name reproaches the Justice League and other heroes who work only to maintain the existing social order rather than improve it. Their name should suggest a shared purpose with the Hand, but in fact the Status Quorum are pawns and victims of that organization. They reside in the Paperverse, a simulated comic book reality created by the Hand to grow and harvest fantastic new concepts; they first appear when Hand agent Moog Mercury enters the comic to steal an advanced weapon and kills two superheroes in the process. This subplot mocks the many forms of coercion and abuse that structure the superhero genre and the American comic book industry: comic book characters who enforce society's laws, comic book writers who take sadistic pleasure in punishing their characters, and comic book companies that exploit characters and writers alike, taking ownership of their employees' creations.

One member of the Status Quorum once attempted to challenge this systemic exploitation and paid dearly for his efforts. At some point prior to the beginning of *The Filth*, Secret Original, a square-jawed hero with a

Superman-esque spit-curl, detected the Hand's tampering with the Paperverse and broke the fictional barrier in an attempt to confront his authors and "restore free will to the universe" (3.17). Broken physically by the forces of the higher universe and mentally by the discovery of his fictionality, Secret Original now haunts the Hand headquarters like a four-color Dr. Strangelove, colluding with his tormentors and reading pornographic versions of his old comic so he can watch his former lover rut in wild abandon. Secret Original is both a failed Animal Man and another Gnostic Superman similar to Weapon XV (who would appear one year later), a hero who breaks out of his illusory prison only to be shattered by his discovery of the world beyond it. Much like Weapon XV—and quite unlike the committed animal rights activist and family man Buddy Baker—Secret Original is compromised by his acceptance of the role and ideology of the superhero, which primes him for his submission to the Hand. He interferes with a plan to sabotage the Hand, a plan that would have resulted in his own rescue and return to the Paperverse, because he no longer wants to go back to his simple, emotionally void existence as "a cheap, derivative superhero" (12.10) in Moog Mercury's scripted fantasies. While his preference for the "agony and blinding, obscene arousal" (12.7) of Mercury's world over the flattened affect (and literal flatness) of the comics page is at least somewhat understandable, his comments also reveal his continued commitment to the conservatism of his old genre formulas. He tells Mercury, "I don't want things to change. [...] I want things to stay this way forever. Status: Q" (12.7–8). As a generic comic book superhero—and a cheap derivation of the Silver Age Superman, that most oneiric and timeless of superheroes—he could want nothing else, and his dedication to maintaining the status quo makes him all too ready a partner for the Hand.

Unable to reconcile his broken body and his perverse self-indulgence with the simplistic moral code he upheld in the Paperverse, Secret Original eventually determines that he is no longer a hero but rather a villain and a monster (12.10). He is not the only character in *The Filth* to confuse these roles. Max Thunderstone, who wants to spend his lottery winnings to become "the world's first ever real-life superhero" (10.6), realizes his mission is meaningless (and most likely illegal) without equally outlandish supervillains to battle. He decides the Hand will fit the bill, describing the series' protagonists as "An organized gang of authoritarian monsters" (10.9) whose advanced technology and color-coded costumes make them "not just organized criminals but well-designed comic book villains" (10.16). Max is soon captured, "recycled"—the Hand's euphemism for co-opting dissidents by programming them with the parapersonalities of Hand agents—and imprinted with the personality of Spartacus Hughes, now reprogrammed to serve the Hand rather than subvert its mission. Hughes proclaims that this union of his artificial mind and Thunderstone's nearly as artificial, "superbly buffed and waxed" body (12.2) has brought Max's dream to life: "I am the world's first super-hero when you stop to think about it" (12.2). This superhero, however, plans to squander his perfect host body in a binge of alcohol, drugs, and unprotected sex, and he gleefully accepts his new duties raping and killing enemies for the Hand, becoming indistinguishable from the villains Max had hoped to combat.

The Filth does not simply suggest, as many genre fictions do, that the roles of hero and villain are ambiguous or interdependent—it argues that these labels are useless in a world where everyone has the capacity for evil and where anyone who behaved like the heroes of formula adventure fiction would be branded as an antisocial menace. A conversation overheard on a bus in the first issue underscores this point while establishing that *The Filth*, for all its investment in the iconography of the super-spy genre, will not be a conventional spy story:

> So what's so good about James Bond? [. . .]
> Well, he knows how to treat a lady for a start. [. . .]
> Gambling all night, knocking her about like a rag doll, using her as a human shield . . . very romantic! (1.6)

The exchange nods to the comic's origins as a subversive take on Nick Fury while reminding readers that even the fictional agents of state power can be less than heroic. Lest any of his readers therefore decide to romanticize the figures who oppose the Hand, Morrison ensures that the subversives are no better. Max Thunderstone and his associates create the Spartacus Hughes parapersona to infiltrate the Hand and disrupt Status: Q, but Hughes does so by murdering innocent civilians and destroying peaceful societies. As Morrison warns Matt Brady, Spartacus only appears to be a sympathetic antihero: "he seems pro-active and willing to change things but the truth is he's a dangerous, ego-driven loon who only ever makes things worse" ("A Healing Inoculation"). The Romantic rebel is as compromised as the superhero, the secret agent, and the police officer; by setting aside genre conventions and looking at the consequences of their actions, *The Filth* acknowledges that the heroes of adventure fiction can be as dangerous and amoral as the enemies they fight.

ENJOY YOUR MICRO-SEPSIS

The Filth's recurring plot of social invasion, containment, and cleansing unfolds in biological as well as sociological contexts, indicating Morrison's ongoing interest in structuring his plots around immunological metaphors and variations in scale. Morrison filled *The Invisibles* with highly charged encounters with viruses and diseases that reflected or anticipated his own health problems. "House of Fun," the final storyline of the first volume, pits the Invisibles against viral invaders from a diseased meta-universe and a cosmic abscess that threatens to destroy their reality; much of the imagery, dialogue, and narration was taken from Morrison's hallucinations when he nearly died of a staph infection (*Invisibles* I.24, "Invisible Ink"). In *New X-Men* Cassandra Nova imagines the X-Men are antibodies, a misinterpretation that is not inconsistent with Charles Xavier's own preference for describing his work through medical metaphors, as when he and the X-Men contain an invasive viral consciousness (*New X-Men* 130). The end of the series applies this medical metaphor on a cosmic scale, dispatching Jean Grey to disinfect potential futures and heal entire universes (*New X-Men* 154). *The Filth*, however, is Morrison's most tangibly, repellently organic exploration of these themes of infection and immune response. Much of the credit goes to Chris Weston, whose pencils (enhanced by the precise inking of Gary Erskine) create disquieting mergers of biological and technological forms as easily as they shift between mundane and fantastic settings. Buildings, vehicles, and uniforms bristle with vaguely organic protuberances while living creatures are outfitted with cybernetic attachments. Weston's art grounds the story in all the sins, vices, weaknesses, excretions, diseases, and pleasures of the flesh.

This fleshiness extends to the organizational structures that shape the series. The Hand are designed along biological lines, of course, though not simply the manual systems their name implies. Morrison told Matt Brady that "The five specialist divisions or gestures which comprise the Hand organization [...] each represent a different type of white [blood] immune cell. The Palm are like Helper T cells, the Fist are Hunter/killer cells" ("A Healing Inoculation"). Casting the Hand as an immune system naturalizes their mission to preserve Status: Q, a far more sympathetic rendering than when the Hand is seen from the perspective of victims like Anders Klimakks and Max Thunderstone. As Morrison told Brady, "Think of Status: Q as the body's natural temperature and threats to Status: Q as fevers or illnesses which have to be contained by our own natural defenses. The 'body' in this case being

Figure 5-1. *The Filth* 12.20-21. Art by Chris Weston. © Grant Morrison and Chris Weston.

Society and the immune system being the Hand" ("A Healing Inoculation"). The Hand relies on this confusion of the body and the body politic to license their work, as when officer Miami Nil tells Greg, "Attacking the Hand is like fighting your own immune system" (13.4).

By that late point in the story, however, Morrison has already suggested that readers might interpret Miami's statement literally as well as figuratively:

> One way to read the series is to see it all happening inside Greg Feely as he slowly loses his mind, his job and his health over the course of the 13 issues. From this perspective, the Hand can be conceptualized as Greg's own immune system and their adventures can be seen as fantasies produced by his own deranged brain as it tries to survive a mid-life nervous breakdown. (Brady, "A Healing Inoculation")

In this interpretation, which is suggested by a dramatic revelation in the penultimate issue, the entire series has been the hallucination of a delusional

Greg Feely, possibly as he overdoses on paracetamol in a suicide attempt.[3] The Hand headquarters and the zone of decay that surrounds it, a devastated landscape known as "the Crack," are exposed as nothing more than the trash scattered across his kitchen floor; the monsters that prowl this inhospitable terrain are only mites and other microscopic lifeforms; and the colossal hand that wields a titanic pen, the appendage that forms the axis mundi of the Hand's cosmology and that they believe to be the hand of God, is Greg's own (fig. 5-1). The radical change in scale both dispels the Hand as figments of Greg's imagination and pardons their lethal cleansing as the work of his immune system, although the final issue does not fully sustain this interpretation.

The series presents other variations in biological scale, as when Tex Porneau assaults Beverly Hills with a swarm of gigantic sperm, but human physiology is not the only area subject to amplification or compression in *The Filth*. The series views human civilization and its own narrative structure through multiple levels of magnification, giving readers several different perspectives on the story and its subjects. The *Libertania*, for example, is both a megaliner and a microsociety whose failure—after careening from libertarian dream to anarchic nightmare to collectivist metaphor—indicts all of humanity's political philosophies, "All the big ideas that always go wrong" (8.19). Morrison arranges these sociological compressions into nested, concentric reflections. The I-Life bonsai planet is a microworld within the world of the Hand, which may itself be another microworld hallucinated by Greg; a scene in which the dying Spartacus Hughes gazes upon the minuscule bonsai planet perfectly anticipates Greg's near-death discovery on his kitchen floor (fig. 5-2). The comic book world of the Paperverse places the transparent fiction of the Status Quorum within the potential fiction of the Hand (and, of course, within the actual fiction of *The Filth*) in exactly the same manner. The pervasive *mise en abyme* plunges readers into a potentially endless abyss of potential realities, no one any more or less certain than the next.

The most significant of these nested narrative compressions reveal the major themes of the series by repeating them at different levels of scale. David Allison notes that the second half of the series quotes and repeats the first half, beginning with the *Libertania* storyline's virtual reenactment of the I-Life story that began *The Filth*:

> Events from the first two issues recur on a different scale and no one seems particularly unsettled by this queasy, stuttering duplication. Let's

Figure 5-2. *The Filth* 2.20. Art by Chris Weston. © Grant Morrison and Chris Weston.

watch the gears grind down: Spartacus Hughes hijacks a pocket utopia and subjects it to his kinky shock doctrine . . . Greg Feely is dragged from his shameful little life to stop his former co-worker. . . Comrade Dmitri 9 ends the show by blowing Hughes' head smooth off. . . . Yeah, we've been here before. ("Déjà Vu")

The parallels do not end there; the *Libertania* issues forecast the ending of the ongoing I-Life subplot just as they recall its beginning. Balanced in the middle of the series (*The Filth* 7–8), they encapsulate its entire narrative arc.

A brief summary of both micro- and macroplot is necessary. Spartacus Hughes destroys the society of the *Libertania* because he wants to trigger its reformation into a new social structure, "The next stage in the evolution of human civilization" (8.16). After the ship carries its implied libertarian fantasy to its ultimate, absurd endpoint, becoming completely lawless and collapsing into rape, murder, piracy, and cannibalism, the *Libertania* regroups as an equally absurd caricature of collectivist society in which citizens share the roles of authority, synchronize their breathing, and flock like birds. (This society is no less threatening to Status: Q, and the Hand exterminate it just as they had planned to wipe out the pirate ship.) The I-Life undergo a similar transformation over the thirteen issues of the series, although they evolve more gradually and do not swing to such ideological extremes. An earlier incarnation of Hughes sells the microbots to Simon, who stages a murderous orgy around the bonsai planet and gloats that he has "transformed an innocent society of gentle healers into vicious viral rapists" (2.16). The I-Life prove more resilient than the *Libertania*, executing a plan to escape their world and kill their tormentor thanks to a variation in temporal scale: while mere days have passed for Simon, the microbots' shorter life cycle has given them generations to devise their counterattack (2.17). The I-Life survive the Hand's rigorous cleansing, thanks in part to Greg's illicit preservation of a small sample, and by the end of the series they evolve into smarter, more humanoid forms with an organizational hierarchy much like the Hand and a similar mission to coordinate Greg's bodily functions and preserve his health (13.21). The final pages of *The Filth* show a world in flux as humans, insects, and plants enter into symbiotic relationships with the I-Life and each other, with Greg acting as the "patient zero" for this viral transformation.

Readers must remember, however, that this guardedly optimistic ending is the result of a chain of events that begins with Hughes murdering the inventor of I-Life and selling the microbots to Simon. The death of their beneficent creator, the degradations under Simon's reign, the separation from their Edenic home, and the terror of finding their way in the larger world have jolted the I-Life out of their original, simplistic programming and forced them to grow. Exposure to social pathogens has made their society healthier; this is the underlying principle of inoculation and, as Morrison explains, of his series:

> *The Filth* can be seen [as] a healing inoculation of grime. I'm deliberately injecting the worst aspects of life into my readers['] heads in small, humorous doses of metaphor and symbol, in an effort to help them survive the torrents of nastiness, horror and dirt we're all exposed to every day—especially in white Western cultures, whose entertainment industries peddle a mind-numbing perverted concoction of fantasy violence and degrading sexuality while living large at the expense of the poor in other countries. [...] *The Filth* is an attempt to 'inject' into my readers

a healing concoction of vile ideas, hurtful emotions and unacceptable images. (Brady, "A Healing Inoculation")

Greg Feely undertakes a similar project, inoculating his debased society through exposure to antigenic I-Life. In the final three pages of *The Filth*, which inhabit a wholly different stratus of surreality from the preceding 284, Greg's society has already begun to view contamination as healthy: vibrant flowers sprout from uncollected garbage and a strange billboard advertising a queasily organic product implores or commands viewers to "Enjoy Micro-Sepsis" (13.20). The sepsis in question could refer to the inflammatory response to bacterial infection or the genus of flies that consumes dung and decaying organic matter; that either one could be a mass commodity is indicative enough of Greg's changed world. The transformation is sudden and jarring, but readers have already seen it played out in miniature among the I-Life, whose evolution is itself reflected in the story of the *Libertania*. These shrinking orders of magnitude, in which the smallest object receives the largest story and vice versa, reflect the goals of the series on multiple narrative scales and enact, with grotesquely biological literalism, the kind of cultural inoculation that Morrison hopes to provide his readers.

IN THE WORLD OF GREG FEELY

Sorting out these shifting orders of magnitude, and the varying levels of reality and fantasy, requires a highly active reader. *The Filth* proposes several different roles for its audience, from engaged interpreters to unwilling participants—anything but passive spectators. The Anders Klimakks story (*The Filth* 5–6) is particularly blatant about this audience positioning, insistently implicating readers in its pornographic content. Klimakks routinely breaks the fourth wall, turning and facing out of the panel to address the reader as he describes his role in the porn industry and explains how he came to work for Tex Porneau. Rather than serve as Brechtian distancing effects, however, these direct addresses draw the reader into the story, eliminating any insulating distance the audience might prefer to keep between itself and the unsettling subject matter. Klimakks's first words—spoken as he penetrates an actress on a film set—are "Hey! Come on in! Don't be shy!" (5.1). The staging, the casual, almost neighborly tone, and Anders's affable personality invite readers to step into his world, with apparent success. As he finishes telling the story of how Porneau brought him to Los Angeles, his auditor

Figure 5-3. *The Filth* 5.11. Art by Chris Weston. © Grant Morrison and Chris Weston.

(and reader surrogate), Hand agent Jenesis Jones, is seen standing inside his flashback while a naked, terrified Anders runs outside of the panel borders, towards the reader; Jones, and by extension the reader, has become more a part of his memories than he is (fig. 5-3).

Anders's antisocial counterpart, Tex Porneau, also implicates the reader in his pornographic fantasies, but where Klimakks is personable and inviting, Porneau is violent and predatory. He and Anders both envelop the other characters in "porn logic" (Allison, "Twisted"), bending the people who come into contact with them into the narrative conventions of porn. While Klimakks's application of this logic may be unintentional (he secretes a "maxi-pheromone" that attracts women—still a manipulation and violation of their consent), Porneau brutally enforces his "Fuck or

Figure 5-4. *The Filth* 6.6. Art by Chris Weston. © Grant Morrison and Chris Weston.

be fucked" motto on everyone who comes to his door, raping delivery men and police detectives as if they were characters in his movies. In his final assault before he receives his poetically appropriate comeuppance, he reaches outside the page to grab someone else's hand, presumably the reader's, as he berates us to "put some goddamn effort into [our] hardcore career!" (fig. 5-4). With Weston graphically pulling us into Porneau's grip, no one can escape the infectious logic of porn. Even the Hand are unable to contain these fantasies; they may kill Anders Klimakks and Tex Porneau, but the story ends with a narrator's voice—presumably Anders's, given that it addresses the audience in the same slightly mangled English syntax—directing our attention to Anders's legacy: 824 children, the results of his many liaisons, each one a perfect genetic copy who has inherited his slightly homely features and his extensive knowledge of porn (6.22). This narrator, disembodied and apparently omniscient now that Anders is no longer alive, asserts that these children will inherit the future and establish a society built on sex and pornography. Just as the readers are pulled into Porneau's films, one day everyone will live in the world of Anders Klimakks.

Most reader involvement in *The Filth* is less coercive, with the series typically encouraging attention rather than demanding participation. Morrison rewards those who read the series retrospectively and asks them to revise their interpretations in light of the new information he provides with increasing frequency as the series progresses. After initially proposing that "Greg Feely" is a parapersonality designed as a temporary refuge for Ned Slade, Morrison begins to hint that "Ned Slade" and the Hand may be delusions of Greg Feely, who is slowly going mad. The I-Life growing in his fishbowl could simply be mold; the chimpanzee assassin who keeps visiting his house could be a figment of his imagination, or worse, a procession of young children Feely has been molesting and murdering (although this is more likely the fantasy of his nosy neighbors, examples of a paranoid culture on perpetual lookout for pedophiles). After allowing readers a few issues to contemplate this scenario, in which a radically unreliable protagonist casts the narrative into epistemological uncertainty, Morrison revises it once again. Max Thunderstone reveals that Greg Feely was once part of his circle of advisors, and the person who alerted him to the existence of the Hand; Greg has apparently been captured by the Hand and infected with the "Ned Slade" parapersonality to undermine Max's plans. Greg then tells his partners "Cameron Spector" and "Moog Mercury" that they and every other Hand agent are also parapersonas used to reprogram dissidents and countercultural types; Mercury, for example, was "a heroin addict in a radical performance collective" (12.10). Just when this interpretation appears to explain everything, however, Morrison throws in another wrinkle: at the end of issue 12, Greg writes a suicide note that once again raises the possibility that he is simply an accountant, and the Hand a delusion concocted to excuse his aberrant behavior (12.17). His dying vision of the surreal topography of the Crack sprouting from the tiles of his kitchen floor implies that the whole series has taken place in his mind, making the Hand nothing more than deranged metaphors for his own immune system's attempts to save him.

As Morrison adds these new and contradictory explanations, he surpasses the epistemological uncertainty of the early issues, in which only Greg's sanity is in question, to propose a superabundance of incompatible realities. This progression echoes the shift from a predominantly modernist epistemological doubt to a predominantly postmodernist ontological doubt that Brian McHale traces in works such as Vladimir Nabokov's *Pale Fire* (McHale, *Postmodernist Fiction* 18–19). Like that novel, *The Filth* proposes several possible narrative worlds and several possible identities for its main character. They are, in the order of their presentation:

1. Greg Feely is a real person with a mundane, depressing life;
2. "Greg Feely" is a parapersonality and Ned Slade, Hand officer, is real;
3. Greg Feely is real, but going mad and imagining "Ned Slade" and the Hand;
4. Greg Feely is real, and "Ned Slade" is a parapersonality used by the Hand to brainwash Greg;
5. Greg Feely is real, but he has been imagining "Ned Slade" and the Hand as he dies on his kitchen floor.

Morrison definitively disproves the second narrative, but refuses to decide between the others. The final issue of *The Filth* suggests that the last two narratives are both true—Greg really does attempt suicide but is saved by the I-Life in his body, an artifact of his adventures as Ned Slade (13.15). Weston's art provides a visual clue that verifies this unification: the length of Greg's hair suggests that the suicide attempt in issue 12 comes after his invasion of the Hand headquarters and confrontation with Hand leader Mother Dirt in issue 13. What appear to be mutually incompatible narratives are actually the result of a disordered chronology. On the other hand, this unified narrative does not explain the Crack's appearance on Greg's kitchen floor or the many suggestions that the Hand are merely a magnification of Greg's own immune system. The Hand is at once real and metaphoric, and Morrison leaves readers no way to prioritize one interpretation over the other.

Readers who crave the certainty of an authoritative explanation will have to settle for Mother Dirt's account of how Greg came to serve the Hand. She tells him they selected him for reprogramming because "A new not-self entered the system; in developing a response, it was necessary to expose you to the antigen" (13.12). Filtering this through the series' prevailing immunological metaphor, it seems that a threat invaded the body or the body politic—most likely Spartacus Hughes, whom Morrison describes as a cancer (Brady, "A Healing Inoculation"), although it could also refer to Max Thunderstone and his group, who created Spartacus. To contain the threat, the Hand exposed Greg to the "Ned Slade" antigen, remaking him into a helper T-cell/super-spy responsible for detecting other threats to the body/society; Greg is an "Anti-person become not-self detector [. . .] One of them who become one of us" (13.1). Because of his attachment to his cat, however, he never quite lets go of his original identity as Greg Feely, resulting in a total psychological breakdown that leaves him unsure of who he is and what he is supposed to do next.

Greg is reduced to scooping up the muck in Mother Dirt's chamber—it could be shit, it could be bone marrow—as he complains about the series' interpretive instability and his own lack of identity:

> I wanted an explanation. Wanted it all to make sense but it's just shit.
> What am I supposed to do?
> [*he holds up the dirt*]
> What am I supposed to do with this? (13.12)

Presumably Greg refers not just to the waste in his hands but also to the general wreckage of his life. Mother Dirt's answer is to "Spread it on your flowers, Greg" (13.13). Calling him "Greg" instead of "Officer Slade," she releases him to use the dirt to nourish new life, and she releases him to be Greg Feely. Mother Dirt recognizes that the manure and the flowers, the infections and the antigens, the antisocial dissidents and the authoritarian police—"the filth" in both senses of the word—are both necessary for a healthy organism and a healthy society. A system that lacks either one will collapse at the first sign of crisis just like all the pocket utopias that litter the earlier issues of *The Filth*. Arguing that exposure to contamination will only strengthen our natural defenses, Morrison insists we do not have to choose between these social, psychological, and biological oppositions. Only by combining them can we confront and survive the worst parts of the human experience.

SEAGUY: BEYOND THE END OF THE WORLD

Ever since Morrison introduced himself to American readers with the metafictions of *Animal Man*, the strange anatomies of *Doom Patrol*, and particularly the dense, oppressive symbolism of *Arkham Asylum*, a small but vocal contingent of comics fandom has accused him of pretension, inaccessibility, and his least favorite label, "weirdness-for-weirdness' sake" (J. Ellis Part 5). Charges of willful incomprehensibility persisted despite his work on more mainstream comics like *JLA* and would continue with his next Vertigo project, *Seaguy* (2004). Labels that might have been tolerable when affixed to best-selling graphic novels became far less so in a shrinking comics market, and *Seaguy* did not perform to Morrison's or Vertigo's expectations, delaying its sequel for nearly five years.[4] Morrison complained about the vanishing audience to Jay Babcock shortly after the miniseries was released, claiming that readers failed to understand his storytelling techniques:

> The comics audience is becoming more and more compressed and unpleasant. It's really sad. After I did *Seaguy* and so many people said they didn't get it, I felt completely exasperated. *Seaguy* is based on medieval quest literature which always has the young hero setting out and he has his companion who gets killed, the questing beast, but many of my readers seem to now be unaware of storytelling structures beyond the Hollywood three-act, and the literalism is so rife that nobody seems to be able to deal with symbolic content anymore. (Babcock 37)[5]

He then compares this purported inability to process symbolism and fantasy to schizophrenia, which he in turn connects to contemporary obsessions with the false realism of celebrity scandals and reality television, hardly endearing himself to readers who had already passed on *Seaguy*—or who do not equate differences of taste with a lack of comprehension.

Morrison's protests about symbolic content also reverse a long trend of disavowing symbolic interpretations of his works. While he has owned up to the elaborate symbolism of *Arkham Asylum*, he more typically insists that his comics do not operate through symbolic codes and must not be read as allegories. He chastised readers for over-reading *Doom Patrol* and assuming symbolism where there is none:

> people seemed to pick up on all the wrong elements of it, and feel that there were things which they couldn't understand, when they were basically things which they didn't have to understand. There weren't any secrets in it, nothing was symbolic in *Doom Patrol*. But I think people thought it was, because I'd built up this reputation, and so they wouldn't read it at face value. [...] *Doom Patrol* didn't represent anything. It was just what it was. (Hasted 70)

These remarks complement Morrison's practice of using hypostasis to craft concrete, multivalent figures rather than abstracted, monovalent symbols. In some respects, this explication of *Doom Patrol* is a better guide to interpreting *Seaguy* than his more timely comments about medieval romances and symbolic content. Its reliance on allegory notwithstanding, *Seaguy* is a story in which everything is exactly what it seems—to the readers, if not to its benighted characters.

Seaguy is a young superhero in a world where heroes have become superfluous since the responsibility for humanity's security and comfort was taken over by a mysterious entity known as the Eye. Aided by the cartoonish art of Cameron Stewart—who presents even the most incongruous objects and locales with the same lucid composure, so that an Egyptian temple complex on the moon appears no more or less plausible than a southern California beach town—Morrison steers his hero through a picaresque tour of surreal landscapes and dreamlike encounters. Easter Island heads smoke giant cigarettes, polar ice caps are coated in dark chocolate, and a beverage erupts out of Seaguy's mouth and begins pleading for help. While these scenes project common images of an exotic and serene world spoiled by mass commodities, these themes generally appear on the narrative's surface, not its subtext. Sometimes a giant cigarette is just a giant cigarette, and most of the symbols are so obvious they don't need decoding; indeed, naming the cartoon mascot of the Eye's surveillance and indoctrination program "Mickey Eye" is a little too obvious on both registers. *Seaguy* is not without its emblematic elements, however, and Morrison would later explain that he structured the Seaguy trilogy as a symbolic narrative of "an entire human life from birth to death," with the first miniseries presenting its protagonist as a figurative child ("Exclusive Interview"). This developmental allegory explains much about the miniseries, from Seaguy's opening game of chess with Death—a symbolic birth on the first page of the story—to his (possibly imaginary) companion Chubby da Choona, a talking tuna fish who externalizes Seaguy's childlike exuberance and timidity and who dies as Seaguy discovers the evil acts that support his world. *Seaguy* is filled with symbols, but they are transparent ones designed to foster interpretation, not to bar it.

Nor does Morrison limit himself to allegory; the story is both a symbolic narrative of one man's childhood and a satirical portrait of an entire society that has lapsed into a childlike naïveté about its leaders and its history. Seaguy and the other residents of New Venice believe the world has achieved peace and stability after an epic war against the forces of evil.[6] The victory was supposedly so complete that the heroes of the previous generation are no longer needed, and in fact most of them appear to have died, disappeared, or lost their powers in the war. The New Venetians' conviction that they have triumphed over the only serious threat to their society recalls similar moments of postwar hubris, including America's military and economic dominance after World War II—Doc Hero, one of the last surviving champions of the heroic age, has traded his ancient Greek armor for a mid-century modern ensemble of plaid trousers and an argyle sweater—or

Francis Fukuyama's argument that liberal democracy became the "final form of human government" in the "end of history" after the fall of the Soviet Union and the conclusion of the Cold War (xi). Morrison presents this vision of the end of history as a false consensus that blinds the people of New Venice to the serious problems within their society; he also depicts it as an antihistorical ideology that has made it impossible for Seaguy's culture to represent the past or to imagine a different future, a condition akin to the "crisis in historicity" (25) that Fredric Jameson ascribes to postmodern culture. Under the Eye's direction, Seaguy's world replaces its past and its future with simulacra, inhabiting an eternal present that admits no possibility for any deviation from its dominant logic.

One of the attractions in the Mickey Eye Park, a Disneyland-style amusement park that seems to be one of the few ways to pass the time in New Venice, is the Future Swamp, in which visitors ride boats through a drowned morass of fallen skyscrapers and downed planes (1.17). The ride presents such apocalyptic fates as objects of fantasy and spectacle, safely avoided and now ready for imaginary consumption, although the simulated landscape may provide a glimpse not of the futures the Eye has averted but of a past it has suppressed. The Eye is engaged in a long-term project to rewrite history, with increasing success between the two *Seaguy* series. In the first miniseries, Seaguy knows enough history and astronomy to recognize the glaring anachronism when he discovers the Earth is being bombarded by five-thousand-year-old moon rocks covered in hieroglyphics. If Morrison is complicit in authenticating that particular impossibility, since the third issue's "secret origin of the moon" reveals that the celestial body is actually a massive tomb constructed by a vain pharaoh and launched into space with fireworks, at least his hero realizes something is amiss.

This playfully fictitious history becomes a much more serious plot point in the second miniseries, *Seaguy: Slaves of Mickey Eye* (2009), when Professor Silvan Niltoid, an ostensibly reformed supervillain, reveals that he has been compiling disturbing evidence that history, as taught by the Eye, is a fake:

> **Niltoid:** Everything we hold dear teaches us that Mickey Eye created the world out of bubblegum and flame, does it not?
> **Seaguy:** That's kid's stuff. Everyone knows the world's made of science and history. (*Slaves* 1.18–19)

Seaguy's response is hardly more reassuring than Niltoid's précis of the Eye's curriculum. Nor can historically minded readers take much solace in

Professor Niltoid's unveiling of his carefully accumulated evidence, "The Cabinet of the Crypto-Saurs," a paleontological exhibit featuring reconstructions that combine dinosaur bones with twentieth-century technology to fashion creatures such as the cyclosaurus and the autoraptor; it's a clever joke about the fast-approaching end of our own society's fossil-fueled automotive dinosaurs, but it suggests that New Venice's few dissidents know as little about their history as the children raised on the Eye's propaganda.[7] Niltoid indicates why that history has become obscured when he says he pieced the crypto-saurs together from "various bones and other odd body parts we discovered down there in the deepest, hardest gum layers" (*Slaves* 1.20). Seaguy's world sits atop layer upon layer of impenetrable gum, a hint of some bizarre cataclysm and a barrier that has collapsed all history before the Eye into prehistory.

If the Eye teaches that Seaguy's world postdates the end of history then it also claims to sit at the end of narrative. Seaguy begins the first miniseries desperate to find an adventure so he can impress She-Beard, a woman warrior with a full, curly beard who has vowed to give herself to the first hero she meets. Seaguy, convinced that he must perform some heroic deed to attract her attention, laments that "everything's been done" (1.14). Narrative has been extinguished by the supposed perfection of the Eye's society, which has removed all incitements to action. Seaguy believes the need for heroes ended with the last war, although those beliefs are belied by the many narratives that accrue around him: a mysterious lunar bombardment, giant balloon animals attacking ocean liners, kidnappings at the Mickey Eye Park, and a new foodstuff that turns out to be sentient, not to mention Seaguy's own romantic aspirations. These narratives may be familiar or even exhausted for contemporary audiences—Seaguy's quest for love and adventure, his voyage around the globe, and his journey to the moon have already been done by protagonists from Don Quixote to Candide to Baron Munchausen—but they are new to Seaguy and they contradict the Eye's teachings that all stories, like all histories, are over.

Any novelty Seaguy's odyssey might generate in our world, however, comes from Morrison's surrealist style and from his decision to graft his hero's picaresque ramblings onto another exhausted genre, the superhero comic. Some commentators such as Joe McCulloch have been quick to identify *Seaguy* as a critique of contemporary superhero comics and the companies that publish them ("New Popular Suicides"). In this reading, Seaguy's home in New Venice and the Mickey Eye Park serve as tropes for the stasis of the never-ending corporate superhero franchise, in which nothing ever changes and nobody dies forever; Seaguy himself plays a game of chess with Death every week, and he always wins (1.3–4). Superhero comics have become as repetitive and as tightly circumscribed as the Eye-Go-Round that Doc Hero rides to regain the sensation of flight. While Seaguy tries to escape this system by seeking out new adventures, his voyages end with the status quo all but restored; on the last page, he is once again playing chess with Death (3.32), though there have been a few minor changes for the better (Seaguy has disrupted the consumption of the Xoo creatures) and for the worse (Chubby has died and been replaced with Lucky el Loro, a new sidekick who serves the Eye). These developments are the *Seaguy* equivalent of the ceaseless convolutions of plot that provide mainstream superhero comics with the illusion of progress without enacting any fundamental changes to the characters or their series. McCulloch argues that it is "difficult not to read the series in the context of Morrison's troubled relationship with Marvel, particularly surrounding the production of his top-lined continuity book *New X-Men*," in which several major changes "were reversed almost as soon as he left" ("New Popular Suicides").

Such readings are likely accurate—*Seaguy* was published mere months after Morrison left Marvel and *New X-Men*—but, as is so frequently the case with Morrison's work, it would be a mistake to limit *Seaguy* to a metafictional commentary on the impossibility of changing the American comics industry. The miniseries depicts the impossibility of changing any system, especially through isolated, individual, "heroic" action; the project demolishes not just the superhero but the Romantic hero. Seaguy plays all of the Romantic roles—innocent child, idealistic lover, explorer, rebel—but his search for novelty and adventure accomplishes little more than the death of his animal companion and the loss of his own childlike innocence. The Eye's conquest of past, present, and future continues unabated, and the hero is absorbed back into the ideology and institutions he attempts to challenge. *Seaguy* criticizes Romantic models of the heroic individual even as it deplores the postmodern economic and cultural forces that erode individual autonomy. The miniseries instead turns to literary models from the more communitarian eras that predate the Romantics, deploying allegories, quests, and picaresque heroes to reveal the consequences of our reliance on simulacra, our accelerating consumption and exhaustion of narrative forms, our environmental exploitation, and our pursuit of private comfort at any cost. Seaguy is an early modern hero lost in a postmodern world.

VIMANARAMA: BOLLYWOOD KIRBY

Like *Seaguy*, *Vimanarama* (2005) combines a whimsical tone with a pessimistic assessment of contemporary society, but it does so through a very different mixture of genres and styles. *Vimanarama* is the story of Ali, a young British Asian Muslim whose dilemmas are at once more personal and more cosmic than those of the protagonists in Morrison's other Vertigo miniseries. A moody but dutiful son, Ali watches over his family and their corner shop for his father, who has also arranged his marriage to a young woman named Sofia. Ali has never met Sofia, and he contemplates her impending arrival with adolescent histrionics: since he believes that "everything is preordained and occurs by God's will," if Sofia is "ugly or stupid or boring" then it must be a sign that God hates him, which he views as grounds for suicide (1.8). Sofia turns out to be beautiful, intelligent, and courageous, but she faces her own predetermined responsibilities when she discovers she is the descendent and reincarnation of another, ancient Sofia who was the lover of Prince Ben Rama, leader of the heroes of the Ultrahadeen. Ben Rama returns after a six-thousand-year absence to defend the human race against Ull-Shattan and his devils, who were until recently entombed in a hidden city buried beneath the family corner shop, but he also expects Sofia to join him as his consort just when Ali becomes attracted to her. Ali and Sofia both grapple with divinely ordained destinies, whether real or imagined, and with decisions that others have made or attempt to make for them.

Unlike its contemporaries, however, *Vimanarama* conveys these struggles against divine and familial authority as a romantic comedy. Philip Bond's art, like Cameron Stewart's, invests the sunken cities and flying saucers with the same solidity and weight it gives to the council houses and corner stores, but Bond's figures are slightly more exaggerated, the better to express the characters' seesawing emotional states. Morrison's script plays along with the comedy; characters stare out of the page to berate Ali for his mistakes (2.1) and schoolgirls appear to break out into dance as he rides by (1.2–3), giving *Vimanarama* something of the air of a Bollywood musical.[8] Its three issues follow the formulaic Hollywood three-act structure of setup, confrontation, and resolution that Morrison bemoaned to Jay Babcock after *Seaguy*'s mixed reception, but the musical film is only one of many genres at play in the miniseries. Morrison combines the musical and the romantic comedy with gruesome scenes of war, heavy-handed political commentary, Kirbyesque superhero and supervillain designs, Hindu and Muslim legends, and a few metafictional gestures reminiscent of *The Invisibles*. Even the title combines names from ancient Sanskrit epics with the *-rama* suffix that graced so many neologisms in twentieth-century American mass culture, such as the Cinerama widescreen projection system.

Unfortunately, the generic pastiche leads to a more problematic cultural pastiche. The miniseries attempts to diversify the world of Anglo-American comics by focusing on South Asian characters, but creates a fantasy culture that combines Muslim and Hindu divinities into a single mythology of an exotic and undifferentiated East. Ull-Shattan and his lieutenant Ull-Blizz are near-homophones for Shaitan and Iblis, Islamic names for Satan, while the Horn of Jabreel that destroys them evokes Jibril, the Arabic name for the angel Gabriel, who revealed the Qur'an to Muhammad. The eponymous vimanas, on the other hand, are flying machines mentioned in the Hindu epics of the *Ramayana* and the *Mahabharata*, and Prince Ben Rama's name derives from Rama, the hero of the *Ramayana*—though it is preceded by *ben*, a Hebrew patronymic that translates into Arabic as *bin* or *ibn*. The comic's language is as confused as its mythology: *vimana* is Sanskrit, while "Ultrahadeen" alludes to the Arabic *mujahideen*, "struggler" or "justice fighter," a term that has only been applied in Pakistan and Afghanistan since the twentieth century. Morrison has created either a postmodern bricolage or an Orientalist fantasy that combines Muslim, Hindu, Arabic, and Sanskrit cultures without acknowledging the distances in time, space, language, and religion that separate them. The miniseries' overall genre fusion and the presence of non-Eastern elements like Jack Kirby comics suggests *Vimanarama* is at least partially the former; being postmodern, of course, does not mean it cannot also be Orientalist fantasy.

Morrison does work some reversals on common Orientalist depictions of the East. Instead of positing an Orient ripe for colonization and conquest, *Vimanarama* envisions powerful Eastern heroes and demons who overwhelm a weak and decadent West. To some extent, this change simply animates post-September 11 fears of a deadly clash of civilizations between the Islamic world and the West, fears that informed earlier drafts of the miniseries. In an interview conducted a year and a half before the first issue was released (and thus very early in *Vimanarama*'s production cycle), Morrison said the story would include "gigantic spider-mosques war[ring] with cathedral tanks on the green fields of England and the question is finally answered: Islam or Christianity—which is the strongest?" (Brady, "Inside Morrison's Head"). The Ultrahadeen's arsenal includes a walking mosque with multiple mechanical legs, but the cathedral tanks and the promised holy war—which should probably be read as Morrison's tongue-in-cheek parody of comics fans' constant arguments over which superhero is the strongest—are nowhere in evidence. The comic instead offers a caustic and unsubtle commentary on the wars fueled by this clash-of-civilizations rhetoric, and the fuels that have embroiled these civilizations in two wars. Ull-Shattan and his devils are "Dead trees [...] pressurized into fossil form, as tar and oil and hatred" (2.17)—in other words, walking, talking fossil fuels who seek to pervert the natural world and who can only survive on the Earth's surface because humanity has polluted the air with acid and carbon dioxide (3.13). The environmental commentary turns explicitly political when these evil fossil fuels conquer London and New York in a vicious reversal of America and Britain's invasions of Iraq and Afghanistan.

If the devils of Ull-Shattan upend the West's military superiority, the heroes of the Ultrahadeen overturn its assumption of cultural supremacy. They promise to lend their technological, spiritual, and moral guidance to repair what they view as a corrupted, fallen world by introducing "The machines and philosophies of the ancient world [to] light your cities and guide your minds" (2.21). Under their protection the West becomes the object rather than the agent of cultural imperialism, which is delivered (as always) in the guise of a beneficent humanitarian intervention. Even if the rampaging devils make that intervention necessary, Morrison makes it clear that humanity is not yet ready to handle the technology the Ultrahadeen provide for their defense, particularly when Bond illustrates groups of British Asians and white skinheads using the advanced weaponry to kill each other (2.30). As with America and Britain's own foreign interventions, superior technology and a sense of purpose are no proof against long-running ethnic and sectarian divisions.

The Ultrahadeen are ultimately successful, however, perhaps because they only seek to transform human society rather than govern it. The world adapts to their technology, though with some difficulty; in the final pages of *Vimanarama*, Ali's family struggles to operate their new robot workers while joyriding teenagers crash a vimana on the moon. The explosion of super-science contradicts Ali's implication that the story ends with a superhero comic's typical restoration of the old social order, or a comedy's typical restoration and continuation of the family. Ali tells the readers, "I suppose you're wondering what lesson I learned on my trip to paradise and back. Well, the more things change [...] the more they stay the same" (3.30). As the story concludes, Ali has begun a relationship with Sofia and he is still bailing others out of trouble, but he now does so as a science fiction superhero, having assumed Ben Rama's powers and responsibilities. He is the perfect man

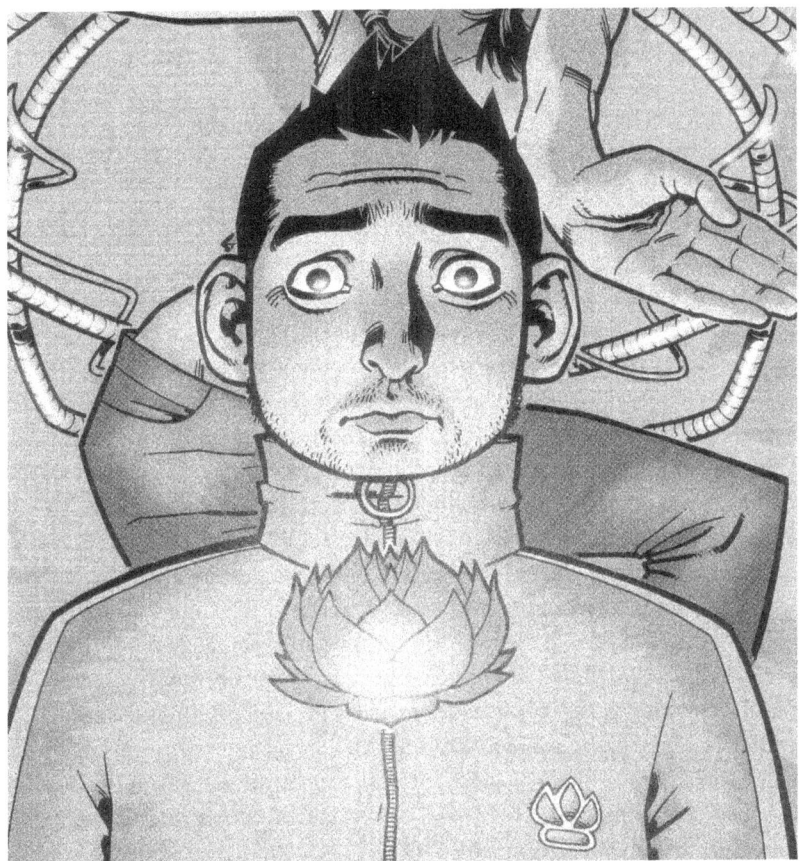

Figure 5-5. Detail from the cover to *Vimanarama* 1. Art by Philip Bond. © Morrison and Philip Bond.

for the job since he and Ben Rama already fulfilled nearly identical roles: both loved the same woman, both watched over the people in their care, and both played the traditional neurotic, hypersensitive Morrison protagonist.[9] Ali also makes an ideal liaison between his world and the world of the Ultrahadeen because, as a British Asian Muslim, he already straddles two cultures at the beginning of the story. Like the icon on his track jacket, which resembles both the original Adidas logo and the sacred lotus flower, Ali comes to bridge all the oppositions that structure the miniseries, guiding humanity into a new culture that fuses the ancient and the modern, the East and the West, the supernatural and the realistic (fig. 5-5). If *Vimanarama*'s narrative structure is unusually cinematic and formulaic, if its political commentary is unusually blunt, its replacement of binaristic and antagonistic civilizations with a culture of fusion and cooperation is pure Morrison.

WE3: THE VOCABULARIES OF CONTROL

We3 (2004–05) also fuses a variety of styles as it seeks to open new spaces for formal experimentation and ethical development. The title is an abbreviation of Animal Weapon 3, the name a United States Air Force research program has given to a trio of former house pets used as test subjects in a grotesque experiment. The program has modified a dog, a cat, and a rabbit (designated 1, 2, and 3 respectively) with cybernetic enhancements, outfitted them with state-of-the-art military ordnance, and trained them to kill as a team with the ultimate goal of developing remote-controlled animal weapons who will replace human soldiers. When the order comes down to kill We3—in part because one doctor has taught the animals to speak a crude, limited English vocabulary, much to the horror of some visiting dignitaries—the doctor turns them loose and inadvertently begins a deadly cross-country pursuit. *We3* thrives on the contrast between its sympathetic animal protagonists, whose attempt to return home recalls the children's book and Disney movie *The Incredible Journey*, and its decidedly unsentimental scenes of high-tech combat and bloody violence, which owe more to video games, anime, and manga; Morrison calls this unwholesome combination "Disney with fangs" (Brady, "Disney With Fangs"). With the assistance of Frank Quitely, he merges Japanese and Western comics styles to push familiar narrative conventions in new directions. One of the most ambitious Morrison-Quitely collaborations, *We3* extends the struggle for personal and creative independence that runs throughout Morrison's later Vertigo work into the realm of language and ethics, depicting characters who fight to build their own moral codes with the limited tools that nature and technology have given them. Hybrids of the animal and the machine, the creatures of We3 strive to enter an ethical space and a mode of selfhood that humanity normally reserves for itself.

In a comparable formal strategy, the miniseries blends narrative and design elements from other media and other cultures to develop a visual style that is not dependent on the practices of the American comics industry. Video games shape everything from the linear plot structure—the animals proceed through escalating combats with increasingly deadly enemies before confronting a single, intimidating "boss" figure—to the design of the modified game controllers that the Air Force uses to guide its animal weapons.[10] The creators also acknowledge their influences in film animation: Morrison praises Jamie Grant's vivid colors in one pivotal scene as "*Toy Story* coloring" and Quitely draws Dr. Trendle, the chief scientist of the animal weapons program, to resemble acclaimed anime director and manga artist Hayao Miyazaki (Brady, "Disney With Fangs"). Yet while the lifelike simulations of video games and animation inspire the writer and artist, they also lead the human characters to make a number of faulty assumptions. Viewing the animals simply as remote-controlled weapons or avatars, the scientists and soldiers tacitly adopt a video game metaphor that allows them to exploit their test subjects without troubling their consciences. Because Dr. Trendle regards the animal weapons as simulated combatants rather than living creatures in their own right, he cannot imagine they could ever slip free of their handlers or turn against the soldiers whose lives they were supposed to save. The miniseries regards the postmodern detachment of the simulation (and the simulator) with suspicion even as it creates its own fantastically detailed, gamelike simulations for the readers' entertainment.

Morrison and Quitely show less apprehension about their comics influences. Most comics featuring animal protagonists belong to the "funny animal" genre—a somewhat misleading name as the genre is defined not by its humor but by the presence of anthropomorphized animals who walk, speak, and act like human beings. Joseph Witek observes that the genre is distinguished by a "curious indifference to the animal nature of the characters" (109) in which "the 'animalness' of the characters drops away entirely" (110). Carl Barks, the legendary creator of Disney's Donald Duck comics, viewed Donald as "a human being who happened to be shaped like a duck" (Witek 109); the cast of Art Spiegelman's *Maus* are actual human beings (mostly Spiegelman's own relatives) rendered as anthropomorphic cats and mice. Morrison violates this convention in *We3*, refusing to anthropomorphize his protagonists and seizing every opportunity to demonstrate their animality. Even though they have been taught to speak English, We3 still think and act like animals: the dog is a loyal pack animal who tries to keep his group together and wants to please his human masters, the cat a solitary hunter who stalks and plays with her prey, the rabbit a creature of limited intelligence who bolts at the first sign of danger and can focus on little more than his next meal (Brown 83). Morrison researched animal communication and behavior to make the creatures as plausible as their military hardware, grounding the story with a veneer of biological and technological verisimilitude; he told Matt Brady, "I've tried to keep this one very real. I wanted to do to funny animal comics what Alan Moore did to superhero comics in *Miracleman*" ("Disney With Fangs"). His plan to introduce realism to the genre came a few decades too late—Witek inventories the many funny animal parodies and deadly serious animal stories that appeared in the underground comix, all of which laid the groundwork for *Maus* (110–11). Nevertheless, Morrison reverses an even more fundamental convention of the genre through his insistence on treating animals as animals.

Rather than follow in the footsteps of funny animal comics, Morrison and Quitely look to manga for guidance, studying the visual styles and narrative techniques of Japanese comics to create their own formal language; Morrison calls *We3* "a vehicle to demonstrate the 'Western Manga' storytelling style Frank and I are trying to develop" (Brady, "Disney With Fangs"). They slow down the pacing, focusing on the most minute details while they dilate the passage of time even in the midst of violent action scenes. Panels alternate between richly rendered environments that establish the setting and blank, spare backgrounds that highlight the characters' interior states. Blurred objects, superimposed images, and other subjective motion effects allow readers to experience the action from the animals' perspectives, while long wordless sequences force readers to linger over the art.[11] At the same time, Morrison and Quitely combine these manga techniques with the more compressed narratives and realistic figure drawing of Western comic books. The end result is not a conventional Anglophone or Japanese comic but a formalist experiment that deploys its graphic and narrative features for carefully considered effect.

One episode from the first issue will serve to illustrate this dynamic. The sequence begins as Dr. Trendle prepares to euthanize the animal weapons while his subordinate Dr. Roseanne Berry, the animals' language tutor, sets them free in a belated fit of conscience. This information is conveyed through six all-but-wordless pages of security camera images, arranged in regular eighteen-panel grids that resemble banks of monitors (fig. 5-6). When the animals break out of the facility they also break free of the tight focus and oppressive repetitions of the panel grids, flying into a double-page spread and a luminous night sky (fig. 5-7). The next page cites this break in the panel grid by focusing on the broken fencing that marks the animals' getaway—another rigid, rectilinear lattice that has been destroyed by their escape. The subsequent panel offers an even more direct quote of the preceding page layouts, but with a crucial difference: it shows Dr. Trendle coordinating the hunt for We3 as he stands in front of one bank of security monitors, with another bank reflected in his eyeglasses (fig. 5-8). The ranks

Figure 5-6. *We3* 1.24. Art by Frank Quitely. © Grant Morrison and Frank Quitely.

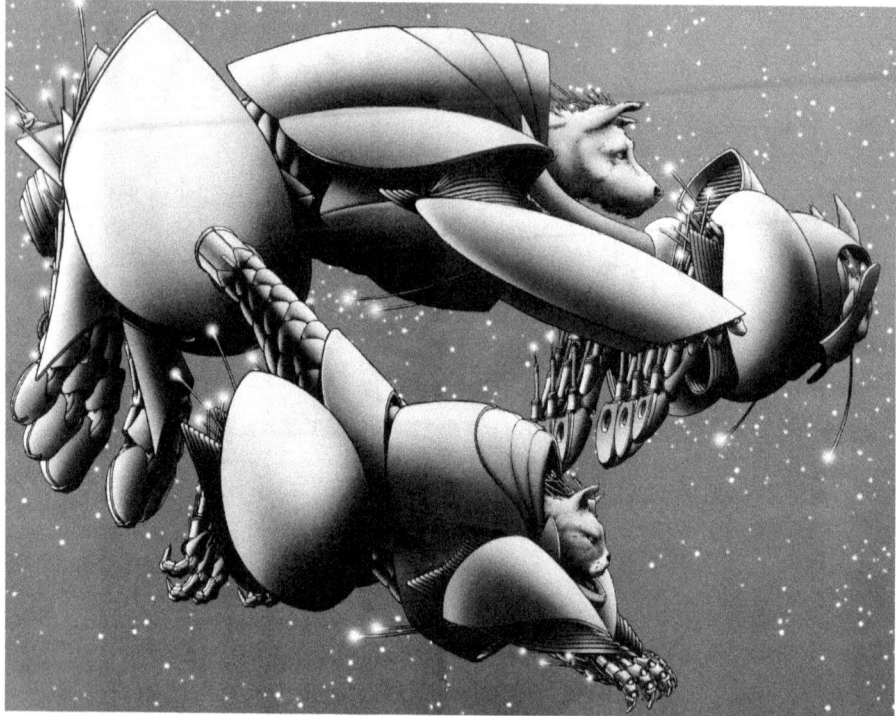

Figure 5-7. *We3* 1.26-27. Art by Frank Quitely. © Grant Morrison and Frank Quitely.

of monitors re-create the panel grids of previous pages even as Dr. Trendle begins his desperate efforts to contain and kill the animals, suggesting that a violent restoration of order is soon to follow. At every stage of the sequence, the page layout, pacing, and panel design match the characters' actions and desires in a seamless integration of form and content.

The escape sequence is a bravura passage, but not an isolated one. The rest of the miniseries applies the same formalist care, particularly when it represents the animals' subjective experience of time. In the second issue, Trendle warns his military superiors that "even their senses are different from ours. They're much faster than any human. They experience time and motion differently" (2.4). Two pages later Quitely confirms the doctor's warning, illustrating how the animals differ not only from their human pursuers but also from each other. In a wordless two-page spread, 1 launches himself through a personnel carrier and kills its occupants while 2 scales a tree and ambushes a squad of troops on the ground beneath her. Such simple descriptions cannot do these pages justice, however, as Quitely subdivides both of these scenes

Figure 5-8. *We3* 1.28. Art by Frank Quitely. © Grant Morrison and Frank Quitely.

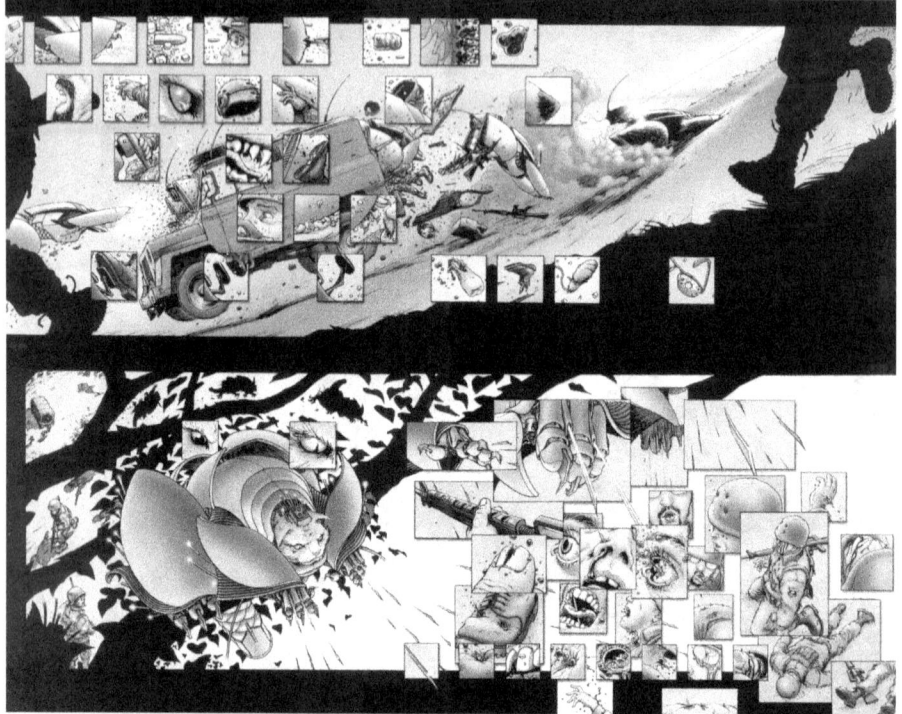

Figure 5-9. *We3* 2.6-7. Art by Frank Quitely. © Grant Morrison and Frank Quitely.

into cascades of smaller panels, turning what could be single, static images into micro-narratives that reflect both the frenetic experience of combat and the animals' radically different perceptions of time and space (fig. 5-9).

The upper tier superimposes a procession of inset panels whose layout is as relentlessly linear as 1's passage through the troop carrier. Each inset focuses on some smaller detail of 1's assault, primarily on incidents and objects inside the troop carrier that are not visible in the larger, external view that forms the background. These insets advance in the standard Western left-to-right, top-to-bottom reading order, and most of the rows depict events at the same levels of elevation, moving from the soldiers' heads down to their feet; because each inset focuses on only a single part of the body, the graphic representation of the battle is as fragmented and disassembled as the soldiers themselves are after their unfortunate encounter with the canine weapon. The dog, on the other hand, more than retains his bodily integrity. While a few of the insets show isolated, terrifying glimpses of his eyes, teeth, and mechanical claws, the background panel displays multiple

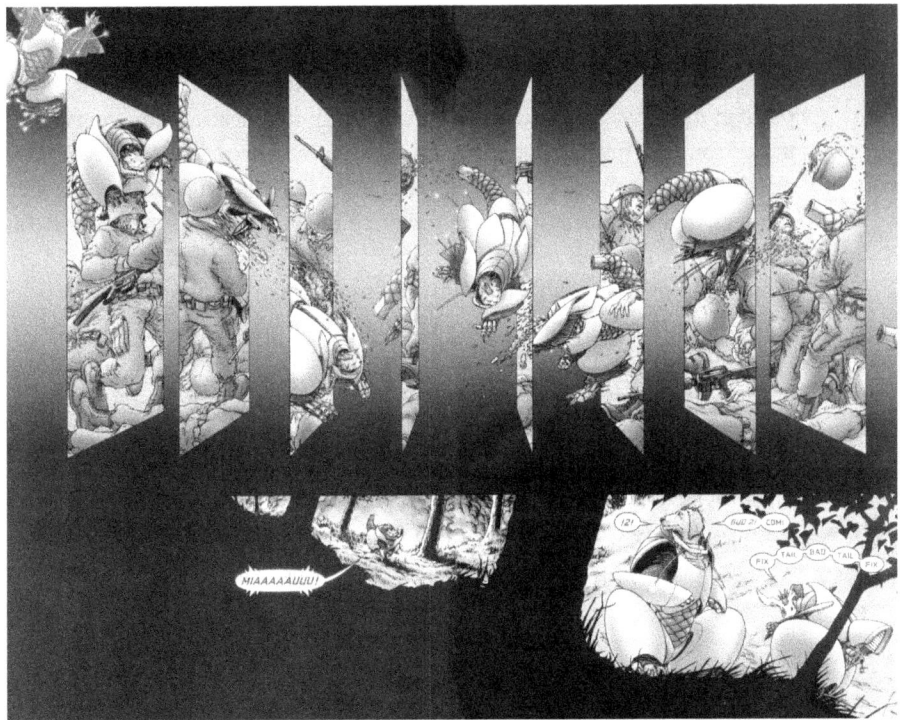

Figure 5-10. *We3* 2.10-11. Art by Frank Quitely. © Grant Morrison and Frank Quitely.

images of 1 moving through a single, continuous setting. The juxtaposition of a sequential 1 against a static background allows the dog to lunge through the panel with inhuman speed while the human onlookers and even the vehicle appear to stand still. If the inset panels imply 1 has a keen awareness of his surroundings, freezing the action and taking in all the scattered details of his combat, the background demonstrates the accelerated time sense and heightened reflexes that Dr. Trendle dreads.

The lower tier applies these same principles but adds a few new techniques to demonstrate the comparable but distinct perceptions of the feline 2. Quitely shows several images of 2 climbing the tree in silhouette, but rather than superimpose them over a continuous background, he uses the branches of the tree to divide them into separate panel-like spaces. Since the gutters that frame and divide the panels are as black as the silhouetted branches, and the branches extend into the gutters, the limbs effectively become panel borders themselves, transforming the lower tier into a sequence of panels that depicts several moments in time—not only for the cat but also for the much slower line of hapless human soldiers trudging down the left side of the page. The cat compensates for this slower panel progression with a burst of inset panels that explode out from her vantage point at different sizes and different levels of magnification, showing everything from full human figures to close-ups of ruptured fingernails and corneas. These panels rain down like the projectiles she fires on the doomed soldiers, demonstrating both the frenzy of the ambush and the cat's eye for detail. While 2 herself remains stationary in this tier's primary image, she is, if anything, even faster than her canine comrade in arms. A few pages later, Quitely sends her plunging into a column of soldiers and diving between the panels that depict them: the troops remain trapped within the panel borders, locked into a slower passage of time, while the cat moves freely outside and between them at a pace they cannot even perceive, let alone match (fig. 5-10). She is equally unconstrained by that most basic and seemingly inviolable barrier, the boundaries of the page. This two-page sequence begins with the cat dropping in from the upper left-hand corner and ends with her tail disappearing off the right-hand edge, granting her a freedom of movement that no formal device, not even the physical limits of the comic, can contain.

Because the rabbit is far less intelligent than the other two animal weapons, his point of view receives a far less elaborate representation. One two-panel sequence shows the rabbit scattering mines in mid-leap and then reveals the effects of those mines, a line of destroyed vehicles and dismembered bodies (2.9). Neither panel is further complicated or subdivided, but readers can draw a few inferences about 3 from these images. The simple panel presentation suggests the rabbit is not as cognitively sophisticated as his teammates, and his complete absence from the second panel, which unfolds after his passage, may indicate that he ignores the consequences of his actions. In fact, the blank background in the panel that does show 3 in action could imply that he is almost completely oblivious to his surroundings and is acting on pure fight-or-flight instinct, even as it also places him in the same featureless zone that Quitely uses to indicate the cat's accelerated time sense. The rabbit is just as fast as his teammates, but less able to think about the past or the future.

All of these experiments take formal elements that have become naturalized by convention, elements that are almost completely invisible in the typical comics text, and call the reader's attention to their artificiality. The cat's rampage between panels, for example, graphically defies the normally unspoken assumption that the panel constitutes a frame that opens into a representational space (Abbott 156–57) rather than being part of the representation itself (Eisner 44–49). The scene sabotages the "mimetic illusion" (Brooks 13) that pretends texts simply view or report on the worlds they depict rather than create them.[12] Placing the cat outside a sequence of window-like panels and extending the action beyond the borders of the frames, Morrison and Quitely remind us that these panels and pages are not windows into another world but narrative fabrications, arbitrary devices that can be altered at will and turned to other purposes. They defamiliarize these conventions in order to break out of the confines of the comics form, pushing against its boundaries just as the animal protagonists push back against their captivity.

We3 experiments with comics' textual conventions as well as their pictorial ones, largely by limiting its dependence on text. The animals' limited vocabulary necessarily forces Morrison and Quitely to rely on visual narrative techniques, but even the human characters often drift through wordless scenes. Sometimes they speak in textual symbols (musical notes, check marks, squiggles that denote an angry grumble) or their word balloons frame pictorial elements; more often they do not speak at all. Instead of marginalizing language, this verbal restraint stresses its power and magnifies its impact when it is spoken. Like Victor Frankenstein's unfortunate creation, whose acquisition of the "godlike science" (Shelley 112) of language enables his moral and intellectual development but also leads to his murderous rebellion against his creator, the animals of We3 are both endangered and liberated by words.[13] The general in charge of the animal weapons program orders their death in part because he is disturbed by their command of language. He asks Dr. Trendle, "What kind of lunatic would teach a killing machine to talk?" (1.19), perhaps because once they can talk, there is a chance they will no longer remain compliant killing machines. That is certainly the consequence of one particular word, the final word Dr. Berry teaches to 1 in an attempt to save him from the military by reminding him of a life before the animal weapons program: "The name on your collar was 'Bandit.' U. R. Bandit." (3.13). Soon after, when his armored "coat" begins to peel off following damage sustained in battle, 1 applies this new term and realizes that his technological shell "Is coat not 'Bandit.' [. . .] Is coat not we" (3.25). The rediscovery of his name allows him to separate himself from "1" and his role as a remote-controlled assassin. By giving the animals the power of language, Dr. Berry has also given them the tools to develop new selves and new ethical codes independent from their instincts as animals and their training as killers.

As in *Animal Man*, Morrison's sympathy for animals does not lead him to romanticize an idyllic nature in which creatures coexist in harmony. Nature is harsh and unforgiving in *We3*, as seen in the carrion creatures that feast on dead bodies or in We3's own murder of a civilian hunter and his loyal dog. Dr. Trendle warns his superiors that We3 are dangerous not simply because of their advanced weaponry but because "They are instinctual, amoral" (1.29). On the other hand, Trendle may be rationalizing his attempts to kill the animals—or projecting some of his own amoral conduct onto them—since at least one of the creatures does display a rudimentary morality. At the beginning of the miniseries 1 is eager to be recognized as a "gud dog" (1.17), whether as a result of his training, his species' long history of sociability, or his faint memories of his past as a house pet with a good home and a beloved owner. (All of We3 were once domesticated; the covers to each issue are designed as "missing pet" posters circulated by their former owners.) The violent events of the miniseries provoke a crisis of conscience as 1 decides his murder of the hunter and his failure to protect 3 make him a "bad dog" (2.29), yet he is unable to play the part of the vicious killer for long, particularly after he encounters the real thing in the form of Animal Weapon 4, a mastiff whose next-generation enhancements give him the size and build of a gorilla. The battle with Weapon 4, Dr. Berry's restoration of his name, and the actions of his team motivate 1 to resume his role as a "gud dog" who protects his teammates and innocent civilians. The choice between being a good dog and a bad one may seem like a simplistic or contrived moral dilemma for us, but to 1 it is monumental: a dog—not an anthropomorphized character in the manner of Barks or Spiegelman but an actual dog—has not only decided what kind of moral code he will follow and what kind of identity he will choose, he has made the responsible choices despite all the forces pressuring him to take the selfish or angry ones.

His teammates reach their own moral decisions, though their dilemmas are neither as complicated nor as fraught with emotion. The cat, who spends the entire miniseries challenging 1's authority and rejecting any allegiance to the team, rejoins him at a crucial moment and demonstrates her teamwork, while the panicky rabbit earns a moment of defiance before he goes out in a blaze of glory against the vastly more powerful Weapon 4. These scenes in which the animals overcome their own worst attributes and defend their teammates follow superhero formulas that are otherwise absent or at least deeply suppressed in *We3*. The cat's struggles for dominance with the dog read like primal versions of the perpetual conflicts between the rebellious loner Wolverine and the strait-laced team leader Cyclops, or any of the other fractious superheroes influenced by Claremont's X-Men.[14] In a similar vein, 2's triumphant rescue of 1 is a splash-page combat pose backlit by a lightning bolt that could have come straight out of *The Dark Knight Returns* (3.18). Both cognitively and ethically less advanced than 1, the cat and the rabbit undergo simpler character arcs that owe more to superhero conventions than to any exploration of language, ethics, or identity.

The human characters, however, also reach ethical breakthroughs in contexts more removed from genre formulas. *We3* refuses to demonize its human antagonists just as it resists sentimentalizing its animal heroes; each of the major human characters sacrifices themselves or their objectives to do the right thing. Dr. Berry's initial liberation of We3 might appear to be one such act, but as Morrison points out to Brady, it is in fact a rash and self-destructive gesture, an attempt to evade responsibility for her own role in exploiting and abusing the animals ("Disney With Fangs"); it also results in the deaths of dozens of people. Filled with remorse, Dr. Berry atones by returning 1's name and giving her own life to save him from an ambush. Shortly afterwards, Dr. Trendle and the general allow 1 and 2 to escape once again in order to prevent more fatalities, killing Weapon 4 after he starts attacking police officers. Trendle's guilt carries him one step further, leading him to blow the whistle on the animal weapons program and destroy the presidential ambitions of the senator who wants to take the project into mass production. Nearly every character acts against their own interests to take a moral stand and protect some other creature's life.

The major exception is Weapon 4. The mastiff is guided by remote control and should be incapable of autonomous action, although his operators' control is far from perfect; he lashes out with an aggression that places human bystanders and even his own handlers in jeopardy. Governed by a dangerous mixture of military technology and animal instinct, Weapon 4 has no mediating self like the We3 team. He also lacks the power of speech—he cannot even bark or hiss like his animal opponents, and when he howls, letterer Todd Klein grants him only a jagged balloon filled with black ink, a graphic expression of formless rage (3.21). This speechlessness is one of the mastiff's most prominent traits, first advertised when Morrison unveils Weapon 4 with Dr. Trendle's declaration that "the time for talking is done," followed by a wordless full-page image of the mastiff drooling in his cage (2.31–32). The silent spectacle and the gentle double-entendre highlight the creature's lack of language as the factor that sets him apart from We3 and makes him their truly amoral reflection. The contrast reinforces Morrison's argument that language defines selfhood and that both are necessary prerequisites for the development of ethical codes. Long before language helps Bandit discover the difference between his body and his armored coat, or between his ethical self and his training as a conscripted killer, it prevents him from becoming a mindless killing machine like Weapon 4.

Morrison would touch on these arguments in his other Vertigo projects. Greg Feely's moral sense is tied to his identity as Greg Feely (and to his affection for his cat); Mickey Eye speaks in a crude pidgin that dumbs down viewers by inhibiting complex thoughts; and Ali discovers he literally consists of language when he journeys to the afterlife (*Vimanarama* 3.5). All four of these series examine the difficulties of defining the self and the challenges of resisting the natural, social, or institutional forces that attempt to dictate its definition. All feature heroes who reject externally imposed identities, and while none allow for a complete escape from social or personal responsibility, these comics do permit their protagonists to develop their own ethical codes in contravention of their societies' ongoing destruction of the individual. Each series approaches these problems through its own unique combination of genres and styles, but *We3* offers the most explicit illustration of their collective desire for independence because it extends that desire to its form and design. Although the project would not inaugurate the new "Western Manga" style Morrison envisioned—even his other collaborations with Frank Quitely would not sustain this level of formal experimentation—*We3* demonstrates what he can accomplish when he is not constrained by corporate ownership or genre expectations, and when he works with a talented and trusted collaborator.

Chapter 6

A TIME OF HARVEST

While Vertigo completed Morrison's troika of genre-bending miniseries with the publication of *Vimanarama*, his next project returned to the more conventional territory of the DC universe of costumed superheroes. February 2005 saw the debut of *Seven Soldiers* (2005–06), a project that sought to renovate several obscure or underutilized DC characters while reinventing one of the most formulaic modes of storytelling in comics, the multi-title crossover.[1] *Seven Soldiers* is written entirely by Morrison but it constitutes a crossover unto itself, almost an entire continuity unto itself: seven miniseries and two bookends that interlock to tell the story of the Sheeda, a predatory race determined to ravage twenty-first-century society, and the Seven Soldiers, a septet of unusual heroes who can stop the invasion only if they never meet or join forces. Accordingly, Morrison does not construct the issues as consecutive chapters in a linear thirty-part story but distributes the narrative across seven more or less freestanding miniseries created in collaboration with nine different artists.

Seven Soldiers combines Celtic myth, Arthurian legend, horror, science fiction, westerns, and more to revitalize superhero comics by infusing them with elements of other genres. *Shining Knight,* with art by Simone Bianchi, relocates the last knight of Camelot to modern Los Angeles. *Guardian*, with Cameron Stewart, gives a disgraced ex-cop a shot at redemption as a private in-house superhero for a sensationalist tabloid newspaper. In *Zatanna*, with Ryan Sook, a second-generation magician overcomes her guilt over past misdeeds and her grief at her father's death after she takes on an apprentice. *Klarion*, with Frazer Irving, follows a willful and impetuous fugitive as he leaves a lost subterranean colony for a series of disastrous encounters with the modern world. *Mister Miracle*, with art by Pasqual Ferry, Billy Dallas Patton, and Freddie E. Williams II—the series was plagued by Ferry's sudden departure and the scramble to find a replacement—focuses on a celebrity escape artist who reevaluates his life after he encounters a race

Figure 6-1. *Seven Soldiers* 1.38. Art by J. H. Williams III. © DC Comics.

of extradimensional gods and becomes caught in their struggles. *Bulleteer*, with Yanick Paquette, introduces a reluctant superhero to the seamier side of comic book culture, and *Frankenstein*, with Doug Mahnke, sends the vengeful, Milton-quoting creature from Mary Shelley's novel on a rambling odyssey from the southwestern United States to Mars to the distant future, to slaughter every other monster in sight.

The project is bookended by two issues featuring the frighteningly versatile art of J. H. Williams III. Williams draws *Seven Soldiers* 0, the first chapter in the narrative, in a pastiche of other famous comics artists, notably Frank Miller and Jean "Moebius" Giraud. Williams's ability to copy these artists' styles by varying his inking, line weight, and figure drawing is uncanny, but he outdoes himself in *Seven Soldiers* 1, the final issue in the series, which he draws in a pastiche of the other *Seven Soldiers* artists: any given page might paint the Sheeda with Simone Bianchi's lush inks while etching Klarion in Frazer Irving's heavy lines, reminiscent of a woodcut print (fig. 6-1). Blending his fellow artists' styles within the same pages and sometimes even the same panels, Williams brings the project to a completion and unity that Morrison's plot explicitly rules out.

In a genre where most of the leading characters are still white men, the Seven Soldiers stand out for their diversity. Most of these heroes are either black or female, with only the blue-skinned Klarion, scion of an interbred race descended from Puritan settlers, and gray, cadaverous Frankenstein, that hideous assembly of whatever corpses were available to Victor Frankenstein in eighteenth-century Geneva, qualifying as white men, and then only on the barest of technicalities. This demographic inclusiveness, like the project's generic and artistic variety, is part of Morrison's attempt to modernize and rejuvenate superhero comics, a mission he narrativizes through multiple storylines about rehabilitation, transformation, and growth. Several of the heroes, most notably Zatanna and the Guardian, seek redemption for past mistakes or tragedies; others, like Klarion or the Shining Knight, are adolescents on the threshold of maturity, transitioning into adulthood as their series unfold. All of the Seven Soldiers undergo ordeals of trial and initiation, crises of conscience or of will that force them to examine their principles while Morrison himself examines the assumptions and conventions of the superhero genre. As is frequently the case with Morrison, however, this metacommentary only accounts for part of the story. *Seven Soldiers* uses its time travelers and clashing cultures to search for criticisms of modernity that are not politically reactionary, while it applies its superheroes, witch queens, and fallen gods to develop new strategies of signification capable of articulating these critiques. The project combines the fantastic and the realistic in a manner that Morrison suggests is necessary if either superhero comics or Western culture as a whole are to reach a state of healthy, sustainable maturity.

CRYPTIC CONNECTIONS

As the first issues were published, the connections between miniseries amounted to little more than a few shared settings. Several of the series take place in a Manhattan filled with visionary architectural projects that were proposed but never realized in our own world, such as Frank Lloyd Wright's Ellis Island Key Project, Antoni Gaudí's Hotel Attraction, or Robert Moses's Mid-Manhattan Expressway (Starr 1, 26). The three heroes based in Manhattan are always on the verge of bumping into each other, although they never quite meet: Klarion and the Guardian almost cross paths in the second issues of their respective titles as they both explore a secret network of subway tunnels, and in *Mister Miracle* 3, Shilo Norman stumbles through the moments of crisis that Klarion and the Guardian experience in the third issues of their own series. The characters converge temporally as well as spatially—some series begin days or even weeks before the disastrous mission in *Seven Soldiers* 0 that kicks off the narrative, but most of the third issues happen simultaneously, within a few days of the finale. By *Seven Soldiers* 1, every hero arrives in Manhattan to fight the Sheeda invasion.

Mostly, though, the stories of *Seven Soldiers* are linked by their common antagonists, their shared mythology, and the million little cross-references and in-jokes that Morrison has seeded throughout the crossover. Even when these references are not themselves significant, they indicate the type of cross-textual reading *Seven Soldiers* requires. When occult store owner Cassandra Craft mentions that she's been fabricating and selling magical forgeries in *Zatanna* 2, it explains why Dyno-Mite Dan, who bought a pair of fake rings from her, didn't accomplish much of anything in *Seven Soldiers* 0; similarly, a throwaway quip in the first issue of *Guardian* about using a horse to get around Manhattan doesn't see its payoff until *Seven Soldiers* 1, when the Guardian finally gets his steed. Two major parental mysteries are buried so deeply in the background that they are only resolved in the cryptic crossword Morrison embeds in a facsimile of the Guardian's newspaper in *Seven Soldiers* 1—one of them is not even hinted at until the crossword makes a stunning revelation. More than establishing a richly textured world, these details reward reader attention and involvement; it's no surprise that *Seven Soldiers* sparked a lively community of online discussion as readers attempted to sort out its mysteries. The Barbelith community's *Seven Soldiers Annotations* are especially thorough, taking full advantage of the web's hyperlink capabilities to track the many allusions and interconnections of this networked narrative. Rather than attempt to duplicate their annotative work in a medium far less suited to charting every link between issues, I will focus on the formal strategies that unify the project and communicate its concerns.

Beginning with *Seven Soldiers* 0, in which a team of seven aspiring superheroes is forced to ride into the field with only six members, the narrative is organized around absence and absent figures. Characters are haunted by memories of colleagues, lovers, and especially missing patriarchs: from Klarion's father, who fled Limbo Town years before his son followed suit, to Zatanna's dead father, to the dead King Arthur, to the absent god Croatoan, nearly every male authority figure is either gone before the narrative starts or dead soon after they enter it. The few who are not, like the deposed Sheeda king Sebastian Melmoth (who claims some form of paternity to two different Soldiers), are undead revenants who refuse to relinquish their power; they must be removed before their children can assume the authority necessary to face Gloriana Tenebrae, the Sheeda's wicked fairy queen. Soldiers like Zatanna seek atonement with the more benevolent fathers and rapprochement with their legacies, while others like Frankenstein or Klarion—this project's version of the rebellious Horus avatar—depose or murder the lingering fathers who overstay their welcome. If Gloriana is a conventionally nightmarish representation of female power, combining traits of every witch queen from Morgan le Fay to Snow White's evil stepmother, the dead and undying patriarchs are equally problematic incarnations of paternal authority who must be laid to rest, peaceably or violently, so their children can reach maturity.

Perhaps the most surprising absences, in a project called *Seven Soldiers*, are the sevens. Sixfold configurations abound instead, from the mysterious pair of dice that float through the narrative to the teams of six that inevitably meet grisly fates. The Vigilante sets the tone when his first, doomed attempt to revive the Seven Soldiers of Victory (a 1940s superhero team) nets only six members, most of whom die horribly in the incident that summons the Sheeda to the twenty-first century. Other groups of six—Zatanna's team of magical investigators, the surviving knights of the Broken Table, the Newsboy Army, the Deviants—fare no better, forming a pattern so prominent that even the amateur crimefighters gathered at a superhero convention have noticed six is an unlucky number (*Bulleteer* 3.11).² Ed Stargard, the Guardian's editor and sponsor, explains why at the narrative midpoint: Gloriana, knowing that legends say she will be overthrown by seven soldiers, has been targeting heroes before they can reach that magic number to prevent her destined enemies from uniting. Morrison introduces another obstacle to his characters' assembly when Stargard reveals that he and a few other survivors of the Newsboy Army have been cultivating a new team of Seven Soldiers who don't know each other, will never meet one another, and might therefore escape the Sheeda's attention (*Guardian* 4.19). The villains attempt to prevent the narrative from reaching completion, while the heroes actively avoid it. This distrust of narrative integration is reinforced when Morrison incorporates Jack Kirby's New Gods into the narrative; Darkseid's slogan, "All is one in Dark Side" (*Seven Soldiers* 1.39), promises that his mode of autocratic control lies at the end of any drive for unity or order, perhaps even narrative order. With every dramatic agent and thematic resonance working against a completed, unified narrative, only the distributed network of *Seven Soldiers* can hope to bring all of Morrison's various plots together without yielding to the brutal simplicity Darkseid embodies.

Fortunately, Morrison provides a couple of model readers who demonstrate how we might navigate this network. The first is FBI agent Helen "Sky-High" Helligan, who explains her nickname and her methodology as follows: "I see things from a high altitude, metaphorically speaking. I make structured cognitive leaps based on long-range pattern recognition. [. . .] It's not so much the details I deal with. I'm looking at the satellite picture" (*Shining Knight* 3.11). Helligan comes as close as any single character can to apprehending the overarching plot of *Seven Soldiers*; when she reconstructs the events of *Seven Soldiers* 0 for a group of FBI colleagues, she tells them, "Stay with me. I know it's a lot of information, but that's the way I work. Everything at once" (*Bulleteer* 2.2). After Helligan dies, her role as model reader is briefly assumed by the Bride, a government agent based on the reanimated Bride of Frankenstein from Shelley's novel and James Whale's film. The Bride takes a similar high-altitude view, "spotting repeated patterns in all the incoming crisis data" (*Frankenstein* 4.6)—data that includes Agent Helligan's report.³ Helligan and the Bride propose that we read *Seven Soldiers* holistically as a single narrative connected by its repeating patterns, not as seven separate stories nor as one more conventionally linear narrative structured around unities of setting, character, or action.

This reading strategy is not perfect, however, as Morrison warns us not to ignore the details either. Helligan's sky-high vantage allows her to piece together the *Seven Soldiers* macro-narrative, including a key discovery about the origin of the Sheeda, but she does not realize until it is far too late that Gloriana has already infiltrated one of her interrogations as the antiquarian Gloria Friday. Gloriana leaves Helligan with "a last detail she may have overlooked" (*SK* 3.20), a poisonous and ultimately fatal kiss that removes the almost-perfect reader from the narrative. Morrison confronts us with a daunting task, to appreciate the bigger picture without missing the details it comprises. He makes this task somewhat easier by building *Seven Soldiers* with the same holographic or fractal structure he used in *Animal Man* and *The Invisibles*, in which the parts synecdochically contain and reflect the themes of the narrative as a whole. *Seven Soldiers* brings the details and the satellite picture into alignment by condensing the macro-narrative into individual, more easily apprehensible installments. Close readings of a few select issues can therefore reveal the ideas that shape the larger project.

DIRTY REALISM

Guardian 3, "Siege at Century Hollow," drops the Guardian into a theme park that depicts the world population through one hundred demographically representative animatronic robots. When Century Hollow founders Jorge and Hannah Control have a bitter falling out, Jorge feigns a terrorist attack that turns the robots into merciless killers and sets them loose on the visitors. He justifies his actions by ranting, "The world is not a playground, my dear, it's a battlefield. Century Hollow was to be my 3-dimensional map of political and social reality, not your tawdry theme park!" (3.5). He then adds, "Leaving out the guns just seemed so dishonest" (3.5). He also reminds himself that the fake terrorist attack "has to look real" (3.5) and wonders whether killing all his human staff was "a verisimilitude too far" (3.4). Jorge casts his marital problems as a struggle between childish pleasure and sober-minded realpolitik, utopian fantasy and realistic representation. He succeeds in introducing violence to Century Hollow, but achieves little else: a world in which "everyone is a terrorist" (3.9) is no more realistic than a world in which no one is violent, and his army of terrordroids garbed in stereotypical national dress (an Italian gondolier, a Spanish toreador, a British Buckingham palace guard) conjures the ludicrous image of Disneyland's "It's a Small World" gone kill-crazy. Nor are his motives as high-minded as he pretends: he's just angry at Hannah because she's been having sex with the animatrons. Later, a brief cameo in *Seven Soldiers* 1 reveals that Hannah was herself a more advanced android (*SS* 1.22), presumably built for Jorge's pleasure—he only rejects the childish playground or theme park aspects of Century Hollow once the toys are no longer under his control. Hannah tells the Guardian that Jorge "has a lot of repressed anger left over from his childhood" (3.13), suggesting that his pretenses to realism and maturity only mask more juvenile feelings of possessiveness, betrayal, and rage.

"Siege at Century Hollow" might appear to be a complete and relatively self-contained adventure, but later issues recast it as a holographic concentration of the themes of *Seven Soldiers* as a whole; Century Hollow's reflection of the world in miniature also reflects the concerns of the *Guardian* series and the larger *Seven Soldiers* narrative. Morrison makes this holographic function clear in the next and final issue of *Guardian*, which dramatizes the same concerns even more explicitly through fantasy and allegory. "Sex Secrets of the Newsboy Army!" divulges much of the background and history of *Seven Soldiers* through the sordid tale of the Newsboy Army, a kid gang in the style of Jack Kirby creations like the Newsboy Legion. When this multicultural band declares a "United Nation of Kids" (4.6) in front of the United Nations Headquarters, they form a smaller and even more intimate distillation of the world population than Century Hollow—and like Century Hollow, they also fall apart in a spiral of sex, murder, and betrayal that is exacerbated (though not created) by an artist with dogmatic views on the value of realism in art.

Each member of the Newsboy Army dresses in a child's imitation of some glamorous adult profession—quarterback, magician, Hollywood starlet, mobster—but as their final case begins, some of them are preparing for the transition to genuine adulthood; at least one member, Captain 7, is getting ready to go to college. Team genius Baby Brain, an intellectually brilliant but physically stunted boy trapped in a perpetually infantile body, throws a tantrum and insists they tackle one last case before accepting their adult responsibilities. This last-ditch effort to preserve their childhood—Morrison aptly sets the investigation at summer's end—leads to a traumatic encounter that will split the team along these growing fissures of youth and maturity. They encounter both Gloriana and Zor, the Terrible Time Tailor, who creates grim futures for them: under-age sex, teen pregnancy, and murder split the team apart and scandalize the survivors for decades (4.17). Zor's narrative is even more grisly than Jorge Control's marital troubles, but it is inflicted for essentially the same reasons. Zor tells the Newsboy Army "My world has no place for smart-ass kids," and Baby Brain—now revealed as Ed Stargard—laments, "In the end the world just got too big and too wide and

Figure 6-2. *Seven Soldiers* 0.9. Art by J. H. Williams III. © DC Comics.

too real for our little band of neighborhood heroes" (4.16). Zor has assumed Jorge's role, purging the childish, impossible fantasies of the Newsboy Army in favor of a debased realism. Morrison's later revelation that all of the Seven Unknown Men, in-text agents of revision who once counted Zor among their number, are fictional versions of DC comic book writers (Brill) only cements the critique of revisionists who equate sex and violence with realism and maturity.

That critique had been building since *Seven Soldiers* 0, an issue that revolves around reinventions of comic book superheroes. Shelly Gaynor, a writer who has decided to become a violent, fetishistic vigilante named the Whip as an act of George Plimpton-style participatory journalism, has self-consciously modeled herself after the revisionist superheroes. J. H. Williams III draws her with the heavy shadows, noirish lighting, and extreme close-ups of Frank Miller's comics (fig. 6-2) while Morrison crafts her first-person narration in terse two- or three-word captions that parody Miller's writing style (and recall Morrison's similar parody in *Animal Man*). These captions begin with ominous, pretentious celebrations of violence—"In the world of the super-cowboys, there's always blood" (*SS* 0.9)—but they shift to another voice and another mood when Shelly stops rehearsing her next column and ponders her future as a superhero:

> I've taken this whole morally ambiguous urban vigilante thing about as far as I can. And now, god help me, I want to visit other planets and dimensions and fight rogue gods. [...] In my deepest, darkest moments at 3 am, I imagine dying to save the universe. I picture the face of a moon, carved into a memorial likeness. Entire bereaved worlds weeping at my grave. (*SS* 0.11)

Miller's gritty, street-level revisionism must be played out if a Miller imitator like Shelly Gaynor longs for a return to the more fantastic Silver and Bronze Age plots and settings that revisionism supplanted.[4] Shelly will get her wish, as *Seven Soldiers* will feature other dimensions and rogue gods, time-traveling parasites and wicked fairy queens, and it will even include a redemptive, sacrificial death—though not Shelly's, which accomplishes nothing and is not commemorated by any lunar memorials. Morrison might reject Miller's revisionism, but *Seven Soldiers* does not return to the old Silver Age tropes Shelly pines for.

This is fortunate, since the nostalgic critique of revisionism is already familiar both from *Animal Man* and from the retro comics that followed in its wake, promoting conservative reactions against the revisionists. Morrison is well aware of the dangers of nostalgia, having incarnated them in the underdeveloped form of Ed Stargard/Baby Brain. As a former member of a Kirby-style kid gang who oversees the rehabilitation of the Guardian, another Kirby creation, Ed would appear to be a stand-in for Kirby himself; his comment that he once created a team of four elemental golems to fight crime, a clear allusion to the Fantastic Four, seals the connection (*Guardian* 1.14). Jack Kirby looms large over *Seven Soldiers*, and with good reason: he created the original versions of Klarion, Mister Miracle, and the Guardian, not to mention affiliated characters like the New Gods and the Newsboy Legion, and much of the project is dedicated to revamping and updating his work. But the discovery that Ed Stargard is a developmentally arrested baby makes the commentary far more biting than most such Kirby tributes; Morrison implies that the superhero genre Kirby shaped is itself arrested, mired in childish conventions and in need of new directions.[5] *Seven Soldiers* does not offer the nostalgic or reactionary critique of revisionism seen in the retro comics, nor even the idealist critique of realism seen in *Animal Man*. Morrison is equally dissatisfied with Baby Brain's permanent childhood and Zor's tawdry, cynical parody of maturity, seeking a third option that negotiates or sidesteps these extremes. The Seven Unknown Men telegraph this ambition, citing a passage from "The Ballad of Thomas the Rhymer" on the path of righteousness and the path of wickedness (*SS* 0.3), then insisting, in the first and final issues of *Seven Soldiers*, "There's a third road" (*SS* 0.5, 1.37).

Morrison may open *Seven Soldiers* with a shot at Frank Miller, but in the spirit of that third road his treatment of the other preeminent revisionist of the 1980s is more complex. Just as his portrayal of Jack Kirby's legacy is not entirely favorable, neither is his assessment of Alan Moore's influence purely critical. After Morrison's many public criticisms of Moore, however, not to mention the parodies and visual jokes that surface as far back as *Doom Patrol*, readers have been primed to see digs at Moore's work in Morrison's comics. *Zatanna*, which takes its protagonist and her young apprentice on a tour of the theory and practice of magic, was widely read as a response to Moore's similarly themed *Promethea*, largely because the first issue ends with Zatanna's new protégé telling her, "I love the way you write about magic. It's so like, down-to-earth and not preachy" (*Zatanna* 1.21). Joe McCulloch, among others, interprets this line as a shot at *Promethea*'s didacticism ("So many more books"). The final issue's revelation that the miniseries has been metaphorically structured around the four elements only increases the similarities, as an early *Promethea* arc (issues 5–8) featured a similar if more transparent tour of the elements' magical significance. McCulloch even speculates that the series' inking by Mick Gray is meant to evoke Gray's work with J. H. Williams III on *Promethea*.

Even if *Zatanna* is written as a response or corrective to *Promethea*, it also acknowledges a debt to an earlier Moore work and, by extension, to Moore himself. Zatanna spends the series searching for the legacy of her father, Zatara, and dealing with her unresolved grief over his death. Zatara died saving his daughter's life in the final chapter of "American Gothic" (*Swamp Thing* 50), one of the major storylines of Alan Moore, Steve Bissette, and John Totleben's *Swamp Thing*. The first issue of *Zatanna* both quotes Zatara's death scene and restages it with another disastrous ritual in the house of Baron Winter, but the prevailing mood is one of loss and regret, not satire or censure. The hero's emotional problems neatly parallel the author's creative dilemma; if Zatanna is to come to terms with her father's legacy, then Morrison must come to terms with Moore's influence over all subsequent superhero comics. That Zatara's bequest should be preserved, Zatanna believes, in a set of books only brings text and metatext that much more in alignment. Author and character must both reconcile themselves with their literary precursors, if only to lay them to rest.

On the other hand, Morrison uses the memory of Moore's older work to criticize his newer material: *Zatanna* places itself in the tradition of ambitious, substantive, but still action-packed genre fiction like "American Gothic" and *Swamp Thing* while mocking the illustrated lectures of *Promethea*.[6] It culminates not in reconciliation with Moore but in a revisitation of Morrison's own tradition. In the final issue Zatanna breaks the ontological barriers of her own comic book, falling like Buddy Baker between and behind the panel borders to meet the Seven Unknown Men, whom penciller Ryan Sook draws to resemble Grant Morrison. In this interstitial space between her world and ours, Zatanna is reunited with her father, who tells her that his books must be understood metaphorically as qualities written into her (*Zatanna* 4.20). His text, his legacy, is his successor. The reunion both acknowledges an artist's debt to his or her predecessors and closes it out, validating the role of the inheritor in a scene that replaces the earlier allusions to Moore's past work with immediately recognizable quotations of Morrison's comics. In this sense *Zatanna* might be read as charting a progression from Moore's influence to Morrison's style.

Morrison also circumvents Moore by acknowledging his obligations to other artists in far less ambivalent terms. In one of his many online interviews during the release of *Seven Soldiers*, Morrison names one influence that had escaped most reviewers:

> Some have seen [the project] as an ode to the King, Jack Kirby, and in so many heartfelt ways it is, but *Seven Soldiers* is also my personal hymn to the poetic imagination of Len Wein, whose 70s work turned me into a teenage fanboy. A great deal of *Seven Soldiers*—as with so much of the work I've done for DC—relates directly to, and expands upon, continuity established by Len. I owe an immense imaginative debt to Wein, who is humble, bemused and patient every time I collar him to tell how much his work meant to me. The way a hero ought to be. (Offenberger)

The genre fusions of *Seven Soldiers* owe much to Wein's mergers of superhero and horror comics. Morrison's Frankenstein is loosely based on Wein's "Spawn of Frankenstein" character, who appeared in a handful of *Phantom Stranger* comics in the early 1970s, but his adventures in *Seven Soldiers* are more indebted to Wein's most enduring creation, the Swamp Thing. Frankenstein's first confrontation with Sebastian Melmoth and his grub-like freaks is highly reminiscent of the Swamp Thing's battles with Anton Arcane and his Un-Men. The creature's peripatetic habits and tendency to encounter updated versions of classic monsters like zombies, golems, mutants, or body-snatchers owe as much to Wein's *Swamp Thing* stories as they do to Moore's later, more celebrated renovation of the character. *Swamp Thing* was the comic that introduced Alan Moore to American readers, but Morrison effectively trumps Moore by looking beyond him, back to the author whose creations enabled Moore's first American work.

Wein is also the writer who brought the original Seven Soldiers of Victory, including the Vigilante and the first Shining Knight, back into modern DC continuity in *Justice League of America* 100–102. That story introduced Nebula Man and the godlike Oracle, whom Morrison transforms into Neh-Buh-Loh the Huntsman and Aurakles, incorporating Wein's work into his own, more elaborate cosmology. Aurakles, the first superhero, is himself a troubling influence, the figurative (and, in one case, literal) ancestor who sets the template for all subsequent heroes. In his prime, he is drawn by J. H. Williams III to resemble a Kirby character (*SS* 1.4–7). In his modern-day appearances, however, he is mad, broken, chained, hirsute, bearded, suggestive of William Blake's Urizen—or possibly Alan Moore. When he is not utterly abject and helpless, Aurakles is haughty and demanding, visually and dramatically another demiurgic creator like Urizen or Ialdabaoth: a stern and frowning dad who requires sacrifice from his petitioners and successors (fig. 6-3). He promises to free the heroes, but instead Mister Miracle frees him twice while the Seven Soldiers assume responsibility for themselves. Whether he alludes to Wein's work, Kirby's, or Moore's, Aurakles is a figure of decrepit influence; Morrison acknowledges his debts to his predecessors but narrativizes the importance of moving beyond them.

With the exception of the brief Miller parody in *Seven Soldiers* 0, most of the criticisms of cynical revisionism and tawdry realism are not aimed at any particular comics creators, but are instead attributed to various characters within the story who either conduct revisionist readings or force them upon innocent heroes. One of the most striking if ultimately flawed examples of such intratextual revisionism is Ramon Solomano, an aging criminal who arranges the murder of his old nemesis the Vigilante and thus inadvertently sets the events of *Seven Soldiers* into motion. In the second issue of *Bulleteer*, Solomano justifies his actions by declaring the Vigilante "was a racist! He deserved to be punished!" and he adds, with defiant pride, "My

Figure 6-3. *Mister Miracle* 4.10. Art by Freddie E. Williams II. © DC Comics.

own people will call me a hero" (2.12). A flashback appears to confirm this reading, showing the Vigilante threatening another Latino criminal with murder if he doesn't clear out of town: "I catch you or any more of your filthy kin round here come moonrise, I'll flay your hides and hang 'em out to dry" (2.13). The moonrise deadline echoes the infamous sundown signs that warned blacks and other minorities "Don't let the sun set on you" in myriad white-only towns across America.[7] The Vigilante—superhero, singing cowboy, founding member of the Seven Soldiers of Victory—seems to have threatened a man with lynching. After witnessing this scene, readers may well share Solomano's outrage that "this cowboy bigot was hailed a 'hero' and I was the villain!" (2.13).

If any crimefighter were suited for revision as a racist, it would be the Vigilante, whose generic name and costume—he hides his identity behind nothing more exotic than a bandana—suggest not the flagrant individualism of the superhero but the dangerous anonymity of the Ku Klux Klan. But after venturing this alarmingly plausible reading, Morrison undercuts it almost immediately. Solomano's reversal of the roles of hero and villain is grounded in his scorn for the very concept of heroism:

> To me, all men are equal: equally deserving of my scorn, equally witless, equally gullible and servile! But this cowboy bigot was hailed a "hero" and I was the villain! Proof there are no such things as heroes, only weak fools who want to believe in them! (*Bulleteer* 2.13)

Since the *Seven Soldiers* project and Morrison's career in general treat superheroes as vehicles for generating meaning, and regard belief in them as a force that can motivate real-world political and social action, it is safe to conclude that Morrison introduces this rant to discredit Solomano. The convict's misanthropy exposes him as a morally compromised criminal, not a revisionist hero.

To defend the Vigilante from his accusations, however, Morrison has to go considerably further, resorting to a fantasy genre trope entirely at odds with Solomano's realistic reading. Agent Helen Helligan reveals that the Vigilante and the criminal he was threatening were both lycanthropes; the bullets in his gun were silver and the "filthy kin" he referred to were werewolves (2.14). This explanation might let the Vigilante off the hook, but it does not answer the eminently reasonable suspicions Solomano raises about the political valences of a masked man who rides across the Southwest shooting at Mexicans. Morrison performs a similar substitution later in *Bulleteer* when Sally Sonic, a superhero who has already been brought to the brink of sexual degradation through personal tragedy, emotional manipulation, and her own naïveté, is pushed over the edge by the transparently ridiculous plot device of "Doctor Hyde's Evil Serum" (4.16). Excusing these heroes' misbehavior through convenient and outlandish genre tropes smacks of the same refusal to grow up that is so often a focus of criticism in *Seven Soldiers*. Arguably, the Vigilante's lycanthropy might serve as a telling metaphor for the destructive effects of suppressed rage, even the rage of bigotry, but Morrison deploys it to indemnify the figure of the masked rider against more realistic, skeptical, and historically minded interpretations.

By projecting a cynical revision onto another simple Golden Age character, Solomano acts as a more mundane version of Zor. Morrison reinforces the parallel when he attributes the summoning of the Sheeda to both Zor (*Guardian* 4.15, *Zatanna* 4.19) and Solomano (*Bulleteer* 2.12), with Zor providing their extratextual origin and Solomano supplying the event within the narrative diegesis that calls them to the twenty-first century. Significantly, both summonings are ascribed to revisionist figures. If Zor is a comic book writer who imposes his corrosive interpretations on the heroes, then Solomano is a reader who infers them because he cannot see through his own contempt. Yet their claims to realism are undermined both by the decadence of the narratives they institute and by the tools they use to implement them. Mystical horns that summon cosmic huntsmen and sewing machines that stitch the future are even less realistic than the kid gangs and singing cowboys that so infuriate the revisionists. Their ultimate fates also reinforce the power of fantasy: Solomano is haunted by the Vigilante's ghost, and the Seven Unknown Men punish Zor by stitching him into DC Comics' hopelessly, irrevocably unrealistic continuity.[8] Solomano and Zor make poor spokesmen for realism, and their failures imply that writers and readers must accept the fantastic as an intrinsic part of superhero comics.

ETERNAL SUPERTEENS

Garish violence and cynical realism are not the only components of revisionist comics. Their treatment of sexuality ranges from the frank, genuinely adult sex scenes of Moore and Gibbons's *Watchmen* to the hyperactive arousal of Howard Chaykin's *American Flagg!* to the leering debauchery of Miller's *Sin City*. Morrison is therefore more ambivalent about the role of sexuality in superhero comics, treating it as a potential sign of maturity, an

A Time of Harvest 237

Figure 6-4. *Bulleteer* 1.18. Art by Yanick Paquette. © DC Comics.

adolescent atavism, and an implement of decadent revisionism. The Newsboy Army tears itself apart over its members' illicit sexual activity, but the Bulleteer's curvaceous figure and Zatanna's increasingly erotic outfits—by the end of her series, she wears a costume that is almost completely translucent—neither limit their agency nor overshadow the qualities of intellect, compassion, and determination that make them heroes. To be fair, none of the male heroes see such attentions lavished on their appearance. *Seven Soldiers* presents its pulchritudinous heroines for viewing pleasure, but it also works to reclaim a healthy adult sexuality for superhero comics by dragging all the genre's fetishes out into the sunlight, where they can either blossom or wither. Sexuality itself is not the problem.

The problem is the dehumanized, merchandized sexuality on display in *Bulleteer*, a series that equates superhero comics with pornography. Alix Harrower, the Bulleteer, learns that her late husband Lance was a regular visitor to "Eternal Superteens," a pornographic web site featuring perpetually adolescent girls in revealing costumes, but most of the comparisons don't need to be that overt; Morrison makes the point that superhero comics are already pornographic. He finds the perfect collaborator for this project in artist Yanick Paquette, an adept at drawing voluptuous women who love to contort their bodies into unnatural positions. Alix certainly fits the bill, spending most of the first issue in her underwear and striking—sometimes unconsciously, sometimes quite self-consciously—the same cheesecake poses as the Superteens (fig. 6-4). The series mocks comic books' hyper-sexualized representations by gleefully indulging in them; as Morrison told one interviewer, "I think of this one as my 'Bendis book' but it's drawn like Penthouse" (Contino, "*Seven Soldiers*"). Brian Michael Bendis writes comics that strive for a veneer of realism by locating superheroes within contemporary media culture and merging them with other genres, typically crime stories. The media critique is equally prominent in *Bulleteer*, but the other genre is porn.

The series assesses superhero conventions and concludes they're all either overtly or covertly pornographic. Women wear cleavage-baring costumes, men pay good money for pictures of bullets bouncing off heroines' ample chests, and superhero team-ups are presented as euphemisms for more intimate liaisons. But these simple observations pale in comparison to Morrison's erotic interpretation of an even more basic convention, the fight scene. The Bulleteer is an unwilling superhero who doesn't seek out combat: she rescues accident victims, assists Agent Helligan on a case, and works as a bodyguard for a Hollywood star, but she doesn't throw a punch until the final issue of her miniseries. The fight scene, not the many pin-up poses of Alix and other half-naked superheroines, is the climax of this pornographic narrative, a point made clear when Helligan refers to video footage of an earlier fight scene (from *Seven Soldiers* 0) through that convention common to every porn movie: "Now here comes the money shot" (*Bulleteer* 2.7). The shot in question is grotesquely penetrative, showing a monster impaling two superheroes on a spear, but not sexualized in the manner of Paquette's cheesecake. The genius of *Bulleteer* lies in its argument that such distinctions don't matter; Morrison and Paquette apply the imagery, terminology, and narrative structures of porn to demonstrate that every superhero comic is locked into a set of conventions just as codified, just as limiting, and nearly as explicit as those of pornography.

These restrictive conventions are maintained by a comics culture that rewards formula and dreads change. Morrison transposes that culture into the comics themselves, filling *Seven Soldiers* with minor-league superheroes, fans, and wannabes—Shelly Gaynor calls them "hero-vestites" (*SS* 0.19)—who fear aging and fetishize their own youth. Baby Brain is only the most literal example of arrested development; *Seven Soldiers* teems with characters who either cannot age or are terrified of growing old or dying. Kid Scarface, the Newsboy who supports Baby Brain's insistence on one last, destructive childhood adventure, will later discover a magical cauldron of rebirth that he uses to prolong his life. Li'l Hollywood, another Newsboy Army survivor, uses her super-impressionist abilities to appear much younger than she is. Gimmix, a second-generation superhero desperate to break into the big time, has gotten a facelift and lies about her age. Lance Harrower develops a metallic "smartskin" because he wants to stay young forever; the smartskin kills him, sparing him from the ravages of time, though not before he transforms Alix into the Bulleteer. Alix's nemesis Sally Sonic is a corrupted superhero whose power (a Mary Marvel-style transformation into an alternate body) has kept her eternally adolescent even at the age of seventy-five, a paradox that drives her mad.

Some of the antagonists conform to this pattern as well. Gloriana searches for the cauldron of rebirth, looking to restore her youth and vitality, and Billy Beezer, leader of the teenage gang the Deviants, tries to postpone the graduation to Team Red that will come with his impending sixteenth birthday (sensibly, since Team Red turns out to be a hard-labor gang). On the other hand, Zor and his allies co-opt and redirect natural processes of growth and change by sewing grisly fates for the Newsboy Army, perverting naïfs like Sally Sonic, working their young charges to death, and turning an

Figure 6-5. *Bulleteer* 3.16. Art by Yanick Paquette. © DC Comics.

entire high school full of teenagers into hosts for Sheeda larvae. Whether they resist change or twist it to serve their own ends, these figures prevent individual characters and the superhero genre as a whole from evolving in healthy directions. The "oneiric climate" (17) Umberto Eco describes in "The Myth of Superman," the seemingly timeless narrative that always returns Silver Age stories to their status quo, is refigured here as a threat to the genre's long-term maturity and viability, no less dangerous than the debasements of the revisionists.

Morrison unites this argument with his critique of juvenile, pornographic sexuality in the third issue of *Bulleteer*, set in a superhero convention that serves as a scathing stand-in for comics conventions. While he skewers the convention for supporting the sexist objectifications that *Bulleteer* wallows in—even the requisite panel on female superheroes is called "Sweethearts and Supervixens" (3.8)—his criticisms revolve primarily around the nostalgia that fuels modern superhero comics. In a lucid moment, one aspiring hero and convention-circuit regular complains that he is "caught up in a nostalgia freakshow that never ends. Look at us. Selling our precious memories for bed and board, reliving the times when our hopes reached the high water mark . . . and then just receded . . ." (3.16). Lest anybody miss the bitter metacommentary, Paquette has drawn the character to resemble Grant Morrison (fig. 6-5). This is easily Morrison's least flattering self-incarnation, a needy, insecure amateur dissatisfied with his meager success but too afraid to break out of the nostalgia freakshow. He accuses every superhero comics writer, Morrison included, of mining a rich history for paltry and diminishing returns instead of making something new.

In this respect, they are not so different from the Sheeda.

CIVILIZATIONS IN DECLINE

In *Shining Knight* 3, Gloriana, posing as Gloria Friday, tells Agent Helligan, "when a civilization reaches its peak, there comes a time of harvest, let's say. After the ripening comes inevitable decay. With predictable and grim implications for your own civilization" (3.7). Her narrative of civilizations' rise and fall is eerily reminiscent of the "life cycle" of genre development proposed by John Cawelti in "*Chinatown* and Generic Transformation in Recent American Films" (510–11), a pattern of generic articulation, self-awareness, exhaustion, and self-parody. Thomas Schatz offers a similar model of genre evolution in *Hollywood Genres*, adapting Henri Focillon's theory of the life span of cultural forms to outline a cycle of experimentation, stabilization, refinement, and exhaustion in which mature genres must embellish or raid their own conventions to remain fresh. These genres become increasingly self-conscious and mannerist until they break down and either begin the cycle anew or die off (Schatz 36–38). The Sheeda and Zor act as agents of mannerist revisionism, undermining naïve conventions of heroism and overwriting them with knowing decadence. Crucially, however, Morrison does not restrict their threat to the superhero genre, which would itself be a prime example of mannerist self-reflexivity—a comic with no subject other than other comics. Gloriana's comments to Helligan instead match genre history to world history, casting *Seven Soldiers* as a narrative of civilizations in decline.

It is no accident that most of the Seven Soldiers are strangers to modern society. Frankenstein and the Shining Knight are relics of past eras; Klarion comes from an isolated community governed by seventeenth-century social structures; and Shilo Norman, Mister Miracle, only becomes a superhero after a close encounter with a race of extradimensional gods alienates him from his hollow celebrity lifestyle. These heroes emerge from other cultures, times, or worlds to save a twenty-first-century society that is being destroyed by postindustrial capitalism. Time and again, *Seven Soldiers* depicts a society on the brink of collapse: a government experiment with weaponized water goes terribly wrong, turning every human and animal in Salvation Valley into a bloodthirsty killer. Children are traded in underground markets and worked to death in gold mines. Wealthy, depressed Manhattanites inhale drugs that flatten affect and undergo surgeries to convert their skin to plastic. Bored husbands surf for barely legal superhero porn and everybody is obsessed with a shallow celebrity culture. A secret agent's assessment that Salvation Valley has entered "total social and environmental breakdown" (*Frankenstein* 3.12) applies just as well to the project's portrayal of Western civilization as a whole; the worldwide violence of Jorge Control's reprogrammed Century Hollow does not seem so far off. This critique becomes especially pointed after Morrison reveals that the Sheeda are not alien invaders from some other planet or dimension, but distant descendants of the human race from a dying future Earth long stripped of natural resources. Incapable of creating anything themselves, unable even to sustain themselves, the Sheeda survive by harvesting past societies, "Consuming their own history" (*SS* 1.22), allowing their ancestors to develop vital cultures and technologies and then sweeping in to plunder them once they pass their zenith. As both exploiters of contemporary Western society and the ultimate extension of its exploitations, the Sheeda constitute a repugnant trope for modern society's cultural and environmental exhaustion. They signal that we are a ripened and self-destructing civilization, facing nothing but decay.

With harsh judgments such as these, *Seven Soldiers* could easily be mistaken for a conservative critique of modernity, especially when it contrasts a debased modern culture with the supposed golden age of the past, whether that age is located in the optimistic postwar years of the Newsboy Army or the legends of King Arthur's Camelot. This critique is most legible in *Shining Knight*, the story of Justin, a young Arthurian knight accidentally transported to modern Los Angeles. The second issue juxtaposes scenes of contemporary crime and violence with ancient prophecies of a dark age: "Women would be shameless, men strengthless. [...] Old men would give false judgments. Legislators would make unjust laws. Warriors would betray one another. Men would become thieves. And virtue would vanish from the world" (*SK* 2.20). When Justin vows the prophecy will not come true "while one knight of Camelot endures" (2.21), a conservative defense of lapsed virtues seems imminent. Morrison never quite mounts a case for the feudal social order, however, and in fact has already begun to undermine any such reading. The prophet's palpable disgust at shameless modern women and weak modern men might appear to call for a renewal of old gender roles in which men show their dominance and women know their place, but a surprising revelation in the final issue of *Shining Knight* calls these roles into question. Justin is exposed as Justina, a girl posing as a boy so she can fight for Camelot. In a subsequent and even more graphic rebuttal to feudal patriarchy, Justina then kills a broken and corrupted Galahad who has been twisted into serving Gloriana. This completes a progression that began in the series' first issue, when she slew the reanimated corpse of King Arthur himself. In order to preserve the ideals and legacy of the Round Table, Justina must kill its survivors, two decaying old men who have betrayed everything they once stood for. This is hardly an endorsement of archaic social structures or gender roles.

The conservative implications of *Shining Knight*'s critique of modernity are directly countered in another series, *Klarion*. Klarion is a Witch-Boy from Limbo Town, a subterranean lost colony descended from Puritan settlers.[9] As the series begins, Limbo Town is caught in a power struggle between the Submissionaries, religious authorities who advocate isolation, and the Witch-Men, innovators who trade with the outside world and who have recently developed a parliament and a steam engine. These inventions, along with the general seventeenth-century flavor of the town's customs and fashions, mark Limbo Town as a civilization at the beginnings of modernity and cast the Submissionaries as enemies of progress. When the Submissionaries learn of the coming Sheeda invasion they seize upon it as a pretext to seal off the town; Ezekiel, a Witch-Man and Klarion's stepfather, explains that Judah, the head Submissionary, "fears that trade with the higher towns might change our lives forever" (*Klarion* 1.13). Ezekiel is right to be wary of the Submissionaries, who have an even more sinister purpose: keeping themselves in business. Judah frets that "If the Sheeda return, we will be retired from duty, deleted. After such long and faithful service our purpose will be at an end" (1.18). The Submissionaries consolidate their power by playing on the town's fear of the Sheeda, but if the threat they guard against ever materialized they would be exposed as purposeless, perhaps even powerless. Their true mission is not to protect Limbo Town but to ensure the town remains isolated and fearful—which explains why, after they reassert their authority and seal the town gate, their first act is to murder their rivals, the Witch-Men.

As theocrats who rule by invoking holy tradition and stoking fears of an alien enemy, the Submissionaries are a fairly obvious critique of fundamentalist Christian and neoconservative political leaders, with the threat of Sheeda invasion replacing the threat of terrorist attack. This critique grows more complex with the second issue of *Klarion*, when Klarion discovers the foundation of the Submissionaries' authority. Judah claims his orders come directly from their god, Croatoan (1.15), but Klarion soon learns the truth: "There is no Croatoan. Croatoan is an absent god" (2.12). He fled his underground prison long ago, abandoning his people, leaving behind only his chains. This is the secret of the Witch-Men's initiation, the truth that has motivated them to invent democracies and embrace modernity: God is either absent or dead. Presumably the Submissionaries also know this secret, for they certainly exploit it, passing their edicts off as divine commandments from a god who is no longer around to contradict them. Morrison's revelation undermines the theocrats' claims to authority and explains the Witch-Men's pursuit of humanistic political systems and scientific discoveries.

Even in the pages of *Klarion*, however, modernity can bring new dangers. Klarion is initially delighted by his discovery of our world, viewing it from an outsider's perspective that re-enchants modernity; candy bars are manna from heaven in miraculous wrappings and even a trip through fetid sewer tunnels fills him with glee. As Sebastian Melmoth, now a Fagin-like trainer of young criminals, explains to his associates, "Everything is new in his sight. Everything is holy" (3.2). But the glow fades quickly—first when Klarion is nearly betrayed by another fugitive from Limbo Town who would sell him to child slavers for a sackful of liquor, guns, and pornography, then when he discovers that Melmoth has been exporting his pupils to toil the rest of their short lives in a gold mine on Mars. Melmoth may cut a distinctly Victorian figure—equal parts dandy, sweatshop owner, and Dickensian villain—but to the denizens of Limbo Town he is nevertheless a modern one, the agent and instrument of the change they fear. In the final issue of *Klarion* he invades Limbo Town, intending to ride out the Sheeda invasion there and establish a power base in the world to follow. After announcing his intentions to use the women as breeding stock he leers at one of them, "I intend to modernize. You'd look good in a bikini" (4.14).

For all their royal titles and trappings, Melmoth and his former wife Gloriana think and act like Gilded Age industrial capitalists and adherents of social Darwinism. Gloriana believes the Sheeda are entitled to ravage the twenty-first century both by their evolutionary superiority and by the precedent humanity has set for exploiting the planet: "Humankind has ever preyed upon the Earth, and we are only the last link in that chain— we super-survivor organisms. [. . .] We are the end result of natural selection, the winner of a savage and bloody struggle for planetary dominion" (*Frankenstein* 4.15, 4.17). Melmoth says he created Limbo Town as a "little experiment in eugenics" (*Klarion* 4.15), and he brags, "We Sheeda-folk, we were born to cling fiercely to life in the most hostile of environments" (*Klarion* 4.8), suggesting the Sheeda are both manipulators and beneficiaries of natural selection. His methodology is more transparently capitalist than Gloriana's: he delivers boardroom presentations to organized crime families and conscripts children to mine the gold he will use to finance his internecine war against his ex-wife. Neither villain presents an entirely contemporary figure, the late-Victorian Melmoth no more so than the quasi-medieval Gloriana, but they both pose distinctly contemporary threats, recalling the last age of unrestrained capitalism to suggest that our own era has similarly run out of control.

As always in *Seven Soldiers*, Klarion's challenge is to find a third path that avoids the fearful obedience of theocracy and the dehumanizing exploitations of modern capitalism. Typically for Morrison, he has already collapsed these nominally opposed systems into one another: Melmoth is not only the progenitor of Limbo Town, the tempter who seduced their Puritan ancestors and drove them underground, he is also the inventor of the Submissionaries—actually sophisticated robot watchmen who have been keeping the town in good order for his return. Religious zealotry, isolationist xenophobia, and decadent, unrestrained capitalism go hand in hand in *Seven Soldiers*, although the capitalist Melmoth is very much in charge. Rather than issue the conservative critique of modernity implied by parts of *Shining Knight*, *Klarion* attributes modernity's depredations to capitalism's conversion of human beings into commodities. Morrison dismisses any suggestion that nostalgia, isolation, or other modes of cultural conservatism offer effective modes of escape; in fact, *Klarion* exposes them as part of the final degradation, political strategies that only prime a population for even worse exploitation.

ABSOLUTE MEANING

Gloriana is evidently no fan of modernity herself. When Justina asks why modern English sounds so guttural and mangled to her ear, the wicked queen replies, "all men are liars in this age. [. . .] Words can mean anything and everything, that is why they have no proper shape here. What once was truth is pliable, untrustworthy, and slippery now. Words cannot be trusted in this age. Only deeds" (*SK* 3.15). She invokes this linguistic instability once again when she attempts to dissuade Frankenstein from opposing her, saying, "In your bright world, there is black and there is white, yes, we've seen it. But here [in her dying future world], there are only subtle shades, deceptive appearances. Words that slither" (*Frankenstein* 4.16). She follows this appeal to linguistic indeterminacy and moral relativism with her case for the Sheeda's evolutionary and capitalistic right to prey on twenty-first-century humanity. It would be easy to read these statements as an exercise in guilt by association—to conclude that since the villain embraces verbal ambiguity and applies it toward her own selfish ends, the narrative must be rejecting linguistic indeterminacy and valorizing a mythical, prelapsarian golden age in which words held constant and absolute meanings. Morrison himself has supported such readings, telling Ian Brill, "my idea here was that in Sir Justin's day there was no such thing as lying—a word was a bond, a magical thing. In our times, however, the word is no longer sacred or magical in the same way. [. . .] Hence, the idea of the Word becoming shapeless and slippery, and whoring itself out to every stray ideology." Just as his critique of modernity turns out to be grounded in a progressive critique of capitalism, however, the view of language Morrison presents in *Seven Soldiers* is also more complex than it first seems. Poststructuralists in particular are liable to read the narrative's calls for certainty and fixity in language as conservative appeals, but *Seven Soldiers* instead asks readers to rethink some of the assumptions that have guided literary and linguistic theory for nearly a century.

The linguistic turn of twentieth-century critical theory proposed that verbal and written signs do not enjoy any absolute correspondence with the concepts they represent; the relationship between signifier and signified is essentially arbitrary, determined by the signifier's relationship to and differences from other signifiers (J. Berger 343–44). Poststructuralist theorists of the 1960s and 1970s associated the liberation of the sign from its object with the project of political liberation so powerfully that many contemporary literary critics still link the two. James Berger, in the course of charting a "counter-linguistic turn" (344) in contemporary literature, characterizes yearnings for fixed meanings and semantic or moral absolutes as essentially reactionary desires, which he describes as "the characteristic post-apocalyptic symptomatic response: the world of semantic and moral ambiguity has fallen and been swept away; the world of simplicity and clarity has taken its place" (343). Berger believes semantic ambiguity accompanies the "dividedness [and] multiplicity" of linguistic diversity, while univalent signs are implements of violent fundamentalisms (343); he cites as examples of the latter both the attacks of September 11, 2001 and the Manichaean narratives of good and evil that the Bush administration deployed in their wake. Berger writes, "The logic and desire both of terrorism and of antiterrorism are to restore the imagined former state: of social harmony and perfect correspondence between word and thing" (343). In his view, this "impulse to restore language from a fallen, ambiguous condition to one of certainty has always been a traumatized, or opportunistic, attempt to destroy language as an instrument of thought" (354). The only counterlinguistic projects Berger praises are those that turn "toward forms of unrepresentable alterity" (354), recognizing that some concepts exist outside language but valuing the ambiguous or inconceivable over the certain and concrete.

Berger's account is not without its own ideologically freighted, Manichaean oppositions between polysemic, progressive, liberatory ambiguity and univalent, reactionary, oppressive certainty. Fortunately, *Seven Soldiers* manages to challenge this logic without falling into the postapocalyptic narrative patterns Berger describes, even though Morrison writes about some of the same apocalypses. An early indicator comes when Justina battles the corrupted Galahad and a delighted Gloriana, reminiscing about the fall of Camelot, remarks, "This age will fare no better. Its heroes will betray one another, its monuments will topple. Can you see the pretty metaphor I make of this combat?" (*SK* 4.3). Morrison all but dares us to read the line about toppling monuments as an allusion to the September 11 attacks. Contrary to Berger's formulation, however, Gloriana seizes this postapocalyptic moment of vulnerability not to cement language, but to break it down even further. In addition to her rhetorical deployment of "words that slither," one of her weapons, Gwydion, is a living language capable of assuming any form—a floating signifier untethered to any referent. In the world of *Seven Soldiers*, the characteristic response to apocalyptic trauma is not the removal of semantic ambiguity but Gloriana's indulgence in language's capacity to deceive.

Berger does not consider that religious fundamentalists and other political and cultural conservatives might exult in the same free play of unfixed meanings that he and other poststructuralist theorists celebrate. Morrison offers a more astute assessment of the politics of the linguistic turn with his recognition that political leaders have thrived on the exploitation of semantic ambiguity, particularly in the post-September 11 period. Redefining torture as "enhanced interrogation techniques" elicits neither simplicity nor clarity, but these words might fairly be said to slither. Indeed, one of Berger's own examples of monologic certainty, the phrase "homeland security" (343), has proven to be a particularly versatile euphemism with jurisdiction over any number of real or imagined threats, reactions, security measures, and abuses, from counterterrorism to immigration enforcement to the suppression of political dissent.[10] In such a climate, reconnecting words to externally verifiable objects, actions, and events may serve to *restore* language as an implement of thought and an instrument of critique. Far from promoting a fundamentalist model of language, *Seven Soldiers* provides an important reminder that severing words from their referents is not always an act of liberation.

Against such deceptions, *Seven Soldiers* searches for one last middle ground, perhaps the ultimate one for any literary text: the third road between the tyranny of univalent meaning and the tyranny made possible when words hold no meaning at all. Gloriana's weapons include the formless language of Gwydion, which can be anything, and the hypostatized emotion of Guilt, which can be nothing else. The New Gods in *Mister Miracle* carry this concretization of symbolic systems one step further, from language to mathematics. Metron, a god of knowledge and technology, tells Shilo Norman, "We have telescopes that can probe the furthest reaches of a man's spirit, profound equations to explain the meaning of love and hate. We are absolute meaning" (*MM* 1.6). Hypostases themselves, the New Gods are capable of quantifying the human psyche in symbolic form and weaponizing these quantifications. Darkseid attempts to destroy Shilo by whispering the Anti-Life Equation, an ego-destroying formula so terrible that letterer Phil Balsman can only represent it as a swirl of ink, a black hole collapsing in on itself (fig. 6-6). Although it consists of verbal and mathematical symbols, the Anti-Life Equation is also beyond symbolization, an inverted hypostasis that incarnates the terrors of intersubjective trauma in the pure abstractions of math. As in *The Invisibles*, symbolic language and absolute meaning can be tools of interpellation and authoritarian control.

Unlike *The Invisibles*, however, *Seven Soldiers* also sees a renewed possibility that concretized symbols, especially the hypostatic figures of superhero comics, can generate more emancipatory readings. Shilo's therapist, Doctor Dezard—actually a mortal shell for a sadistic god working for Darkseid—encourages him to dismiss his encounter with the warring New Gods as a metaphor of "The war within a man's soul [. . .] that might be a more

Figure 6-6. *Mister Miracle* 3.12. Art by Freddie E. Williams II. © DC Comics.

realistic way of looking at what you're going through. [. . .] Demons and angels are all within us. Their titanic campaigns are fought over and over again in the churning mud of human hearts and minds" (*MM* 1.18, 1.19). Morrison's suspicion of applying realism to superhero comics is already well established by this point in *Seven Soldiers*, but *Mister Miracle* both supports and contradicts Dezard's interpretation. Within the world of the series the gods are real, as Dezard well knows, and his figurative reading is intended to cause Shilo to doubt his recent revelations. But in our world, the New Gods, Shilo, and the rest of the *Seven Soldiers* cast are fictional characters—outsized, impossible, fantastic characters who only hold meaning as figures that embody human drives and desires. As Shelly Gaynor writes in her final column, "the themes may seem unfamiliar but trust me, those are human stories, writ large, dressed in capes and riding magic carpets to other universes" (*SS* 1.15). Dezard may attempt to mislead Shilo, but he provides an important guide for our own reading.

By the end of *Mister Miracle*, Shilo becomes one of these hypostatic figures himself. Darkseid has trapped him in Omega, "the fundamental force that is restriction" (4.13), where he is condemned to live out a series of increasingly degrading lives and deaths in a torment that combines the dharmic concept of samsara, the cycle of suffering and reincarnation, with the dying fantasy and imagined future life of *The Last Temptation of Christ*.[11]

Shilo escapes this endless repetition by telling Omega, "there's a fundamental force in me, too. I gave my life over to representing something that's in all of us" (4.16). Given that Shilo is an escape artist, and that the original Mister Miracle is widely read as a personification of Jack Kirby's own struggles for artistic independence (Evanier 4), that fundamental force can only be the desire for freedom. Shilo delivers his appeal not only to Omega but also to the audience, staring out of the panels and inviting the readers to join him in throwing off our chains and escaping whatever pressures, external or internal, hold us down. While Morrison acknowledges the restrictive potential of absolute meaning, *Mister Miracle* ends with a confident assertion that hypostasis can also be liberating depending on the particular meanings it embodies. By emphasizing the valences of the referent, and not just the act of signification, Morrison rehabilitates hypostasis and the counterlinguistic turn more broadly as strategies that can express diverse ideas, including humanistic as well as reactionary or fundamentalist ideologies.

He does so in the process of rehabilitating superhero comics, and fantasy genres in general, by highlighting their ability to generate meaning. In a flashback to humanity's prehistory, the New Gods instruct Aurakles, the first superhero, "To bring order and meaning where incoherence reigns" (*SS* 1.5). Because they personify human traits and desires, the heroes can also illuminate meanings already present but unrecognized in the ubiquity of mundane experience. After one encounter with a group of New Gods, Shilo says he felt "like human life, all human life, was so precious . . . and every individual human story was worthy of . . . I don't know . . . mythology" (*MM* 2.16). For Morrison, superheroes supply that mythology, representing the best aspects of human nature: courage, selflessness, determination, compassion. Shilo shakes off the Anti-Life Equation and regains his faith in humanity as he glimpses a sign for the Manhattan Superhero Museum (*MM* 3.15); this museum will later serve as a rallying point for humanity's resistance to the Sheeda invasion. Despite their best efforts to extinguish the superhero ideal, and so remove an obstacle to their harrowing, the Sheeda cannot quite stamp it out. At one point Kirby stand-in Ed Stargard tells the Guardian, "We're telling stories about human dignity, Jake. Stories of how human beings make culture and meaning for ourselves, even down there in the garbage" (*Guardian* 2.21). It makes as good a mission statement as any line in *Seven Soldiers*: toiling away in the gutters of genre fiction, Morrison and his partners have told a story about childhood and maturity, stasis and transformation, realism and fantasy, modernity's wonders and its horrors, all through the meaning-making forms of the superhero.

Chapter 7

WORK FOR HIRE

While Morrison was rehabilitating the superhero in *Seven Soldiers*, he was also becoming increasingly central to DC Comics and to superhero comics in general. Although he had already worked on DC and Marvel's leading franchises in *JLA* and *New X-Men*, he spent the second half of the decade writing Superman and Batman, renovating minor and underused characters for DC, guiding readers on a year-long tour of the DC universe, and ultimately steering DC's continuity as part of a linewide crossover. This period completed Morrison's move from the fringes of the comics industry to the center and cemented his status as one of the most important writers in mainstream American comics. It also reaffirmed his interest in populating his works with reflections and analogues of existing characters, a style that has dominated superhero comics from the late 1990s into the new millennium.

This propensity for multiplication is only the latest in a series of narrative logics that have shaped the history of superhero comics. Umberto Eco described the "oneiric climate" and the "iterative scheme" ("Myth" 17, 19–21) that governed the Superman comics of the early Silver Age, in which the narrative begins anew with each new story as a means of arresting the passage of time while preserving the illusion of the potential for progress. Henry Jenkins notes that by the 1970s, superhero comics had shifted to longer, serialized stories and elaborate narrative continuities (20), and proposes that they have changed once again to "a period of multiplicity" (21) that presents numerous, frequently incompatible versions of the same franchises. Some are analogues and homages published by creators and companies who do not own the rights to the familiar characters they mimic; licensed variants, such as Marvel's Ultimate line or DC's All Star line, simply place the same time-tested characters—Spider-Man, the X-Men, Superman, Batman—in new titles that are shorn of decades of accumulated continuity.

Duncan Falconer, troping on fandom's propensity for dividing the history of superhero comics into different ages, has identified this period as "the Prismatic Age" for its proliferation of copies, reflections, and variants of existing heroes. While duplication, imitation, and the expansion of popular heroes into families of similar characters have been part of the genre since its inception, Falconer traces the contemporary dominance of the prismatic style back to the retro comics of the nineties, which not only revisited past comics but also created simulacra of their characters and histories in series such as *Supreme* and *Astro City*. The retro movement's classicist repudiation of modern superhero comics faded, soon to be replaced by the jubilant taboo-breaking of widescreen, but the prismatic reflections remained; most of the Authority, for example, are minor variations if not thinly disguised copies of other superheroes. Jenkins attributes this ceaseless reduplication of existing properties to the exhaustion of old genre conventions, to readers' and creators' increasing awareness of the genre's history, and to their attendant demand for new takes on familiar heroes (22–26). Falconer, however, notes the market and industry incentives that discourage the creation of original characters: "creators are not overly invested in pushing new creations because the readership is generally unresponsive and because, they know by now, they will not be adequately rewarded for their efforts should they make such a breakthrough." Because the major comics companies would own any new characters created under their work-for-hire policies, creators might as well work with the properties the company already owns; because the shrinking audience for superhero comics has demonstrated little interest in new heroes, creators and companies both find more success with new variations on established characters.

Although Benjamin Woo's warnings about the utility of "Age"-based historical schemas remain pertinent, Falconer's "Prismatic" label is useful not because it presumes to offer a systematic logic for organizing all of comics history—it does not—but rather because it identifies and distills the most salient features of the style it describes. As a hermeneutic tool, and not a historiographic one, the "Prismatic Age" is particularly relevant to Grant Morrison's work, which both inspires and responds to Falconer's terminology. Falconer introduces the term with an image from Morrison and Mark Millar's *Flash* in which a giant prism splits the Flash into seven identical beings, each one a different color of the visible light spectrum (fig. 7-1); this image becomes a metaphor for the period's multiplication of familiar characters. Falconer later cites Morrison's *JLA* as an example of a superhero team that constantly encounters alternative versions of itself, from extradimensional doubles to future inheritors to ethical foils like the Hyperclan or the Ultramarines.

Work for Hire 253

Figure 7-1. *The Flash* 133.4. Art by Paul Ryan. © DC Comics.

If Morrison's late nineties superhero comics set the tone for the coming trend, his postmillennial work would embrace it. *52*, a weekly comic written in collaboration with Geoff Johns, Greg Rucka, and Mark Waid, featured a collection of spin-offs, analogues, and supporting characters who attempted to fill in for an absent Superman, Batman, and Wonder Woman; it culminated in the reintroduction of the DC multiverse of parallel worlds, a development designed, in Morrison's words, to create "a number of big new franchise possibilities" for alternative versions of established characters (Brady, "The 52 Exit Interviews"). Morrison's other comics from this period are even more committed to the prismatic style, contrasting their heroes against arrays of reflections and situating them within textual palimpsests that consolidate decades of comics history into single narratives. *All Star Superman* measures its protagonist against a number of failed imitations to make a case for his continued importance not only in the comics market but also in our own world. *Batman*, on the other hand, conjures its prismatic variations as part of a project to rebuild and reintegrate its hero into a healthier, less damaged individual, although the series puts him through a psychological ordeal that repeats, rather than corrects, the hallmarks of the revisionist comics it initially rejects. The self-referential commentary intensifies in *Final Crisis*, a crossover whose metafictions suggest that just as Morrison's work has become central to DC Comics, so have the rarefied concerns of contemporary superhero comics become far too central to Morrison's work.

ALL STAR SUPERMAN: HISTORY UNDER GLASS

Superman is perhaps the ideal subject for a prismatic treatment. As the definitive superhero, he has inspired a legion of analogues and knock-offs such as Supreme, Apollo, Icon, Hyperion, Majestic, and countless others; in one sense, every superhero created after 1938 follows in his footsteps. Beyond this gallery of imitators, Superman's own history is already filled with reflections. In his introduction to "Travels in Hyperreality," Eco cites the Silver Age Superman's Fortress of Solitude, filled with robot doubles and life-size wax statues, as a revealing example of America's fascination with the simulacrum (4–5). *All Star Superman* (2005–08), a twelve-issue limited series with art by Frank Quitely, is less preoccupied with re-creating this museum of simulations and more interested in expanding its doubles outside the Fortress of Solitude and beyond mere physical similarity. The mementos of past achievements and relics of Superman's lost Kryptonian homeworld are similarly released from the Fortress in a series that abounds with references to past Superman comics. *All Star Superman* is not simply a self-referential pastiche, however. Morrison and Quitely craft a series of "science fiction fables" (Thill) that harness the outsized, universally recognized characters of the Superman myth to tell stories rich in emotional resonance. Superman confesses his love for Lois Lane, confronts the death of his adoptive father, Jonathan Kent, and faces his own impending mortality after an overexposure to solar radiation triggers a fatal cellular breakdown. Drawing on his own grief over his father's death in February 2004, Morrison attempted to translate his sorrow into stories that would speak to his readers' experiences of "these simple human feelings" (Smith Part 10). *All Star Superman* is a tender, emotionally vulnerable story, but not a depressing one; Morrison and Quitely present an idealistic and humanistic interpretation of Superman while they argue that he and other fictions are important for their ability to guide human aspirations.

That argument reveals itself gradually, and *All Star Superman* begins far more modestly with a tour of Superman's world and supporting cast. As it spotlights Lois Lane, Jimmy Olsen, Lex Luthor, Jonathan Kent, Metropolis, Smallville, the Fortress of Solitude, the DNA P.R.O.J.E.C.T., and other familiar elements, the series comes perilously close to a storytelling model Morrison had previously derided as "commercial strip-mining":

> The current vogue in superhero comics [...] is for the 'definitive' take, which tends to manifest itself as creators playing it safe by cherry-picking and re-packaging all the best and most popular elements of an already successful feature. It's a commercial strip-mining kind of approach to a given property that seems to make a lot of sense until you realize it can really only work once before you find yourself in the awful position of having to make up stuff again. (Brady, "Grant Morrison's Big-Time Return")

Had *All Star Superman* stayed in this mode it might well have amounted to yet another derivative "definitive" take, but the second half of the series returns the focus to Superman and assembles the disparate stories into a unified narrative. Morrison marks the change by starting the series over again: issue 7 opens with scientist Leo Quintum's spaceship breaking up from the stresses of a dangerous expedition into an inhospitable environment, repeating the scenario that begins the first issue.

Rather than merely survey the most popular parts of the Superman franchise, Morrison organizes *All Star Superman* around his protagonist's encounters with a series of doppelgangers and reflections. The series is replete with duplicate Supermen, mostly flawed ones who reproduce some aspects of Superman's character but fall far short in other areas. In issue 3 Superman encounters Samson and Atlas, two mythical strongmen who lack his ethics and compete with him for Lois Lane's attentions; in issue 4 a chunk of "black Kryptonite" transforms Superman into a hostile, cowardly, Bizarro-like inversion; and in issue 6 he meets a team of his own descendants who travel through time to fight evil as the Superman Squad. In his civilian life as Clark Kent he must work with Steve Lombard, a swaggering, overcompensating jock who constantly compares himself to Superman and constantly comes up short. After Morrison restarts the series, however, the reflections intensify until they dominate every issue. The second half of the series features Bizarro, Superman's twisted and imperfect duplicate; Zibarro, a copy of a copy, an imperfect duplicate of Bizarro; Bar-El and Lilo, two Kryptonian astronauts who briefly usurp Superman's mission as Earth's protectors; Superman's cousin Van-Zee and the Kandor Emergency Corps, natives of the shrunken Kryptonian city that Superman keeps under glass in his Fortress of Solitude; and in the final issues, Lex Luthor himself, who copies Superman's powers and uses them to initiate a reign of terror.

Contrasting Superman with these incomplete copies, Morrison identifies the qualities that make the original great by demonstrating the disastrous consequences when they are removed. Bizarro possesses Superman's power but lacks his intellect and inverts his morals; Zibarro, on the other hand, matches his intellect but lacks his powers. He sulks on the Bizarros' backwards Earth and laments his lot as the only intelligent being on a planet of idiots, a classic self-centered neurotic boy outsider. Superman grants him a sense of purpose by charging him with telling the story of his planet, effectively making him a journalist; if Zibarro does not have Superman's power, he can at least enjoy the dignity of Clark Kent's job. Other reflections like Samson, Atlas, and Luthor rival Superman's powers but lack his sense of responsibility, or, in the case of the Kryptonian astronauts, his restraint. Bar-El and Lilo believe their super powers and the "uncontested superiority and grandeur of Kryptonian culture" (9.8) entitle them to rebuild that culture on Earth. They berate Superman for disguising himself as a human and failing to impose his values on a defenseless planet until a sudden ailment demonstrates the value of human compassion. As in *JLA*, Morrison contrasts his hero against a series of ethical and philosophical foils to create a nonauthoritarian, nonimperialist superhero who does not believe that physical might justifies political domination. This Superman is not a conqueror but a scientist like his father, Jor-El. "I am a scientist's son," he tells Bar-El. "It's in my nature to observe and to learn ... and not to interfere too much" (9.18). Bar-El and Lilo prompt him to do more to benefit human and Kryptonian culture in the limited time he has left, but they cannot make him abandon the self-restraint and the trust in humanity's ability to determine its own future that defines Morrison's progressive, noninterventionist superheroes.

Van-Zee may be the most perfect copy, duplicating Superman's powers, his judgment, his selflessness, and even, by Silver Age tradition, his appearance. Unfortunately, as a miniaturized citizen of the bottle city of Kandor he is simply too physically unimposing to make an adequate replacement for his cousin. He takes part in another one of the series' organizing structures, however, a pattern that combines elements from every part of Superman's seventy-year history to form a palimpsest of all prior Superman comics. Just as *All Star Superman* extends its protagonist's reflections beyond the physical simulacra of the Silver Age, so does it expand the reproduction of his history outside the memorial atmosphere of the Fortress of Solitude and onto the plotting and cast. The series is particularly indebted to the Superman comics edited by Mort Weisinger in the 1950s and 1960s, formulaic stories in which Superman routinely performed miraculous labors and met strongmen of myth and legend, Lois Lane gained super powers, Jimmy Olsen transformed into a succession of monsters, and Lex Luthor spent most of his time plotting revenge from prison. In addition to paying homage to these stock plots, Morrison also retells specific tales from the Weisinger years: Bar-El and Lilo's brief stay on Earth and abrupt exile into the Phantom Zone repeats the story of the Daxamite astronaut Mon-El in "Superboy's Big Brother" (*Superboy* 89, 1961), and the overarching plot in which Superman hurries to complete his life's work before he dies recalls "The Last Days of Superman" (*Superman* 156, 1962). Morrison has cited the fanciful comics of the Weisinger era as an inspiration and justification for his own fantastic, antirealistic take on Superman (Brady, "Talking *All-Star Superman*") with specific reference to "Superman's New Power!" (*Superman* 125, 1958), in which the Man of Steel gains the unusual ability to shoot another, miniature Superman out of his palm—an image Morrison would re-create in issue 10 of *All Star Superman* with Van-Zee and his Kandorian colleagues standing in for the minuscule double.

Morrison maintains, however, that the series is more than a simple homage to the Silver Age. He told Zack Smith, "I never intended *All Star*

Superman as a direct continuation of the Weisinger or Julius Schwartz-era Superman stories. The idea was always to create another new version of Superman using *all* my favorite elements of past stories, not something 'Age' specific" (Smith Part 8; Morrison's emphasis). Rather than re-create the Weisinger years, the series assembles an eclectic pastiche of every era of Superman history, including more recent characters like Steve Lombard, who tormented Clark Kent in the Julius Schwartz-edited comics of the 1970s and early 1980s; Cat Grant, the oversexed gossip columnist created in Marv Wolfman and John Byrne's 1986 revamp; Doomsday, the monster who killed Superman in 1992; and Solaris, the tyrant sun Morrison created for *DC One Million* in 1998. Morrison nods to Alan Moore's Superman stories of the mid-eighties and to his own future history of Superman in *DC One Million*. By the end of the series, the palimpsest has grown to include *All Star Superman* itself. A quick tour of the Fortress of Solitude in issue 11 includes mementos of the first ten issues, signaling that these comics are now themselves part of Superman's history (11.4–5). Finally, Morrison contributes new characters like Leo Quintum and Zibarro, ensuring that the Superman story continues to grow in the twenty-first century. The result is not a re-creation of any single period in Superman's history but a summation and synthesis of the most notable elements from every period.

That synthesis is most visible in Morrison and Quitely's portrayal of Krypton. While the appearances of Superman and his earthly supporting cast have remained relatively stable over the decades, Krypton has seen many dramatic revisions, all of which resurface in *All Star Superman*. A brief glimpse of Krypton in issue 12 combines the crystal canyons of John Barry's sets for the 1978 *Superman* film with the Fire Falls of Silver Age comics and an allusion to the Scarlet Jungle fever of a 1985 Alan Moore story. Kryptonian culture proves equally multivalent, as seen in a meeting of the Kandorian council in issue 10. One of the councilors declares they are "dedicated to preserving the last living remnants of an ancient, lordly culture" (10.13), a mission they seem to have incorporated into their own dress: their clothing ranges from the headbands and chest emblems of the Silver Age to the elaborate robes and headdresses of John Byrne's revamp and the snug bodysuits of Quitely's own retro-modernist designs (fig. 7-2). The council constitutes a living exhibition of Kryptonian history, yet they unwittingly demonstrate the dangers of fetishizing the past. Van-Zee, Bar-El, and Leo Quintum all recognize that life under glass has stifled Kandorian development, and Quintum calls the Kandorians an "endangered species" if they insist on remaining isolated in their bottle, where they can only look back on past glories (10.13).

Figure 7-2. *All Star Superman* 10.13. Art by Frank Quitely. © DC Comics.

Superman and Quintum resolve the problem by taking Kandor out of its bottle and relocating it to Mars, where it is still miniaturized but free to grow in new directions. This solution could serve as a trope for the series as a whole; because *All Star Superman* is not bound by the regular Superman continuity and not obligated to continue the story beyond its twelve issues, Morrison is free to let all of Superman's history out of the bottle. He may quote past eras incessantly but he also works substantial changes on their long-established status quo. By the end of the first issue, Superman learns he is dying and reveals his secret identity to Lois; by the end of the series, he has left Earth for good and charged Leo Quintum with creating his successor. Morrison's debts to the past notwithstanding, *All Star Superman* is fundamentally antinostalgic in its insistence on progress and change.

SECULAR MYTHOLOGIES

Morrison's pastiche extends beyond comics to create a blend of myth, fable, and fairy tale that he calls "science fiction folk tales" (Brady, "Talking *All-Star Superman*"). In the first issue, Leo Quintum prompts Superman's rescue and accidentally precipitates his death by solar radiation poisoning when he leads an expedition "to steal fire from the sun" (1.15). Here Morrison combines the myths of Icarus and Prometheus to invert part of the myth of Superman, which had long established the sun as the source of his power. The next issue, a paranoid Lois fears Superman has brought her to his Fortress of Solitude to breed with her or kill her in a perverse restaging of the story of Bluebeard—fortunately, she is wrong—and Superman himself spends the series attempting to complete twelve challenges before he dies, an obvious echo of the labors of Hercules. The series as a whole is structured around the monomyth of the hero's descent into and return from the underworld, with that descent occurring over several issues in the middle of the series: a subterranean river beneath Luthor's prison cell in issue 5, Jonathan Kent's death in issue 6, and the Bizarro "Underverse" in issues 7 and 8 all offer metonymic examples or symbolic proxies for Superman's confrontation with his own mortality. Morrison makes no distinction between retelling these myths and retelling the story of Mon-El or "The Last Days of Superman." All of his intertexts are absorbed into the same mythic framework.

Interviewers such as Matt Brady and Zack Smith have tried to read that mythic framework in a Christian context, with some justification. Other creators have treated Superman as a Christ figure, as in Bryan Singer's film *Superman Returns*, and *All Star Superman* does not exactly discourage such readings. Superman cures a hospital ward full of sick children in issue 10, dies in issue 11, and briefly returns in issue 12 before he ascends to the sun to save the human race once again. But Morrison resists any interpretation that reduces Superman to a narrow Christian allegory. In interviews, he stresses the many differences between these figures—"Superman is by no means a pacifist in the Christ sense" (Smith Part 9)—and emphasizes the secular dimensions of Superman's character. Before the series was published, he called Superman "a much more progressive figure than Jesus [. . .] a science fiction savior rocketed to Earth from a world of wonder [. . .] the character has the potential to transcend his humble origins and say something quite profound to those of us living in the secular 21st century" (Brady, "Talking"). After the series' completion, Morrison continued to describe Superman as "a secular messiah, a science redeemer" (Smith Part 9), while suggesting he and his fellow superheroes were the "only secular role models for a progressive, responsible, scientific-rational Enlightenment culture" (Thill). These comments display Morrison's characteristic hyperbole but the series upholds their secular interpretation, presenting a Superman who identifies himself as a scientist. Many of his feats revolve around making scientific breakthroughs, devising new inventions, rescuing Leo Quintum's expeditions, or finding new solutions to intractable problems like the enlargement of Kandor. Morrison's Superman is a model of rational scientific inquiry, not an object of religious veneration.

Morrison attributes the religious and mythical elements in *All Star Superman* to archetypal patterns rather than any single divinity. He told Smith, "It's not that [Superman]'s based on Jesus, but simply that a lot of the mythical sun god elements which have been layered onto the Christ story also appear in the story of Superman. I suppose I see Superman more as pagan sci-fi" (Smith Part 9). He disavows direct parallels with Christ, Hercules, or any other mythological figures, explaining that the comic creates "the contemporary 'superhero' version of an archetypal solar hero journey, which naturally echoes numerous myths, legends and religious parables. At the same time, we didn't want to do an update or a direct copy of any myth you'd seen before, so it won't work if you try to find one specific mythological or religious 'plan' to hang the series on" (Smith Part 2). He instead aligns the series' structure with the solar calendar, noting that Superman's descent into the underworld occurs at the winter solstice, in the middle of the night, and at the midpoint of the series (Smith Part 2). Evoking diverse sources both secular and religious, ancient and modern, *All Star Superman* operates according to several complementary narrative logics. These overdetermined origins account for everything from the multiple underworlds Superman passes through at the series' midpoint to the three separate origins of the Bizarros (who appear at different times as failed clones of Superman, an evil inversion triggered by black Kryptonite, and infectious zombies from the Underverse). In this respect *All Star Superman* is highly reminiscent of *JLA*, another Morrison comic that features a superabundance of metaphysics without attempting to rank, organize, or even distinguish between them (Klock 124–27). *All Star Superman* is as "joyful in overdetermination" (Klock 134) as its predecessor, presenting a multivalent, multiply redundant, prismatic mythology rather than a single symbolic organizing scheme.

From its cosmic story structures to its panel transitions, *All Star Superman* is one of Morrison's most meticulously plotted comics. Morrison may have disparaged his ability to construct a plot in his final issue of *Animal

Figure 7-3. *All Star Superman* 5.10-11. Art by Frank Quitely. © DC Comics.

Man (*AM* 26.11), but the last issue of *All Star Superman* has Superman declaring, "I had the whole thing paced out to end pretty much exactly like this" (12.12), all but boasting on his author's behalf. Morrison's clockwork execution is assisted by the equally measured art of Frank Quitely, who generally eschews the formal pyrotechnics of *We3* to focus on the subtleties of body language and page layouts. His Clark Kent is a slouching, stumbling misfit in the tradition of actor Christopher Reeve's interpretation of the character, a performance that might plausibly fool Superman's closest friends. Much of the series is set in courtrooms, laboratories, the Fortress of Solitude, and other locations that match Quitely's austere design sense (and, not inconsequentially given his notoriously slow pace, relieve him of the burden of drawing detailed backgrounds); Superman even quips that his armory looks like a modern art gallery (2.9). When Clark visits Lex Luthor in prison, Quitely's rigorous layouts become part of the stark utilitarian design as his regular grids of evenly-spaced panels double for the prison's architecture (fig. 7-3). Quitely is not afraid to disarrange his layouts but he

Figure 7-4. *All Star Superman* 5.18. Art by Frank Quitely. © DC Comics.

does so only to reflect the action on the page, knocking panel grids off-kilter to duplicate the violent motions of combat (9.10) or twisting and collapsing panel borders to suggest a tremor (fig. 7-4). Quitely's formalist restraint ensures that even the most dramatic images focus the reader's attention back on the comic's content and themes. Morrison has explained that he and Quitely "agreed [the art] had to be about grids, structure, storybook panel layouts, an elegance of form, a clarity of delivery. 'Classical' in every sense of the word. The medium, the message, the story, the character, all working together as one simple equation" (Smith Part 7).

ENDING THE NEVER-ENDING BATTLE

Morrison may reject Christian allegories but he does concede that Superman is similar to Jesus "In the sense that he inspires us towards our best" (Brady, "Talking"), an interpretation *All Star Superman* advances in scenes rife with religious overtones. In the final issue—which Morrison titles "Superman in Excelsis," a reference to the hymn "Gloria in Excelsis Deo"—a dying Superman hallucinates the life he never lived on Krypton, a last temptation akin to the worlds of illusion that torment other Morrison messiahs like Dane McGowan and Shilo Norman. Jor-El, acting as both the subconscious voice of reason that undoes the fantasy and the heavenly Father who sends his son back to Earth to save the human race, tells Superman, "You have given [humanity] an ideal to aspire to, embodied their highest aspirations" (12.6). In addition to alerting readers to the hypostases at work in *All Star Superman*, Jor-El restates an earlier argument about the purpose and significance of the Superman character. In issue 10, Superman tests whether the human race can survive without his protection by creating life on Earth-Q, a duplicate Earth in the micro-universe of Qwewq. The glimpses of this pocket world, which is functionally identical to our own, trace the evolution of humanity's aspirations from early religions to Pico della Mirandola's *Oration on the Dignity of Man* and Nietzsche's *Thus Spoke Zarathustra*, a humanist trajectory that culminates in Jerry Siegel and Joe Shuster's creation of Superman. Morrison's Superman is at once a godlike creator and a human creation, a paradox the series presents not as a theological claim but as a case for the dignity and worth of human imagination and the value of Superman and other fictional heroes. *All Star Superman* suggests that Superman's most important power—the only one he possesses in the real world—is the power to inspire people by modeling their best qualities of courage, altruism, reason, and hope; through such inspiration, fiction can shape the world, an influence Morrison magnifies and literalizes into Superman's creation of our own world. Depicting our planet and our species as the creations of a fictional character whom we have in turn created, Morrison establishes a reciprocal, inseparable relation between the material and the ideal.

Not every character in *All Star Superman* is willing to acknowledge this reciprocity. Lex Luthor is Superman's archenemy not only because of his formidable if amoral intellect but because he espouses a radical, reductive materialism that denies and despises the power of ideals. He claims to oppose Superman out of pride in human accomplishments, expressing his resentment that "We all fall short of that sickening, inhuman perfection, that impossible ideal" (5.8). He also claims he has been building a model society in prison, offering an alternative to "truth, justice and all the other things you can't weigh or carry! To every abstract [Superman] represents" (5.11). With its refusal of all the things that cannot be touched and quantified, Luthor's materialist utopia would constitute an alternative not just to Superman but to idealism itself. While Morrison tacitly undercuts Luthor's utopian pretenses (the other prisoners do not think nearly as highly of Luthor or his "model society" as he thinks they do), he also implies the criminal scientist's rivalry with Superman is rooted in a general disdain for the ideal and immaterial; Luthor demands that a priest be dismissed from his execution because he "stinks of the irrational" (11.1). He expresses equal contempt for secular ideals in this exchange with Perry White, editor of the *Daily Planet*:

> **Perry White:** The truth sent you to the chair, Luthor!
> **Luthor:** Is that right, Mister White? Funny, I don't see the truth anywhere around, do you? I mean, what color is it? Can I touch it? (12.5)

Morrison connects this fanatical empiricism to his favorite example of rationalism and utopianism gone wrong, the French Revolution. When Luthor's inventions briefly overrun Metropolis following Superman's apparent defeat, his niece Nasthalthia proclaims "This is Science Year Zero" (12.14), indicating a desire to rebuild society along the same rigidly rationalistic principles that led the Jacobins to institute the French Republican Calendar. With her allusion to the Revolution and her threats to try and presumably execute the "traitors" of the *Daily Planet*, Nasthalthia completes the portrayal of Luthor as a figure of rationalism and materialism run amok.

In his final battle with Superman, however, Luthor belatedly learns to recognize the power of ideas. Temporarily in possession of Superman's enhanced senses, Luthor accidentally discovers the key to a unified field theory that links the four fundamental forces of the universe: "The fundamental forces are yoked by a single thought. [...] It's thought-controlled" (12.15). His realization that thought unifies and directs the fundamental interactions of elementary particles echoes the mission of one of Leo Quintum's genetically engineered workers, who seeks to describe the unified field in a haiku: "If we can first unify the fundamental forces in our imagination, you see, all else will follow" (4.6).[1] Luthor achieves this imaginary unification, conceding the primacy of thought over matter and learning to see the universe as Superman sees it, both literally and figuratively. This triumph for idealism is punctuated with a decidedly material punch as Superman tells Luthor, "You were right, Lex... brain beats brawn every time" (12.15–16). The maxim is both appropriate to the circumstances (Superman, ever the scientist, has just used Einstein's general theory of relativity to rob Luthor of his artificial powers) and a sarcastic restatement of an earlier boast by Luthor (5.11); the punch, however, is more than mere genre window-dressing. Providing a physical counterpart to Luthor's ideological failure, the punch graphically resolves the series' conflict of ideas—optimism and idealism sock cynicism and materialism in the jaw—while it demonstrates superhero comics' facility for concretizing the abstract and embodying our ideals just as Jor-El describes. The ideological conflict and the material punch that incarnates it form a meta-hypostasis of comics' knack for hypostatic representation.

All Star Superman does not end with one belief system simply defeating the other but, much more characteristically for Morrison, with these systems finding common ground. Luthor's hostility to Superman may be a classic example of the clash between beneficial science and misapplied, destructive science typical of the superhero genre since its inception (Reynolds 20–24), but Morrison reconciles these oppositions in a third figure, Leo Quintum. While the gifted geneticist can be read as the latest character to fill the role of Superman's scientist friend in the tradition of Phineas Potter, Jasper Pepperwinkle, Emil Hamilton, and so forth, he shares many of Luthor's more destructive qualities, including the theatricality, recklessness, and hubris that lead Quintum to steal fire from the sun and inadvertently kill Superman. These similarities have prompted some readers to postulate that Leo Quintum is in fact a repentant Lex Luthor who has traveled back in time and adopted a new identity to atone for his sins, although Morrison has not confirmed this interpretation in the text of *All Star Superman* or in his many interviews.[2] Even if Quintum is not literally a redeemed Luthor, he figuratively presents a Luthor analogue who has learned from Superman's example. As Morrison explains, "Science so often goes wrong in Superman stories, and I thought it was important to show the potential for science to go right or to be elevated by contact with Superman's shining positive spirit" (Smith Part 3). This fusion of traits is legible in the characters' color schemes. Superman has worn the three primary colors—red, yellow, and blue—since his 1938 debut. Morrison and colorist Jamie Grant associate Luthor with the secondary colors, clothing him in an orange prison jumpsuit and a green-and-purple costume. Quintum, however, wears a rainbow-colored coat that combines the primary and secondary colors into a single spectrum, indicating his combination of Superman's selflessness and social responsibility with Luthor's intellect and pride.

The world will need Quintum's potent blend of altruism and ingenuity since it can no longer depend on Superman's protection. With his body converting into stored solar energy—"pure energy, pure information" (12.17) and therefore pure idea—Superman leaves Earth forever to repair a sun poisoned by Luthor's schemes. His distant but still beneficent interactions with the Earth duplicate his earlier relationships to Kandor and Earth-Q; he is once again the custodian who presides over the planet from afar and, in his absence, the purely ideal being who can only influence the world by inspiring others to do better. The ending revisits two of Morrison's customary techniques, a sudden variation in scale that likens Earth to the microworlds it contains and a blurring of ontologies that makes Superman's fictional world more like our own. Both manifest Morrison's overarching interest in the power of fictions to shape the world. Contrary to popular but reductive Christian readings and Morrison's own religious allusions, the finale offers a humanist and egalitarian interpretation of Superman in which the hero not only saves humanity but challenges us to take responsibility for our safety and our future. The final image shows not Superman but Leo Quintum expressing confidence in our ability to rise to the occasion.

BATMAN: THE MANY LIVES OF THE BATMAN

Months before his first issue of *Batman* (2006–08) saw print, Morrison told a comics convention audience that his interpretation of the character would be "more of a 'fun guy, more healthy,' more like the 'Neal Adams, hairy-chested, love-god' version of Batman" ("WonderCon"). Repeating a phrase he had used in his annotations to the *Arkham Asylum* 15th Anniversary Edition, where he said he preferred to think of Batman "as Neal Adams drew him—the hairy-chested globetrotting love god of the '70s stories" (61), this pithy description suggested that Morrison's forthcoming series would reject revisionist treatments of Batman in favor of earlier, more well-adjusted renditions. In a subsequent interview, Morrison told Matt Brady,

> Personally, I wanted to see a psychologically "healthier" Batman—the last couple of decades have seen the character in the comics deconstructed almost to the point of no return and the Bat-books were heavily-laden with an extended family of characters, many of whom existed only to stand in for some part of Batman's personality that had been lost or suppressed over the last twenty years. It seemed like the right moment to step in and start gluing him back together again. (Brady, "Morrison in the Cave")

In fact, Morrison would reassemble more than just the confident, generically versatile Batman of the Neal Adams years. His *Batman* draws upon elements from every period in the character's history, mixing the Gothic tales of the 1930s with the noirish crime stories of the 1940s, the weird science fiction of the 1950s, the self-conscious camp and pop art of the 1960s, the globetrotting adventure and macho romance of the 1970s, and the grim and gritty revisionism of the 1980s and 1990s. In his "Introduction" to *Batman: The Black Casebook*, a collection of oddball stories from the fifties and sixties that inspired his own *Batman* storylines, Morrison writes, "I decided to treat the entire publishing history of Batman as the events in one man's extraordinarily vivid life. [...] I imagined a rough timeline that allowed me to compress 70 years' worth of Batman's adventures into a frantic 15 years in the life of an extraordinary man." Instead of selecting and synthesizing his favorite elements for a private continuity, as he did in *All Star Superman*, Morrison accepts every story in his protagonist's seventy-year history and attempts to incorporate all of them into his narrative.

This inclusivity extends even to those eras that most embarrass fans, the science fiction of the 1950s and the camp of the 1966–68 *Batman* television series. Morrison begins his tenure on *Batman* with a sly nod to the television series and to other, roughly contemporaneous appropriations of comic book iconography. In his second issue (*Batman* 656), Batman battles foes inside an art gallery filled with Roy Lichtenstein-style paintings whose comic book captions and word balloons interact with the combat and re-create the

Work for Hire   269

Figure 7-5. *Batman* 656.10. Art by Andy Kubert. © DC Comics.

Figure 7-6. *Batman* 658.22. Art by Andy Kubert. © DC Comics.

superimposed sound effects from the television series (fig. 7-5). Two issues later, Morrison drops the ironic mediation of the paintings and incorporates Lichtenstein's pop art aesthetic directly into the comics when artist Andy Kubert draws an exploding submarine with the flat composition, colossal lettering, and heavy brushstrokes of Lichtenstein's *Whaam!* (1963); the image also works as a narrative sequel to *Torpedo . . . Los!* (1963), showing the consequences of a torpedo launch similar to the one depicted in Lichtenstein's painting (fig. 7-6). Rather than fret over comics' appropriation by high art or their mockery by mass media, Morrison's allusions display his comfort with all the periods in Batman's history and all of the culture's adaptations of comic book conventions.

With so many conflicting influences, however, the tone fluctuates wildly from storyline to storyline, issue to issue, and sometimes even from page to page. *Batman* 664 leaps from a jet-set romance and a ski chase in the Alps, the stuff of the globetrotting love god, to a sordid plot involving police corruption and dead prostitutes; the next issue reverses this lurching change in tone with equal abruptness. *Batman* 672 includes two visual citations of *The Dark Knight Returns*, but it also references the hallucinatory alien giant from "Robin Dies at Dawn" (1963), the alien planet from "Batman—The Superman of Planet X!" (1958), and Bat-Mite, the magical pest who bedeviled Batman and Robin in the late fifties and early sixties. Far from emphasizing Batman's sanity, the stylistic whiplash results in a series as schizoid and unstable as its protagonist. Morrison's attempts to restore Batman's mental health are further undermined by his decision to incorporate the science fiction and fantasy elements within a more realistic framework of psychological manipulation. His climactic storyline, "Batman R.I.P." (*Batman* 676–681), writes the forgotten sci-fi adventures back into Batman continuity but it also attributes most of the zany imps and alien worlds to Batman's exposure to chemical agents, sensory deprivation experiments, and other assaults on his mind, suggesting they are hallucinations or psychological defense mechanisms. The explanation successfully assimilates the otherwise unassimilible science fiction stories, but it also contradicts and overwhelms Morrison's stated interest in rebuilding Batman's psyche.

A storyline featuring the Club of Heroes (*Batman* 667–669) manages Morrison's pastiche more effectively, thanks largely to the artist's versatility. The Club of Heroes, an international group of crimefighters inspired by Batman, have rarely been seen since the 1950s, but J. H. Williams III redesigns each member to look as if they have been illustrated by a different comics artist of the past twenty years: El Gaucho is drawn with the wild

Work for Hire 271

Figure 7-7. A Howard Chaykin Gaucho, a Dave Gibbons Wingman, and an Alan Davis Musketeer. *Batman* 667.11. Art by J. H. Williams III. © DC Comics.

linework and stippled, textured inks of Howard Chaykin, for example, while the Wingman bears the rigid lines and measured hatching of *Watchmen*-era Dave Gibbons (fig. 7-7). As Williams explained to the Barbelith online community, "the whole idea here was to convey characters that have had real history that we haven't been privy to. [. . .] grant wrote them as if they've been having lives and adventures all along and i wanted to see if i could make them seem as if they had stepped out of their own comics and into this one. so i imagined what those comics might currently look like." Williams coordinates these conflicting influences through a robust design sense that treats each page as an integrated, internally consistent image; no single character is allowed to stand out, with the possible exception of Batman, who is rendered in Williams's own style and forms the calm center in the otherwise relentless homage. Morrison did not request Williams's visual citations but he does help manage them by maintaining a consistent plot and atmosphere for three issues, placing Batman and the Club of Heroes in a murder mystery based on Agatha Christie's *And Then There Were None* (1939)—or perhaps more directly inspired by "The Superlative Seven," a 1967 episode of *The Avengers* television series based loosely on Christie's plot. The mystery is at once modern and antiquated, considerably more sinister than the Club's original appearances but still holding realism at arm's length through its formulaic plot and self-conscious theatricality. The story is every bit as retro-modernist as the Club of Heroes themselves; so too is the art, which twists panel borders into angular silhouettes reminiscent of Saul Bass and other postwar graphic designers. Regrettably, few artists possess Williams's uncanny talent for graphic impersonation. Other than a few desultory attempts by Tony Daniel, most of Morrison's collaborators on *Batman* do not reinforce the series' palimpsest of comics styles.

Left largely to his own devices, Morrison writes that palimpsest into the script by confronting Batman with a series of reflections that embody different periods in his history and different aspects of his character. The imitation Batmen of the Club of Heroes form one of the more genial sets of reflections, although each hero illustrates a flaw that has dominated past interpretations of the caped crusader. The Wingman and the Ranger (now the Dark Ranger) have adopted armored suits and grim personas, reflecting the post-Miller trend towards a darker, more violent Batman. Unsurprisingly, the former is exposed as the killer and the latter as one of his victims, delivering an unmistakable commentary on the dead end of revisionism. The Knight is burdened with guilt over the death of his father, much like Batman himself, but that guilt has led to mental illness; Chief Man-of-Bats has alienated his son and partner, mirroring Batman's acrimonious relationships with his sidekicks; and the Legionary and the Musketeer have both cashed in on their careers to become rich, a wry comment on Batman's extranarrative status as a phenomenally lucrative trademark and the star of a cross-media franchise. Less honorable analogues include a trio of Gotham City police officers who were trained to replace Batman but who have descended into corruption and murder, and several warped reflections of Bruce Wayne, Batman's secret identity. The billionaires John Mayhew, Jezebel Jet, and the secretive members of the Black Glove, a consortium of gamblers, are jaded elites who dwarf Wayne's considerable wealth but lack his defining mission and use their money to ruin innocent lives as a form of decadent entertainment.

Bruce Wayne and Batman are both reproduced in Damian, the son Batman conceived with Talia, the daughter of his adversary Ra's al Ghul.[3] Raised by terrorists and trained to assume his grandfather's place as the leader of an international cartel of assassins, Damian is a spoiled and petulant brat, but he doesn't just take after his mother's side of the family; when he storms out of the Batcave after throwing a profane tantrum, Bruce's butler Alfred sighs, "Memory lane" (657.8). Presumably Alfred refers to Bruce Wayne's own troubled childhood, but Damian is not so different from the Batman of recent years, either—the post-*Dark Knight Returns* character that Morrison has called the "sour-faced, sexually-repressed, humorless, uptight, angry, and all-round grim 'n' gritty Batman" (Brady, "Morrison in the Cave").

When Batman briefly attempts to raise Damian, he has a rare opportunity to avoid past mistakes and correct past representations, although Morrison unfortunately chooses to keep father and son apart for most of his time on the series. If the reflections of *All Star Superman* fall short of their original because they lack one or more of his most important qualities, the imitators in *Batman* carry their hero's qualities to destructive extremes. Morrison forces Batman to confront and defeat his own worst attributes, investing the commercial practice of prismatic brand proliferation with dramatic and psychological import.

One other character in Morrison's *Batman* sports a panoply of identities, although rather than displace them onto a gallery of reflections he contains them all within his own fragmented psyche. It is fitting that a palimpsestic Batman should have an equally palimpsestic archenemy, and Morrison treats the many conflicting portrayals of the Joker as no less valid than the various phases of Batman's own history. He explores these multiple Jokers in "The Clown at Midnight" (*Batman* 663), a story that combines John Van Fleet's plasticine computer-generated art with Morrison's overheated prose. If the issue fails as a lurid parody of hard-boiled crime fiction ("Rain goes clickety-clack-tack through the sticks and branches of bare, bony graveyard elms, the kind that stand as if ashamed, like strippers past their best"), it at least manages to approximate the Joker's deranged perceptions. In this issue, Batman explains that the Joker "has no real personality, remember, only a series of 'superpersonas'" (663.13), canonizing an interpretation Morrison first proposed almost twenty years earlier in *Arkham Asylum*. In that graphic novel, psychotherapist Ruth Adams attempted to rationalize the Joker's behavior to a skeptical Batman:

> In fact, we're not even sure if he can be properly defined as insane. [...] It's quite possible we may actually be looking at some kind of super-sanity here. A brilliant new modification of human perception. More suited to urban life at the end of the twentieth century. [...] Unlike you and I, the Joker seems to have no control over the sensory information he's receiving from the outside world. He can only cope with that chaotic barrage of input by going with the flow. That's why some days he's a mischievous clown, others a psychopathic killer. He has no real personality. He creates himself each day. (*Arkham Asylum*)

The Joker has internalized this interpretation in "The Clown at Midnight," recalling it as he prepares to cast aside an old persona and molt into a new one: "He tries to remember how the doctors in Arkham say he has no Self, and maybe they're right, or maybe just guessing. Maybe he is a new human mutation, bred of slimy industrial waters. [...] Maybe he is the model for 21st-century big-time multiplex man, shuffling selves like a croupier deals cards" (663.16). The Joker demonstrates a dangerous application of the MeMePlex, providing a necessary if chilling correction to Morrison's earlier suggestion in *The Invisibles* that multiple personality disorder could serve as a model for political and existential liberation. The Joker's destruction and multiplication of the self has led not to unity in the supercontext but simply to a psychotic mass murderer "addicted to an endless cycle of self-annihilating violence" (663.16).

The Joker is highly conscious of this succession of psychological transformations, a sequence that parallels his publication history. He has developed names for his earlier selves, branding them with labels like "the Satire Years" (663.16), alluding to a period in the late 1940s and early 1950s when he crafted his own imitations of Batman's Batmobile, utility belt, and other crimefighting accoutrements; "Camp," referring to the 1960s *Batman* television series and the comics that emulated its style; and "New Homicidal," the return of the menacing, murderous Joker that began with "The Joker's Five-Way Revenge" in 1973.[4] Blessed or cursed with a perfect memory—or a metafictional awareness of his past appearances—the Joker punctuates his rebirth by reciting his own best lines, from his first appearance in *Batman* 1 (1940) to *The Killing Joke* and *Arkham Asylum* to the recent storyline "Hush" (2003), recapitulating his own ontogeny (663.16). He emerges from this mental chrysalis as "the Thin White Duke of Death" (663.18), a reference to the drug-addled, megalomaniacal 1976 "Thin White Duke" persona of David Bowie—another aesthete with an endless talent for reinvention. Morrison's contribution to the Joker's history is to imagine him as a self-conscious performance artist who contains all his prior representations in a warped reflection of Batman's own multiplicity.

Elegant though it is, even this schema cannot fully explain the Joker's psychosis. The Joker proudly defies any comprehension or rationalization; in "Batman R.I.P." he tells Batman, "the real joke is your stubborn, bone deep conviction that somehow, somewhere, all of this makes sense! [...] you think it all breaks down into symbolism and structures and hints and clues [...] no, batman, that's just wikipedia" (680.15, 18). The grinning killer not only mocks Batman's attempts to understand him, he also taunts any readers who try to do the same. Those readers conduct much of their interpretive work online, either through the consultation of references or the creation of online communities. Morrison told Patrick Meaney that he wrote "Batman R.I.P." to encourage this kind of extranarrative participation and said he wants readers to track down his allusions on Wikipedia (307–8), yet the Joker's recognition and dismissal of that participation tells readers they will never be able to devise a rational explanation of his character. They will find a similar resistance to interpretation from the primary villain of "Batman R.I.P.," one of the leaders of the Black Glove, Doctor Simon Hurt. At various points in "Batman R.I.P." Hurt is identified as a military psychiatrist, a vengeful film actor, Thomas Wayne (Batman's dead father), Satan, or some other malign spirit or psychological entity called forth by Batman's exploration of the deepest recesses of his own mind; one character even suggests that Batman could have created the Black Glove himself. After Batman dismisses most of these possibilities and settles on the most rational answer, that Hurt is an actor adopting a variety of guises, the doctor says he is "the hole in things, Bruce, the enemy, the piece that can never fit, there since the beginning" (681.25).

Morrison's overall design becomes apparent: in a series dedicated to reintegrating Batman into a healthy, sane character with a single, all-encompassing history, the two most dangerous antagonists are a mass murderer who gleefully resists psychological integration and a mastermind of uncertain origin who cannot be assimilated into any coherent narrative. Even worse, these antagonists insist that Batman is no more rational than they are. The Joker parodies his varied history, suggesting it leads only to madness, while Doctor Hurt exploits his psychological vulnerabilities, and both men confound his attempts to make sense of a senseless world. Morrison's run on *Batman* ends with the failure of his extranarrative project; not only is he unable to overwrite the grim, violent, borderline insane Batman of the revisionist years—who would have survived in any case as one Batman among many in Morrison's diverse history—but he cannot produce the healthy, integrated but heterogeneous Batman he promised in early interviews. The series remains a collection of dissonant pieces as the Joker and Doctor Hurt remind us that Batman's world, like his psyche, remains beyond rationalization.

Morrison recognizes his inability to integrate Batman's many selves. His final issues (*Batman* 682–683), which tie into *Final Crisis*, lament both the prismatic copies he has created throughout the series and the revisionist interpretations he has failed to dispel. In these issues Batman relives his career as part of a ruse perpetrated by Mokkari and Simyan, two agents of Darkseid. The rogue geneticists are attempting to clone Batman into an army of super-soldiers and they need to replicate his traumatic memories in order to ensure their copies will have the same unrelenting drive. Mokkari tells his colleague, "These are traits we must steal, duplicate . . . and mass-produce! [. . .] With this template we will build a production line army of mindless 'Batmen' to fight and pillage and die in the name of our dark empire" (682.23). The rant offers a transparent criticism of "Prismatic Age" imitation and comics companies' demands for new variations on the same proven quantities. Mokkari and Simyan only intend to do what Morrison and countless Batman writers before him have already done: replicate Batman across multiple characters, multiple comics, and multiple media. The next issue, Morrison's last, is equally cynical in its assessment of the readers' complicity in Batman's tormented history. As Batman's recollections reach the comics of the late 1980s—a period that saw the Joker cripple Batgirl and murder Jason Todd, the second Robin—Mokkari gloats, "This is what we want! Raw emotional energy! More pain! Motivation!" (683.13). The implicit critique has expanded from Batman's writers and editors to the readers who rewarded these abusive developments with high sales and critical acclaim. Morrison castigates all of these factions, himself included, for the unremitting violence, the emotional and creative exploitation, and the endless imitations that have governed Batman comics for more than twenty years. The overabundance of prismatic reflections has become one of the problems facing modern superhero comics, although it is a problem Morrison's concurrent project only intensifies.

FINAL CRISIS: CONTAMINATING SELF-CONSCIOUSNESS

A seven-issue miniseries with art by J. G. Jones, Carlos Pacheco, and Doug Mahnke, *Final Crisis* (2008–09) cannot be read simply as the next Morrison work or even as the next stage of his assimilation into DC's most mainstream superhero comics. As a companywide crossover with multiple tie-ins and spin-off titles, some of them written by Morrison and some by other creators, *Final Crisis* was also the culmination of several years of comics focused on the myriad contradictions and revisions of DC continuity. These comics were products of Dan DiDio's supervision of the DC universe of superhero titles, first as vice president-editorial and later as DC's senior vice president-executive editor. Under DiDio's direction, the company revisited Marv Wolfman and George Pérez's *Crisis on Infinite Earths* several times in a series of attempts to sort out or reverse the changes it had wrought.

Wolfman and Pérez had collapsed the DC cosmos from a plenitude of parallel dimensions into a single universe with a single narrative continuity in the interest of attracting new readers (Klock 19–21). Since this consolidation retroactively erased many characters and stories from DC's official continuity, if not from the memories of longtime fans, these revisions generally only made matters more confusing. *Infinite Crisis* (2005–06), a sequel by Geoff Johns and Phil Jimenez, flirted with undoing and restoring the multiverse. That restoration was not made official until *52* (2006–07), in which Morrison, Johns, Greg Rucka, and Mark Waid revealed that *Infinite Crisis* had in fact resulted in the creation of fifty-two parallel universes—most of which were based on the old parallel worlds that had preceded *Crisis on Infinite Earths* or on various out-of-continuity projects that had been published in the decades since. DiDio followed *52* with another weekly comic, *Countdown* (2007–08), which explored these parallel worlds and generated a host of spin-offs that followed suit. By the time *Final Crisis* began in May 2008, the DC line had been dominated for more than three years by comics primarily concerned with DC's cosmology and continuity.

Morrison had come to play an increasingly central role at DC in those years, writing the company's flagship characters in *Batman* and *All Star Superman* and surveying the remodeled DC universe in *52*. After DiDio saw Morrison's revitalizations of minor and forgotten heroes in *Seven Soldiers*, he asked the writer to redesign other underused DC characters ("Grant Morrison on Being the DCU Revamp Guy"). Several of these reinventions were published as miniseries and ongoing series, including *The All-New Atom*, *Uncle Sam and the Freedom Fighters*, and *Metal Men*, although none were written by Morrison and none would last more than two years. *Final Crisis* was Morrison's first opportunity to steer the DC universe on his own, without other writers to act as intermediaries or collaborators; it was also the first time DC's linewide obsession with its own continuity began to dominate his work and crowd out other concerns. While Morrison attempts to build the crossover around issues of human progress, generational change, depression, and ideological extremism, *Final Crisis* collapses into a relentless and repetitive metacommentary more characteristic of its publisher and its moment in the history of superhero comics.

The sprawling plot furnishes enough material for several crossovers. In a direct continuation of the *Mister Miracle* storyline from *Seven Soldiers*, Darkseid and the other evil gods of Apokolips have become loa-like beings who possess mortal bodies. Working behind these mortal guises, Darkseid and his followers initiate a wildly successful invasion of Earth, converting more than three billion people into mindless followers through the soul-destroying power of the Anti-Life Equation. Meanwhile, in a separate plot largely confined to the *Final Crisis: Superman Beyond 3D* tie-in (2008–09), Superman is summoned by one of the extradimensional Monitors to battle a menace that threatens not just Earth but the entire multiverse. With Superman absent and the other leading superheroes incapacitated, Darkseid is resisted by a motley alliance of new and minor heroes, including several who are still teenagers, until the champions return in the final chapter of *Final Crisis* and all of the storylines converge.

The rapid spread of Darkseid's fanatical following echoes the zombie narratives that have captivated twenty-first-century popular culture, expressing shared fears of ideological contagion and social breakdown. Unlike most zombie apocalypses, however, Morrison explicitly links Darkseid's followers to religious extremists. In the *Final Crisis: Submit* spin-off (2008), written by Morrison and drawn by Matthew Clark, a captured superhero who has been brainwashed into joining Darkseid's Justifiers burns a copy of Charles Darwin's *The Origin of Species* while declaring "What disagrees with Darkseid is heresy. What agrees with Darkseid is superfluous" (*Submit* 29). The proclamation echoes the apocryphal words that Christian historians attributed to Caliph Omar, who supposedly ordered the burning of the Library of Alexandria because its collection either contradicted the Qur'an or duplicated it. Morrison paraphrases the fictitious quote not as an attack on Islam but as a criticism of all zealotry; the pyre of burning books would not look out of place at a Nazi rally, or in the postwar anticomics crusade. The same book-burner then shouts "Anti-Life justifies my ignorance!" (*Submit* 29), leaving little doubt as to his author's views on all forms of fanaticism.

Other parts of the crossover hold more personal and psychological resonance. Darkseid's command of the Anti-Life Equation and his ability to possess and corrupt noble personalities make him a figure of depression as well as tyranny and ideological conformity. As with the League of Legions' escape from the Absolute in *Flex Mentallo* or the Justice League's battle against Mageddon in *JLA*, Morrison rallies an army of superheroes to confront one of the hypostases of depression that are so common to his superhero epics. Darkseid wins the early rounds, however, and popular heroes such as Superman, Batman, and Green Lantern are quickly written out of the plot, presenting the remarkably anticommercial prospect of a major crossover that focuses on secondary characters like Mister Miracle and new creations like the Super Young Team, a group of teenaged Japanese fans who seize the opportunity to become the kind of superheroes they have previously idolized. Young and novice heroes take center stage in *Final Crisis*; the crossover opens with an image of Anthro, boy hero of the Paleolithic age, and soon flashes forward to a scene of Kamandi, boy hero of a dystopian future. The temporal arc from Anthro to Kamandi not only encompasses the rise and projected fall of human civilization, it positions *Final Crisis* as a story of heroic youth battling old age, mortality, depression, and societal decline.

Unfortunately, most of these potential themes remain strictly potential. Morrison writes *Final Crisis* in an accelerating parataxis he calls "channel-zapping comics" (Hudson), moving from scene to scene with increasing speed and little to no transition; by the final two issues he condenses entire subplots into one or two panels. This increases the range of subjects the miniseries can address but leaves them little room for development, and nearly all disappear before the grand finale. The changing villains are symptomatic of this narrowing focus: in the last fifteen pages of the crossover, Morrison abruptly replaces Darkseid, the ideal antagonist for a story about fanaticism, depression, or generational rebellion, with Mandrakk the Dark Monitor, a much simpler character who serves only as a vehicle for a transparent and familiar criticism of modern superhero comics. The multiple hypostases of the god of fascism and depression drop away in favor of a monovalent allegory and a metacommentary that Morrison and other writers had been delivering for decades.

This commentary is initially most apparent in *Superman Beyond 3D*, which reveals the history of the multiversal custodians known as the Monitors. In Morrison's retelling, the first Monitor was not the benevolent half of a Manichaean dyad, as he had been in *Crisis on Infinite Earths*, but a being of perfect and all-encompassing nothingness. This primal void soon discovers "a flaw [...] at the heart of Monitor perfection" (*SB* 1.22), a flaw of fractally infinite and ever-changing complexity. Examining this flaw, Monitor experiences something it has never encountered before: events, happenings, stories (*SB* 1.23). The encounter infects Monitor with narratives, and "story, like contagion, spreads unchecked" (*SB* 1.24) through the celestial intelligence. Morrison revises the Wolfman and Pérez creation myth of the DC universe into a Gnostic metafiction in which the perfection of nothingness is stained by the corruption of narrative, although he once again contradicts Gnosticism by celebrating the corrupting material. The propagation of beginnings, endings, and plots through Monitor society may echo the Anti-Life philosophy that spreads like a contagion through human society in *Final Crisis* proper, but Morrison presents the narrative epidemic as a fortunate fall that makes stories, and existence itself, possible.

He also vilifies those characters who attempt to resist or control this profusion of narratives. He reimagines the Monitors, who had been depicted in *Countdown* and its related spin-offs as continuity police who maintained the divisions between DC's parallel universes, as a race of "celestial parasites" and "vampire gods" who survive by consuming stories and draining the multiverse of its vitality (*SB* 2.17). The worst of these vampire gods is Mandrakk, who, in a typically Morrisonian twist, was also the best of them, Dax Novu, a legendary Monitor hero who went mad at the thought of being tainted by narrative. Mandrakk emblematizes the reductive, univalent DC continuity that followed *Crisis on Infinite Earths*. Superman defeats him with the help of a young Monitor, Nix Uotan, and a hastily assembled coalition of outlandish characters from every world in the DC multiverse: an army of Superman analogues from all the parallel Earths, the Green Lantern Corps, Jack Kirby's New Gods, the angels of the Pax Dei, even the funny animals of Captain Carrot and his Amazing Zoo Crew. Most of these characters are little more than onlookers at the final battle, their purpose being not to participate in the plot but to prove an allegorical point. Their victory presents a symbolic triumph over the streamlined continuity and the darker, more cynical tone of the post-1986 comics, a point Morrison hammers home when Nix Uotan tells Mandrakk "Dawn is on its way" (*FC* 7.28) or when the army of Supermen shouts "Let the sun shine in!" (*FC* 7.27) as they incinerate Mandrakk's henchman. The allegory is equally transparent in Nix Uotan's final statement to his fellow Monitors, in which he upbraids them for their attempts to police an ungovernable continuity. When he says "This multiverse of life deserves its freedom from our interference" (*FC* 7.33), Morrison suggests that writers, editors, and even readers should refrain from attempting to limit, consolidate, or codify DC's irreducibly pluralistic cosmology.

Final Crisis ultimately amounts to little more than a simplistic and heavy-handed metacommentary on DC comics. Its arguments have been in circulation since the retro comics of the mid-nineties—or, in Morrison's case, since *Animal Man*, although *Animal Man* presents the restoration of DC's Silver Age cosmology as the misguided and self-destructive project of the unbalanced Psycho-Pirate. *JLA* and *All Star Superman* are similarly skeptical of nostalgia, yet *Final Crisis* is largely unreflective in its rejection of modern comics and uncritical in its call for a return to the multiple narrative ontologies that preceded *Crisis on Infinite Earths*. To be sure, Morrison does not fetishize the past, nor does he simply re-create the Silver Age multiverse; the parallel worlds established at the end of 52 and defended in *Final Crisis* are nominally different from their forerunners, although sometimes those

Figure 7-8. *Superman Beyond 3D* 2.10. Art by Doug Mahnke. © DC Comics.

differences can be hard to discern on the page. *Final Crisis* rarely delivers on the revolutionary changes it promises: while the crossover begins with the death of the New Gods of Kirby's "Fourth World" comics, the "Fifth World" established at the end of the series appears to be functionally identical, populated by deities who are near-perfect copies of their predecessors. *Final Crisis* rejects revisionism and editorially mandated continuity but it does little to chart a new direction for DC Comics, upsetting the balance of classicism and innovation that characterizes Morrison's other superhero projects.

Morrison does mitigate this highly traditionalist scenario with the occasional note of appreciation for certain revisionist comics. One of the parallel-universe heroes featured in *Superman Beyond 3D* is Captain Allen Adam, the Quantum Superman. Nominally another version of Captain Atom (a.k.a. Captain Nathaniel Adam), a Charlton Comics hero acquired by DC in the 1980s, he is written and drawn to resemble Dr. Manhattan from *Watchmen*, who was himself inspired by Captain Atom (fig. 7-8). Allen Adam shares Dr. Manhattan's blue skin, his boundless powers and perceptions, and a nearly identical emblem based on a diagram of the hydrogen atom; his first name is likely a reference to Manhattan's co-creator Alan Moore. Unlike many of Morrison's earlier allusions to Moore, however, Allen Adam pays homage to Moore's work. Adam tells Ultraman, the evil antimatter version of Superman, "I am the endgame of the idea that spawned the likes of you" (*SB* 2.10), a seeming admission that Dr. Manhattan and *Watchmen* are, more than twenty years after their publication, still the final word on the concept of the superhero. Other interpretations of this comment are possible—if the line is addressed specifically to Ultraman, Adam could be declaring himself the final word in greedy, nihilistic, ultraviolent superhumans. This reading is less plausible, however, since Adam also becomes a spokesman for Morrison's views on the reconciliation of opposites when he realizes the key to stopping Mandrakk and saving the multiverse is to combine Superman and Ultraman, moral and physical antitheses, and harness the resulting energy. His insight that "There are no dualities. Only symmetries" (*SB* 2.9–10) expresses Morrison's suspicion of binaries while nodding to the many symmetries that structure *Watchmen*, suggesting that the homage to Moore is gentle and conciliatory. After decades of lamenting Moore's influence on superhero comics, Morrison has finally placed it in a harmonious dialogue with his own work.

That olive branch aside, Morrison devotes considerably more attention to his past work. If *All Star Superman* and *Batman* create palimpsests of their characters' histories, *Final Crisis* assembles a pastiche of Morrison's career at DC Comics. *Superman Beyond 3D* sends Superman to the Limbo of forgotten comics characters Morrison introduced in *Animal Man*, presents a new twist on the Gnostic cosmologies of *Doom Patrol* and *The Invisibles*, and uses Ray Zone's 3D effects to simulate passage into higher dimensions, the latest variation in Morrison's ongoing project to represent multi-dimensional spaces on the two-dimensional plane of the comics page (Wolk 265–66). *Final Crisis* proper continues the New Gods plotline from *Seven Soldiers*, replays Darkseid's conquest of the world in *JLA*'s "Rock of Ages" storyline, and ends with the Monitors' dissolution into a field of negative space, repeating the absorption into the supercontext and the disintegration of the comics page at the end of *The Invisibles*. Even the most fleeting developments originate in other Grant Morrison comics: when a pair of subatomic superheroes tunnel into an alternate dimension to create an emergency shelter for the human race, they recall a similar plot twist from *Flex Mentallo*. Morrison also nods to his longstanding interest in hypostasis and counterlinguistic representation, filling the crossover with divine alphabets whose letters are living symbols (*FC* 6.15) and resolving it with the convenient introduction of the Miracle Machine, a literal *deus ex machina* that "turns thoughts into things" (*FC* 6.2). Unlike the meditations on language in *The Invisibles* or the psychoanalytic embodiments of *Arkham Asylum*, however, the hypostases of *Final Crisis* serve only as plot devices. Morrison calls upon a familiar repertoire of themes and techniques from his previous works, yet he rarely explores them for any greater significance. *Final Crisis* inventories his methods rather than expanding them or taking them in new directions.

Like *Batman* and *All Star Superman*, *Final Crisis* also conjures legions of reflections to generate new perspectives on familiar stories and characters.

Morrison seems well aware of the language and conventions of the "Prismatic Age"; if he has not read Falconer's piece, he is certainly operating on the same wavelength.[5] In the penultimate issue of *Final Crisis*, Darkseid says his son Orion was "Splintered like light through a prism in an infinite number of deaths" (*FC* 6.26)—Morrison's explanation for the discrepancies between *Final Crisis* and some of its lead-ins, which presented multiple and conflicting versions of Orion's death, but perhaps also a nod to the prevailing aesthetic of a story that concludes with the triumphant arrival of more than fifty variations on Superman. A postmortem interview with Matt Brady suggests this choice of words was not accidental; defending his paratactic style as an experiment in narrative form, Morrison calls for more "comics loaded with multiple, prismatic meanings and possibilities" (Brady, "Final Crisis Exit Interview" Part 1). He delivers an impassioned appeal for narrative innovation in mainstream comics, but he fails to consider the creative limitations of an aesthetic built around endless permutations on the same handful of fifty- or seventy-year-old characters. *Final Crisis* is an unmistakable reminder of those limits as the metafictions that are always implicit in such permutations run wild, crowding out or devouring every other possible meaning.

After *All Star Superman* concluded, Morrison told Zack Smith that the series "is not intended as arch commentary on continuity or how trends in storytelling have changed over the decades. It's not retro or meta or anything other than its own simple self. [...] Which is to say, we wanted our Superman story [to] be about life, not about comics or superheroes" (Smith Part 8). The same cannot be said of *Final Crisis*, which is devoted to the concerns and demands of contemporary superhero comics to the exclusion of the other aesthetics and modes of production that once fueled Morrison's work. When the last chapter of *Final Crisis* was released in January 2009, it had been nearly four years since Morrison had published any comics outside the DC universe. *Vimanarama* was his last project from Vertigo; *We3* was the last not to feature superheroes. Without the influence of his creator-owned work, *Final Crisis* is too indebted both structurally and thematically to the never-ending serials, convoluted narrative continuities, and companywide crossovers of corporate superhero comics. Whereas the individual miniseries of *Seven Soldiers* told complete stories while contributing to the larger narrative, no part of *Final Crisis* is legible without reference to other parts of the crossover, or to earlier crossovers like *Seven Soldiers* and *Crisis on Infinite Earths*. Key plot points like the introduction of Mandrakk or Batman's escape from Mokkari and Simyan are displaced onto the tie-ins, re-creating the endlessly interconnected stories of modern superhero continuity at the expense of any narrative or thematic cohesion. While *Seven Soldiers* constructed a similar continuity to deliver a story about crises of modernity and maturity as well as a metanarrative about contemporary comics, *Final Crisis* abandons every other context until only the metanarrative remains. The series is not just another self-conscious, continuity-obsessed crossover: it is a microcosm of superhero comics at the end of the decade and a sign of Morrison's absorption into their aesthetic. In stark contrast to the rest of his career, Morrison was no longer balancing the sensibilities of mainstream and independent comics.

AFTERWORD

Morrison, Incorporated

No matter what direction his comics take, which genres they inhabit or which methods they pursue, Grant Morrison never limits himself to one style for long. Since *Final Crisis* he has worked on a mixture of sequels and new projects, corporate properties and creator-owned series, demonstrating a renewed interest in operating outside the conventions of mainstream comics even as he continues to write one of the oldest and most popular superhero franchises. If the latter half of the last decade saw his writing dominated by the superhero genre, his most recent comics show the beginnings of a return to the fusion of sensibilities and the balance of tradition and innovation that characterized his earlier work.

For his first project, Morrison returned to Vertigo after a four-year absence to complete *Seaguy: Slaves of Mickey Eye* (2009), the sequel to his 2004 miniseries with Cameron Stewart and the second volume in a projected trilogy. The return to Vertigo notwithstanding, Morrison would use the new miniseries to continue his commentary on prevailing trends in superhero comics—although *Slaves of Mickey Eye* is far more cynical about recent directions in the comics industry, in keeping with the tone of the previous *Seaguy* series. As the sequel opens, Seaguy remains at the mercy of a culture industry that offers repetitive and increasingly mindless entertainments to distract citizens from their lack of control over their lives. As he struggles to escape the Eye's authority, he meets three imitators, Threeguy, Treeguy, and Peaguy, profane and violent superheroes who claim to be rebels inspired by his example. Their derivative names and uniforms, polychromatic copies of Seaguy's old costume, mark them as representatives of prismatic brand proliferation, yet they turn out to be anything but revolutionary; their indiscriminate murders and obscene language suggest that prismatic comics have not shed the revisionist influence Morrison deplores, while the revelation that they are secretly agents of the Eye who merely simulate rebellion implies that the prismatic style offers no challenge to reigning genre conventions or industry practices. The trivial variations of Threeguy, Treeguy, and Peaguy cannot conceal the creative bankruptcy of the Eye, which can only imitate and multiply existing properties and seems incapable of creating anything new.

Like its predecessor, however, *Slaves of Mickey Eye* tackles more than just the comics industry. The sequel makes the developmental allegory of the first *Seaguy* miniseries far more explicit; if the first series presented Seaguy as a figurative child, *Slaves* pushes him into adolescence with a story about social dissidence and rebellion against paternal authority ("Exclusive Interview"). It is also a story about sexual maturity and sexual awakening as the characters are pushed into traditional, highly polarized gender roles. Seaguy, thinking he's on the run from Mickey Eye, is steered by the Eye's operatives to assume the new identity of "El Macho," a "bulldresser" in the town of Los Huevos who enters the *corrida* not to slaughter bulls but to dress them in human clothing. (His specialty, in fact, is women's lingerie, which he uses to humiliate and subjugate the bulls.) Meanwhile, back in New Venice, the warrior woman She-Beard is shaved and turned into a giggling bride, forced into a model of femininity every bit as restrictive and condescending as Seaguy's macho posture. The miniseries presents adolescence as a period when everybody is pressured to adopt such caricatured gender roles, although Seaguy grows dissatisfied enough that he will reject the whole system, stripping away his El Macho identity and leaving his beautiful girlfriend Carmen to resume his old life.

As this brief summary of Seaguy's time in Los Huevos should indicate, *Slaves of Mickey Eye* is filled with cultural stereotypes as well as gendered ones. Los Huevos is a collection of romanticized Spanish clichés that owes much to Georges Bizet's opera *Carmen* (McCulloch, "Just a Misunderstood Rebel"), while Seaguy's sidekick Lucky el Loro speaks in a crude parody of a Latino accent. The Eye, which has created both Lucky and Los Huevos to keep Seaguy's rebellion under close supervision, can only construct its world out of stereotypes, pastiches, and other bits of regurgitated culture. To populate this world of juvenile clichés, the Eye and its agents have set out to reduce people to juveniles, molding simpler people for a simpler world. They initially accomplish this by distracting the citizens with cartoons and amusement park rides, dosing the food with drugs, and constructing adventure-filled scenarios to occupy dissidents like Seaguy. Seadog, the Eye's chief human intermediary, plans to take the project further by converting adults into "infantiloids" who do nothing but argue and watch each other on reality television shows that monitor every moment of their lives (3.7). In the final stage of Seadog's plan, these infantiloids will become dependent on the "numminal exo-placenta," a quasi-organic blob that plugs directly into the brain and reduces its wearer to a drooling stupor; Seadog's marketing campaign has made it the most sought-after toy in the world. The criticism of the hegemony of mass culture is hard to miss, but Morrison adapts it into a critique of utopian schemes—including his own.

Seadog says his project "is designed to give everyone exactly what they want. Bliss. Absolute, unending bliss" (3.7), exposing himself and the Eye as dangerous utopians in the vein of so many other Morrison antagonists. His plans even cast suspicion on the highly qualified utopianism of *The Invisibles*. Like the Invisibles, Seadog claims to be giving everybody the utopia they want, although he doesn't appear to leave them any choice about it since the Eye brutally punishes anybody who attempts to opt out of its paradise. The "exo-placenta" can be read as a corrupted and commodified version of Barbelith, the cosmic placenta that was to guide humanity into the unity and plenitude of the supercontext. Warping his earlier work into a nightmare of social conformity and corporate control, Morrison demonstrates that any utopian dream, even his own, can be co-opted through the universalizing and commercializing forces of global capitalism and post-Enlightenment modernity. While the Eye appears to be sincere in its desire to do good and make everybody happy, its attempt to impose this desire turns humanity into nothing more than compulsory consumers of the narcotic bliss it provides. *Slaves of Mickey Eye* finds a terrifying tyranny in the universalist impulses of Enlightenment utopianism even as the series continues to undermine Romantic fantasies of individual resistance and heroic rebellion.

Seaguy's rebellion appears to be much more effective this time around, in keeping with the book's fiery adolescent tone. Unlike the previous series, *Slaves of Mickey Eye* ends with Seadog defeated, the kidnapped slaves of Mickey Eye Park freed, the superheroes of the previous generation making their triumphant return, and Seaguy locked in a kiss with She-Beard. Seaguy briefly adopts the archetypal Morrison role of the teenage destroyer, but he is now wise enough to recognize that apart from Seadog's ouster nothing has really changed (3.29). The Eye's rebranding of itself from "Mickey Eye" to "the New Eye" (3.27) is purely cosmetic, and Seaguy shrewdly declines its offer of Seadog's old job. He is equally suspicious of another offer that he once would have jumped at: Doc Hero's determination to form a new team that will "get things back to normal around here" promises nothing more than superhero comics' traditional restoration of the status quo, yet Seaguy is no longer certain what normal is, let alone whether it is worth restoring (3.29). He achieves personal independence and maturity, but he recognizes that the world is still filled with injustice and still run by the same forces. The superhero genre, the comics industry, and the world at large are largely unchanged, and Seaguy's personal freedom does not translate into social liberation.

Morrison has continued to pursue his own creative freedom both inside and outside the superhero genre. The Vertigo miniseries *Joe the Barbarian* (2010–11), with art by Sean Murphy, offers one of the most literal treatments of his characteristic combination of the worlds of realism and fantasy. The protagonist, Joe Manson, is a diabetic boy who suffers a hypoglycemic attack and hallucinates a fantasy world that he maps onto the rooms of his house. He then embarks on a dual quest to save this magical realm from the forces of "King Death" and to save himself from a potentially fatal hypoglycemic shock by reaching the kitchen and drinking some soda. This superimposition of two normally antithetical discourses does little to complicate the two equally familiar narratives that operate within each of those discourses. The quest elements are so conventional that all the characters seem to know they are living in an epic fantasy: one supernatural being, tasking Joe with his quest, tells him, "The journey—arduous, companions on the way, et cetera! Traditional rules apply!" (2.14). These plot elements need no elaboration; Morrison knows readers will recognize the monomythic dimensions of Joe's odyssey, which leads him on a journey into underworlds both literal and figurative. Never one to privilege realism, Morrison also notes in passing that real life is just as full of clichés and stereotypes, including the school bullies who torment Joe and possibly Joe himself (1.7), who is the latest in a long line of Morrison's sensitive artists and disaffected outsiders. The problems facing Joe in the real world—diabetes, home foreclosure, a father dead in a foreign war—are just as common as the characters who people his fantasy world. That ordinariness in no way diminishes their severity. *Joe the Barbarian* mounts a defense of familiarity, a defense of convention, suggesting that the fantasy stories it echoes are popular because they are emotionally resonant, and resonant because the challenges they embody are so common.

Morrison has shown more innovation in his renewed work on DC's leading superhero franchise. *Batman and Robin* (2009–10) builds on his earlier tenure on *Batman*, but while he maintains that series' historical palimpsest, Morrison revitalizes the franchise by recasting the most familiar duo in comics. With Bruce Wayne presumed dead after the events of *Final Crisis*, Dick Grayson (the original Robin, the Boy Wonder) inherits the role of Batman, while Wayne's illegitimate son Damian becomes the new Robin. The team pairs a cavalier, devil-may-care, generally well-adjusted Batman with a grim, sullen, egotistical Robin, reversing the usual dynamic; Morrison finally

Afterword: Morrison, Incorporated 289

Figure 8-1. *Batman and Robin* 1.1. Art by Frank Quitely. © DC Comics.

achieves his psychologically healthier Batman, even if he has to change the man behind the mask to do so. He also combines several different genres, mixing traditional superhero conventions with science fiction, horror, mystery, and conspiracy literature. Ironically, while the plot revolves around Grayson and Damian's attempts to cope with Bruce Wayne's absence, the series initially focuses on introducing original characters and reconfiguring existing relationships. The references to past Batman comics, although still present, are generally subordinated to the characters' (and Morrison's) exploration of their new roles.

 At the same time, *Batman and Robin* sustains and ultimately perfects Morrison's earlier pastiche, integrating all of Batman's previous eras and interpretations into a single overarching narrative. Frank Quitely illustrates the first storyline with onomatopoeic sound effects incorporated directly into his settings, recalling older superhero comics and the Batman television series without replicating their appearance (fig. 8-1). Other references allude to grimmer and more recent treatments: the opening storyline concludes in the decrepit amusement park from Moore and Bolland's *The Killing Joke*, the next one revisits the telephone poll that killed Jason Todd, and the finale inverts and parodies Morrison's own work in "Batman R.I.P." (Phegley). Morrison cites Batman comics both historical and contemporary, famous and obscure, without forsaking the creeping psychological disquiet of his previous run on *Batman*; he told one interviewer the opening storyline is "more poppy, and more colourful" than his previous series, "but it's also creepier. It's like David Lynch doing the Batman TV show" (George). He would extend the pastiche even further in *Batman: The Return of Bruce Wayne* (2010), a miniseries that abandons all pretenses to realism by hurling the original Batman through time and casting him in a variety of pulp genres to assume the roles of caveman, witch-hunter, pirate, cowboy, hard-boiled detective, and futuristic cyborg. These genre impersonations nevertheless remain part of Morrison's ongoing Batman narrative as Bruce Wayne explores the history of his family and his home and unravels most of the mysteries left at the end of "Batman R.I.P." The miniseries unearths several forgotten stories and supporting characters and restores them to continuity as Morrison finally builds a Batman franchise that can assimilate its entire history and acknowledge its many pulp antecedents without sacrificing a cohesive tone or identity. *Batman and Robin* and *The Return of Bruce Wayne* are deeply indebted to tradition, but they harmonize it within an integrated narrative that can host a reintegrated hero. Bruce Wayne emerges from his ordeal stronger, saner, and ready to acknowledge that he depends on others, a healthier Batman at last.

Appropriately enough, this unification is only possible once Morrison rationalizes the two antagonists who served as barriers to narrative completion and interpretive closure in *Batman*. The Joker discards his schizoid "Thin White Duke of Death" persona to assume the role of the Gravedigger, a crime novelist who pretends to investigate the very murders he commits. As a detective and author, even a false one, the Joker demonstrates a knack for plotting and an obsessive attention to detail—traits that are sometimes lacking in Morrison's comics, although both are very much in evidence here. Morrison also supplies an origin for Dr. Hurt, filling the "hole in things" left by his earlier run on *Batman*. Dr. Hurt is not simply an actor, but neither is he Satan or Thomas Wayne—or rather, he is *a* Thomas Wayne, not Batman's father but an eighteenth-century ancestor who attained immortality after making a deal with a demon. Morrison replaces Hurt's interpretive lacuna with multiple, redundant origins that combine different metaphysics and radically divergent narrative logics: the demon is not a demon, exactly, but a "hyper-adapter" released by Darkseid to torment Batman during the events of *Final Crisis*, and after bonding with it, Thomas Wayne assumes its mission. He also turns out to be yet *another* Thomas Wayne, a forgotten and institutionalized relative from an obscure 1974 Bob Haney story (Phegley). The other revelations of *Batman and Robin* and *The Return of Bruce Wayne* are equally baroque and equally overdetermined, but they conclude dangling plotlines and answer lingering questions from *Batman, Final Crisis, Seven*

Soldiers, and even *52*, uniting all of Morrison's recent work for the DC universe into a single albeit sprawling narrative—almost a personal narrative continuity—that develops over the course of several series and several years.

After reintegrating Batman's psyche and his history, Morrison's next move is to expand the character laterally, imprinting his identity onto other characters. In *Batman, Incorporated* (2010–present), Morrison and Yanick Paquette narrativize the brand proliferation of the previous two decades and take it global as Batman recruits an international army of crimefighters to work under his franchise. Unlike the legions of clones Morrison criticized at the end of his first run on *Batman*, however, he does not simply copy the original. It may be no accident that Batman's first recruit is a Japanese vigilante who operates from a subterranean lair hidden beneath a manga store, or that the premier issue is filled with references to manga artists and works, including Jiro Kuwata's 1966–67 *Batman* manga (Kidd, Spear, and Ferris). Morrison, recognizing manga's growing international appeal, attempts to appropriate and capitalize on it in his new Batman series. He is not just replicating DC's most lucrative franchise; he is transforming it, broadening its scope, introducing new influences, and taking control of its inevitable expansions. In *Batman Unmasked*, Will Brooker predicts that Batman will evolve into a brand, a genre, or a myth (317–33); Morrison's recent Batman comics explore all three possibilities while steering them in more inclusive and heterogeneous directions. As with his earlier work on Superman, the X-Men, and the Justice League of America, Morrison has found ways to innovate within a genre and a set of corporate-owned characters whose core premises he can never change. Like the fractal shape of the Koch snowflake, Morrison continuously creates new complexity within the same bounded territory—though he also pushes against the boundaries, expanding the range of stories that can be told in the superhero genre.

As these projects demonstrate, Morrison remains committed not only to superheroes, fantasy, and other popular genres, but also to the prevailing commercial practices of the comics industry that sustains them. Those practices include the serialized format of the periodical comic book itself. Like many series before them, most notably *The Invisibles* and *New X-Men*, *Batman and Robin* and *The Return of Bruce Wayne* are filled with ongoing mysteries, hidden identities, sudden revelations, and long-deferred payoffs designed to provoke audience speculation and reward or confound readers who follow them every month. While the rest of the industry shifts its attention to graphic novels and the bookstore market, while even the superhero companies are coming to view periodical comic books as proving grounds or loss leaders for the collected editions, Morrison continues to pace his work for monthly serialization. Despite all his innovations, experiments, and challenges to the industry's dominant genres, his pacing and plot structure can be deeply traditionalist, crafted to suit the publishing model of the open-ended series rather than the standalone graphic novels that have gained so much cultural capital and so many new readers in the last decade. Although Morrison's work is now collected regularly into hardcovers and trade paperbacks—nearly everything except for the early British material is in print—the narratives retain the shapes of their original episodic structures. While Charles Hatfield notes that many graphic novels are initially published in installments and bear the traces of their serialization (153–62), Morrison creates something else, not serialized graphic novels but collected and cohesive comic book series. Issued as periodicals, his comics contain integrated and interconnected themes; given finite endings, they are nevertheless long-running stories that can stretch to a thousand pages or more. At their best, they unite some of the best features of the comic book and the graphic novel.

Morrison continues to merge the varied and sometimes conflicting aesthetics that have defined his career. Without abandoning superheroes, he has rediscovered the surreal imagery, the fluid genres, and the creator ownership and authorial control that have allowed him to move beyond the concerns of most superhero comics. He continues to explore the place of the individual in postmodern society, identifying the dangers of mass conformity and Romantic individualism alike. He continues to experiment with forms of representation unique to comics; even a project as commercial as *The Return of Bruce Wayne* can set aside a few pages to discuss nonlinear models of spacetime and the problems of representing them on the two-dimensional space of the comics page. Perhaps most important of all, he continues to develop visual embodiments that sidestep the deferrals of symbolic language while maintaining his efforts to collapse or unite the binary oppositions that have shaped Western culture. These concerns have remained constant even when his genres and techniques have been most in flux. After more than thirty years in the comics industry, Grant Morrison is still looking for the next genre, the next experiment, the next direction as part of his career-long project to combine the diverse, impossible, potentially infinite worlds of contemporary comics.

Notes

Introduction

1. "Frank Quitely" is the pseudonym of Scottish comics artist Vince Deighan.

2. Mark Salisbury's *Writers on Comics Scriptwriting* prints samples of Morrison's thumbnails (214–15) along with a page from one of his full scripts (211). More thumbnails are collected in the *Arkham Asylum* 15th Anniversary Edition, along with a script that Morrison describes as "a monstrous hybrid between the traditional 'Full Script' comic book method and a movie screenplay" (n. pag.) as it lacks panel breakdowns. More typical full scripts are printed in *Batman: The Return* 1 and *New X-Men* 121; although the X-Men comic is nearly wordless, Morrison's script contains detailed panel descriptions.

3. Superhero fans and fan historians use the term "Golden Age" to refer to the period spanning from the genesis of superhero comics in the late 1930s through their wartime popularity in the 1940s, while the "Silver Age" refers to a creative and commercial renaissance in superhero comics from 1956 to the early 1970s. In most fan histories, the Silver Age is followed by a "Bronze Age" of genre consolidation and refinement in the 1970s and early 1980s, and then by a modern period characterized by the revision, destruction, and rebuilding of superhero conventions.

This age-based system of fan historiography creates several problems for comics scholars, including, as Benjamin Woo argues, its pursuit of convenience "at the expense of accuracy, specificity, and analytical rigour" (269) and its lack of applicability beyond superhero comics (271). Nevertheless, these labels provide a "convenient, shorthand notation" (Woo 269) for the history of superhero comics. Contrary to Woo's assertion that there "should be a basic symmetry" (272) between the histories of superhero comics and other genres, publication formats, or national traditions, genres do develop distinct trajectories and sometimes require specific historical markers. While no critical consensus has established a name for the modern period, which may best be understood as a succession of competing movements, styles, or fads, the Golden, Silver, and Bronze Ages remain useful shorthands for three periods in the history of superhero comics—provided that scholars take care not to extend that shorthand beyond the superhero genre or to reify the ideologies and value judgments implied by these names (Woo 270, 272–74).

4. By 2009, Morrison had told the Kathmandu story so many times that he reacted with some exhaustion, if not exasperation ("It becomes like a performance you've done a million times"), when Meaney asked him to tell it again (292).

5. While the phrase "the linguistic turn" originates in analytic philosophy (Rorty 8–9) and describes a separate intellectual tradition, it has become associated with Saussurean linguistics, structuralism, and poststructuralism, especially as they have been applied in

literary theory. For a summation of these literary applications of the linguistic turn, see James Berger.

6. I distinguish hypostasis from the more conventional master tropes of figurative language and discuss its centrality to the superhero genre in my article "Embodiments of the Real" (282–87).

7. Morrison is far from the first writer to associate presymbolic hypostases with gods. In *The New Science*, Giambattista Vico proposes that the symbolic abstractions of figurative language were derived from the ancient poets' "animate divinities" (128), entities that expressed human passions yet preceded symbolization.

8. McHale and Sukenick make similar claims for aleatory games, improvisations, and other techniques that generate narratives through chance and coincidence (McHale, *Constructing* 32, 35; Sukenick 19). Morrison uses these and other nonrational methods, including automatic writing, cut-ups, and séances, in his composition of early comics like *Doom Patrol* and *Bible John*, though they have largely disappeared from his more recent work.

Chapter 1

1. Morrison told Nigel Curson that *Dare* is about Frank Hampson's loss of ownership of his creations (Curson 27)—the story ends with the white hot blast of the fusion bomb turning into a blank page in Hampson's studio (4.17–19)—yet he completely destroys Hampson's characters while protesting his exploitation. The cynical revisions of *Dare* are only possible because Fleetway, not Hampson's estate, owned the rights to Dan Dare.

2. On Thatcher's falling popularity prior to the Falklands War, see Hitchcock 321 and Young 241 ("She was as unpopular as any prime minister since polling began"); on the war's resuscitation of her political fortunes, see Hitchcock 324–25 and Young 297; on her breaking of the miners' strike and trade union power in general, see Hitchcock 325–28, Young 366–78, and Riddell 43–54.

3. Thatcher's policies intensified economic inequalities and regional divisions between the south of England and the north, Scotland, and Wales (Riddell 158–63).

4. Morrison also claims that Kane and Jackson wanted to move on to higher-paying, higher-profile jobs, and used *The New Adventures of Hitler* as a pretext for their resignations (Hasted 81).

5. Morrison, Mark Millar, and Steve Parkhouse would create a similar personification a few years later in *Big Dave* (1993, 1994). Like John Bull, Big Dave is a scatological caricature "showing the Thatcherite man triumphant—this classless, monstrous figure unleashed" (Hasted 80).

6. Morrison has hinted at other, more personal reasons for the softening portrayal of his conservative characters. Decades after he completed *Zenith*, he told Timothy Callahan that its yuppie protagonist is "a cynical acknowledgment of the central contradiction of the times— that so many of we raging left wing opponents of the Iron Lady [Thatcher] were actually making some money, buying nice clothes and generally doing rather well for the first time in our miserable lives under the yoke of the tyrant" (247).

7. Although the British revisionists usually represent right-wing societies far more unproblematically as dystopias (see *V for Vendetta*, *The Adventures of Luther Arkwright*,

or *Nemesis the Warlock*), they typically suggest that any utopian scheme contains the foundations for a dystopia.

8. St. John quotes William Blake's "Auguries of Innocence" (IV.14.5), a bookend to the line from "The Tyger" that figures so prominently in Phase I and an indication of the deceptive paradoxes of scale that he and Morrison have just perpetrated on us:

> To see a world in a grain of sand,
> And heaven in a wild flower,
> Hold infinity in the palm of your hand,
> And eternity in an hour.

Chapter 2

1. The similarities between *Marvelman*, "Whatever Happened to the Man of Tomorrow?" and *Superfolks* are undeniable; the case for *Watchmen* is more strained. However, these accusations came in a period when Morrison, by his own admission, was making a name for himself by "saying cruel things about everybody else in comics" (Salisbury 218). He would later regret this persona and try to escape it, though he remains willing to level barbed criticisms at other creators in his interviews.

2. To cite just a few examples, Warren Ellis and John Cassaday's *Planetary* (1999–2009) comments on the histories of superhero comics and other popular genres through a series of thinly veiled pastiches, while DC Comics crossover events such as *Infinite Crisis* (2005–06) draw their subject matter almost exclusively from the company's history of continuity revisions. Alan Moore's *Supreme* (1996–2000) combines both of these approaches; one of the earlier examples of metafictional superhero comics, it still follows *Animal Man* by several years.

3. Morrison had experimented with metafictional comics prior to *Animal Man*. One of the characters in *Zoids*, a licensed comic based on a line of toy robots, realizes he and the other characters are all toys being manipulated by higher-dimensional beings (*Spider-Man and Zoids* 50); however, the series was canceled before Morrison could develop the plot further. He would later pursue these ideas to fruition in *Animal Man* and *The Invisibles* (Salisbury 208).

4. Morrison may have picked up this trick from Alan Moore, Steve Bissette, and John Totleben, who used it in *Swamp Thing Annual* 2 (1985).

5. Clayface's deranged love for mannequins, which he confuses with real women, dates back to a 1978 story by Len Wein, who also wrote the 1985 *Who's Who: The Definitive Directory of the DC Universe* entry on Arkham Asylum that inspired Morrison's plot. Unfortunately, Morrison's scripted directions that the mannequins be "posed in lingerie" as "Clayface's harem" (38) are not translated into McKean's art, obscuring this convenient illustration of one of the comic's overarching themes.

6. Brooker elaborates on the connections between Morrison's Mad Hatter scene and the life and work of Lewis Carroll in *Alice's Adventures: Lewis Carroll in Popular Culture*.

7. *Arkham Asylum* is unpaginated. When citing Morrison's script or annotations in the 15th Anniversary Edition, I will refer to the handwritten page numbers Morrison provides on the typed script pages.

8. Morrison's use of Clayface—particularly the fetishizing, contagious Preston Payne version of the character seen in *Arkham Asylum*—as a personification of Batman's fear of sexuality seems much more persuasive, more rooted in the character's physicality and history, than Klock's assertion that other, shape-shifting versions of Clayface symbolize "the anti-essential nature of the Batman/Bruce Wayne relationship" (36).

9. One of Morrison's annotations explains, "The construction of the story was influenced by the architecture of a house—the past and the tale of Amadeus Arkham forms the basement levels. Secret passages connect ideas and segments of the book. There are upper stories of unfolding symbol and metaphor. [...] The journey through the book is like moving through the floors of the house itself. The house and the head become one" (2).

10. I discuss Morrison's annotations, and his attempts to defend his own contributions while deflecting responsibility for the comic's faults onto McKean, in more detail in "'A Serious House on Serious Earth': Rehabilitating Arkham Asylum."

11. Shaviro's idea of subversive behavior combines hyperactive consumption with critical passivity. He says postmodernism must be enjoyed "as mindlessly and abjectly as possible," *Doom Patrol* no less than shopping or credit card debt (2); he exemplifies the "rebel consumer" lacerated by Thomas Frank and the other essayists in *Commodify Your Dissent*.

12. The animal experimentation is an innocuous detail in the Drake/Premiani origin of the Chief (*DP* I.88, 1964). Richard Case re-creates these panels almost line for line in his retelling (57.20), but Morrison, still concerned with animal rights, recontextualizes them as evidence of the Chief's amorality.

13. The Chief also reveals a streak of misogyny and a motive of sexual dominance when he admits that he subjected Rita Farr to his experiments because "I wanted to see this fabulous, gilded creature brought low. Impotent in my wheelchair, I wanted to exert control over a beautiful woman" (57.29). The Chief's experiments are not overtly sexualized, but this confession clearly places him in the company of the other abusive fathers.

14. Morrison continues this practice with the second Brotherhood of Dada—one member, the Toy, wears a costume that parodies Cliff's robotic appearance—but for the most part the second Brotherhood is designed as a replication of the first, with members slotted into similar roles such as the devoted acolyte of Nobody or the multipowered utility player.

15. This commitment to liberal democratic values is also typical of the superhero genre. Richard Reynolds observes that superheroes are loyal to the principles of the state, if not to the letter of the law (16), and argues that "Superheroes have been better Americans [...] than most of America's modern political leaders" (74).

16. The religious dispute is loosely patterned after the Hussite wars that divided Bohemia in the fifteenth century and presaged the Protestant Reformation. Huss, the leader of the Geomancers, is named after Jan Hus, the Czech church reformer, and the Ultraquists take their name from the Utraquists, the moderate Hussite faction. Morrison's war begins as a dispute over the communion (38.9), the primary object of Utraquist reforms. On the other hand, the outer space setting, apocalyptic destruction, and perfectly matched combatants seem to be Morrison's first take on the war between New Genesis and Apokolips in Jack Kirby's "Fourth World" comics (*New Gods*, *Mister Miracle*, *The Forever People*, and *Superman's Pal, Jimmy Olsen*), which DC published from 1970 to 1974.

17. Unfortunately, these ideas are not as new as the aliens think. Their next plan, to collaborate on a great tower that will stretch up to the heavens and lift their consciousness

towards divinity (41.21–22), suggests they and the Judge Rock are still imitating Biblical precedent and implies another linguistic fall lies ahead.

18. Josh Lukin observes that several issues of *Doom Patrol* reference a "White Abyss" filled with formative energies, and that this abyss might denote "the space between panels, or the initially blank page" (86). These self-reflexive nods are encoded within the prevailing mythologies of the series and do not prompt the same metafictions that structure *Animal Man*.

19. Colorist Daniel Vozzo depicts this world in muted shades of brown and gray, much like Tatjana Wood's depiction of the "real" Glasgow Buddy visits at the end of *Animal Man*.

Chapter 3

1. Berger describes Young's history with Disney and alludes to Touchmark in the February 1993 "On the Ledge" column (published in all Vertigo comics cover-dated April 1993). She mentions Vertigo's acquisition of the Touchmark properties and the doubling of the publishing plan in "An Interview with Karen Berger" (13).

2. The three chapters of "Entropy in the UK," the first *Invisibles* storyline to focus on King Mob, are titled "Dandy" (I.17), "Messiah" (I.18), and "Assassin" (I.19), at least two of which apply to Sebastian. Additionally, one of the henchmen sent to kill Sebastian greets him with the phrase "Nice and smooth" (*Sebastian O* 2.4), a line from the Kinks song "David Watts" that would become King Mob's catch-phrase (*Invisibles* II.1.6).

3. While the first two volumes follow conventional numbering, the third is numbered as a "countdown" from issue 12 to issue 1. The third volume was supposed to count down to January 2000, but delays pushed the final issue back to April of that year.

4. Early issues of *The Invisibles* mock the speculator and collector culture of the early nineties. The first letter column urges readers to "DESTROY THIS COMIC!" and proclaims "Death to 'speculators'!" (I.1, "Invisible Ink"), asserting that comics should be disposable. The fifth issue parodies cover gimmicks—variant covers, foil covers, die-cut covers, and other ploys to increase collectibility—by releasing several different covers, all of them featuring crudely printed slogans on cheap brown pulp stock (Neighly 29–30). As the market worsened and sales collapsed, these jokes disappeared.

5. Morrison has ample justification for his claims. *The Matrix* copies many elements from the first two volumes of *The Invisibles*: both works feature young men who are inducted into cells of countercultural criminals by bald warriors who believe they are destined to become saviors; both young men undergo initiations by jumping off skyscrapers; both groups battle enemies who are depicted with insectoid imagery; both groups are betrayed by traitors; both works feature the silvery, shimmering magic mirror substance; and both suggest the world is a construct generated by a higher order of being.

6. Morrison tends to conflate all early Christians with the Gnostic sects. His association of the vesica piscis with the Christian ichthys replicates Philip K. Dick's amalgamation of the two symbols, just as the idea of a hologramatic universe comes directly from *VALIS*.

7. This image was deemed important enough that Cameron Stewart was asked to redraw three Ashley Wood pages that deviated from the script and failed to illustrate the life casts. See *The Invisibles* III.2.12–14 and compare to Stewart's revisions in the trade paperback collection, *The Invisibles* vol. 7, *The Invisible Kingdom*, 252–54.

8. Morrison told Patrick Neighly that a female reader gave him the idea of making Ragged Robin the author (Neighly 252).

9. Chris Randle first connected Morrison's work to Afrofuturism in "Worlds of Otherness," his discussion of *Seven Soldiers: Mister Miracle*.

10. Fanny is a cross-dresser, a witch, a prostitute, and an oversexed Latina. Her family hails from Spanish-speaking Mexico and worships Aztec gods, yet they live in Lusophone Rio de Janeiro. While some of these elements combine artfully—the shamanic practice of transvestism dovetails neatly with Fanny's transgendered identity, for example—others simply result in a collision of exoticisms.

11. Morrison would eventually use the idea of refashioning the Whip into a "kind of S&M superhero" (Neighly 15) in *Seven Soldiers*.

12. Many of the Invisibles' codenames reappropriate terms they detest. Thus, the African American Lucille Butler adopts the racist slur "Boy"; another black Invisible names himself "Jim Crow" after America's post-Reconstruction racial laws; the transsexual Hilde Morales calls herself "Lord Fanny" after Alexander Pope's homophobic satire on the effeminate, bisexual Lord Hervey; and Dane McGowan names himself "Jack Frost" after a childhood bogeyman. Not every alias is adopted antagonistically: King Mob takes his name from the British Situationist group of the 1960s and 1970s whose affiliates included Malcolm McLaren and Jamie Reid (Ford 148–49), reflecting the Situationist influence on *The Invisibles* and King Mob's own taste in British punk rock. However, even this name is ambiguous; the King Mob group took its name from graffiti scrawled on Newgate Prison during the anti-Catholic Gordon Riots of 1780 (Ford 148), hardly a positive example of anarchy or mob rule.

13. Altman has since developed a "semantic/syntactic/pragmatic approach" (*Film/Genre* 208), which recognizes that genres are shaped by multiple audiences and institutions outside the texts. This approach augments but does not erase his distinction between semantics and syntax, which continues to provide a useful vocabulary for describing the genre fusions of *The Invisibles*.

14. Stephen Rauch tabulates many instances where the series appears to endorse the Sapir-Whorf hypothesis, although he attributes these ideas to much later work by the counterculture writer Robert Anton Wilson. Rauch is far more credulous of Wilson's linguistic determinism than Wolk is.

15. This numerology is just as significant as Key 17's allusion to the Tower of Babel. The number twenty-three takes on considerable, if arbitrary, significance in conspiracy theory and chaos magic (Neighly 188); it is also one more than the number of trumps in the major arcana, indicating that the Invisibles have developed the drug beyond its origins. Sixty-four is the number of letters in the secret, primal alphabet known to Cell 23 and other initiates.

16. The visual arts can also express these aggregates, as in one remarkable scene where Morrison and Philip Bond show a woman looking at Pablo Picasso's *Guernica* (1937) and seeing not the Cubist painting but a mimetic representation of the bombing of the Basque village (III.9.11). Because the woman's lover died in the bombing, the painting has, in her subjective view, surpassed its own symbolic abstractions.

17. The page is open-ended in another sense as well. Neighly and Cowe-Spigai observe that Dane never closes the quote from Elfayed, suspending the series in incompletion; they believe this signifies "the transition from the fictional universe of *The Invisibles* to our own" (217n.22.6).

18. Or possibly reenacting it. The scene opens with a manuscript of "Julian and Maddalo" blowing from a discarded bag as Byron and Shelley walk through the events that will inspire the poem—just one of many places where *The Invisibles* collapses the distinction between real life and artistic representation.

19. Many theorists of postmodernism have been equally glib, if not downright euphoric, about prescribing mental disorders as metaphoric models for postmodern identity. David Harvey notes that Deleuze, Guattari, and even Jameson ignore the devastating cognitive and psychological effects of the schizophrenic disorders they metaphorize or exalt (Harvey 351–52). Harvey sees nothing to celebrate in such accounts of postmodernism.

20. The Institute of Contemporary Arts held a Situationist International retrospective in 1989, which Ford credits with promoting wider awareness of the Situationists and establishing their reputation (152). Ford also notes the contradictions of enshrining the Situationists within the art institutions they rejected (155–57).

Chapter 4

1. J. M. Tyree and Ben Walters discuss the "magpieism" (17) and the relentless pastiche that were characteristic of 1990s popular culture; David Sigler surveys the decade's pervasive nostalgia for the 1970s (40). The retro comics look back to the 1960s and the Silver Age but otherwise conform to the decade's prevailing interest in nostalgia and recycled culture.

2. Mark Millar likely scripted this issue, as his name is listed first in the writing credits (134.3). However, he and Morrison worked in close collaboration on *The Flash* and the issue's sentiments match those expressed in *Prometheus*, written by Morrison alone.

3. For a record of *JLA*'s commercial success, see the sales charts calculated by John Jackson Miller for *Comics Buyer's Guide*. Barring a few crossovers and other special events, Morrison's *JLA* was nearly always DC's highest-selling comic, and after July 1997 it was regularly one of the top ten titles sold through the direct market.

4. Although the term "widescreen" is commonly associated with Warren Ellis and *The Authority*, Morrison was one of the first writers to apply this label to superhero comics. He told Mark Salisbury that he "kept making [*JLA*] more extreme, more widescreen and more epic" (222) in an interview conducted prior to the publication of the first issue of *The Authority*. A much earlier use of the term appears in a 1995 *Invisibles* letter column, where Morrison refers to *Doom Patrol* as "an out-and-out, widescreen, romping super-hero team book" (I.17, "Invisible Ink"). This usage is idiosyncratic and bears little relation to later applications of the term, but it demonstrates how long Morrison had been thinking about superhero comics in cinematic terms.

5. The Flex Mentallo storyline was followed by "The Beard Hunter" (*Doom Patrol* 45), which parodied the violent superheroes of the 1980s and early 1990s and highlighted Morrison's interest in breaking away from the revisionist style.

6. On fans' overreaction to Wertham's charges, see Brooker, *Batman* 103–07 and Medhurst 151–52. Morrison is hardly the first creator to incorporate Wertham's judgments into his comics, and he follows in the footsteps of works such as Rick Veitch's *Bratpack* (1991). Veitch, however, delivered his Werthamesque interpretations in a self-published comic completed

after an acrid departure from DC Comics; Morrison endorses Wertham's views in a miniseries published by an imprint of DC.

7. The second issue's range of reference is somewhat wider than the others. The cover's design recalls the EC Comics of the 1950s, and Quitely draws a scene in which a junkie overdoses in a public bathroom to resemble the underground comix of the late 1960s and 1970s. These comics bracketed the Silver Age but do not fall within the superhero genre; these references tentatively expand the miniseries' history to include American comics as a whole, but the rest of *Flex Mentallo* does not sustain this expansion.

8. The severity of Wally's suicide attempt is unclear. Wally initially claims to have taken a bottle of the pain reliever paracetamol (known in the U.S. as acetaminophen) along with ecstasy, marijuana, LSD, and a bottle of vodka. The final issue, however, shows a pill bottle that has been filled with M&Ms rather than paracetamol, indicating that he has feigned a suicide attempt as a cry for help (4.8). It would be a misreading, however, to assume that only one of these interpretations is accurate; as Wally explains, "on one parallel Earth my pill bottle had paracetamol in it. On the other, it had M&Ms" (4.14). Like the thought-experiment of Schrödinger's cat, to which Morrison alludes several times over the course of the miniseries, Wally is perfectly safe and he is dying; like the quantum superpositions whose paradoxes are illustrated by Schrödinger's cat, every possible narrative has an equal claim to truth in *Flex Mentallo*.

9. Ironically, Darkseid promises his captive subjects "Freedom from self" (14.2), an offer not so far removed from the Invisibles' promotion of the MeMePlex a few years later. Darkseid is simply exploiting people's fear and uncertainty to make their subjugation appear more palatable; his "Anti-Life Equation" annihilates their personalities and places them under his control rather than liberating them into a plenitude of selves. Nevertheless, in a perverse demonstration of Morrison's ongoing union of opposites—and a sign of just how much his and his characters' philosophies would change over the course of *The Invisibles*—the ultimate freedom fighters share a goal, or at least a slogan, with the god of fascism.

10. In *JLA Classified* 1–3 (2004–05), Morrison models the Ultramarines on Mark Millar's Ultimates (Brady, "Grant Morrison's Big-Time Return") and uses their failures to castigate the both the authoritarian superheroes of the widescreen movement and George W. Bush's policy of preemptive war.

11. Just one month after this story ended, Marvel Comics published a similar storyline in *The Avengers* 57–58 (1968), cementing it as a standard plotline for superhero teams.

12. As just one example, of the seven original members of the Justice League of America, two (Green Lantern and the Flash) had been killed and replaced, one (Aquaman) had a hand amputated, and three others (Superman, Batman, and Wonder Woman) had their memberships retroactively erased from continuity.

13. Quentin's call for a "Year Zero" and his habit of addressing his fellow gang members as "Citizen" (136.5) both evoke the French Revolution, a familiar Morrison touchstone for failed utopias and revolutions that go too far.

14. Quentin's last words are also a double- or triple-entendre that could refer to Magneto's infiltration of the Xavier Institute as Xorn, or John Sublime's infection of Quentin and Magneto through the drug Kick. Morrison disguises important clues to two of his ongoing mysteries by concealing them in a statement that appears, on the first reading, to be purely figurative.

15. *New X-Men* is haunted by the September 11 attacks. The series begins with a disquieting anticipation of the attacks when one of Cassandra Nova's wild Sentinels, a machine cobbled

together from jet engines and airplane fuselages, punches through a Genoshan skyscraper (115.22); the issue was published in July 2001. Months later, once the production schedule allowed Morrison to react to the events of September 11, the series incorporated multiple references to the attacks and their aftermath. *New X-Men* 132, released on September 11, 2002, commemorates the Genoshan genocide with a monument that broadcasts the voices of the victims into space as radio waves, "At the speed of light" (132.22), recalling the Tribute in Light installation that beams two columns of light from the site of the World Trade Center. Later still, Magneto's destruction of Manhattan would indicate his surrender of all moral authority and cement Morrison's portrayal of Magneto as "a mad old terrorist twat [...] an old bastard with daft, old ideas based on violence and coercion" (J. Ellis part 4).

Chapter 5

1. Morrison would elaborate on these statements for Jonathan Ellis, describing at least one attempted suicide and several instances of cutting and self-mutilation (Part 5).

2. Elements of Morrison's planned approach survive in "Nick's World . . ." (2002), a Nick Fury story published by Marvel Knights just one month before Vertigo launched *The Filth*. The story features an assassin who tries and fails to become a perfect duplicate of Nick Fury only to discover that his superior is actually Fury in disguise. The mutable identities, the artificiality of Fury's super-spy persona, and the elaborate simulations—the story ends with SHIELD agents disassembling a set—all prefigure similar themes in *The Filth*.

3. Paracetamol is also Wally Sage's method of choice in *Flex Mentallo*, another series that forces readers to choose between contradictory but equally valid narratives.

4. John Jackson Miller estimates that retailers ordered 21,502 copies of the first issue, and 16,602 of the final issue ("Comic Book Sales Charts & Analysis," May-July 2004). While such figures would be outstanding for most independent comics, and were initially only a few thousand copies below Vertigo's top-selling titles, the sales were low enough to postpone the sequel.

5. Morrison misidentifies the questing beast of Arthurian legend, which is actually a monster and the object of several futile hunts—more Moby Dick than Old Yeller.

6. This war was conducted in the style of comic book crossover events such as DC's *Crisis on Infinite Earths*. The enemy was a monstrous being known as "Anti-Dad," a name that riffs on the Anti-Monitor, the villain of *Crisis on Infinite Earths*, while alluding to Morrison's two favorite categories of antagonists. "Anti-Dad" could be the ultimate bad father or the ultimate rebel against paternal authority—Ialdabaoth and Satan rolled into one.

7. Since one of these crypto-saurs later demonstrates the ability to walk and shoot flames from its headlamp eyes, it is possible Niltoid knows these concoctions are fakes and has been using them as a ruse to build weapons for a planned revolt underneath the Eye's ever-watchful gaze.

8. Olivia Woodward offers a less secular interpretation of the dance number, arguing that the staging re-creates the architecture of a temple or a palace of the gods and moves the rest of the narrative—everything that follows after the second page—into sacred space.

9. With Ben Rama, Morrison carries this trait into overt self-parody. After Sofia rejects him, Ben Rama becomes so sensitive that a fluttering leaf causes him pain and a fall leaves his knee "grazed beyond redemption!" (2.30).

10. Video game narrative structures and avatars also influence "Bad Gumbo" (1994), a *Swamp Thing* storyline Morrison wrote with Mark Millar.

11. On these and other common storytelling practices in manga, see Frederik L. Schodt, *Manga! Manga!* 18–25 and *Dreamland Japan* 22–28, and Scott McCloud, *Understanding Comics* 77–80 and *Making Comics* 216–221.

12. Abbott's assumption that panel borders and text captions merely frame the representation of a separate, pictorial scene parallels the structuralist distinction between story (the events of a narrative as they occur in the world of the narrative) and discourse (the narration of those events as they are presented to the audience); the parallel is hardly surprising given Abbott's interest in "structuralist studies" of comics (155). Even before Abbott transferred this concept to comics scholarship, literary scholars such as Jonathan Culler and Peter Brooks had begun to question the separation of story and discourse, noting that story exists only as a "mental construction" readers derive from the discourse (Brooks 13). Morrison and Quitely's false, inadequate frames both dramatize and debunk this structuralist misconception as it applies to comics.

13. Morrison compares the animals to Frankenstein's creation (Brown 84), though in terms of audience sympathy rather than the powers of language. As products of science that rebel against their creators, the animals have much in common with Shelley's creature.

14. *We3* can be read as an unlicensed extension of Morrison's X-Men work. In one issue of *New X-Men*, Fantomex mentions that early versions of the Weapon Plus program experimented on animals, effectively placing the animal weapons in Wolverine's genealogy (130.4). The issue was published in 2002, the same year Morrison developed the story for *We3* (Brady, "Disney With Fangs").

Chapter 6

1. *Seven Soldiers* was preceded by a more traditional superhero adventure in *JLA Classified* 1–3 (2004–05), illustrated by Ed McGuinness. This story introduced the Sheeda and Neh-Buh-Loh the Huntsman and pitted them against the Justice League. These issues also reintroduced the Knight and the Squire, British versions of Batman and Robin who would later figure prominently in Morrison's tenure on *Batman*.

2. Any teams that expand beyond six tend to end up with an eighth, often hidden member, just as the original Seven Soldiers of Victory had an unofficial "Eighth Soldier." Even the Seven Soldiers who give the narrative its name turn out to have an eighth member in the final issue. Every organizing system in *Seven Soldiers* is either incomplete or overcomplete, like the secret sorcerors' calendar that has an extra, thirteenth month, Arachne: perfect systematic knowledge is impossible.

3. The Bride is also a model reader because she is able to connect to the Internet through a USB port in her forehead, which she uses to download information and context on the enemies she encounters—not unlike the *Seven Soldiers* fans who consult and build online annotations to parse the narrative's many allusions and cross-references.

4. The reference to a moon carved in a memorial likeness is strongly reminiscent of "Superman Under the Green Sun" (*Superman* 155, 1962), in which a grateful people landscape their entire planet in Superman's image.

5. Morrison's former protégé and writing partner Mark Millar had already created a similarly critical figure in the pages of *The Authority*; Dr. Krigstein is a disfigured dwarf who

dreams up super-soldiers, all of whom are transparently based on Marvel Comics characters, for the United States government (*Authority* 13–16).

6. Morrison further positions *Seven Soldiers* as an updated version of "American Gothic" by defining it in relation to a contemporaneous, much more conventional superhero crossover. Just as "American Gothic" unfolded alongside and briefly intersected with *Crisis on Infinite Earths*, Morrison presents *Seven Soldiers* as the more serious, sophisticated crossover running parallel to *Infinite Crisis* (2005–06), a sequel to *Crisis on Infinite Earths*.

7. For more on the sundown towns, see James W. Loewen, *Sundown Towns: A Hidden Dimension of American Racism*.

8. One of the Unknown Men (wearing, in one of Morrison's less subtle nods, a DC logo tie-pin) describes the suit he sews for Zor as "Threadbare and ragged . . . the work of too many hands to ever fit properly" (*SS* 1.34), a fitting description of a DC continuity that has been assembled in piecemeal fashion by hundreds of writers over more than seventy years.

9. Morrison mangles his American history. He says the inhabitants of Limbo Town are descended from "Puritan settlers of the Lost Colony of Roanoke" (*Klarion* 3.1), confusing the Puritans of the Massachussetts Bay Colony with the ill-fated colony Sir Walter Raleigh established on Roanoke Island. Morrison also locates the Lost Colony in West Virginia when Roanoke Island is in fact found along the Atlantic coast in present-day North Carolina.

10. The George W. Bush administration was particularly committed to this kind of free play, decoupling its rhetoric not only from referentiality but from reality itself. Journalist Ron Suskind memorably captured this outlook in this boast from a senior Bush advisor:

> The aide said that guys like me were "in what we call the reality-based community," which he defined as people who "believe that solutions emerge from your judicious study of discernible reality." I nodded and murmured something about enlightenment principles and empiricism. He cut me off. "That's not the way the world really works anymore," he continued. "We're an empire now, and when we act, we create our own reality. And while you're studying that reality—judiciously, as you will—we'll act again, creating other new realities, which you can study too, and that's how things will sort out. We're history's actors . . . and you, all of you, will be left to just study what we do." (Suskind 51)

Poststructuralist celebrations of semantic and moral ambiguity may not inspire this particular example of conservative postmodernism (although they tend to hold Enlightenment principles in about as much esteem), but they can do little to counter it.

11. *Mister Miracle* combines the story of Jesus's temptation, torment, death, and resurrection with the story of the Buddha's spiritual awakening. After escaping Omega and breaking out of samsara, Shilo does not enter nirvana but instead returns to the world to free gods and humans alike, becoming a superhero bodhisattva. Note also the similarities between the Middle Way of Buddhism that renounces extremes and dualities and the "third road" Morrison seeks throughout *Seven Soldiers*.

Chapter 7

1. Morrison has said that Luthor "delivers his own version of the unified field haiku—explaining the underlying principles of the universe in fourteen syllables" (Smith Part 2). He

likely refers to "The fundamental forces are yoked by a single thought," although "it's all just us, in here, together. And we're all we've got" (12.15) could also fit his description.

2. Cole Moore Odell offers the most detailed and persuasive—though still largely circumstantial—argument that Quintum is Luthor in "All-Star Luthor" and his comments to Joe McCulloch's "God's in his Heaven."

3. Mike W. Barr first came up with the idea of Batman and Talia conceiving a child in *Batman: Son of the Demon* (1987), a graphic novel that had long been erased from DC continuity until Morrison took over the Batman franchise.

4. Mark Waid surveys the various stages in the Joker's history from 1940 through the late 1980s in "Stacking the Deck"; Morrison's labels generally conform to the periods Waid identifies.

5. In his interview with Patrick Meaney, Morrison shows considerable familiarity with the *Mindless Ones* website (308), where Falconer first published his essay naming the "Prismatic Age."

Bibliography

Abbott, Lawrence L. "Comic Art: Characteristics and Potentialities of a Narrative Medium." *Journal of Popular Culture* 19.4 (1986): 155–76.

Allison, David. "Déjà Vu." *Vibrational Match* 13 August 2009. http://nearit.blogspot.com/2009/08/deja-vu.html. Accessed 8 December 2010.

———. "Twisted Brainwrongs and One-Off Man-Mentals." *Vibrational Match* 18 October 2008. http://nearit.blogspot.com/2008/10/twisted-brainwrongs-and-one-off-man.html. Accessed 8 December 2010.

Altman, Rick. *The American Film Musical*. Bloomington: Indiana UP, 1987.

———. *Film/Genre*. London: British Film Institute, 1999.

Babcock, Jay. "One Nervous System's Passage Through Time." *Arthur* 12 (September 2004): 28–38.

Barr, Mike W., and Jerry Bingham. *Batman: Son of the Demon*. New York: DC Comics, 1987.

Berger, James. "Falling Towers and Postmodern Wild Children: Oliver Sacks, Don DeLillo, and Turns against Language." *PMLA* 120.2 (2005): 341–61.

Berger, Karen. "Afterword: Changing the Face of Comics." *Batman: Arkham Asylum* 15th Anniversary Edition. New York: DC Comics, 2004. n. pag.

———. "On the Ledge." Vertigo monthly column. April 1993. n. pag.

Bishop, David. *Thrill-Power Overload: 2000 AD—The First Thirty Years*. Oxford: Rebellion, 2009.

Borges, Jorge Luis. "Partial Magic in the *Quixote*." Trans. James E. Irby. *Labyrinths*. Ed. Donald A. Yates and James E. Irby. New York: New Directions, 1962. 193–96.

Brady, Matt. "Disney With Fangs." *Newsarama* 1 September 2004. Archived at http://web.archive.org/web/20071013020107re_/www.newsarama.com/pages/DC/We3.htm. Accessed 8 December 2010.

———. "The 52 Exit Interviews: Grant Morrison." *Newsarama* 8 May 2007. http://forum.newsarama.com/showthread.php?t=111900. Accessed 8 December 2010.

———. "Grant Morrison: *Final Crisis* Exit Interview." *Newsarama* 28 January 2009. http://www.newsarama.com/comics/010928-Grant-Final-Crisis.html. Accessed 8 December 2010.

———. "Grant Morrison: Talking *All-Star Superman*." *Newsarama* 22 December 2004. Archived at http://web.archive.org/web/20041224202859/http://www.newsarama.com/DC/AS/AllStarSuperman_Morrison.htm. Accessed 8 December 2010.

———. "Grant Morrison's Big-Time Return to the DCU." *Newsarama* 2 August 2004. http://forum.newsarama.com/showthread.php?s=5e0f1f3c032b47c7ccc8e981fe4a648a&threadid=15990. Accessed 8 December 2010.

———. "A Healing Inoculation of Grime: Grant Morrison on *The Filth*." *Newsarama* 7 March 2003. Rpt. at *Crack!Comics*. http://www.crackcomics.com/the_filth_questions.htm. Accessed 8 December 2010.

———. "Inside Morrison's Head: Leaving Marvel Vimanarama & More." *Newsarama* 11 August 2003. http://forum.newsarama.com/showthread.php?t=5087. Accessed 8 December 2010.

———. "Morrison in the Cave: Grant Morrison Talks Batman." *Newsarama* 23 August 2006. Archived at http://web.archive.org/web/20060830185703/http://www.newsarama.com/dcnew/Batman/Morrison/Morrison_Batman.html. Accessed 8 December 2010.

Brill, Ian. "Looking Back at *Seven Soldiers* with Grant Morrison." *Newsarama* 14 November 2006. Archived at http://web.archive.org/web/20061115094420/http://www.newsarama.com/dcnew/7Soldiers/7Soldierswrap_Morrison.html. Accessed 8 December 2010.

Brooker, Will. *Alice's Adventures: Lewis Carroll in Popular Culture*. New York: Continuum, 2005.

———. *Batman Unmasked: Analyzing a Cultural Icon*. New York: Continuum, 2000.

———. "Hero of the Beach: Flex Mentallo at the End of the Worlds." Unpublished.

Brooks, Peter. *Reading for the Plot: Design and Intention in Narrative*. New York: Knopf, 1984.

Brown, Lisa. "Grant Morrison: *We3*." *Antennae* 9 (Spring 2009): 82–87.

Bukatman, Scott. *Matters of Gravity: Special Effects and Supermen in the 20th Century*. Durham, NC: Duke UP, 2003.

Burton, Tim, dir. *Batman*. Warner Bros., 1989.

Callahan, Timothy. *Grant Morrison: The Early Years*. Edwardsville, IL: Sequart, 2007.

Campbell, Eddie. "Alan Moore." *Eddie Campbell's Egomania* 2 (December 2002): 1–32.

Carter, Dave. "Comics Bloggers' Poll 2005—Reactions." *Yet Another Comics Blog* 26 January 2006. http://yetanothercomicsblog.blogspot.com/2006/01/comic-bloggers-poll-2005-reactions.html. Accessed 8 December 2010.

Cawelti, John G. *Adventure, Mystery, and Romance: Formula Stories as Art and Popular Culture*. Chicago: U of Chicago P, 1976.

———. "*Chinatown* and Generic Transformation in Recent American Films." 1978. *Film Theory and Criticism*. Ed. Gerald Mast, Marshall Cohen, and Leo Braudy. New York: Oxford UP, 1992. 498–511.

Christie, Stuart. "Morrison, Walter, 1924–2004." *libcom.org* 19 September 2005. http://libcom.org/history/morrison-walter-1924-2004. Accessed 8 December 2010.

Contino, Jennifer M. "Grant Morrison's *Seven Soldiers*." *COMICON.com* 5 September 2005. Archived at http://web.archive.org/web/20060114173259/http://www.comicon.com/cgi bin/ultimatebb.cgi?ubb=get_topic;f=36;t=004150. Accessed 8 December 2010.

———. "A Touch of Vertigo: Karen Berger." *Sequential Tart* January 2001. http://www.sequentialtart.com/archive/jan01/berger.shtml. Accessed 8 December 2010.

Coogan, Peter. *Superhero: The Secret Origin of a Genre*. Austin, TX: MonkeyBrain, 2006.

Culler, Jonathan. "Fabula and Sjuzhet in the Analysis of Narrative: Some American Discussions." *Poetics Today* 1.3 (1980): 27–37.

Curson, Nigel. "Daring Future." *Speakeasy* 109 (May 1990). Rpt. in *Dare* 1 (Monster Comics, 1992). 25–27.

Dean, Michael. "The Image Story." *The Comics Journal* 222, 223, 225, 226 (April, May, July, August 2000). Rpt. at *The Comics Journal: Newswatch Online Index* 25 October 2000. http://archives.tcj.com/3_online/n_image1.html. Accessed 8 December 2010.

"Death to Maggie book sparks Tory uproar." *The Sun* 19 March 1990.

Delany, Samuel R. "Shadows." *The Jewel-Hinged Jaw: Notes on the Language of Science Fiction.* Elizabethtown, NY: Dragon Press, 1977. 51–134.

DeLillo, Don. *White Noise.* New York: Penguin, 1985.

de Man, Paul. "The Rhetoric of Temporality." 1969. *Blindness and Insight.* 2nd ed., rev. Minneapolis: U of Minnesota P, 1983.

Deppey, Dirk. "Eddie Campbell." *The Comics Journal* 273 (January 2006): 66–114.

———. "X-Men . . . Retreat!" Part 1. *The Comics Journal* 262 (Aug./Sept. 2004): 46–50.

Dery, Mark. "Black to the Future: Interviews with Samuel R. Delany, Greg Tate, and Tricia Rose." *Flame Wars: The Discourse of Cyberculture.* Ed. Mark Dery. Durham: Duke UP, 1994. 179–222.

Dick, Philip K. *Time Out of Joint.* 1959. New York: Vintage, 2002.

———. *VALIS.* 1981. New York: Vintage, 1991.

Di Liddo, Annalisa. *Alan Moore: Comics as Performance, Fiction as Scalpel.* Jackson: UP of Mississippi, 2009.

Drake, Arnold, Bob Haney, and Bruno Premiani. *My Greatest Adventure* 80–85 and *Doom Patrol* vol. 1 86–121. New York: DC Comics, 1963–68.

Eco, Umberto. "The Myth of Superman." 1962. Trans. Natalie Chilton. *Diacritics* 2.1 (1972): 14–22.

———. *The Search for the Perfect Language.* Trans. James Fentress. Oxford: Blackwell, 1995.

———. *Serendipities.* Trans. William Weaver. New York: Columbia UP, 1998.

———. "Travels in Hyperreality." 1975. *Travels in Hyperreality.* Trans. William Weaver. San Diego: Harcourt Brace, 1986. 3–58.

Eisner, Will. *Comics & Sequential Art.* Expanded ed. Tamarac, FL: Poorhouse Press, 1985.

Ellis, Jonathan. "Grant Morrison: Master & Commander." *PopImage* 5 July 2004. http://www.popimage.com/content/grant2004.html. Accessed 8 December 2010.

Ellis, Warren. "Come in Alone" 28. *Comic Book Resources* 9 June 2000. http://www.comicbookresources.com/?page=article&id=13349. Accessed 8 December 2010.

Ellis, Warren, and Bryan Hitch. *The Authority* 1–12. La Jolla, CA: WildStorm, 1999–2000.

Epstein, Daniel Robert. "Grant Morrison." *Suicide Girls* 4 March 2005. http://suicidegirls.com/interviews/Grant+Morrison/. Accessed 8 December 2010.

Evanier, Mark. "Introduction." *Jack Kirby's Mister Miracle.* New York: DC Comics, 1998. 4.

"Exclusive Interview and Preview: Grant Morrison creator of *Seaguy*!" *MySpace Comic Books* 17 March 2009. http://www.myspace.com/comicbooks/blog/477293507. Accessed 8 December 2010.

Falconer, Duncan. "A hall of mirrors II: the Prismatic Age." *Mindless Ones* 3 August 2008. http://mindlessones.com/2008/08/03/a-hall-of-mirrors-ii-prismatic-age/. Accessed 8 December 2010.

"The Fauves." *Spirophone.* http://homepage.ntlworld.com/ulric.kennedy/Spirophone/The%20Fauves.htm. Accessed 8 December 2010.

"The Filthy Thoughts of Grant Morrison." *Newsarama* 4 June 2002. Archived at http://replay.waybackmachine.org/20020802122640/http://www.comicon.com/cgi-bin/ultimatebb.cgi?ubb=get_topic&f=12&t=000186. Accessed 8 December 2010.

Ford, Simon. *The Situationist International: A User's Guide.* London: Black Dog, 2005.

Frank, Thomas, and Matt Weiland, eds. *Commodify Your Dissent: Salvos from* The Baffler. New York: Norton, 1997.

Fukuyama, Francis. *The End of History and the Last Man.* New York: Free Press, 1992.

Gabilliet, Jean-Paul. *Of Comics and Men: A Cultural History of American Comic Books*. 2005. Trans. Bart Beaty and Nick Nguyen. Jackson: UP of Mississippi, 2010.

George, Richard. "Grant Morrison Discusses Batman & Robin." *IGN Comics* 11 March 2009. http://comics.ign.com/articles/961/961488p1.html. Accessed 8 December 2010.

"Grant Morrison on Being the DCU Revamp Guy." *Newsarama* 20 June 2005. Archived at http://web.archive.org/web/20050601-20050630re_/http://www.newsarama.com/dcnew/MorrisonDCU.htm. Accessed 8 December 2010.

Harris, John Glyndwr. *Gnosticism: Beliefs and Practices*. Brighton: Sussex, 1999.

Harvey, David. *The Condition of Postmodernity*. Oxford: Blackwell, 1990.

Hasted, Nick. "Grant Morrison." *The Comics Journal* 176 (April 1995): 52–82.

Hatfield, Charles. *Alternative Comics: An Emerging Literature*. Jackson: UP of Mississippi, 2005.

Hitchcock, William I. *The Struggle for Europe*. New York: Anchor, 2003.

Hudson, Laura. "Grant Morrison: The Comic Foundry Interview." *Comic Foundry* 5 (Spring 2009). Rpt. at http://comicfoundry.com/?p=1693. Accessed 8 December 2010.

Hugnet, Georges. "Dada" and "In the light of Surrealism." Trans. Margaret Scolari. *Fantastic Art, Dada, Surrealism*. Ed. Alfred H. Barr, Jr. New York: Museum of Modern Art, 1936. Rpt. Arno Press, 1968. 15–53.

"An Interview with Karen Berger." *Advance Comics* 49 (January 1993): 13–14.

"Interview with an Umpire." *Barbelith Interviews* 2 September 2002. http://www.barbelith.com/old/interviews/interview_1.shtml. Accessed 8 December 2010.

James, Nick. "Opting for Ontological Terrorism: Freedom and Control in Grant Morrison's *The Invisibles*." *Law, Culture and the Humanities* 3.3 (2007): 435–54.

Jameson, Fredric. *Postmodernism, or, The Cultural Logic of Late Capitalism*. Durham, NC: Duke UP, 1991.

Jenkins, Henry. "'Just Men in Tights': Rewriting Silver Age Comics in an Era of Multiplicity." *The Contemporary Comic Book Superhero*. Ed. Angela Ndalianis. New York: Routledge, 2009. 16–43.

Jennings, Dana. "At House of Comics, a Writer's Champion." *New York Times* 15 September 2003: C8.

Jones, Chuck, dir. "Duck Amuck." Warner Bros., 1953.

Jones, Gerard, and Will Jacobs. *The Comic Book Heroes*. New York: Crown, 1985.

Kidd, Chip, Geoff Spear, and Saul Ferris, eds. *Bat-Manga!: The Secret History of Batman in Japan*. New York: Pantheon, 2008.

Klock, Geoff. *How to Read Superhero Comics and Why*. New York: Continuum, 2002.

Kristeva, Julia. "Women's Time." 1979. Trans. Alice Jardine and Harry Blake. *The Kristeva Reader*. Ed. Toril Moi. New York: Columbia UP, 1986. 187–213.

Landon, Richard. "A Half-Naked Muscleman in Trunks: Charles Atlas, Superheroes, and Comic Book Masculinity." *Journal of the Fantastic in the Arts* 18.2 (2007): 200–16.

Lien-Cooper, Barb. "Punching Holes Through Time: Grant Morrison." *Sequential Tart* August 2002. http://www.sequentialtart.com/archive/aug02/gmorrison2.shtml. Accessed 8 December 2010.

Loewen, James W. *Sundown Towns: A Hidden Dimension of American Racism*. New York: New Press, 2005.

Lukin, Josh. "Childish Things: Nostalgia and Guilt in Grant Morrison's Comics." *The Comics Journal* 176 (April 1995): 83–87.

Malcolm, Cheryl Alexander. "Witness, Trauma, and Remembrance: Holocaust Representation and X-Men Comics." *The Jewish Graphic Novel: Critical Approaches*. Ed. Samantha Baskind and Ranen Omer-Sherman. New Brunswick, NJ: Rutgers UP, 2008. 144–60.

McCloud, Scott. *Making Comics*. New York: HarperCollins, 2006.

———. *Understanding Comics*. Northampton, MA: Kitchen Sink, 1993.

McCulloch, Joe. "Just a Misunderstood Rebel." Review of *Seaguy: Slaves of Mickey Eye* 2. *Jog—The Blog* 12 May 2009. http://joglikescomics.blogspot.com/2009/05/just-misunderstood-rebel.html. Accessed 8 December 2010.

———. "New Popular Suicides." *Comixology* 15 June 2009. http://www.comixology.com/articles/251/New-Popular-Suicides. Accessed 8 December 2010.

———. "Please God, Send Your Angels to Shoot Me in the Back, For My Education is Done." Review of *The Mystery Play*. *Jog—The Blog* 29 August 2005. http://joglikescomics.blogspot.com/2005/08/please-god-send-your-angels-to-shoot.html. Accessed 8 December 2010.

———. "So many more books, but here's all I have time for . . ." Review of *Zatanna* 1. *Jog—The Blog* 7 April 2005. http://joglikescomics.blogspot.com/2005/04/so-many-more-books-but-heres-all-i.html. Accessed 8 December 2010.

———. "Thoughts as Tuesday drifts to bed . . ." *Jog—The Blog* 26 January 2006. http://joglikescomics.blogspot.com/2006/01/thoughts-as-tuesday-drifts-to-bed.html. Accessed 8 December 2010.

McHale, Brian. *Constructing Postmodernism*. London: Routledge, 1992.

———. *Postmodernist Fiction*. New York: Methuen, 1987.

Meaney, Patrick. *Our Sentence Is Up: Seeing Grant Morrison's* The Invisibles. Edwardsville, IL: Sequart, 2010.

Meaney, Patrick, dir. *Grant Morrison: Talking With Gods*. Respect Films, 2010.

Medhurst, Andy. "Batman, Deviance and Camp." *The Many Lives of the Batman: Critical Approaches to a Superhero and his Media*. Ed. Roberta E. Pearson and William Uricchio. New York: Routledge, 1991. 149–63.

Mellard, James M. "Inventing Lacanian Psychoanalysis: Linguistics and Tropology in 'The Agency of the Letter.'" *Poetics Today* 19.4 (1998): 499–530.

Merivale, Patricia, and Susan Elizabeth Sweeney, eds. *Detecting Texts: The Metaphysical Detective Story from Poe to Postmodernism*. Philadelphia: U of Pennsylvania P, 1999.

Miéville, China. "Floating Utopias: Freedom and Unfreedom of the Seas." *Evil Paradises: Dreamworlds of Neoliberalism*. Ed. Mike Davis and Daniel Bertrand Monk. New York: New Press, 2007. 251–61.

Millar, Mark, Frank Quitely, et al. *The Authority* 13–29. La Jolla, CA: WildStorm, 2000–02.

Miller, Frank. *Batman: The Dark Knight Returns*. New York: DC Comics, 1986.

Miller, John Jackson. "Comic Book Sales Charts & Analysis." *CBGXtra.com*. http://cbgxtra.com/comic-book-sales-charts-analysis. Accessed 8 December 2010.

Mitchell, W. J. T. *The Last Dinosaur Book*. Chicago: U of Chicago P, 1998.

"The Mixers." *Spirophone*. http://homepage.ntlworld.com/ulric.kennedy/Spirophone/The%20Mixers.htm. Accessed 8 December 2010.

Moore, Alan. "The Mark of Batman: An Introduction." *Batman: The Dark Knight Returns*. New York: DC Comics, 1986. n. pag.

Moore, Alan, and Brian Bolland. *Batman: The Killing Joke*. New York: DC Comics, 1988.

Moore, Alan, and Dave Gibbons. *Watchmen*. New York: DC Comics, 1986–87.

Moore, Alan, Garry Leach, et al. *Marvelman*. London: Quality Communications, 1982–84. Rpt. and cont. as *Miracleman*. Forestville, CA: Eclipse Comics, 1985–89.

Morrison, Grant. "Afterword." *Kill Your Boyfriend*. New York: DC Comics, 1998. n. pag.

———. *Captain Clyde*. Glasgow: Govan Press, 1979–82.

———. "Drivel." *Speakeasy* 111 (July 1990): 55.

———. *Gideon Stargrave* and other stories. *Near Myths* 2–5. Edinburgh: Galaxy Media, 1978–80.

———. "Intro." *Animal Man* vol. 1. New York: DC Comics, 1991. n. pag.

———. "Introduction." *Batman: The Black Casebook*. New York: DC Comics, 2009. n. pag.

———. "Introduction." *Zenith Book One*. London: Titan Books, 1988. n. pag.

———. "It was the 90s." *Fortune Hotel*. Ed. Sarah Champion. London: Penguin, 1999. 246–60.

———. "Morrison Manifesto." *New X-Men* vol. 1: *E is for Extinction*. New York: Marvel Comics, 2002. Rpt. in *New X-Men Omnibus*. New York: Marvel Comics, 2006. n. pag.

———. "Pop Magic!" *Book of Lies: The Disinformation Guide to Magick and the Occult*, ed. Richard Metzger. New York: Disinformation, 2003. 16–25.

———. "Preface." *Book of Lies: The Disinformation Guide to Magick and the Occult*, ed. Richard Metzger. New York: Disinformation: 2003. 9.

———. "A Word from the Author." *Doom Patrol* vol. 2 20, 1989. Rpt. in *Doom Patrol* vol. 1: *Crawling from the Wreckage*. New York: DC Comics, 1992. n. pag.

Morrison, Grant, and Simone Bianchi. *Seven Soldiers: Shining Knight* 1–4. New York: DC Comics, 2005.

Morrison, Grant, and Philip Bond. *Kill Your Boyfriend*. New York: DC Comics, 1995. Rpt. 1998.

———. *Vimanarama*. New York: DC Comics, 2005.

Morrison, Grant, and Richard Case. *Doom Patrol* vol. 2 19–63. New York: DC Comics, 1989–93.

Morrison, Grant, Richard Case, et al. *Doom Force Special* 1. New York: DC Comics, 1992.

Morrison, Grant, and Matthew Clark. *Final Crisis: Submit*. New York: DC Comics, 2008.

Morrison, Grant, and Duncan Fegredo. *Kid Eternity* 1–3. New York: DC Comics, 1991.

Morrison, Grant, Pasqual Ferry, et al. *Seven Soldiers: Mister Miracle* 1–4. New York: DC Comics, 2005–06.

Morrison, Grant, and David Finch. *Batman: The Return* 1. New York: DC Comics, 2011.

Morrison, Grant, and Ian Gibson. *Steed and Mrs. Peel* 1–3. Forestville, CA and London: Eclipse Comics and Acme Press, 1990–92.

Morrison, Grant, and Paul Grist. *St. Swithin's Day*. *Trident* 1–4. Leicester, UK: Trident Comics, 1989. Rpt. in *St. Swithin's Day*. Portland, OR: Oni Press, 1998.

Morrison, Grant, and Manuel Gutierrez. "Nick's World . . ." *Marvel Knights Double Shot* 2. New York: Marvel Comics, 2002.

Morrison, Grant, and Rian Hughes. *Dare*. *Revolver* 1–7 and *Crisis* 55–56. London: Fleetway, 1990–91. Rpt. in *Dare* 1–4. Seattle: Monster Comics, 1992.

Morrison, Grant, and Frazer Irving. *Seven Soldiers: Klarion* 1–4. New York: DC Comics, 2005.

Morrison, Grant, and Klaus Janson. *Batman: Gothic*. *Legends of the Dark Knight* 6–10. New York: DC Comics, 1990.

Morrison, Grant, Geoff Johns, et al. *52*. New York: DC Comics, 2006–07.

Morrison, Grant, and J. G. Jones. *Marvel Boy* 1–6. New York: Marvel Comics, 2000–01.

Morrison, Grant, J. G. Jones, et al. *Final Crisis* 1–7. New York: DC Comics, 2008–09.

Morrison, Grant, and Arnie Jorgensen. *Prometheus* 1. New York: DC Comics, 1998.

Morrison, Grant, Andy Kubert, et al. *Batman* 655–658, 663–683. New York: DC Comics, 2006–09.
Morrison, Grant, and Jae Lee. *Fantastic Four 1234* 1–4. New York: Marvel Comics, 2001.
Morrison, Grant, and Doug Mahnke. *Final Crisis: Superman Beyond 3D* 1–2. New York: DC Comics, 2008–09.
———. *Seven Soldiers: Frankenstein* 1–4. New York: DC Comics, 2005–06.
Morrison, Grant, and Ed McGuinness. *JLA Classified* 1–3. New York: DC Comics, 2005.
Morrison, Grant, and Dave McKean. *Batman: Arkham Asylum: A Serious House on Serious Earth*. New York: DC Comics, 1989.
———. *Batman: Arkham Asylum* 15th Anniversary Edition. New York: DC Comics, 2004.
Morrison, Grant, Mark Millar, and N. Steven Harris. *Aztek: the Ultimate Man* 1–10. New York: DC Comics, 1996–97.
Morrison, Grant, Mark Millar, and Phillip Hester. "Bad Gumbo." *Swamp Thing* 140–143. New York: DC Comics, 1994.
Morrison, Grant, Mark Millar, and Steve Parkhouse. *Big Dave*. *2000 AD* 842–849, 869–872, 904–907. London: Fleetway, 1993, 1994.
Morrison, Grant, Mark Millar, Paul Ryan, et al. *The Flash* 130–141. New York: DC Comics, 1997–98.
Morrison, Grant, Mark Millar, and Steve Yeowell. *Skrull Kill Krew* 1–5. New York: Marvel Comics, 1995–96.
Morrison, Grant, and Sean Murphy. *Joe the Barbarian* 1–8. New York: DC Comics, 2010–11.
Morrison, Grant, and Jon J. Muth. *The Mystery Play*. New York: DC Comics, 1994.
Morrison, Grant, and Yanick Paquette. *Batman, Incorporated*. New York: DC Comics, 2011–present.
———. *Seven Soldiers: Bulleteer* 1–4. New York: DC Comics, 2005–06.
Morrison, Grant, Howard Porter, et al. *JLA* 1–41. New York: DC Comics, 1997–2000.
Morrison, Grant, and Frank Quitely. *All Star Superman* 1–12. New York: DC Comics, 2005–08.
———. *Flex Mentallo* 1–4. New York: DC Comics, 1996.
———. *JLA: Earth 2*. New York: DC Comics, 2000.
———. *We3*. New York: DC Comics, 2004–05.
Morrison, Grant, Frank Quitely, et al. *Batman and Robin* 1–16. New York: DC Comics, 2009–11.
———. *New X-Men* 114–154. New York: Marvel Comics, 2001–04.
Morrison, Grant, and Val Semeiks. *DC One Million* 1–4. New York: DC Comics, 1998.
Morrison, Grant, and Ryan Sook. *Seven Soldiers: Zatanna* 1–4. New York: DC Comics, 2005.
Morrison, Grant, Chris Sprouse, et al. *Batman: The Return of Bruce Wayne* 1–6. New York: DC Comics, 2010.
Morrison, Grant, and Cameron Stewart. *Seaguy* 1–3. New York: DC Comics, 2004.
———. *Seaguy: Slaves of Mickey Eye* 1–3. New York: DC Comics, 2009.
———. *Seven Soldiers: Guardian* 1–4. New York: DC Comics, 2005.
Morrison, Grant, and Chas Truog. *Animal Man* 1–26. New York: DC Comics, 1988–90.
Morrison, Grant, and Daniel Vallely. *Bible John: A Forensic Meditation*. *Crisis* 56–61. London: Fleetway, 1991.
Morrison, Grant, and Chris Weston. *The Filth*. New York: DC Comics, 2002–03.
Morrison, Grant, and J. H. Williams III. *Seven Soldiers* 0–1. New York: DC Comics, 2005–06.
Morrison, Grant, and Steve Yeowell. *The New Adventures of Hitler*. *Cut*. 1989. Rpt. in *Crisis* 46–49. London: Fleetway, 1990.
———. *Sebastian O* 1–3. New York: DC Comics, 1993.

———. *Zenith* Phases I–IV. *2000 AD* 535–550, 558–559, 589–606, 626–634, 650–662, 667–670, 791–806, 2001, *Sci-Fi Special 1988, Winter Special 1, Annual 1990.* London: Fleetway, 1987–92, 2000.

Morrison, Grant, Steve Yeowell, et al. *The Invisibles.* 3 vols. New York: DC Comics, 1994–2000.

———. *Zoids. Spider-Man and Zoids* 19, 30–31, 36–37, 40–51. London: Marvel UK, 1986–87.

Morrison, Grant, and Leinil Francis Yu. *New X-Men Annual 2001.* New York: Marvel Comics, 2001.

Murray, Christopher. "Subverting the Sublime: Romantic Ideology in the Comics of Grant Morrison." *Sub/versions: Cultural Status, Genre and Critique.* Ed. Pauline MacPherson et al. Newcastle, UK: Cambridge Scholars, 2008. 34–51.

Ndalianis, Angela, ed. *The Contemporary Comic Book Superhero.* New York: Routledge, 2009.

Neighly, Patrick, and Kereth Cowe-Spigai. *Anarchy for the Masses: The Disinformation Guide to the Invisibles.* New York: The Disinformation Company, 2003.

Ness, Alex. "A Chat About Craft with Grant Morrison." *PopThought.com* 5 September 2005. Archived at http://replay.waybackmachine.org/20051221160317/http://www.popthought.com/display_column.asp?DAID=861. Accessed 8 December 2010.

Odell, Cole Moore. "All-Star Luthor: Xs and Os." *Mountain of Judgment* 22 September 2008. http://mountainofjudgment.blogspot.com/2008/09/all-star-superman-xs-and-os.html. Accessed 8 December 2010.

———. Comments to Joe McCulloch, "God's in his Heaven—All's right with the world!" Review of *All Star Superman* 12. *The Savage Critics* 17 September 2008. http://www.savagecritic.com/jog/gods-in-his-heaven-alls-right-with-the-world/. Comments archived at http://www.haloscan.com/comments/lazybastid/3356879661032346268. Accessed 8 December 2010.

O'Donnell, Tony. "Captain Clyde—His Life, Death, and Life and Death." *Fusion* 7 (October 1985). Rpt. at *Fish1000 Comics: Lost and Found* 1 January 1999. http://homepage.ntlworld.com/fish1000/index/lostcontent/gm-fusion7-oct85.txt. Accessed 8 December 2010.

Offenberger, Rik. "Uniquely Original: Grant Morrison." *Silver Bullet Comics* 6 September 2005. http://www.comicsbulletin.com/features/112602239631900.htm. Accessed 8 December 2010.

Orwell, George. *Nineteen Eighty-Four.* London: Secker and Warburg, 1949.

Ouspensky, P. D. *The Symbolism of the Tarot.* Trans. A.L. Pogossky. 1913. New York: Dover, 1976.

Parkin, Lance. *The Pocket Essential Alan Moore.* Harpenden, UK: Pocket Essentials, 2001.

Phegley, Kiel. "The Bat Signal: Grant Morrison." *Comic Book Resources* 13 October 2010. http://www.comicbookresources.com/?page=article&id=28872. Accessed 8 December 2010.

Popper, Karl R. *The Logic of Scientific Discovery.* 1934. Trans. by the author. New York: Basic Books, 1959.

Pustz, Matthew. *Comic Book Culture: Fanboys and True Believers.* Jackson: UP of Mississippi, 1999.

Pynchon, Thomas. *The Crying of Lot 49.* 1965. New York: HarperCollins, 1999.

"Q&A: Grant Morrison." *The Big Issue* [Scotland] 12 February 2009. http://www.bigissuescotland.com/features/view/16. Accessed 8 December 2010.

Raine, Kathleen. *Yeats, the Tarot, and the Golden Dawn.* 2nd ed. rev. Dublin: Dolmen Press, 1976.

Randle, Chris. "Worlds of Otherness." *Gutteral* 8 July 2008. http://gutteral.blogspot.com/2008/07/worlds-of-otherness.html. Accessed 8 December 2010.

Rauch, Stephen. "'We Have All Been Sentenced': Language as Means of Control in Grant Morrison's *The Invisibles*." *International Journal of Comic Art* 6.2 (2004): 350–63.

Raviv, Dan. *Comic Wars*. New York: Broadway, 2002.

Reynolds, Richard. *Super Heroes: A Modern Mythology*. Jackson: UP of Mississippi, 1992.

Riddell, Peter. *The Thatcher Decade*. Oxford: Blackwell, 1989.

Robinson, James, and Peter Snejbjerg. *Starman 1,000,000* (November 1998). New York: DC Comics.

Rogers, Mark. "Understanding Production: The Stylistic Impact of Artisan and Industrial Methods." *International Journal of Comic Art* 8.1 (2006): 509–17.

Rollin, Lucy. "Guilt and the Unconscious in *Arkham Asylum*." *Inks: Cartoon and Comic Art Studies* 1.1 (1994): 2–13.

Rorty, Richard, ed. *The Linguistic Turn: Recent Essays in Philosophical Method*. Chicago: U of Chicago P, 1967.

Sabin, Roger. *Adult Comics: An Introduction*. London: Routledge, 1993.

———. *Comics, Comix & Graphic Novels*. London: Phaidon, 1996.

Salisbury, Mark. *Writers on Comics Scriptwriting*. London: Titan, 1999.

Sattler, Peter R. "Past Imperfect: 'Building Stories' and the Art of Memory." *The Comics of Chris Ware: Drawing Is a Way of Thinking*. Ed. David M. Ball and Martha B. Kuhlman. Jackson: UP of Mississippi, 2010. 206–22.

Schatz, Thomas. *Hollywood Genres: Formulas, Filmmaking, and the Studio System*. New York: McGraw-Hill, 1981.

Schodt, Frederik L. *Dreamland Japan: Writings on Modern Manga*. Berkeley: Stone Bridge, 1996.

———. *Manga! Manga! The World of Japanese Comics*. Tokyo: Kodansha, 1983.

Seven Soldiers Annotations. Barbelith 17 March 2007. http://www.barbelith.com/faq/index.php/Seven_Soldiers_Annotations. Accessed 8 December 2010.

Shaviro, Steven. *Doom Patrols: A Theoretical Fiction about Postmodernism*. London: Serpent's Tail, 1997.

Shelley, Mary. *Frankenstein*. 1818. Oxford: Oxford UP, 1998.

Shyminsky, Neil. "Mutant Readers, Reading Mutants: Appropriation, Assimilation, and the X Men." *International Journal of Comic Art* 8.2 (2006): 387–405.

Sigler, David. "'Funky Days Are Back Again': Reading Seventies Nostalgia in Late-Nineties Rock Music." *Iowa Journal of Cultural Studies* 5 (2004): 40–58.

Singer, Bryan, dir. *Superman Returns*. Warner Bros., 2006.

———. *X-Men*. 20th Century Fox, 2000.

Singer, Marc. "Embodiments of the Real: The Counterlinguistic Turn in the Comic-Book Novel." *Critique: Studies in Contemporary Fiction* 49.3 (2008): 273–89.

———. "'A Serious House on Serious Earth': Rehabilitating Arkham Asylum." *International Journal of Comic Art* 8.2 (2006): 269–82.

Singh, Arune. "The End of an X-Era: Morrison Talks Finishing 'New X-Men,' Sex & DC." *Comic Book Resources* 26 September 2003. http://www.comicbookresources.com/?page=article&id=2707. Accessed 8 December 2010.

Skir, Robert N. "X-ing the Rubicon." *The Unauthorized X-Men*. Ed. Len Wein. Dallas: BenBella, 2005. 19–28.

Smith, Zack. "All Star Memories: Grant Morrison on *All Star Superman*." *Newsarama* 3 November 2008. http://www.newsarama.com/comics/110803-Grant-Superman-10.html. Accessed 8 December 2010.

Starr, Alexandra. "It's a Bird! It's a Plane! It's Architecture!" *New York Times* 31 July 2005: AR 1, 26.

Stewart, Cameron. "13 questions with Cameron Stewart." *Mindless Ones* 9 April 2009. http://mindlessones.com/2009/04/09/13-questions-with-cameron-stewart. Accessed 8 December 2010.

Sukenick, Ronald. *Narralogues: Truth in Fiction*. Albany: State U of New York P, 2000.

Suskind, Ron. "Faith, Certainty and the Presidency of George W. Bush." *New York Times Magazine* 17 October 2004: 44+.

Talbot, Bryan. *The Adventures of Luther Arkwright*. 1978–89. Milwaukie, OR: Dark Horse Comics, 1997.

Thill, Scott. "Grant Morrison Talks Brainy Comics, Sexy Apocalypse." *Underwire* 19 March 2009. http://www.wired.com/underwire/2009/03/mid-life-crisis. Accessed 8 December 2010.

Todorov, Tzvetan. *The Fantastic: A Structural Approach to a Literary Genre*. 1970. Trans. Richard Howard. Ithaca, NY: Cornell UP, 1973.

Tondro, Jason. "An Imaginary Mongoose: Comics, Canon and the Superhero Romance." Diss. U of California, Riverside, 2008.

Tong, Ng Suat. "The Symbolism of the Ungodly: *The Mystery Play*." *The Comics Journal* 168 (May 1994): 49–51.

Tyree, J. M., and Ben Walters. *The Big Lebowski*. London: British Film Institute, 2007.

Vico, Giambattista. *The New Science of Giambattista Vico*. 1744. Trans. Thomas Goddard Bergin and Max Harold Fisch. Ithaca, NY: Cornell UP, 1968.

Wachowski, Andy and Larry, dir. *The Matrix*. Warner Bros., 1999.

Waid, Mark. "Stacking the Deck: The *Other* Joker Stories." *The Greatest Joker Stories Ever Told*. Ed. Mike Gold. New York: DC Comics, 1988. 278–83.

Waugh, Patricia. *Metafiction: The Theory and Practice of Self-Conscious Fiction*. London: Methuen, 1984.

Weiland, Jonah. "Marvel confirms Buckley as new Publisher." *Comic Book Resources* 15 October 2003. http://www.comicbookresources.com/?page=article&id=2746. Accessed 8 December 2010.

Wilber, Ken. "Introduction to Volume Two." *The Collected Works of Ken Wilber* vol. 2. Boston: Shambhala, 1999. 1–12.

Williams, J. H. III. Comment to "Grant Morrison's *Batman*." *Barbelith Underground* 11 August 2007. http://www.barbelith.com/topic/23776/from/735#post724924. Accessed 8 December 2010.

Wilson, Richard. "Furore over the Fuhrer—How Hitler has started a new war of words." *Guardian* 19 June 1989: 23.

Witek, Joseph. *Comic Books as History*. Jackson: UP of Mississippi, 1989.

Wolfman, Marv, and George Pérez. *Crisis on Infinite Earths*. New York: DC Comics, 1985–86.

Wolk, Douglas. *Reading Comics: How Graphic Novels Work and What They Mean*. Philadelphia: Da Capo, 2007.

"WonderCon '06: DC—The Best Is Yet to Come Panel." *Newsarama* 11 February 2006. Archived at http://web.archive.org/web/20070929141605re_/www.newsarama.com/WonderCon2006/DCU/besttocome.html. Accessed 8 December 2010.

Woo, Benjamin. "An Age-Old Problem: Problematics of Comic Book Historiography." *International Journal of Comic Art* 10.1 (2008): 268–79.

Woodward, Olivia. "Sunday Slugfest—Vimanarama #1." *Silver Bullet Comics* 13 February 2005. http://www.comicsbulletin.com/reviews/110835274421815.htm. Accessed 8 December 2010.

"Work Outside Comics 2008." *grantmorrison.com*. http://www.grant-morrison.com/index.php?option=com_content&view=article&id=31&Itemid=24. Accessed 8 December 2010.

Young, Hugo. *The Iron Lady*. New York: Farrar Straus Giroux, 1989.

Zani, Steven. "It's a Jungle in Here: Animal Man, Continuity Issues, and the Authorial Death Drive." *The Contemporary Comic Book Superhero*. Ed. Angela Ndalianis. New York: Routledge, 2009. 233–49.

"Zenith Phase Three Scorecard." *International Superheroes*. http://www.internationalhero.co.uk/s/scorcard.htm. Accessed 8 December 2010.

Žižek, Slavoj. *Looking Awry: An Introduction to Jacques Lacan through Popular Culture*. Cambridge, MA: MIT, 1991.

Index

Abbott, Lawrence, 216–17, 302n
Adams, Neal, 25, 66, 267–68
adolescence, 40, 44, 49, 51, 134–35, 144–46, 164, 167–69, 172, 204, 223, 238–40, 286–87
Afrofuturism, 107–8, 298n
Allison, David, 184, 190–91
alternative comics, 3, 5, 9, 21, 24–25, 27, 93
Altman, Rick, 110, 298n
America, 78, 101, 107, 113, 200, 205–6, 235, 254, 296n, 298n, 303n
Anderson, Brent, 137
Anderson, Lindsay, 4
animals, 59, 78, 181–82, 203, 208–20, 296n, 302n; animal rights, 19, 59, 62–63, 186, 296n; anthropomorphic "funny animals," 55, 209–10, 280
authorities and authoritarian politics, 41–43, 77–87, 101, 116, 126, 130, 183, 186–87, 198, 204, 225, 243–44, 248, 285–86, 300n, 301n; and narrative authority, 106–7, 226; and superheroes, 138–40, 150–53, 180, 256–58

Babcock, Jay, 49, 199, 204
Balsman, Phil, 248
Barks, Carl, 209, 218
Barnes, Peter, 89
Bendis, Brian Michael, 238
Berger, James, 246–48
Berger, Karen, 52–53, 64, 92–93, 297n
Bianchi, Simone, 221, 223
binaries. *See* dualism
Bissette, Steve, 63, 88, 136, 231, 295n
Blake, William, 33, 41, 111, 126, 233, 295n
Bohm, David, 58–59, 61, 69
Bolland, Brian, 52, 64, 68, 71, 113, 289

Bond, Philip, 16, 99, 134, 204, 206, 298n
Borges, Jorge Luis, 59, 86, 89
Brady, Matt, 260
Britain: comics industry, 8, 20, 24–30, 33, 40; comics writers, 26–27, 29, 52, 92, 111; culture, 4, 9, 30, 35, 43, 134–35; national identity, 36–37, 41–43; politics, 33, 36–44, 206, 294n
Brooker, Will, 65, 71, 142, 291, 295n
Brooks, Peter, 217, 302n
Broome, John, 5, 154
Buckley, Dan, 180
Bukatman, Scott, 17
Bulwer-Lytton, Edward, 173
Burton, Tim, 17, 64–65
Bush, George W., 247, 300n, 303n
Busiek, Kurt, 63, 137
Byrne, John, 72, 163, 258
Byron, George Gordon, Lord, 89–90, 126–29, 299n

Callahan, Timothy, 5, 55, 60–61, 88, 294n
Campbell, Eddie, 6, 14
Case, Richard, 73, 75, 77, 88, 296n
Cawelti, John, 116, 241
Chaykin, Howard, 236, 271
Claremont, Chris, 72–73, 88, 138, 163, 167–68, 180, 219
Cockrum, Dave, 72
comic books, 3, 6–7, 99–100, 104, 291–92
comics industry (U.S.), 7–8, 24, 27–29, 51–52, 92–93, 147, 202–3, 208, 251, 285–86, 288, 291–92; collapse in direct market, 99–100, 136; ownership practices, 140, 180–82, 185, 252
Coogan, Peter, 109–10, 151
Cowe-Spigai, Kereth, 5, 98, 298n

317

Crisis, 20, 27, 33, 96
Cut, 20, 27, 40

Dadaism, 80, 90–91
Daniel, Tony, 272
DC Comics, 3, 21, 23, 30, 52–53, 65–66, 72, 92–93, 138, 147, 150, 156–57, 221, 251, 254, 276–77, 281–83, 291, 299n, 300n; Morrison's centrality, 251, 277; Morrison's recruitment, 52–53; narrative continuity, 29, 57, 61, 137, 236, 251, 254, 276–77, 279–81, 283–84, 295n, 303n
DeLillo, Don, 118
de Man, Paul, 16–17
De Quincey, Thomas, 89, 126
Dery, Mark, 107
de Sade, Donatien Alphonse François, 128–29
Dick, Philip K., 4, 98, 107, 118, 120, 297n
DiDio, Dan, 276–77
Di Liddo, Annalisa, 14–15
Disney: comics, 92, 209, 297n; Disneyland theme park, 201, 227; films, 208
Drake, Arnold, 72–74, 78, 80, 296n
dualism, 19–20, 73, 75, 80, 83–87, 101–2, 116–17, 135, 142–43, 166, 207–8, 231, 282, 292, 303n

Eco, Umberto, 121, 240, 251, 254
Eisner, Will, 137, 217
Ellis, Warren, 138, 159–60, 295n, 299n; *The Authority*, 138–39, 143, 151, 153, 159–60, 252, 299n
embodiment. *See* hypostasis
Enlightenment, 77–78, 81, 128, 261, 287, 303n
epistemologies, 96–98, 196
Erskine, Gary, 188
Ezquerra, Carlos, 30

Falconer, Duncan, 251–52, 283, 304n
Fauves, the, 5, 96
Ferry, Pasqual, 221
film, and Morrison's writing, 4, 108, 111–13, 138, 159, 163–64, 199, 204–5, 209, 238–39, 299n
Fox, Gardner, 154

fractals, 19, 57–59, 73, 102, 129, 227, 279, 291
French Revolution, 127, 128, 265, 300n
Fukuyama, Francis, 201

Gaiman, Neil, 111
gender, 33, 65, 83, 107–8, 167–68, 170–71, 243, 286, 298n
genre: cycles of development, 241; semantics and syntax, 110, 150, 163, 183, 298n
Gibbons, Dave, 27, 30, 52, 108, 236, 271
Giordano, Dick, 92
Glasgow, 5, 7, 9, 25, 58, 61, 96, 144, 297n
Gnostics, 10, 85–86, 101–2, 176, 186, 279, 282, 297n
graphic novel, 3, 6–7, 64, 91, 291–92
Grant, Alan, 30
Grant, Jamie, 209, 267
Gray, Mick, 231
Grist, Paul, 40, 44
ground level comics, 3, 20, 24–25, 27

Haney, Bob, 72, 290
Hardt, Michael, 132
Harras, Bob, 162
Hasted, Nick, 72, 94
Hatfield, Charles, 292
Hernandez, Gilbert and Jaime, 108
Hitch, Bryan, 138
holograms, 19, 57–58, 69, 101–3, 115, 129, 131, 151, 166, 227–28
Horus avatars, 49, 160–61, 225
Hughes, Rian, 33–39, 147
hypostasis, 16–19, 21, 36, 42–43, 49, 53, 67–68, 71–73, 75, 82–88, 96, 119, 122–23, 140, 146, 160–61, 176–77, 199, 248–50, 264, 266, 278–79, 282, 288, 292; defined, 16–17, 294n

Ialdabaoth, 79, 85–86, 233, 301n
idealism, 12, 18, 20, 36, 46–48, 61, 86–87, 102, 127, 129, 175–77, 231, 264–67
identity, 96, 130–32, 134, 170, 175, 183–84, 197, 220, 273–74, 299n, 301n; the MeMePlex, 131–32, 134, 274, 300n; minority identity, 107–8, 167–71
Image Comics, 108, 136–38, 147, 150, 157

implicate order, 58–59, 61, 96–97, 129
Irving, Frazer, 221, 223

Jameson, Fredric, 209, 299n
Janson, Klaus, 72
Jemas, Bill, 162–63, 180
Jenkins, Henry, 251–52
Jimenez, Phil, 7–8, 16, 99–101, 104, 113, 119, 123, 277
Johns, Geoff, 254, 277
Jones, J. G., 159, 276

Kahn, Jenette, 92
Kane, Pat, 40, 294n
Kirby, Jack, 5, 22, 82, 88, 163, 181–82, 204–5, 226, 228, 230–33, 250, 280–81, 296n
Klein, Todd, 124–26, 219
Klock, Geoff, 5, 67, 153, 155–56, 261, 296n
Kurtzman, Harvey, 137
Kuwata, Jiro, 291

language, 14–18, 118–24, 246–50; and identity, 19, 119, 219–20; the linguistic turn, 16, 246–48, 293–94n
Larkin, Philip, 4, 64
Lee, Jae, 161
Lee, Stan, 88, 163
Lennon, John, 12–13, 46; the Beatles, 47
Lichtenstein, Roy, 268–70
Liefeld, Rob, 88, 108
Lukin, Josh, 77–78, 297n

Mahnke, Doug, 223, 276
manga, 138, 147, 182, 208–10, 291, 302n
Marvel Comics, 22, 25–26, 30, 72–73, 100, 136–37, 157–58, 161, 172, 183, 203, 251, 303n; leadership changes, 162–63, 180
materialism, 20, 86–87, 102, 265–66
McCarthy, Brendan, 30
McCay, Winsor, 137
McCloud, Scott, 104, 302n
McCulloch, Joe, 6–7, 95, 202–3, 231, 304n
McGuinness, Ed, 302n
McHale, Brian, 19, 196, 294n
McKean, Dave, 64, 66, 68–71, 295–96n
Meaney, Patrick, 5, 10, 293n

Medhurst, Andy, 65–66, 299n
metafiction, 18–20, 55–59, 61–63, 86, 102, 104, 124, 137, 140–44, 179–80, 202–3, 241, 274–76, 279–80, 283, 295n, 297n
Millar, Mark, 137, 139, 157, 160, 162, 252, 294n, 299–300n, 302n; *The Authority*, 151, 153, 160, 162, 302–3n
Miller, Frank, 30, 52–53, 61, 64–65, 72–73, 108, 223, 229–31, 233, 236, 272; *Daredevil*, 30, 72; *The Dark Knight Returns*, 30, 34, 52–53, 64, 72, 147, 151, 219, 270, 272
Mills, Pat, 27, 30
mimesis, 16–20, 72, 118–23, 217, 298n
Mitchell, W. J. T., 167
Mixers, the, 5, 96
modernity, 22–23, 97, 128, 223, 242–46, 250, 284, 287
monomyth, 111, 260–61, 288
Moorcock, Michael, 4, 25, 94, 98, 115
Moore, Alan, 5, 14–15, 20, 27, 52–53, 61, 63, 65, 88–90, 111, 136–37, 231–33, 258, 281–82, 295n; *The Killing Joke*, 34, 64–65, 71, 274, 289; *Marvelman/Miracleman*, 25–26, 28, 30, 32, 47–48, 52, 90, 151, 210, 295n; *Promethea*, 231–32; *Swamp Thing*, 30, 48, 52, 55, 88, 92, 231–33, 295n; *Watchmen*, 30, 32–34, 48, 52, 55, 62, 88–90, 151, 198, 236, 271, 281–82, 295n
Moore, Stuart, 100
Morrison, Grant: authorial self-representations, 9, 14, 32, 55–63, 90, 106, 141, 144–46, 232, 240–41; autobiographical material, in comics, 9–10, 40, 99, 144–46, 255; depression, 44, 146, 278–79; family, 9–10, 144, 255; influences, 4–5, 25–26, 52–53, 88–91, 98, 111, 126, 130, 208–10, 230–33, 281–82; Kathmandu experience, 10–11, 99, 151, 293n; magical beliefs, 10–15, 18–20, 98–100, 182–83; music career, 4–5, 144; relationship with readers, 5–6, 12, 64, 72, 100, 193–96, 198–99, 224–25, 274–75, 291; scripting methods, 6–9, 66–71, 293n; work outside comics, 4

Works:
All Star Superman, 8, 16, 23, 254–68, 273, 277, 280, 282–83, 303–4n
Animal Man, 5, 8, 19, 21, 51, 53–63, 65, 73, 86, 90–93, 104, 136, 186, 198, 218, 227, 230–31, 280–81, 295n, 297n
Arkham Asylum, 16, 21, 52, 63–72, 88, 90–91, 95–96, 198–99, 268, 273–74, 282, 293, 295–96n
Aztek: the Ultimate Man, 139
Batman, 8, 23, 245, 267–76, 277, 282, 288–91, 302n
Batman: Gothic, 72, 90
Batman, Incorporated, 291
Batman: The Return, 293n
Batman: The Return of Bruce Wayne, 290–92
Batman and Robin, 288–91
Bible John: A Forensic Meditation, 96–97, 294n
Big Dave, 51, 294n
Captain Clyde, 25–26, 52
Dare, 20, 33–40, 48, 51, 107, 129, 294n
DC One Million, 154–55, 258
Doom Patrol, 16, 21, 72–93, 109–10, 136, 140–41, 183, 198–99, 231, 282, 294n, 296–97n, 299n
Fantastic Four 1234, 22, 139, 161–63 52, 254, 277, 280, 291
The Filth, 22, 181–98, 220, 301n
Final Crisis, 23, 254, 275–85, 288, 290
The Flash, 137–39, 252, 299n
Flex Mentallo, 21, 140–50, 180, 278, 282, 299–301n
Future Shocks, 26–27
Gideon Stargrave, 25, 94, 106
The Invisibles, 5, 7–10, 12–14, 16, 19, 21, 49, 93–94, 98–135, 146, 150–51, 157, 174, 179, 181–83, 188, 204, 227, 248, 274, 282, 287, 291, 295n, 297–300n
JLA, 8, 16, 21–22, 63, 137–39, 146, 150–57, 159, 180–81, 185, 198, 251–52, 256, 261, 278, 280, 282, 299–300n
JLA: Earth 2, 139, 153
JLA Classified, 153, 300n, 302n
Joe the Barbarian, 288

Kid Eternity, 49
Kill Your Boyfriend, 93, 134–35
Marvel Boy, 22, 49, 139, 157–63, 183
The Mystery Play, 21, 93, 95–98
The New Adventures of Hitler, 20, 40–46, 51, 129, 183, 294n
New X-Men, 8, 22, 139, 162–81, 183, 188, 203, 251, 291, 293, 300–302n
Seaguy, 22, 181, 198–204, 220, 285–86, 301n
Seaguy: Slaves of Mickey Eye, 201–2, 285–88, 301n
Sebastian O, 21, 93–95, 98, 297n
Seven Soldiers, 22, 221–51, 277, 282, 284, 298n, 302–3n; *Bulleteer*, 223, 226, 233, 235–41; *Frankenstein*, 223, 225–26, 232–33, 242, 246; *Guardian*, 221, 223–24, 226–30, 236, 250; *Klarion*, 221, 223–25, 242–45, 303n; *Mister Miracle*, 221, 224, 233–34, 242, 248–50, 277, 298n, 303n; *Seven Soldiers* (bookends), 222–31, 233, 239, 242, 249–50; *Shining Knight*, 221, 223, 226–27, 241–43, 245–47; *Zatanna*, 221, 223–25, 231–32, 238
Skrull Kill Krew, 157
Steed and Mrs. Peel, 94
St. Swithin's Day, 20, 40–41, 43–44, 46, 49, 51, 183
Swamp Thing, 302n
Vimanarama, 16, 19, 22, 181–82, 204–8, 220–21, 283, 301n
We3, 19, 22, 181–82, 208–20, 262, 283, 302n
Zenith, 20, 27–33, 46–52, 94, 102, 126, 151–52, 294–95n
Zoids, 26, 295n
Morrissey, Steven Patrick, 5, 31, 46; the Smiths, 85
Murray, Christopher, 126
Muth, John J., 95

Nabokov, Vladimir, 196
Near Myths, 24–25, 106
Negri, Antonio, 132
Neighly, Patrick, 5, 10, 98, 133, 298n

nostalgia, 8–9, 21, 32, 63, 136–38, 141, 144, 146–47, 150, 153–57, 163, 180, 230–31, 241, 245, 259, 280, 299n

O'Neill, Kevin, 27, 30
ontologies, 3–4, 19–20, 58–59, 86–88, 94–95, 232, 267, 280, 288; ontological confusion, 60–61, 98, 140–42, 176–77, 196–97
Orwell, George, 118

palimpsests, 9, 147, 254, 257–58, 272–74, 282, 288–89
Palmiotti, Jimmy, 157, 159
Paquette, Yanick, 223, 238–39, 241, 291
Parkhouse, Steve, 294n
Parkin, Lance, 26–27
pastiche, 9, 23, 29, 46, 73, 108, 137, 182, 204–5, 223, 258, 260, 270–71, 282, 286, 289–90, 295n, 299n
Patton, Billy Dallas, 221
Pérez, George, 276–77, 279
Perlmutter, Ike, 162
personification. *See* hypostasis
pornography, 183–86, 193–95, 238–39
Porter, Howard, 150, 153
postmodern capitalism, 22, 37, 39, 78, 132–33, 160–61, 167, 184–85, 203, 242, 245–46, 287
postmodernism, 3–4, 18–19, 23, 29, 57, 141, 182, 196–97, 201, 203, 205, 209, 292, 296n, 299n, 303n
poststructuralism, 4, 16–17, 19, 22, 119–21, 246–48, 293–94n, 303n
Potter, Dennis, 4
Premiani, Bruno, 72–73, 78, 80, 296n
prismatic style, 252–54, 261, 273, 275–76, 283, 285–86, 304n
punk, 5, 61, 298n
Pustz, Matthew, 57
Pynchon, Thomas, 107

Quesada, Joe, 157, 159, 162–63
Quitely, Frank, 7–8, 124–26, 141–42, 147, 163–64, 208–17, 220, 254–55, 258, 262–64, 289, 293n, 300n, 302n

rationalism, 33, 75, 77–79, 81, 87, 128, 261, 265, 274–75
realism, 3–4, 17, 25–26, 29, 32–33, 40, 92, 209–10; combined with fantasy, 107–8, 141–42, 144–46, 207, 270–71, 288; Morrison's rejection, 9, 21, 39, 53, 55, 57, 61–63, 72–73, 96, 143–44, 199, 224–27, 229, 231, 233, 235–36, 249
Reeve, Christopher, 262
reification. *See* hypostasis
retro comics, 21–22, 63, 136–39, 141, 147, 151, 153, 157, 161, 163, 230–31, 252, 280, 283, 299n
revisionist superheroes, 29–30, 48, 52–53, 136–37, 151, 294–95n; Morrison's criticisms, 21, 52–53, 55, 61–66, 73, 90–91, 140–41, 143–44, 156–57, 161–62, 229–36, 240–41, 272, 275–76, 280–81, 285, 299n; Morrison's participation, 20–21, 24–26, 30–34, 48, 51–55, 64–66, 72; Morrison's reconciliation, 268, 281–82
Revolver, 20, 27, 33
Reynolds, Richard, 67, 109–10, 167–68, 266, 296n
Robinson, James, 155
Roeg, Nicolas, 4
Rogers, Mark, 6–8
Rollin, Lucy, 66–67, 71
Romanticism, 4, 72, 79, 90, 126–31, 183, 187, 203, 287
Ross, Alex, 63, 137
Rucka, Greg, 254, 277
Rudkin, David, 4

Sabin, Roger, 29–30, 34, 53
Salisbury, Mark, 10, 293n, 299n
Sapir-Whorf hypothesis, 118–19, 121, 298n
scale, variations in, 4, 19, 57–59, 94, 101–3, 151, 184, 188–93, 267, 295n
Schatz, Thomas, 241
Schwartz, Julius, 63, 258
September 11, 2001 attacks, 177, 205, 247–48, 300–301n
sex and sexuality: in Morrison's comics, 24,

32–33, 65–67, 79, 84, 94–95, 101, 113, 115, 128, 142–43, 170–71, 182, 184, 192–95, 227–28, 236–41, 286, 296n, 298n; in revisionist comics, 29–30, 33–34, 53, 62, 91, 136, 143, 229; in X-Men comics, 167–68, 170–71
Shaviro, Steven, 5, 77–78, 296n
Shelley, Mary, 217, 223, 226, 302n
Shelley, Percy Bysshe, 89–90, 126–27, 129, 299n
Shuster, Joe, 264
Shyminsky, Neil, 167–69
Siegel, Jerry, 264
sigils, 12, 14–15, 20, 100
simulations and simulacra, 29, 58, 94–95, 118, 133, 185–86, 201, 209, 252, 254, 256–57, 285–86, 301n
Singer, Bryan, 163, 260
Situationists, 98, 131, 133–34, 298n, 299n
Smith, Zack, 260
Sook, Ryan, 221, 232
Spiegelman, Art, 209, 218
Spielberg, Steven, 167
spy genre, 10, 21, 94, 98, 108, 110–12, 115, 117, 131, 181, 183, 187, 301n
Starlin, Jim, 5, 25
Steranko, Jim, 25
Stewart, Cameron, 7, 200, 204, 221, 285, 297n
suicide, 34, 87, 146, 183, 190, 196–97, 204, 300–301n
Sukenick, Ronald, 19, 294n
superhero genre: definitions, 109–10; Morrison's criticisms, 46, 50–51, 62–63, 74–75, 109–10, 143, 151–53, 163, 178–80, 185–87, 202–3, 230, 238–41, 285–86; periods, 8–9, 143–44, 251–52, 293n; semantics, in other genres, 109–10, 218–19; as vehicle for generating meaning, 9, 16–18, 235, 249–50

Talbot, Bryan, 5, 20, 25, 30, 98
Taylor, Aaron, 142–43, 152–53
television, influence on Morrison's writing, 4, 94, 183, 268–71, 289

Thatcher, Margaret, 20, 25, 33, 36–44, 47, 129, 294n
Thompson, Jill, 7, 12, 99, 108, 112
time and space, in comics, 103–6, 212–16, 292
Tondro, Jason, 151
Totleben, John, 88, 136, 231, 295n
Touchmark, 92–93, 297n
Trident Comics, 20, 27, 40
Truog, Chas, 55
2000 AD, 20, 26–28, 30, 51–52, 136, 157

underground comix, 5, 20, 24–25, 210, 300n
utopias, 41, 47–48, 126–30, 171–72, 184–85, 191, 227, 265, 287, 294–95n, 300n

Vallely, Daniel, 96–97
Veitch, Rick, 63, 136–37, 299n
Vertigo, 3, 8, 21, 27, 92–93, 98–99, 108–11, 140–41, 159, 180–81, 183, 198, 283, 285, 297n, 301n
video games, 4, 102, 107, 132, 182, 208–9, 302n
Vozzo, Daniel, 297n

Wachowski, Andy and Larry, 102; *The Matrix*, 102, 297n
Wagner, John, 30
Waid, Mark, 137, 254, 277, 304n
Waugh, Patricia, 18
Wein, Len, 5, 232–33, 295n
Weisinger, Mort, 257–58
Wertham, Fredric, 143, 299–300n
Weston, Chris, 99, 182, 188, 195, 197
widescreen comics, 21–22, 138–39, 151, 153, 157, 159–60, 162, 252, 299–300n
Wilber, Ken, 130
Williams, Freddie E., II, 221
Williams, J. H., III, 222–23, 229, 231, 233, 270–72
Wilson, Robert Anton, 12, 98, 298n
Witek, Joseph, 209–10
Wolfman, Marv, 258, 276–77, 279; *Crisis on Infinite Earths*, 29, 57, 61, 276–77, 279–80, 283, 301n, 303n
Wolk, Douglas, 5, 118, 124, 298n
Woo, Benjamin, 9, 252, 293n

Wood, Ashley, 297n
Wood, Tatjana, 297n

Yeowell, Steve, 30, 40, 42, 46, 93–94, 99, 157
Young, Art, 92, 297n
youth vs. age, 28, 41, 49–50, 175, 228, 239–40, 278–79

Žižek, Slavoj, 17, 68
Zone, Ray, 282

www.ingramcontent.com/pod-product-compliance
Lightning Source LLC
Chambersburg PA
CBHW070300240426
43661CB00057B/2596